The Forms of Renaissance Thought

The Forms of Renaissance Thought

New Essays in Literature and Culture

Edited by

Leonard Barkan
Arthur W. Marks '19 Professor of Comparative Literature
Princeton University

Bradin Cormack
Associate Professor of English
University of Chicago, USA

Sean Keilen
Associate Professor of English
The College of William and Mary, USA

palgrave
macmillan

First published 2009 by
PALGRAVE MACMILLAN

Palgrave Macmillan in the UK is an imprint of Macmillan Publishers Limited,
registered in England, company number 785998, of Houndmills, Basingstoke,
Hampshire RG21 6XS.

Palgrave Macmillan in the US is a division of St Martin's Press LLC,
175 Fifth Avenue, New York, NY 10010.

Palgrave Macmillan is the global academic imprint of the above companies
and has companies and representatives throughout the world.

Palgrave® and Macmillan® are registered trademarks in the United States,
the United Kingdom, Europe and other countries.

ISBN-13: 978–0–230–00898–4   hardback
ISBN-10: 0–230–00898–4   hardback

This book is printed on paper suitable for recycling and made from fully
managed and sustained forest sources. Logging, pulping and manufacturing
processes are expected to conform to the environmental regulations of the
country of origin.

A catalogue record for this book is available from the British Library.

Library of Congress Cataloging-in-Publication Data
The forms of Renaissance thought : new essays in literature and culture /
    [edited by] Leonard Barkan, Bradin Cormack and Sean Keilen.
        p. cm.
    Includes index.
    ISBN 0–230–00898–4 (alk. paper)
      1. English literature – Early modern, 1500–1700 – History and criticism.
    2. Literature and society – England – History. I. Barkan, Leonard.
    II. Cormack, Bradin. III. Keilen, Sean.

    PR413.F67 2008
    820.9′003–dc22   2008015876

10   9   8   7   6   5   4   3   2   1
18   17 16 15 14 13 12 11 10 09

Printed and bound in Great Britain by
CPI Antony Rowe, Chippenham and Eastbourne

For Stephen Orgel

Contents

List of Illustrations

Notes on the Contributors

Leonard Barkan has been a professor of English, Art History, and Comparative Literature at Northwestern, NYU, and Princeton. He is the author of *The Gods Made Flesh: Metamorphosis and the Pursuit of Paganism* (1986) and *Unearthing the Past: Archaeology and Aesthetics in the Making of Renaissance Culture* (1999) and *Satyr Square: A Year, a Life in Rome* (2006).

Anston Bosman is Associate Professor and Director of Studies in English at Amherst College. He is completing a book on transformations of English Renaissance theatre in the North Sea world.

A. R. Braunmuller teaches early modern and modern drama at UCLA. He has written books and essays on Shakespeare and many of his fellow dramatists and edited their plays.

Bradin Cormack is Associate Professor of English at the University of Chicago. He is author of *A Power to Do Justice: Jurisdiction, English Literature, and the Rise of Common Law, 1509–1625* (2007); and co-author of *Book Use, Book Theory: 1500–1700* (2005) (with Carla Mazzio).

Margreta de Grazia is the Sheli Z. and Burton X. Rosenberg Professor of the Humanities and Professor of English at the University of Pennsylvania. Her books include *Shakespeare Verbatim* (1991) and *Hamlet without Hamlet* (2007). She has also edited the *Cambridge Companion to Shakespeare* (2001) (with Stanley Wells) and *Subject and Object in Renaissance Culture* (1996) (with Maureen Quilligan and Peter Stallybrass).

Jonathan Goldberg is Arts and Sciences Distinguished Professor at Emory University. His most recent book is *Tempest in the Caribbean* (2004).

Peter Holland is McMeel Family Professor of Shakespeare Studies in the Department of Film, Television, and Theatre at the University of Notre Dame. He is editor of *Shakespeare Survey* and currently President of the Shakespeare Association of America.

Ann Rosalind Jones, Esther Cloudman Dunn Professor of Comparative Literature at Smith College, is the author of *The Currency of Eros: Women's Love Lyric in Europe, 1540–1620* (1996); *The Poems and Selected Letters of Veronica Franco* ((1999) translated with Margaret F. Rosenthal); *Renaissance Clothing and the Materials of Memory* ((2001) with Peter Stallybrass);

and *The Clothing of the Renaissance World (Europe, Asia, Africa and America): Cesare Vecellio's "Habiti Antichi"* (also with Margaret Rosenthal, 2008).

Sean Keilen is the author of *Vulgar Eloquence: On the Renaissance Invention of English Literature* (2006) and an editor of *Shakespeare: The Critical Complex* (1999). A recipient of fellowships from the John Simon Guggenheim Foundation and the National Humanities Center, he teaches in the English Department at the College of William and Mary.

William H. Sherman is Director of the Centre for Renaissance and Early Modern Studies at the University of York and Associate Editor of *Shakespeare Quarterly*. He is the author of *John Dee* (1997) and *Used Books* (2007) and the editor of plays by Shakespeare, Jonson, and Marlowe.

Peter Stallybrass, Walter H. and Leonore C. Annenberg Professor in the Humanities and Professor of English of Comparative Literature and Literary Theory at the University of Pennsylvania, is the author of *The Politics and Poetics of Transgression* ((1986) with Allon White); *O Casaco de Marx: Roupas, Memória, Dor* (1999), trans. Tomaz Tadeu da Silva (Essays on Marx, Materiality, and Memory); *Renaissance Clothing and the Materials of Memory* (with Ann Rosalind Jones); and *Benjamin Franklin, Printer and Writer* ((2006) with James Green).

Valerie Traub is Professor of English and Women's Studies at the University of Michigan. She is the author of *The Renaissance of Lesbianism in Early Modern England* (2002), which won the Best Book Award from the Society of the Study of Early Modern Women in 2002, and *Desire and Anxiety: Circulations of Sexuality in Shakespearean Drama* (1992), as well as co-editor of *Feminist Readings of Early Modern Culture: Emerging Subjects* (1996) and *Gay Shame* (2008).

Michael Wyatt is the author of *The Italian Encounter with Tudor England: A Cultural Politics of Translation* (2005), the editor of *The Cambridge Companion Guide to the Italian Renaissance* (2009), and co-editor of *The Politics of Writing Relations: American Scholars in Italian Archives* (2008). He teaches at Stanford.

Introduction: "The Form of Things Unknown": Renaissance Studies in a New Millennium

Leonard Barkan, Bradin Cormack, and Sean Keilen

> And as imagination bodies forth
> The forms of things unknown, the poet's pen
> Turns them to shapes, and gives to airy nothing
> A local habitation and a name.
> – *A Midsummer Night's Dream* (5.1.14–17)

This collection situates itself at the boundary between context and intertext – between the social and material grid envisioned by the new historicism, on the one hand, and, on the other, a less deterministic mapping of the literary work within a cross-textual and cross-disciplinary space that is now emerging in early modern literary studies. Without distancing ourselves from the historical work that has so enriched how we approach cultural and artistic expression and its interpretation, we nevertheless welcome a disciplinary speculation that grants to authors and cultures the grounding force also of a free and productive imagination. One reason "form" might stand at the conceptual center of a collection with this double aim is that form is itself animated by a tension between freedom and determination. When Raymond Williams wrote that the word means both "a visible or outward shape" and "an inherent shaping impulse," and as such "spans a whole range from the external and superficial to the essential and determining," he was pointing out that form has a vexed place in the relation between a culture and its representations, since it describes both the limits of what is thinkable and a potential for passing beyond those limits.[1]

Form for Williams is "inevitably a relationship" between producer and consumer, a kind of pre-text that makes the composition and transmission of thought possible by shaping what can be said.[2] And this is equally true of political and administrative forms, social norms and roles, the material forms of domestic and civic life, book forms such as the codex, margin or index, and the whole range of literary form that includes genre, prosody, figures of speech, and the sound of words. If form can be understood generally as the horizon of a culture's political aesthetics, as a shifting infrastructure for thought, it nevertheless does more than direct us to a specific culture's implicit limits.[3] It also stands for a potential within any culture to reshape what can be said or known. For Williams this force is most visible in relation to those forms that are "not already shared and available, and in which new work is something much more than variation." Here, "[a]s in the case of language, new formal possibilities, which are the possibilities of a newly shared perception, recognition, and consciousness, are offered, tested, and in many but not in all cases accepted."[4] We would suggest that this potential in "new" forms for changing the boundaries of a culture's thinking belongs to form in general, since no form can ever be said to be simply given, but must always be understood as the historical product of its instantiations in time. This means that what Williams calls external form (which because of its availability to the senses has always had a special relation to the imagination, to desire, and to aesthetic appreciation) might itself generate thought rather than only express it in response to a determining force imagined as elsewhere. The forms that make thought historical also make history the source of change. Critical attention to form is one activity in which that potential may be detected and indeed activated.

Walter Benjamin addresses the place of the critic or historian in the process of activation when (in 1931) he writes that "[w]e are now very far from grasping the fact that the existence of a work of art in time and the understanding of it are but two sides of the same thing."[5] Meaning flows in Benjamin's sentence in two directions, toward history and away from it. If the recent scholarly work that has so enriched the discipline of literary studies has focused on the "existence of a work of art in time," on its otherness, its embeddedness, its estrangement into the local and the contingent, it is now possible to see how historically responsible work might aim also at what Benjamin calls the "understanding" of the artistic work. Indeed, that is the work he describes when he asserts that literary historians must "struggle above all with the works," whose "entire life and ... effects should have the right to stand alongside the history of their composition." In this extraordinary vision for literary history, Benjamin asserts that history remains historical to the extent that it risks anachronism by staying open to the demands and desires of the present: "What is at stake is not to portray literary works in the context of their age, but to represent the age that perceives them – our age – in the age during which they arose. It is this that makes literature into an organon of history; and to achieve this, and not to reduce literature to the material of history, is the task of the literary historian."[6] Benjamin's lesson is worth taking because, even as we attend scrupulously to the empirical details that the historical past throws in our scholarly way as its objects, we are still always on the verge of forgetting the shaping power of our own historical being. Far from being a deficit or impediment to historical understanding, that existence is the ground from which a truly historical knowledge becomes imaginable.

We are supposing that these sentiments about historical knowing are broadly shared in the discipline today, and also that their implications have not been completely absorbed. One benefit of accepting the risk Benjamin outlines would presumably be the reinvigoration of pleasure as a category of disciplinary activity and of historical understanding. For the pleasure in confronting a work of art is not solely personal even if it is particular. That distinction defines how the aesthetic response of a particular body might also be exemplary.[7] Roland Barthes, for example, makes his pleasure historical at the moment it becomes peculiarly his own and for that reason of interest to others:

> Whenever I attempt to "analyze" a text which has given me pleasure, it is not my "subjectivity" I encounter but my "individuality," the given which makes my body separate from other bodies and appropriates its suffering or its pleasure: it is my body of bliss I encounter. And this body of bliss is also *my historical subject*; for it is at the conclusion of a very complex process of biographical, historical, sociological, neurotic elements ... that I control the contradictory interplay of (cultural) pleasure and (non-cultural) bliss, and that I write myself as a subject at present out of place, arriving too soon or too late ... [an] anachronic subject, adrift.[8]

Barthes' vision of historical being as almost entirely unmoored from history lies at one end of a spectrum whose other end gives us a historical subject determined by forces and bound within limits that can scarcely be imagined, much less transcended.

The essays in this volume are situated between those poles. Or they are on an altogether different spectrum in which the historical need not reduce ultimately to the deterministic. Our anthology concerns form because in form we are looking for a way to integrate the claims of anachronism and of pleasure into the discipline's way of making history. It is not a book of, nor an argument for, a new formalism, even if many of the essays mobilize a close reading now almost universally associated with formalism narrowly conceived. Like form, close reading for us reflects instead a trust in the various powers that an aesthetic object comes to possess through the relation it mediates between artist and audience. Form seduces. Which is to say that, in the play of its potential, it points to a plural history in whose details we might contemplate meanings that, not ours, were also already our own.[9]

* * *

The essays in this volume are organized under three headings, with each group providing four perspectives on a single category that, at the boundary between the material and immaterial, can be said to give thought form. All the contributions are animated by a need to find methods adequate to the task of reaching a conceptual object lying slightly beyond comprehension. These are essays about invention, in the double sense of illuminating the "forms of things unknown" by looking for new objects and for the knowledge forms adequate to them.

The first section – Reception, Renovation, Renaissance – treats mediation itself, by reflecting on the technologies through which artworks and the apparatuses for interpreting them are transmitted in time. The case studies look, respectively, to lost artworks that survive in the textual history of their appreciation; to the place of mythology in the emergence of literary historical consciousness; to translation; and to editorial practice. The volume's second section treats desire as a dynamic that disorganizes the bodies it inhabits, even as it positions them as subjects and objects. Identifying in desire's excess an intrinsic resistance to normativization, the four essays differently argue that desire's potential as a social and ethical force depends on its not being foreclosed by any tradition – whether artistic, philosophical, critical, or pedagogical – that brings it only selectively into view. Our third section on "intimate matters" addresses in material culture a disciplinary subfield that in the last few decades has reshaped how we approach writing and reading, the use of books, and their relation to worlds of practice. Our four case studies are concerned, however, with a still understudied horizon for that work, since each takes up a material form – beard, leather, busk and dust – that signifies by pointing to the body on which it grows, from which it is taken, to which it is added, or into which it decays. This third section thus fits itself to the earlier two by casting the scintillating potential of mediating signs and of desire both in terms of choice objects in the *Wunderkammer* of Renaissance materiality and in terms of the material world's always fluid interaction with body, mind, and imagination. In addressing forms for the world that do fit into familiar schemes, all the essays in this volume are concerned with *conceptual objects* that might be cast as *conceptual things*, things being understood here, in Bill Brown's formulation, both as "the amorphousness out of which objects are materialized by the (ap)perceiving subject" and as "what is excessive in objects, as what exceeds their mere materialization as objects or their mere utilization as objects."[10] Thought for us flows out of and into the forms that seek to make it patent.

From even so brief a description, it can be appreciated that our volume means to bring into conversation disciplinary fields as apparently disparate from one another as textual studies (including editing), gender and queer studies, and the history of theater and performance. In each of these fields, the work of Stephen Orgel has seemed to us a case study for how historical concerns can be illuminated by a close attention to form's capacity for producing meaning. Stephen's career is marked as much by the range of his concerns as by the consistent rigor of a method that transforms his archive of pictures, portraits, textual lacunae and textual cruxes, titlepages, margins and all the rest into a breathtakingly creative history-making. From his seminal analysis of the printed masque as the textual remainder of political and poetic spectacle, and his engagements with emblem, illustration, and the varied history of theatrical performance; through his penetrating accounts of authorship and its others, and of gender and its others; to his groundbreaking work on the reader's and spectator's place in the formal production of meaning, whether in the theater or in the margins of a book – in all of these, Stephen has helped define the boundaries and, if you will, the form of the field in which the different essays collected here could take shape.[11]

Our volume opens with a generative absence. In his essay on the lost *Aphrodite* of Praxiteles, Leonard Barkan offers a history of the "aesthetic impulse" rather than a history of the "aesthetic" per se. This other history takes the form, not of genealogy in the sense of the anti-teleological projects we associate with Nietzsche and Foucault, but rather of what Barkan calls an etiology, a "myth about origins." At the center of his project is the insight that narrative is one place where the aesthetic impulse becomes visible in history, in excess of its social, political, and ideological aspects. Barkan's methodological approach thus converts anecdotes that might be treated in anthropological terms into consequential events in a symbolic history. As a form of historical discourse that is in excess of literal truth, myth, he finds, fits itself to the description of the excessive libidinal experiences that constitute the history of aesthetic appreciation.

For Sean Keilen, the classical allusions and mythical thinking that pervade English Renaissance writing are the forms of a literary historiography that looks upon vernacular composition with mixed appreciation. He interprets the appearance of the Midas myth in works by John Lyly and Thomas Nashe as a meditation on antiquity's influence upon England's vernacular literary culture. Keilen shows that in the story of Midas's immoderate desire for gold and power – a desire that is extinguished in its very fulfillment – these authors had occasion to contemplate the ambivalent attitude of their culture toward a past that promised to enrich vernacular composition and define its authority, even as it threatened to diminish the achievement too. Keilen's essay thus opens a new perspective on an old story about the place of antiquity in the movement from a premodern to a modern sensibility. When the myth of Midas is seen to be a fable about imitation as a dynamic between past and present, Renaissance literature reveals itself as a field of anachronistic play in excess of those binary distinctions – ancient and modern, same and different, self and other – that suggest its "early" modern character.

In his essay on John Florio's translation of Boccaccio's *Decameron* and on the Stuart implications of one *novella* about an earlier moment in Anglo-Italian relations, Michael Wyatt shows how fictional narration, and specifically the gendered plotting of crisis and resolution, might be understood as a way of thinking about history and culture. For this reason, the translation or adaptation of a story can be seen as a process that shapes cultural norms by exemplifying what textual forms are possible or tolerable in a given place or time. Translation is not just linguistic, but necessarily geographical, political, and ethical. Wyatt gives a privileged point of view on that process to Florio himself, for the reason that he stands at the point of departure and arrival of Boccaccio's migrant tale. In the biographical details of Florio's precarious double life as an Italian in England and in the English court, Wyatt finds an analogy for the precarious fate of the work of art whose transmission Florio oversaw.

Continuing her work on Shakespeare's sonnets (1609) and on the editorial shaping of their reception, Margreta de Grazia wonders whether John Benson's 1640 anthology of Shakespeare's poems, a scandal in the history of publishing, would not be more appropriately understood as the product of a highly inventive reader, one scrupulously attuned to the norms and forms of organization that characterized the setting in which the poems would be circulating. If historical distance is now an impediment to our understanding a book such as Benson's, that distance is for de Grazia also a source of illumination, insofar as texts are for her always historical negotiations both with an earlier past and, inevitably, with the futures that will receive them. In drawing on such forms as paratext, organization of part and whole, and the fitting of thought to proverb or commonplace, Benson, De Grazia shows, stands in a pivotal place in the history of Shakespearean textual scholarship, as the exponent of a very different editorial sensibility from that associated with the conspicuously modern practices ushered in by Edmond Malone and his contemporaries. As against Benson's attention to the text's rhetorical function and the probable "interests of [a] readership," these later practices would ground themselves in the idea of an authentic author and in the collation of "authentic texts and documents centered on the author." Measured against Benson, Malone's editorial norms (and our own) come to seem less a natural way of accounting for a text's material life than a choice to include particular forms and to exclude others from the domain of interpretation and, indeed, of authenticity itself.

The volume's second section opens in a *locus amoenus* for the renaissance erotic imagination and a *locus classicus* for its critical reception. Jonathan Goldberg's essay on Spenser turns to the Garden of Adonis and the Bower of Bliss in order to revisit the question of what Lucretius is doing in *The Faerie Queene*. In dialogue with Lucretius, Goldberg argues, Spenser's poem "join[s] a materialist vocabulary to sexual representation," so as to explore "sexuality and materiality together and outside of the spiritualized, masculinized, Christian, marital, juridical framework." Reading Spenser out of the neoplatonizing tradition in which he has been embedded, and in response ultimately to the late Foucault, Goldberg thus discovers a Spenser open to the possibility that the proper use of pleasure "does not mandate marital coupling as its only realization." In so charging the Lucretian subtext of Spenser's representation of desire, Goldberg shows how the Garden of Adonis discloses a vision of sexual fulfilment open to possibilities other than the heteronormative. This is a point about the claims of materialism on the text and, more generally, about the work that a queer historiography might do. For desire in Goldberg's view is wanton in the sense of pointing to a play between spirit and matter in which the latter might exert claims not reducible to the former as its true horizon.

Allowing eros its full, wanton scope means making history the field for a fully erotic aesthetics.

Bradin Cormack's essay on the literary afterlife of Echo and Narcissus is centrally concerned with subject and object, as Shakespeare brings that relation into view in *Romeo and Juliet* and in the sonnets. In contrast to readings that abstract Narcissus from the time of his narrative, Cormack argues for Echo's centrality to the myth, in order to suggest that the diffuseness of Ovidian desire – its fungibility and excess, its sudden derangement of the body in relation to itself and other bodies – regrounds where a sexual ethics might lie. If Goldberg suggests that in *The Faerie Queene* sexuality is found "in couples, whether of the same sex or not, whose sex is not bound to the institutional form (marriage) that supposedly makes sex valid," Cormack finds that in Shakespeare the couple is best seen as always incomplete, always looking to shore up the meaning it seems formally to promise. He describes this incompletion in terms of a gap between the forms of repetition and reciprocation, as that emerges through the play of eye and ear. In validating Narcissus's desire for his image as, visually, an instance of the melancholic dynamic that, aurally, keeps Echo apart from him, Shakespeare (and Ovid) turn out to be describing desire in terms of the adequacy of poetic and social forms to express the relations toward which they reach.

In an essay on *Coriolanus*, Peter Holland fashions a criticism that, "driven by a profound awareness of contextual issues," nevertheless also works "inwards," towards the play's sensory effects, as these emerge in time through a linguistic superflux in which desire's excess reveals itself. Fusing performance studies with close reading, the method lands on close listening as a primary mode for detecting arguments dependent on the play's movement across line and scene, "its meaning shaped by its forms." Like Barkan and Goldberg, Holland is concerned with the unruly body, but here it is the textual body that is at issue: in the playful instability of Coriolanus's name; in the instability of the five-act structure; in the unruliness of rhythm itself as that sustains the play's linguistic analysis of power, desire, and social relation. For Holland, drama's attractiveness lies in its refusal to *predict* the outcome of interpretation, and *Coriolanus* thematizes the fact that drama is always more than the sum of its parts. In this abundance, Holland finds what he calls the remainder: that which "is left over when divisions are made" and which, as the opposite of exhaustion, figures the richness of the whole, even as it makes its ongoing interpretation possible.

This section on the productive circuits of desire concludes with Valerie Traub's essay on desire as a pedagogical form. Traub looks to one episode in Richard Brome's 1638 play *The Antipodes*, in order to describe the dynamics that may be said to constitute an intimate public sphere and thereby bridge "the historical divide separating the queer past from the queer present." In the play's representation of Martha Joyless's half-transparent memory of her erotic encounter with another woman, and in her half-ignorant attempt to use that memory to "transform her joyless state," Traub finds between the Foucauldian arts of discipline and imitation a space for a quite other erotic regime, this one grounded in the unstable and provisional, but also instrumental field of pedagogy. This is a capacious pedagogy, because it opens a space for the epistemological production of a sexual ethics grounded in "sexual variation" that cannot be reduced to a "set of sexual contents." Asking what a knowledge of sex is by asking how a culture produces that knowledge, Traub insists that sex is a "knowledge relation." If sex education as we usually experience it works by normatively constraining us, the only sex pedagogy worthy of its name, she shows, is one that, freely and fully pluralistic, would teach us how to live with each other and with the past, and in that way fit itself to the disorganizing opacities of sex itself.

The third section opens with a material form that is both generative and embarrassing. In his essays on decorous and indecorous beards, A. R. Braunmuller is concerned, like Traub, with the relation of sexual difference to certain binary categories that cannot do it justice. Tracing the dramatic and social representation of the bearded lady, he argues that the distinction between male and female is fraught with sexual possibilities that are in excess of the normative relation the distinction ostensibly imposes. Braunmuller finds that when a beard is present on women or absent from boys, these limit cases both derange the experience of masculinity and make visible the beard's capacity to determine the gender of a body, regardless of its biological sex. The shape of the body thus limns an ideological reality, a point he unfolds mainly in relation to the operation of shame in the public sphere. More than simply a stabilizing or destabilizing social force, shame for Braunmuller is an event that points to the priority of the body's forms for making the social, since shame operates to exclude certain forms from certain bodies and thereby to invent a normative order through the imaginative production of a natural one. If the distinctions made among bodies are in this sense the source of constraining norms, the forms on and of the body are for that reason also pedagogical in Traub's sense, a starting point from which to rethink what we have been taught to think about the body.

Taking us to the heart of the discipline's preoccupation with the relation between word and thing, Anston Bosman's essay pursues a method for approaching a pre-Cartesian world in which the relation of spirit and matter was so different from what it is for us. Addressing leather as a material integral to theatrical performance, to printing technology, and to the work of the early modern imagination, Bosman demonstrates the "intimate and changeable relation" between early modern discourse and materiality. "To separate leather-as-material from leather-as-metaphor would be to misinterpret this culture," he argues, by denying the early modern imagination's fundamental implication in the phenomenological world. The importance of John Shakespeare's craft for his son's writing cannot therefore be measured only in terms of the wildly inventive metaphoric use that the plays make of leather. For Bosman, Shakespeare's writerly achievements must be seen instead as being on a continuum with his father's practice as a craftsman and manufacturer. And what matters in this formulation is the capacity in the early modern discourse around leather not just to make language material, but also to insist that matter itself – the stuff of the household, the workshop, the theater – is articulate, resonant, meaningful.

William H. Sherman meditates on "the materials and metaphors that frame our work in archives" and on "the peculiar place of dust" therein, in order to build a bridge between dirt and light, between the past's minimal substances and the evanescent promise of a digital future. Dust for him is a heuristic, a remainder in Holland's sense that tells us about the condition of the city or hero or author or archive responsible for it. As a material on the verge of becoming nothing, and as the event horizon where the material world gives way to the imagination, dust is the limit case for thinking both about what scholars do and about how that work might be continuous with the memorializing work of librarians, editors, biographers, preachers, writers, artists, programmers. In the digital age that has given us unprecedented access to historical material, Sherman observes, that same technology in fact "*de*-materializes the text." Databases such as EEBO were created in part to satisfy our longing for a physical contact with the past, and yet, as he point out, at their most seductive they turn out to provide only an image of the *desideratum* that prompted us to create them. In other words, the promise and limits of digitalization make visible as forms for thought the matter that digitalization cannot itself show.

In the volume's final essay, Ann Rosalind Jones and Peter Stallybrass focus their attention on the busk as the body's disciplining scaffold, adornment and prosthesis, and as a locus for a complex social exchange between genders and within the category of gender itself. Gendered female but available for broader use, the busk's materiality for them is phantasmatic in its capacity for "turning women into men and men into women and even dissolving sexual norms entirely." Their essay is concerned, then, with how things signify on their way to becoming objects. Like the dust, leather, beards, gold, and statues that occupy others in this volume, busks are a material form that produce knowledge and organize experience and identities, even as they disorganize the very norms on which identity seems to depend. In this obsolete artifact of sexual and domestic life, Jones and Stallybrass show, the early modern period contemplated the possibility of a world so unlike theirs as to exhilarate and horrify by turns. As an object of commerce, relation, and disguise that threatened through its Ovidian work "to upset the whole balance of nature," the busk is a material catalyst for a scene of unpredictable transformation in which the culture could imagine a freedom it scarcely knew how to articulate.

Notes

1. Raymond Williams, *Marxism and Form* (Oxford: Oxford University Press, 1977), 186. In sympathy with Williams, our collection concerns the productive capacity of form. Some notable recent collections have addressed more explicitly the related question of history's relation to formalism. See for example *Renaissance Literature and Its Formal Engagements*, ed. Mark Rasmussen (New York: Palgrave, 2002); and *Shakespeare and Historical Formalism*, ed. Stephen Cohen (Aldershot: Ashgate, 2007). For an earlier project on the relation of historicism and formalism, see *The Historical Renaissance: New Essays on Tudor and Stuart Literature and Culture*, ed. Heather Dubrow and Richard Strier (Chicago: University of Chicago Press, 1988). A further collection suggests new historicism's own investments in accounting for form in history; see *The Power of Forms in the English Renaissance*, ed. Stephen Greenblatt (Norman, OK: Pilgrim Books, 1982).
2. Williams, *Marxism and Form*, 187.
3. On aesthetics as an immediately political mode of delimiting the phenomenal world, see Jacques Rancière, *The Politics of Aesthetics: The Distribution of the Sensible*, trans. Gabriel Rockhill (London: Continuum, 2004).
4. Williams, *Marxism and Form*, 188–9.
5. Walter Benjamin, "Literary History and the Study of Literature," in *Selected Writings, Vol. 2, Part 2*, trans. Rodney Livingstone et al., ed. Michael Jennings, Howard Eiland, and Gary Smith (Cambridge: Belknap Press, Harvard University Press, 1999), 463.

6. Benjamin, "Literary History and the Study of Literature," 464.
7. On the example, and more generally a "whatever" or *quodlibet* being, in relation to the distinction between singularity and specific content, see Giorgio Agamben, *The Coming Community*, trans. Michael Hardt (Minneapolis: University of Minnesota Press, 1993).
8. Roland Barthes, *The Pleasure of the Text*, trans. Richard Miller (New York: Hill and Wang, 1975), 62–3.
9. For Dipesh Chakrabarty, the history that recognizes that the past can tend to more than one future also gives us a present that is "irreducibly not-one." See Chakrabarty, *Provincializing Europe: Postcolonial Thought and Historical Difference* (Princeton: Princeton University Press, 2000), 249.
10. Bill Brown, "Thing Theory," in *Things*, ed. Bill Brown (Chicago: University of Chicago Press, 2004), 5.
11. See Stephen Orgel, *The Jonsonian Masque* (Cambridge, MA: Harvard University Press, 1965); *The Illusion of Power: Political Theater in The English Renaissance* (Berkeley: University of California Press, 1975); *Impersonations: The Performance of Gender in Shakespeare's England* (Cambridge: Cambridge University Press, 1996); *The Authentic Shakespeare and Other Problems of the Early Modern Stage* (New York: Routledge, 2002); *Imagining Shakespeare: A History of Texts and Visions* (Basingstoke: Palgrave, 2003); also Ben Jonson, *The Complete Masques*, ed. Orgel (New Haven: Yale University Press, 1969); William Shakespeare, *The Tempest*, ed. Orgel (Oxford: Oxford University Press, 1987); William Shakespeare, *The Winter's Tale*, ed. Orgel (Oxford: Oxford University Press, 1996).

Part I

Reception, Renovation, Renaissance

1

Praxiteles' *Aphrodite* and the Love of Art

Leonard Barkan

"A fifteenth-century painting is the deposit of a social relationship": so begins an epoch-making book by Michael Baxandall.[1] In other words, the work of art is to be understood as the consequence, the remains, the residue from a set of practices within society, especially the power exercised by patrons, institutions, and finances. It is a brilliant, but disturbing, metaphor that seems to diminish agency and turn art objects into pieces of automatic writing dictated by one particular strand of public culture. Now, this very compelling account of art has been extraordinarily fruitful, notably by providing a vital corrective on the methodological lamenesses of connoisseurship, formalism, and the cult of personal inter-pretation – not to mention the fact that great scholars like Baxandall have always succeeded in bringing their awareness of social relationships into a dialogue with other factors.

Yet as a master narrative that has done such salutary work in cross-examining previous assumptions, it continues to need its own question-ing. The extraordinary range in Stephen Orgel's scholarship stands as a reminder of what it means both to practice and to question. Attempting to follow that example by looking back on my own work, I discover that I began with a resistance to the social master narrative that was uncon-scious and uninterrogated; then, inspired, or pressured, by intellectual movements that insisted on that narrative but also theorized it, I began to be more conscious of what I was myself assuming and, as time went on, more willing to argue it. In 1985, when I composed the preface to *The Gods Made Flesh*, at the end of twelve years spent writing the book, I tried to formulate a narrative for the persistence of metamorphosis by saying that "Artists confront their past (especially the work of other artists) partly within the limits of their own historical moment and partly at the level of a personal encounter that is as unique and outside of time as the creative gift itself."[2] In 1998, when I wrote the introduction to *Unearthing the Past*, after thirteen years on that book, I came yet further out of the closet:

> The cultural production that results [from rediscovering ancient sculpture in the Renaissance] becomes a sign that art can be made not only out of dogma, out of natural observation, or out of historical events but also out of what we might in the fullest sense call *aesthetics* – which is to say, a philosophy, a history, and a phenomenology proper to art itself.[3]

The problem is, that even to a confirmed art appreciator like myself, aesthetics doesn't quite seem to cut it as a master narrative; it seems, in other words, to beg the question of what drives and needs are satisfied by artistic production and reception.

The present essay, then, attempts to stop begging that question. We might call it the early history of the aesthetic impulse: early in that I am seeking to locate my subject within some fundamental human impulses and early in the sense that I am postulating a particular moment within Greek and Hellenistic culture for the emergence of a set of responses to artistic beauty. What I am offering is a sort of etiology: a myth about origins. In fact, my point of beginning is also a deposit, but quite different from that which Baxandall has so memorably pictured.

"They say," Pliny the Elder tells us in his discussion of Praxiteles' *Cnidian Aphrodite* (Figure 1.1), "that a certain man was once overcome with love for the statue and that, after he had hidden himself [in the shrine] during the nighttime, he embraced it and that it thus bears a stain, an indication of his lust."[4] A couple of centuries later, the Lucianic author of the *Erotes* turns this event into a full-blown romance. The lover would spend his whole day in Aphrodite's shrine, in an appearance of religious piety while in fact murmuring secret love chat to her. He played games of chance in the hopes of getting lucky. He wrote amorous messages all over the walls of the temple and on the bark of trees (shades of Mad Orlando). He started worshipping Praxiteles as much as Zeus. Finally one evening when the temple was about to be closed,

> quietly and unnoticed by those present, he slipped in behind the door and, standing invisible in the inmost part of the chamber, he kept still, hardly even breathing. When the attendants closed the door from the outside in the normal way, this new Anchises was locked in. But why do I chatter on and tell you in every detail the reckless deed of that

Figure 1.1 After Praxiteles, *Cnidian Aphrodite* (Colonna type), Museo Pio Clementino, Vatican Museums
Photo credit: Scala/Art Resource, NY

unmentionable night? These marks of his amorous embraces were seen after day came and the goddess had that blemish to prove what she'd suffered. The youth concerned is said, according to a popular story told, to have hurled him self over a cliff or down into the waves of the sea and to have vanished utterly.[5]

The story, however, does not vanish.

Indeed, in one form or another we find it *passim* in the ongoing mythology of art, especially sculpture. Just in the immediate Plinian context, and regarding the same sculptor, we have the *Eros of Parion*, which

> is equal to the Aphrodite at Knidos, both for its fame and for the injury it suffered; for Alketas the Rhodian fell in love with it and also left upon it the same sort of trace of his love.[6]

At least in regard to male desire, then, it is an equal opportunity story, offering both homo- and hetero- possibilities. Athenaeus in his *Deipnosophistae* produces several instances of men who got up close and personal with sculpture. A delegate to a Delphic festival left a wreath in payment for the pleasure he took with the statue of a boy; apparently, his effort was more successful than that attempted by Cleisophus of Selymbria, who,

> becoming enamoured of the statue in Parian marble at Samos, locked himself up in the temple, thinking he should be able to have intercourse with it; and since he found that impossible on account of the frigidity and resistance of the stone, he then and there desisted from that desire and placing before himself a small piece of flesh he consorted with that.[7]

Even in Rome, where we might expect more decorous behavior, we learn from Varro (*apud* Pliny) that the knight Junius Pisciculus fell in love with one of the Muses sculpted on the Temple of Felicity (probably also by Praxiteles).[8] And, in an anecdote as sinister as it is revealing, Pliny explains how the dissipated emperor Tiberius caused Lysippus' statue of the *Apoxyomenos*, or the Boy Scrubbing himself with a Strigil, to be taken out of public space and transferred to his own bedroom; only when the Roman populace clamorously demanded its return was the emperor prevailed upon to restore the statue, *quamquam adamatum* – despite how much he had fallen in love with it.[9]

How are we to comprehend this strand in the history of art appreciation? One approach is to consider these anecdotes as chapters in the history of abnormal psychology – a Kraft-Ebbing of aesthetics. For Athenaeus, sex with statues belongs in a catalogue of perversions that includes military rape and a rooster falling in love with a sommelier, while the exploits of Tiberius are part of a whole tendency toward *luxuria* and the privatization of art.[10] We are talking, in other words, about a territory that, depending on different cultural definitions of unorthodox sexual practices, connects the experience of art to activities understood as bestiality, sodomy, and masturbation. Alternatively, these stories get processed by rationalizers who seek to debunk anything bizarre, miraculous, or aberrant that appears in myth or legend and fix it instead in the realm of quotidian history. Stained sculpture can be explained away as some sort of justification regarding blemishes in the perfect whiteness of Parian marble or Cyprian ivory. The story becomes one of those mythological etiologies, in the style of some Ovidian metamorphoses, that manages to absolve the legendary artist from incompetence or poor choice of raw material at the same time as it reassures later viewers that they are in the presence of the very object upon which the master worked his chisel. Indeed, the narrator of the *Erotes*, before hearing about the true origin of the stain, has made precisely this wrong assumption, misguidedly admiring Praxiteles for managing to hide the marble flaw in what he considers the less visible private parts of the figure.[11] Whether the private parts are also the least observed by viewers is a question he does not ask.

Then there are those who, faced with this blot, look up rather than down. I quote not from an anonymous Hellenistic author but from the superbly annotated Gian Biagio Conte edition of Pliny. Readers seeking further information on the passage describing the stain find the following:

> The concept of the statue as an echo on earth of divine beauty, to whose vision mortals are finally admitted, had to give place to the desire to go beyond the limits of the human condition and to "appropriate for oneself" forms of the divine.[12]

A curious description, to be sure, of what transpired that night in the temple. If the abnormal psychology route is too clinical and the rationalist route too reductive, this one-way travel to ecstatic forms of heavenly contemplation seems a bit precipitous in leaving behind the material of statues, and of life.

What happens if we take the *Cnidian Aphrodite* as the model of the art object and try to understand how this story might be fundamental to the history of art?

I begin with a counter-example: the great gold and ivory statue of Hera by Polyclitus, located in the goddess's temple at Argos, which we know from verbal descriptions, though nothing even remotely resembling a full replica survives. According to an epigram from the *Greek Anthology*, credited to Parmenion,

> Polycleitus of Argos, who alone saw Hera with his eyes, and moulded what he saw of her, revealed her beauty to mortals as far as was lawful; but we, the unknown forms beneath her dress's folds, are reserved for Zeus.[13]

The greatness of the statue demonstrates that the artist was vouchsafed a unique mortal view of the goddess, *up to a certain point*. His representation of that vision is magnificent, but it remains within the law. The speakers of the lines, as it turns out, are the *agnostoi morphai* – forms unknown, both to the sculptor and to us, that lie in some unchartable space between art and life, or mortal and divine, underneath the covering that Polyclitus has so masterfully executed. In these strange and beguiling verses (perhaps the earliest known vagina monologue?), artistic genius emerges as both glorious and boundaried. This is highly appropriate to the place of Polyclitus in the traditional history of Greek art – a tradition that stretches from Pliny to Winckelmann and beyond – as the supreme rule-giver but lacking something in the sophistication and grace that the sculptural masters of the next age would achieve.[14]

And indeed Praxiteles decisively breaks through the boundaries that held Polyclitus back. By general scholarly agreement, the *Cnidian Aphrodite* was the first colossal female nude in the history of art.[15] In that simple fact – and its all too elementary connection with the story of the stain – our aesthetic counter-narrative begins. Declared by Pliny to be "superior to all the works, not only of Praxiteles, but indeed in the whole world" (*Nat. Hist.* 36.20), the *Aphrodite* is one of the supremely canonical artworks of all time, but it raises a mass of unanswerable questions. As with all the legendary masterpieces – and I lay stress on that word "legendary" – attributed to the most famous names in Greek sculpture, it is known to us only in copies that were generally made in Rome almost five hundred years later. The evidence of all these replicas leaves us in a tantalizing uncertainty regarding major questions about Aphrodite's pose, but we must despair of ever getting the chronologically definitive word, for instance, on the relation between the turning of her body and the turning of her head (Figures 1.2, 1.3).[16]

That is only the beginning of the perplexities. So long as we understand this figure as a religious icon within rigorous limits of such a culture circa 340 BCE – let's call it an instrument in the civic self-assertion of Cnidos as a center for worship of Aphrodite – we have a lot of explaining to do. What, to review some of the most persistent questions, is the goddess doing here? Aphrodite was born with sea-foam all over her; perhaps she has come to the port city of Cnidos to wash it off. Hence the water-jug and the garment, which may be a recently shed piece of clothing or even a bath towel. Or is it absurd to place such a figure in the midst of a quotidian narrative? Should we rather see her as a symbolic figure of divine force, a cult object in the service of some particular subset of godliness – perhaps love, perhaps fertility? If so, by what system of religious symbolism shall we understand the fundamental and interrelated features of his composition: the gesture of covering her pubis and the semi-averted *contraposto* stance, which seems to most commentators a sign that she is reacting to an intrusion upon her privacy? Do goddesses have ordinary experiences, like personal hygiene and disconfiture in the presence of prying eyes?

If I look at the work through my own pair of prying eyes, what I see is not so much a goddess or a myth as an overwhelming assertion of nakedness. I say "assertion" not just because we know Praxiteles was making a revolutionary choice in presenting the figure unclothed but because the statue so aggressively declares nudity to be its subject. In previous sculpture, female divinities could expose body parts only where the arcana of their divine power were aggressively present, so as to shift the representation decisively away from any resemblance to the mortal, like the Artemis of Ephesus (Figure 1.4). Far more often, as in the Athena from the Acropolis (Figure 1.5), of course, it is the mark of representing a goddess – or indeed any female figure – that she be swathed in vast quantities of drapery, like the folds under which Hera's private parts were speaking in Parmenion's epigram.[17] Indeed, from an aesthetic standpoint, what happens in the high classical age of Greek sculpture (and it will be replicated in both Italian and Northern Renaissances) is that by what we might call the logic of fetishism, the elaborate rendering of these covering garments becomes the focal point where artists flaunt their skill, as though in recompense for what cannot be rendered. That is the Polyclitan economy of the artist: a magnificent achievement that stops short of both divine secrecy and mortal shame.

Figure 1.2 After Praxiteles, *Cnidian Aphrodite*, Glyptothek, Staatlich Antikensammlung, Munich
Photo credit: Bildarchiv Preussischer Kulturbesitz/Art Resource, NY

Figure 1.3 After Praxiteles, *Cnidian Aphrodite* (Belvedere type), Museo Pio Clementino, Vatican Museums
Photo credit: Deutsches Archäologisches Institut, Rome

Figure 1.4   Artemis of Ephesus, Museo Capitolini, Rome
Photo credit: Erich Lessing/Art Resource, NY

Figure 1.5 *Varvakeion Athena*, Acropolis Museum, Athens
Photo credit: Scala/Art Resource, NY

The Praxitelean economy is different. That Aphrodite wears no clothes is only the beginning of the revolution here. The choice of depicting her nude derives its power and meaning first from the fact that she is holding a wad of drapery that *could* cover her if only she were not brandishing it at a distance. Balancing her rounded form is a correspondingly sensuous artificial structure, the jug, that is being lavished with a surplus of covering – unnecessarily, since jugs have no modesty. The outstretched fabric is perfectly poised in relation to the goddess's exposed parts, which could revert to their traditional secret positioning with a mere turning of her arm; but the placement of the strut, which may or may not have been part of the Praxitelean original, seems definitively to disallow this potential act of *pudeur*. Aphrodite's nakedness, in other words, is staged in the imminent presence of its opposites.

Then there is the complex matter of her stance. When the contraposto of the Polyclitan *Doryphoros* (Figure 1.6) is recast as the posture of an unexpectedly naked goddess, all the intricate postural harmonies of the Polyclitan canon turn into instabilities.[18] At the heart of this matter, of course, is the question of gender. I would hazard to say that it is a feature common to antiquity itself, to the Renaissance revival of antiquity, and to pre-feminist modern scholarship about antiquity that naked gods are just naked while naked goddesses need to have a reason or a story or an excuse to be naked.[19] In this instance, what was for the *Doryphoros* a mixture of purposiveness and balance turns into the disequilibrium of multiple and uncertain purposes in the Cnidian statue; what was active becomes reactive. And because there is a drama about nudity here, in which beholding is itself thematized – not to say rendered thrilling and dangerous – it is inevitable that the different directions implied by left leg, right leg, and turned head should construct viewership as integral and necessary to the represented object.

And finally, there is the astonishingly equivocal gesture of the right hand. Does it conceal or emphasize the genital area? Does it speak to the vulnerability of the figure, or to the source of her power? What is certain is that it captures the visible and the invisible in a tangle of ambiguity. Aphrodite's hand atop a pubic region that itself appears to be undeveloped is like the famous curtain in Pliny's story about the Parrhasius painting that fooled his rival Zeuxis.[20] It appears to be a cover, but if you look under it, all you end up observing is your susceptibility to the trickery of art; you've been caught peeping, and there's nothing there. Parrhasius, said Pliny in another context, followed the dictum that the artist should "*ostendat etiam quae occultat*" ("disclose

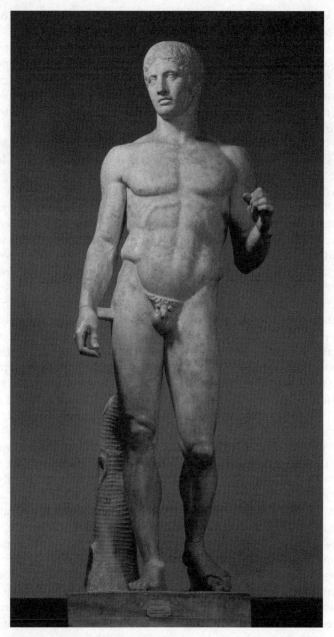

Figure 1.6 After Polykleitos, *Doryphoros*, Museo Archeologico, Naples
Photo credit: Scala/Art Resource, NY

even what he hides") (*Nat. Hist.* 35.68). The same goes for Aphrodite, and for her maker Praxiteles.

Regarding these questions of pose, perhaps the most salient sign of how the *Aphrodite* plays itself out in the tradition is the sequence of sculptures that follows upon the Praxitelean invention. As a student of the longer classical tradition, I find it interesting that so many works within this lineage have played a significant role in the continuing imaginative life of classical statuary from the Renaissance onwards. The *Medici Venus*[21] (Figure 1.7), famous from the seventeenth century when it was placed in the Uffizi Tribuna, where it remains, makes it clear – or, at the very least, its restorations do – that the Cnidian original's gesture of sexual concealment/emphasis was a decisive feature: why merely cover one private region when you can cover two? The equally famous *Capitoline Venus*[22] (Figure 1.8) (whose arms are not restored but original), contemporary and Roman competitor of the Florentine work, includes the Praxitelean jug and garment, even though they have less logic and sensual effect when the goddess's hands are not free to integrate them. Another seventeenth-century import to the Uffizi, sometimes called the *Venus Victrix*[23], also a restores logic by maintaining the double *pudica* gesture but locating the garment – uselessly, from the point of view of concealment – around the back of the body. And the *Venus Felix*[24] (Figure 1.9), which had found its way to the Pope's Belvedere courtyard by the early sixteenth century, completes the narrative of drapery and modesty by returning the cloth to its Praxitelean position on the statue's left but attaching it to the right hand, where it augments the familiar gesture of protecting the figure's genital region.

But these images, though they may be worth a thousand words apiece, must be discursively filled out with the *Aphrodite*'s paper trail, the great flood of verbal responses from which the story of the stain is only the most enticing detail. As I have argued elsewhere, long-enduring works of art present difficulties in decoding both because of historical distance and because visual representations are intrinsically enigmatic, even in the moment of their origin.[25] Praxiteles' work, like other canonical landmarks of the fifth and fourth century, comes with no contemporary documentation. But more than most other art objects from its milieu, it develops, beginning about two hundred years later, a very considerable textual response. As soon as we read the statue through the testimony of so many ancient eyes, something very obvious but very true emerges: the *Cnidian Aphrodite* is neither a god nor a human being; it's a statue. It is thus equally absurd to say that this piece of

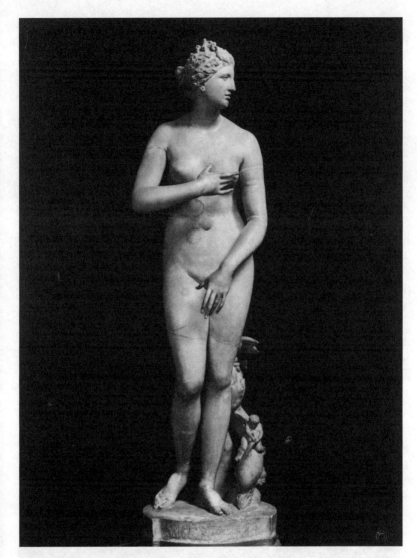

Figure 1.7 *Venus Medici*, Uffizi, Florence
Photo credit: Alinari/Art Resource, NY

stone is a god-and-only-a-god as it is to say that this piece of stone has complex emotions going on inside its marble head. The appearance of the paper trail coincides with and signals precisely this re-definition – let's call it the "modern" definition – of the *Aphrodite*, not as a god

Figure 1.8   Capitoline Venus, Museo Capitolini, Rome
Photo credit: Scala/Art Resource, NY

Figure 1.9 Venus Felix, Museo Pio Clementino, Vatican Museums
Photo credit: Scala/Art Resource, NY

Figure 1.10   Capitoline Venus seen from behind, Musei Capitolini, Rome
Photo credit: Alinari/Art Resource, NY

and not as a person but as a work of art. Or, to put it another way, it is a work of art that partakes of human and divine in such a way that the story of the stain seems at once to stretch and define all these terms.[26] It is the possibility of a sexual response (mixed with the impossibility of its consummation) that gives life to art as the *tertium quid* of the human and the divine.

I take as paradigmatic here the first piece of art appreciation in this later history – and it is repeated several times in the epigrams of the *Greek Anthology* – which imagines the goddess personally journeying to Cnidos to look at herself. The epigrammatists take delight in the notion of a mirroring event between Aphrodite and her representation, while at the same time they doubtless reflect a local cultic tradition that the statue was able to conjure up the authentic divinity in its temple. But their real interest lies elsewhere, as we can see from the often repeated punchline that climaxes these visits:

Cypris, seeing Cypris in Cnidos, said, "Alas! Alas! where did Praxiteles see me naked?" (16.162)

Or:

Paphean Cytherea came through the waves to Cnidos, wishing to see her own image, and having viewed it from all sides in its open shrine, she cried, "Where did Praxiteles see me naked?" (16.160)

Or in the goddess's own voice:

Paris, Anchises, and Adonis saw me naked. Those are all I know of, but how did Praxiteles contrive it? (16.168)

This is what – at least in the retrospect of the tradition – sets the fourth-century Aphrodite by Praxiteles apart from the fifth-century Hera by Polyclitus. The queen of the gods could not "visit" her effigy in Argos, or at least not as a museum-goer: she was of an incommensurable order of being, and that effigy could only be a reminder of its own representational and ontological limitations. But Praxiteles *did* see all, and he told all. Whatever the historical Praxiteles may have had in mind in originating the colossal female nude, his later viewers see him as having entered into some sort of mythic and sacred space where he gained an authentic view of divine nakedness, which he was then able to realize in the sightlines of all human beings. The statue becomes, in consequence, a privileged site for the notion of a work of art that is independent from both the mortal that it materially replicates and the divine that it invokes, and that quality derives its etiological grounding from a myth about the artist's experience, which is itself eroticized.

We may learn as much about that myth when it is viewed negatively as when it is celebrated. The early third-century *Life of Apollonius of Tyana* by Philostratus chronicles the wanderings of a Pythagorean ascetic-philosopher-mystic-miracle worker with ports of call from Greece to India. A contemporary of Jesus (later understood as a rival), Apollonius seems to represent a paganism that has been transformed into a spiritualized, perhaps Platonized, religion. Two of his triumphant encounters are of interest to us. At one point, he is arguing with the Egyptians about the animal forms in which their gods are represented; the Greek deities, he declares contrariwise, have been sculpted "in the most honorable and pious way." To which Thespesion, the Egyptian spokesman, replies,

> "Your Phidias ... and your Praxiteles, they did not go up to heaven and make a cast of the gods' forms before turning them into art, did they? Was it not something else that set them to work as sculptors?" "It was," said Apollonius "and something supremely philosophical." "What was that?" asked the [Egyptian], "you cannot mean anything but Imitation [mimesis]." "Imagination [phantasia] created these objects," replied Apollonius, "a more skilful artist than Imitation. Imitation will create what it knows, but Imagination will also create what it does not know, conceiving it with reference to the real."[27]

Apollonius' "imagination," though it may sound glorious and liberating, insists on a program of broad doctrinal correctness that minimizes the fact of representing a god's body as human. Thespesion, equally uninterested in the body, responds by arguing in favor of a religious iconography that rests upon deeper and more mystical symbolism; his culture's statues of their gods, he says, have "profound inner meaning." On the one hand, then, theological allegory (*à la* the crown on Polyclitus' statue of Hera); on the other, artistic representations legible only by the initiates. Most significant to us is the aesthetic that both combatants essentially dismiss: the notion of a direct physical apperception of the divine that becomes mimetic art.

What is at stake here becomes clear from another episode in the life of Apollonius. Among his miscellaneous adventures in problem-solving, he arrives in – of all places – Cnidos, where he is confronted with the spectacle of a young man who is in love with none other than

Praxiteles' statue of Aphrodite. The townspeople themselves are quite tolerant of this aberration – they think the "the goddess would be more celebrated if she had a lover" (6.40) – but, noting Apollonius' negative reaction, they ask him if he means to reform their systems of religious observance. No, he replies, "'I will correct your eyesight but the customs of the sanctuary may remain as they are" (ibid). After this enigmatic assertion, Apollonius demands of the lovesick young man whether he believes in the existence of the gods. Oh, yes, comes the reply: "he revered them so much as to fall in love with them, and mentioned the wedding which he was planning to celebrate" (ibid). In response, Apollonius begins to lecture the lovelorn swain not about the impropriety of mortal unions with statues but about the impropriety of mortal unions with gods, after which the young man goes away cured, having made appropriate – rather than inappropriate – sacrifices to his favorite divinity.

The message, I think, is contained in that strange comment about correcting their eyesight. It is right to believe in the gods, and it may even be right to believe in statues, but it is wrong to see the statue as the god and (perhaps more fundamentally) wrong to see the statue as the *Greek Anthology* epigrams imagined Praxiteles seeing the god. Insofar as the *Cnidian Aphrodite* declares its independence from mortal and divine significations, insofar as it is something other than an alle-gorized divinity or a hermetic symbol or a liturgical mediator, it is understood to embody desire.

How does a statue embody desire? The epigrams about catching illicit sight of Aphrodite are self-consciously mythic; but there is a more earthbound tale of origins as well. Indeed, the verbal lore that follows in the statue's wake has one simple, direct, and often repeated answer: he was in love with the model who posed for the statue – the courtesan Phryne – and that passion is transferred to the work itself. Even before the time of Praxiteles, *Phryne*, or toad, is a comic or disparaging term for a prostitute, but the life of a famous courtesan by that name who is supposed to have been contemporary with and lover of Praxiteles *inter alios* is mostly a construct of later times – in other words, part of the same legendary matter that surrounds the statue.[28] From numerous sources, we are given to understand that she had a beautiful body and that she was a great patroness of the arts, in effect, a public personage. What is most intriguing are the interrelations among these attributes. There are many versions of a story in which she is on trial for her life; things are not going well in the courtroom, whereupon she (or, in some versions, her lawyer) bares her breasts. No less an authority than Quintilian cites this event, and, though he wishes to demonstrate that lofty masculinist oratory, which is his subject, must be separated from the more vulgar category of persuasion (such as women baring their breasts), the parallels to other courtroom ploys already make it clear that Phryne was being understood as not just an artist's model but a body artist in her own right.[29]

That becomes even clearer in the detailed account of her life by Athenaeus, in the same *Deipnosophistae* which contains lists of individuals enamored of sculpture. The legal victory, he says, was owing to the fact that "Phryne was more beautiful in the unseen parts. Hence one could not easily catch a glimpse of her naked; for she always wore a tunic which wrapped her body closely, and she did not resort to the public baths" (13.590). If these acts of partial denuding do not already establish a connection to the Cnidian goddess, we have only to read on, as Athenaeus recounts the story of Phryne's semi-exhibitionist performance at the Eleusinian festival:

> In full sight of the whole Greek world, she removed only her cloak and let down her long hair before stepping into the water; she was the model for Apelles when he painted his Aphrodite Rising from the Sea. So, too, the sculptor Praxiteles, being in love with her, modelled his Cnidian Aphrodite from her. (Ibid.)

It may be, in fact, that the Apelles painting is a Praxitelean source, occupying what is essentially a middle term of nakedness between the heavily draped females of previous art and the revolutionary step of the Cnidian figure.[30] Here, that same story is told in the key of eros: Phryne bestows on the statue the art of the naked body. It is no surprise that in another Hellenistic text, Alciphron's *Letters of Courtesans*, Phryne is imagined as begging the sculptor to join her next to a representation of herself as Aphrodite so that they can make love in the temple; [31] or that Pliny will say of yet another Praxitelean version of his *innamorata* that "connoisseurs detect in the figure the artist's love of her and the reward promised him by the expression on the courtesan's face" (*Nat. Hist.* 34.70). Whether that bashful *mercedem* is the statue that he will present to her or some other type of reward that she will present to him in return, it is clear that art objects born of desire perpetuate desire.

And they perpetuate desire because of the way they are on public view. The Praxitelean Aphrodite is, as we have seen, a very monument to exposure. With considerable eloquence, Andrew Stewart places himself in the picture:

> Praxiteles constructs the spectator as both worshipper and voyeur. In fact, he seems to construct *two* spectators, linking them and her in a triangular relationship of voyeuristic complicity and erotic rivalry. One of these individuals (me) sees her frontally as he enters the temple, while the other (already present off to my right) apparently provokes her sidewise glance and smile. For I can interpret these to mean that she is either modestly turning away from me or ignoring me in favor of this notional third party.[32]

Though this narrative is compelling, it begs questions regarding the gendered basis of this whole kind of analysis without confronting it directly. There is no doubt that from the glimpse of female nakedness to the stain on the statue, we are in masculinist territory. But there is some risk in assigning to simple binary categories the operations of eros, whether we take them for granted or condemn them.[33]

Pliny's account of the statue's installation is, fittingly, more inclusive than that of Andrew Stewart, both in regard to optics and to desire:

> The shrine in which [the *Aphrodite*] stands is entirely open so as to allow the image of the goddess to be viewed from every side, and it is believed to have been made in this way with the blessing of the goddess herself. The statue is equally admirable from every angle. (*Nat. Hist.* 36.21)

We might follow the archaeologists in searching out the kind of fourth-century BCE temple structure that would allow multiple ways of looking,[34] or we may note the fact that the statue itself does not entirely support such viewing in the round. But what I find most interesting is "the blessing of the goddess herself." As in the epigram from the *Greek Anthology*, Aphrodite seems to have visited this shrine; in the process, she transfers the act of artistic viewership from the individual, male, peeping Tom to a response governed by her own divine aegis. If Venus smiles upon this form of exhibition, that is presumably because it is likeliest to inspire love. The triumph of art is also the triumph of love.

Which makes Pseudo-Lucian's contradictory account of the installation all the more intriguing:

> The temple had a door on both sides for the benefit of those also who wish to have a good view of the goddess from behind, so that

no part of her be left unadmired. It's easy therefore for people to enter by the other door and survey the beauty of her back. And so we decided to see all of the goddess and went round to the back of the precinct. (*Erotes* 13)

Praxiteles' Aphrodite, in other words, is not installed in an arena for 360° viewing. Rather, the sculptor's artistry expresses itself in staging her from two opposing points of view. Once again, the archaeologists pursue this possibility with great seriousness, pointing out that there was in this part of Asia Minor a two-sided type of shrine known as a *naiskos*; though in earlier times it would not have actually had a door with a key, that might have been added in the Hellenistic period.[35] Perhaps that change confirms the more "sophisticated" tastes of later times. More to the point, the fact that the front of the shrine was open while the back required a special key also speaks volumes about the structures of eros in culture.

And that is where the heart of the issue lies. The *Erotes* is, essentially, a sexual debate within a sexual debate. In the framing story, a man who is indiscriminately greedy in his taste for both women and boys provokes the narrator, who doesn't care for either, into recounting the experience of judging an oratorical contest between two other men, one who liked women and the other boys. In the context of that traditional Hellenistic *querelle*, the trip to Cnidos undertaken as part of the debate becomes a sort of litmus test for the operations of desire. On the one hand, it is a pilgrimage to Aphrodite in her role as an overarching divinity of love and hence appropriate to both combatants; on the other hand, it is a celebrated site for appreciating female beauty, which would seem to prejudice the case heterosexually. And indeed the boy-lover, from Athens, is far less happy to undertake this part of the voyage than is the woman-lover, from Corinth. But on the third hand, even if Aphrodite is female, the subject that brings all these people together is *eros* – not just a masculine noun but also a beautiful boy. Nor is it an accident that Praxiteles' most famous other statue is the *Eros of Thespiae*, which seems to be a future part of their itinerary.

Now we can understand what it means in this text to look at the *Aphrodite*:

When the door had been opened by the woman responsible for keeping the keys, we were filled with an immediate wonder for the

beauty we beheld. The Athenian who had been so impassive an observer a minute before, upon inspecting those parts of the goddess which recommended a boy, suddenly raised a shout ... (cf. Figure 1.10) "Heracles!" he exclaimed, "what a well-proportioned back! What generous flanks she has! How satisfying an armful to embrace! How delicately moulded the flesh on the buttocks, neither too thin and close to the bone, nor yet revealing too great an expanse of fat! And as for those precious parts sealed in on either side by the hips, how inexpressibly sweetly they smile! How perfect the proportions of the thighs and the shins as they stretch down in a straight line to the feet! So that's what Ganymede looks like as he pours out the nectar in heaven for Zeus and makes it taste sweeter."
(*Erotes* 14)

The Cnidian Aphrodite becomes the center of this homosexual/heterosexual debate not only because she is the goddess of love and not only because she has a pendant Cupid in Thespiae but also because she is installed in a front door/back door temple. What was for Pliny polymorphous erotic connoisseurship becomes here the aesthetic definition of alternative sexualities.

Do these strange texts, and this singular statue testify to a whole aesthetics of desire? One statue, however foundational, cannot make the full case. Let us say, at least, that in the retrospect of the classical tradition we are presented with opposing alternatives. It is no coincidence that Philostratus' *Life of Apollonius* should wish to shunt the artistic experience away from the desiring and desirable body, nor that the contemporary Christian convert Arnobius should cite Praxiteles as having based his goddess on a courtesan and therefore having debased religion into whoredom.[36]

On the other hand, we have Pliny, whose work is the principal channel for the diffusion of classical art into the tradition. In the previous book of the *Natural History* to that where the *Cnidian Aphrodite* is discussed, Pliny tells the story of the painter Protogenes, whose artistic achievements are so significant to King Demetrius that he abandons a battle plan that might harm the artist's studio. This leads to a not so free association about Protogenes' artistic tastes; Aristotle, Pliny goes on to say, kept advising Protogenes to paint the achievements of Alexander the Great, on account of their eternal significance. But "the impulses of the mind, and a certain artistic desire [*impetus animi et quaedam artis libido*]" led him instead to subjects like the *Satyr Reposing* and the *Tragic Poet in Meditation* (*Nat. Hist.* 35.105). Indeed, throughout his account of ancient art, Pliny goes a long way to celebrate the libidinous – which is to say both imaginative and pleasurable – aesthetic over against other systems of defining the force of art.

Of course, within the space that encompasses imagination and pleasure, there is much room for movement, and for confusion. In the long run, if one wishes to characterize aesthetics as the encounter of love and art, then the story of the nocturnal visitor to Aphrodite's temple must stand as an extreme example, at once defining the relationship and also setting its boundaries. In one sense, he is the supreme art lover who gives his all in an unmediated relationship to the aesthetic object. In another sense, he is like those birds who fly down to peck at the painted grapes of Zeuxis,[37] performing the ultimate compliment to the master's artistry but also revealing themselves to have a highly primitive – indeed, beastly – notion of the relation between art and life. What is essentially missing from the story of the stain (the reason, in effect, that I previously referred to my concern here as the *early* history of the subject) is the aesthetic impulse to separate art from life, without sacrificing its erotic charge.

On that subject, Pliny recounts a circumstance in regard to the *Aphrodite* that may be even more significant than the tale we have concentrated on here. He reports, in a case parallel to that of Protogenes and Alexander, that King Nicomedes offered to pay off the immense public debt of Cnidos if only the citizens would cede him the Praxitelean statue, but Pliny applauds their refusal, he says, "for with this statue Praxiteles made Cnidus a famous city." And then he tells a story about the statue (not found anywhere else) that seems to locate art in a more complicated space of eros. Praxiteles, he says,

> had made two figures, which he put up for sale together. One of them was draped and for this reason was preferred by the people of Cos, who had an option on the sale, although he offered it at the same price as the other. This they considered to be the only decent and dignified course of action. The statue which they refused was purchased by the people of Cnidus and achieved an immeasurably greater reputation. (*Nat. Hist.* 36.20–1)

The tale of the two Venuses in a statuary showroom is generally thought to be historically implausible. It certainly testifies to that strange sense of clothing and unclothing that we have seen in the "real" single Aphrodite. More than that, it tangles up this twosome with an even more famous pair of Venuses – *ouranos* and *pandemos*, heavenly and earthly[38] – so that we are in a destabilized realm where it is not automatically clear whether nudity belongs on earth and clothing in heaven or vice versa. But most of all, it traps the poor citizens of Cos. They get first choice. They wish to act in a manner that is *casta* and *severa*, so they sensibly elect the Aphrodite that is *casta* and *severa*. But they go wrong in failing to recognize that the rules of art are different from, indeed perhaps opposite to, the rules of life. On the scale of citizenship, you may be well advised to admit clothed ladies rather than naked ones into your town, but on the scale of art, it is nudity and not civic decorum that produces ultimate value. If art is the deposit of a social relationship, there is something that escapes the stain – indeed, both the Baxandallian and the Cnidian stains – something naked, exposed, gazing, gazed upon, and responding to the gaze, "admirable from every angle," occupying the whole range from illicit to extraordinary experience.

Notes

1. Michael Baxandall, *Painting and Experience in Fifteenth-Century Italy* (Oxford: Clarendon Press, 1972), 1.
2. Leonard Barkan, *The Gods Made Flesh: Metamorphosis and the Pursuit of Paganism* (New Haven: Yale University Press, 1986), xiv.
3. Leonard Barkan, *Unearthing the Past: Archaeology and Aesthetics in the Making of Renaissance Culture* (New Haven: Yale University Press, 1999), xxxii.
4. Pliny the Elder, *Natural History* 36.21. Citation is to LCL edition, trans. D. E. Eichholz, 10 vols. (Cambridge, Mass.: Harvard University Press, 1938), 10: 17. Subsequent references will be to this edition, by chapter number only.
5. Pseudo-Lucian, *Erotes* 16. Citation is to LCL edition, trans. M. D. MacLeod, 8 vols. (Cambridge, Mass.: Harvard University Press, 1967), 8: 177–9. Subsequent references will be to this edition, by chapter number only.
6. Pliny, *Natural History* 36.22.
7. Athenaeus, *Deipnosophistae* 13.605ff. Citation is to LCL edition, trans. C. B. Gulick, 7 vols. (Cambridge, Mass.: Harvard University Press, 1999), 6: 265–57. For yet more instances of unconventional loves in this vein, and a broadly informed view of the love for images, see Maurizio Bettini, *The Portrait of the Lover*, trans. L. Gibbs (Berkeley and Los Angeles: University of California Press, 1999), esp. 59–74.
8. Pliny, *Natural History* 36.39. The attribution to Praxiteles depends on a reading of Cicero's *Verrine Orations* 2.4.2.4.
9. Pliny, *Natural History* 34.62.
10. On this general theme in the *Natural History*, see Jacob Isager, *Pliny on Art and Society* (London and New York: Routledge, 1991), passim.
11. Pseudo-Lucian, *Erotes* 15.
12. Gaio Plinio Secondo, *Storia Naturale* (Torino: Einaudi, 1988), 5.549.
13. *Greek Anthology* 16.216. Citation is to the LCL edition, trans. W. R. Paton, 5 vols. (Cambridge, Mass.: Harvard University Press, 1920), 5: 289. Subsequent references will be to this edition, by book and epigram number only.

14. For Pliny, see *Natural History* 34.55–6, where Polyclitus is credited for having perfected art but also rendered sculpture quadrata and monotonous. For Winckelmann, see A. A. Donohue, "Winckelmann's History of Art and Polyclitus," in *Polykleitos, the Doryphoros, and Tradition*, ed. W. G. Moon (Madison, 1995), 338–41.

15. See, for example, Christine Mitchell Havelock, *The Aphrodite of Knidos and Her Successors* (Ann Arbor: University of Michigan Press, 1995), 1: "The female nude as a subject for art in three-dimensional and monumental form was introduced by the late classic sculptor Praxiteles"; and M. Robertson, *A History of Greek Art* (Cambridge: Cambridge University Press, 1975), 2.391: "Praxiteles created something profoundly new: a figure designed from start to finish, in proportion, structure, pose, expression to illustrate an ideal of the feminine principle."

16. Here, as elsewhere in the study of ancient sculpture (and still more in the study of ancient painting), scholars must remain aware that they are writing about art objects that they have never seen. Such an awareness entails both a sense of humility in the face of limited data and a careful methodological attention to the largely discursive, non-visual channels – in other words, language, often composed with little or no interest in documentary precision – through which the notion of the ancient original is transmitted. As for the non-linguistic evidence of Praxiteles' *Aphrodite*, which (as usual) consists of replicas at several removes, Andrew Stewart (*Greek Sculpture: An Exploration* [New Haven and London: Yale University Press, 1990], 177) goes so far as to say, "Today she survives only in a few dozen rather graceless copies." Among these examples, the principal contenders have been two versions in the Vatican, the "Colonna" and the "Belvedere," shown in the present article as Figures 1.1 and 1.3, along with another in Munich, here seen as Figure 1.2. For discussions of their various claims, see C. S. Blinkenberg, *Knidia: Beiträge zur Kenntnis der praxitelischen Aphrodite* (Copenhagen: Levin & Munksgaard, 1933), esp. 47–52; and M. Pfrommer, "Zur Venus Colonna: Ein späthellenistische Redaktion der Knidischen Aphrodite," *Deutsches Archäologisches Institut Abteilung Istanbul Abhandlungen* 35 (1985): 173–80.

17. The bibliography on nudity is vast, beginning with the classic (and still valuable) work of Kenneth Clark, *The Nude: A Study in Ideal Form* (Garden City, New York: Doubleday, 1956). Of enormous value, both for its arguments and for its bibliography, is Andrew Stewart, *Art, Desire, and the Body in Ancient Greece* (Cambridge: Cambridge University Press), esp. 24–42, 238–41. See also several of the essays in A. O. Koloski-Ostrow and C. L. Lyons, eds., *Naked Truths: Women, Sexuality and Gender in Classical Art and Archaeology* (London: Routledge, 1997), especially those by Beth Cohen ("Divesting the Female Breast of Clothes in Classical Sculpture") and Joan Reilly ("Naked and Limbless: Learning about the Feminine Body in Ancient Athens"); Larissa Bonfante, "Nudity as a Costume in Classical Art," *American Journal of Archaeology* 93 (1989): 543–79; and Robin Osborne, "Men Without Clothes: Heroic Nakedness and Greek Art," *Gender and History* 9 (1997): 504–28.

18. A particularly eloquent comparison of the two canonical figures, rather different from mine, is to be found in Rhys Carpenter, *Greek Sculpture* (Chicago: University of Chicago Press, 1960), 173–4.

19. See, by way of contrast, Nanette Salomon, "Making a World of Difference: Gender, Asymmetry, and the Greek Nude" in Koloski-Ostrow and Lyons (eds.), *Naked Truths*, 197–219; and Robin Osborne, "Looking on – Greek Style: Does the Sculpted Girl Speak to Women Too?" in *Classical Greece: Ancient Histories and Modern Archaeologies*, ed. I. Morris (Cambridge: Cambridge University Press, 1994) 81–96. More cautious approaches to these questions may be found in Havelock, *Aphrodite of Cnidos*, 36–7, and Brunilde Ridgway, "Some Personal Thoughts on the Cnidia" available at http://www.archaeologie-sachbuch.de/Fleischer/index1.htm?/Fleischer/Texte/Ridgway1.htm.

20. See Pliny, *Natural History* 35.65.

21. On the reception history of this work, one of the most widely copied pieces of art in the classical tradition, see Francis Haskell and Nicholas Penny, *Taste and the Antique* (New Haven and London: Yale University Press, 1981), 325–8. For an account of its origins and condition, see Guido A. Mansueli, *Real Galleria degli Uffizi: Le Sculture* (Rome, 1958), 1.71–3.

22. On the history of this statue, see Haskell and Penny, *Taste,* 318–20; and Wolfgang Helbig, *Führer durch die öffentlichen Sammlungen klassischer Altertümer in Rom* (Tübingen, 1966), 2.128–30.

23. The name is given as canonical by Haskell and Penny (*Taste*, 332–3), though many statues in different poses have also been referred to by that title. This work has a very extensive history of restoration, for which see Mansuelli, *Sculture*, 1.127–8, but the position of the clothing behind the figure seems to have belonged to it in its original form.

24. See Phyllis Pray Bober and Ruth Rubinstein, *Renaissance Artists and Antique Sculpture* (London: Harvey Miller, 1986), 61–2; and H. H. Brummer, *The Statue Court in the Vatican Belvedere* (Stockholm: Almqvist & Wiksell, 1970), 122–9, 227–34.

25. See Barkan, *Unearthing the Past*, 128.

26. On these distinctions – understandably more complex than my brief outline of them here – see the magisterial article by R. L. Gordon, "The Real and the Imaginary: Production and Religion in the Graeco-Roman World," *Art History* 2 (1979): 5–34. The argument that the *Aphrodite* must be construed solely as a divinity has represented one strand of the archaeological debates concerning the body positions of the original: if viewers of the original did not see her as in any way human, then she could not have been performing any human actions like washing herself or reacting to an intrusion on her privacy. In this vein, see Gerhart Rodenwaldt, "*theoi rheia zoontes*," *Abhandlungen der deutschen Akademie der Wissenschaften zu Berlin* 14 (1943). Given the number of stories, throughout the classical period, about divinities engaged in human actions and threatened by humans, this hardly seems historically plausible.

27. Philostratus, *Life of Apollonius of Tyana* 6.19. Citation is to LCL edition, trans. C. P. Jones, 3 vols. (Cambridge, Mass.: Harvard University Press, 2005), 2: 155.

28. The best summary of the sources – interpreted in a more naturalistic vein than would be my wont – is in Havelock, *Aphrodite of Cnidos*, 42–7.

29. The nudity ploy appears in a set of anecdotes concerning courtroom successes not due to rhetoric: "Many other things have the power of persuasion, such as money, influence, the authority and rank of the speaker, or even some sight unsupported by language" (Quintilian, *Institutio oratoria* 2.15.6).

30. On the relation between these works and the possibility of a sculptural afterlife of the Anadyomene, see Havelock, *Aphrodite of Cnidos*, 86–93. See also the historiographical reflections on these connections in Brunilde Sismondo Ridgway, *Hellenistic Sculpture I* (Madison: University of Wisconsin Press, 1990), 60–1.

31. Alciphron, *Letters to Courtesans* 1. Citation is to LCL edition, trans. A. R. Benner and F. H. Fobes (Cambridge, Mass.: Harvard University Press, 1949), 251–3.

32. Stewart, *Art, Desire, and the Body*, 103. Though I may offer some challenges to this reading, I should also express my great indebtedness to the account of the *Aphrodite* offered both here and in the same author's *Greek Sculpture*, 177–8.

33. Perhaps it is unseemly, in a volume honoring a scholar who has done so much to open up historical questions regarding sexuality, that the critical debates surrounding gender in regard to the Aphrodite be mostly relegated to a footnote. Whatever that may indicate about the present author's priorities, it should certainly be noted that, among its other provocations, the Praxitelean statue has induced many twentieth- and twenty-first century scholarly observers to feel a special immediacy regarding their own gender concerns. This is as true when Andrew Stewart decides that he is himself entering Aphrodite's temple as it is when Nanette Salomon concludes her essay by saying that the statue "continues to serve as a shared bond which ultimately gives access to membership in the hegemonic club of cosmopolitan manly heterosexuals" ("Making a World of Difference," 212). I am a little more hesitant about painting myself into the picture. Granted, works of art do, and should, inspire us to feel that we live in their permanent presence, and in a permanent present. Still, an abyss separates us from Praxiteles or Pliny or, for that matter, Winckelmann; and we need to exercise some caution about applying our own notions of gender construction to the past – starting with the very concept of gender construction. That having been said, if I *were* to attempt to cross this gap and enter the gender debate from where I stand, I would say, first of all, that neither the traditional view of the statue (which, let us say, assumes a masculinist viewpoint) nor the ideologically informed feminist view pays sufficient attention to homoerotic aesthetics of antique culture, which arises out of a very different set of assumptions and actions regarding what we call "homosexuality" and "heterosexuality." In other words, the assumption that indissolubly links a female statue with a heterosexual male observer, whether it is taken for granted or deplored, needs to be interrogated just as much as any other essentializing assumption. Equally worth challenging on historicist grounds is the assumption that a sexualized representation, including an emphasis on a female's genitals or (just as prevalent) on a boy's buttocks, is *ipso facto* degrading. For valuable work on the subject of the "gaze," in addition to Osborne (cited in note 19), see John Elsner, "Naturalism and the Erotics of the Gaze: Intimations of Narcissus," and Françoise Frontisi-Ducroux, "Eros, Desire and the Gaze," both in *Sexuality in Ancient Art: Near East, Egypt, Greece, Italy*, ed. N. Kampen (Cambridge: Cambridge University Press, 1996); and Simon Goldhill, "The Erotic Experience of Looking: Cultural Conflict and the Gaze in Empire Culture," in *The Sleep of Reason: Erotic Experience and Sexual Ethics in Ancient Greece*

and Rome, ed. M. Nussbaum and J. Sihyola (Chicago: University of Chicago Press, 2002).

34. For an extensive account of archaeology at what may have been the original site, see I. C. Love, "A Preliminary Report of the Excavations at Knidos," *American Journal of Archaeology* 74 (1970): 149–55; 76 (1972): 61–76, 393–405; and 77 (1973): 413–24. More recent excavation has suggested that Love was uncovering a temple from a later period; still, it may have replicated the earlier original. See Havelock, *Aphrodite of Cnidos*, 58–63.

35. See A. H. Borbein, "Die griechische Statue des 4. Jahrhunderts v. Chr: Form-analystische Untersuchungen zur Kunst der Nachklassik," *Jahrbuch des deutschen Archäologischen Instituts* 88 (1973), esp. 188–94.

36. See Arnobius, *Against the Heathen* 6.13: "Who does not know ... that Praxiteles, putting forth his utmost skill, fashioned the face of the Cnidian Venus on the model of the courtesan Gratina, whom the unhappy man loved desperately? Nor is this the only Venus to whom there has been given beauty taken from a harlot's face."

37. Pliny, *Natural History*, 35.65.

38. This extraordinarily persistent strand of mythic material goes back to Pausanias' speech in Plato's *Symposium* (180d–181d) and to an account given by Socrates in Xenophon's *Symposium* 8.

2
English Literature in its Golden Age

Sean Keilen

The Golden Age is a topic of perennial interest for scholars of Renaissance art and culture, but the notion that the Renaissance itself was a golden period has been much less resilient to changes in academic taste. When C. S. Lewis cited a distinction between English literature's "golden" and "drab" ages more than half a century ago, he was trying to resurrect an idea whose life-force had waned. More than 150 years earlier, Thomas Warton had observed that "golden" was merely a commonplace way of referring to the "POETICAL" features of the Elizabethan age, meaning "the predominancy of fable, of fiction, and fancy, and a predilection for interesting adventures and pathetic events."[1] Declining from scholarly axiom to common cliché, despite Lewis's efforts to prop it up, the notion that Renaissance writing constitutes an ideal condition of literary composition in English – and therefore is worth more than the writing of other periods, as gold is more precious than silver, bronze, and iron – eventually fell into disfavor during the canon wars of the 1980s and '90s, at which point it disappeared entirely from the lexicon that English professors share.[2] This minor change in professional discourse may have indicated a major shift in sensibilities about the craft of literary scholarship, and measured the degree to which the discipline of literary studies then lost interest in some of the tasks that had defined it until that moment: establishing which pieces of writing were "literature" and which "literary" texts merited recognition as "the best."

In the context of the different priorities that most scholars and critics of English literature espouse today, it may be risible to describe the sixteenth century as a golden age, but our suspicion of obsolete critical metaphors such as this one, and our embarrassment about the kind of value judgments that they imply, blind us to a critical history of remarkable interest and complexity. For example, when Lewis asserts that there are important differences between the overlapping periods of English literary history that he calls "the Late Medieval [Age], the Drab Age, and the 'Golden' Age," he takes the unusual step of twice instructing the reader that the "epithet *golden* is not eulogistic." "By golden poetry," he writes, "I mean not simply good poetry, but poetry which is, so to speak, innocent or ingenuous. In a Golden Age, the right thing to do is obvious: 'good is as visible as green'." Associating "the whole Golden achievement" of English Renaissance writing with innocence and ingenuousness and with the self-evidence of the good (moral and aesthetic), Lewis not only fits vernacular literary history to the golden age of ancient myth, which Greek and Roman writers described as a utopia of contentment, simplicity, peacefulness, and order.[3] He also adapts the eighteenth-century scholar Richard Hurd's idea that the superiority of the Elizabethan age inhered in its social decorum, as opposed to its revival of ancient learning, its reformation of religious belief, or its artistic virtuosity. Speaking through the character of John Arbuthnot in a dialogue titled "On the Golden Age of Queen *Elizabeth*," Hurd argues that "throughout her kingdom there was every where that reverence of authority, that sense of honour, that conscience of duty, in a word that gracious simplicity of manners, which renders the age of *Elizabeth* truly GOLDEN: as presenting the fairest picture of humanity that is to be met with in the accounts of any people." In a footnote to the phrase "the reverence of authority," Hurd expands upon Arbuthnot's claim by quoting Henry Wotton, for whom the late-sixteenth century was "an ingenuous and uninquisitive time, when all the passions and affections were lapped up in such an innocent and humble obedience, that there was never the least contestation ... with the queen ..."[4] Here again, the excellence of England's golden age is tantamount to a conviction that it is in the nature of authority to be self-evident, internally consistent, logically unassailable, and compelling, wherever and however it manifests itself.[5]

When they look back to Renaissance England from the vantage of their later periods, and when they ascribe ideal qualities to an earlier age and allow it to exercise authority in their own time, largely on the basis of the golden attributes that they themselves bestow on it, Hurd and Lewis exhibit an attitude toward the past that is typical of the Renaissance itself.[6] Handed down from texts such as Hesiod's *Works and Days*, Virgil's *Eclogues*, and Ovid's *Metamorphoses*, the golden age topos presented an idealized picture of humanity in its primitive condition, essentially civilized before the foundation of cities and the formulation of laws, and obedient to authority by instinct. "The first age was golden," writes Ovid, "and, wanting both law and someone to enforce it, of its own will cherished loyalty and what's right" (*Aurea prima sata est aetas, quae vindice nullo, | sponte sua, sine lege fidem rectumque colebat*) (*Met.* 1.89–90). English Renaissance writers were quick to use such ideas as a way of sanctioning their own devotion to Antiquity at a time when the Reformation had put the prestige of Rome as a cultural ideal in jeopardy.

On the other hand, it is also in their nature to be more ambivalent than either Hurd or Lewis about the adequacy of "gold" and "golden" as metaphors for the excellence of Greek and Roman literature and of their own art too. As a myth of ideality, the golden age provided an equivocal way of placing modernity in relation to its archaic origins. Available for satire as well as encomium, the golden age topos was as malleable as the physical substance to which it was linked by metaphor: It could be fitted to the present time either as the first chapter in a story about human progress, leading from humble pastoral beginnings to the superb achievement of modern civilization ("from here, things will only get better"); or as the beginning of humanity's inevitable decline and fall ("from here, things will only get worse").[7] At what point, the topos would appear to ask, are human beings really in their prime?

The ambivalence of Renaissance writers toward the golden age, in this sense, may also have been born of the extraordinary metaphoric range of the terms "gold" and "golden" in ancient sources. Virgil, in the fourth *Eclogue*, famously celebrates the advent of a new Augustan age, teaming with a golden Roman race (*aurea gens*); and just as famously, in the *Aeneid*, he deplores the fact that the metal gold brings out the worst in human nature, observing the murder of Priam's son by his guardian with proverbial economy: "O accursed hunger for gold, to what will you not drive human hearts?" (*quid non mortalia pectora cogis, | auri sacra fames*) (*Ecl.* 4.9, *Aen.* 3.56–7). Ovid's messages about gold are similarly mixed. On the one hand, the *Metamorphoses* establishes that the golden age is categorically better than every period that followed it, and therefore uniquely worthy of having the epithet "golden" attached to it. On the other, the *Amores* perversely holds that the golden age was golden precisely because it was ignorant of gold. "[W]hen old *Saturne* heavens rule possest," writes Ovid (in Marlowe's English), "All gaine in darknesse the deepe earth supprest. | Gold, silver, irons heavy weight, and brasse, | In hell were harbourd, here was found no masse. | But better things it gave, corne without ploughes, | Apples, and hony in oakes hollow boughes." Now, however, "Gold from the earth in steade of fruits we pluck," violence floods the world with blood, and "wealth gives estimation" (*Elegy* 7.36–40, 53, 55, translating *Amores* 3.8.35–40, 53, 55).

Such contradictions found issue in a wide variety of Renaissance texts, not all of them English or literary, from Erasmus's *Adagia*, to the episode of Mammon's Cave in the *Faerie Queene*, to Timon's reflections on the volatility of wealth in Shakespeare's play, to the *De re metallica* of Georgius Agricola – though the meaning of "gold" and "golden" is never more protean than it is in Renaissance poems.[8] Geffrey Whitney neatly captures the extreme reversibility of "gold" in the emblem "*Aureae compedes*" (Golden fetters), a stoical meditation on the difference between happiness and privilege that ends with a line that juxtaposes gold as a value concept with gold as a valuable substance: "I like the goulden libertie, let goulden bondage rest" (16).[9] Donne's ninth elegy, "The Autumnal," uses "gold" as a way of drawing our attention to the close relationship of the antithetical categories "best" and "worst" and to other, related dichotomies of value, such as "young" and "old" and "old" and "new." As Donne tallies up the worth of his aging lover in this poem, the golden age appears to lie in the past and in the future and to signify enrichment as well as decline: "Were her first years the golden age? That's true, | But now she's gold oft tried and ever new" (*Elegy* 9.7–8). Here, several centuries after Petrarch first invented the Renaissance, we find Donne paying tribute to Petrarchan lyric in the form of a portrait, as it were in middle age, of the ideal girl whose name means "gold" and signifies Petrarch's laureate achievement (Laura). We also find him echoing an anthropomorphic idea about the development of poetry from ancient times that James VI articulated during the 1580s, writing "Thairfore, quhat I speik of Poesie now, I speik of it as being come to mannis age and perfectioun, quhair as then [in Antiquity] it was bot in the infancie and chyldheid."[10] Presumably, Donne's portrait of a cherished lover entering the autumn of her life tells us that the golden age is now.

Arising from Greek and Roman literature as an image of ideal origins, the golden age represented Antiquity's radical difference in time, place, language, sensibility, and value from the Renaissance that admired it. At the same time, it also gave the period a mirror for speculating what its own modernity might look like if the ancient world was restored, in all of its alien plenitude, just as humanism promised. For many English writers, this was an equivocal prospect at best, and particularly for two of them – Thomas Nashe and John Lyly – the golden age had different implications from the ones that we have been taught to recognize by studies connecting the golden age to the pastoral genre; or to utopian thinking about Eden and the New World; or to the ideological projects of Renaissance monarchs, like Elizabeth Tudor and James Stuart, who used golden age iconography in order to establish that they themselves had fulfilled the prophecy of the *Fourth Eclogue*, restoring peace and bringing Justice back from the heavens to which she had fled at the beginning of the Bronze Age.[11] For Nashe and Lyly, the idea of the golden age was indelibly associated with another ancient narrative – the myth of Midas – and from their meditations on this text arose the strain of thinking about imitation and its promise of literary authority that concerns me here.

Nashe

It is not difficult to see why Midas was attractive to Nashe and Lyly as a symbol for the process and the problems of imitating ancient literature. At least from the moment that he appears in Ovid's *Metamorphoses*, Midas is the figure for a certain transition between literatures and cultures that are alien to each other and an embodiment of the confusion of different kinds that ensues from this movement. Not coincidentally, he is also a figure of extremely vexed authority. Ovid's character may or may not be related to Mita, an eighth-century Phrygian king in central Anatolia, but as the fictional monarch of Lydia, Midas stands in between the Roman empire and Thrace, a more remote territory whose name was synonymous (for Romans) with barbarity, though Orpheus lived there.[12] In his pivotal situation between the center and the periphery of the Roman world, Midas figuratively presides over the transmission of strange knowledges and tradition into civilization, a passage that Ovid reenacts in the structure of his poem, placing the Midas myth directly after the myth of Orpheus. According to an esoteric mythographical tradition of which Ovid was evidently aware (*Met.* 11.92–3), Midas studied the orgiastic rites of Bacchus at Orpheus's feet on Mount Pieria, the site of a spring that was sacred to the Muses.[13]

Midas's ontological situation "in between" one thing and another made him a favorite subject of Renaissance visual art. Frequently the shape of his body draws attention to the different orders of being in which he stands on unsure footing. While Midas's crown and his golden touch make him more than a man but less than a god, his ass's ears make him less than a man but more than a beast. Illustrations of the myth in early printed editions of the *Metamorphoses* commonly underscore Midas's resemblance to Pan, a minor deity who is himself half-a-man and half-a-goat. In this way, they make the point that by preferring Pan's pipes to Apollo's lyre, Midas has turned himself into the kind of hybrid composition that he admires. In a superb engraving by Melchior Meier, which conflates the Midas myth with the myth of Marsyas, Midas appears in the right-hand corner, leaning on a stump, turning inward toward Apollo (Figure 2.1). Ass's ears, already sprouting from his head, link him visually to the long-eared fawns and satyrs who stand in the background at the left and ventilate their grief about the awful fate of Marsyas – who, having lost the fabric of his own humanity, is dissolving into the landscape, becoming one with the tree on which his body is splayed. Midas's ears also link him to a figure looming just above and behind him at the right side of the image: Tmolus, the god of the mountain on which the scene is taking place. In the Midas myth, Tmolus joins the nymphs in judging that Apollo's music is the better composition, and here he seems fascinated by the god himself, who stands forth naked in the center of the image as a portrait of the artist-

Figure 2.1   Melchior Meier, *Apollo and Marsyas and the Judgment of Midas, 1581,*
The Metropolitan Museum of Art, New York

as-engraver and also as the utmost achievement of Meier's engraving as a life-like work of art. Midas points toward Tmolus with his right hand, as if to protest to Apollo that he is equal to the mountain god as a judge and therefore that his judgment, though different, is equally valid. In response, Apollo demands that Midas understand that he is more like Marsyas than Tmolus. Confronted with the skin that the god has flayed from his opponent, who lies opposite the king in a symmetrical but inverted posture, Midas appears to contemplate his own reflection in the face of an empty hide that is a literal extension of his bad judgment, having neither eyes to see nor ears to listen.[14]

In a letter that Thomas Nashe addresses to readers of the first and unauthorized edition of *Astrophel and Stella* (published in the same year as Lyly's play), Midas stands in the forefront of a contest between Philip Sidney and his poetic predecessors.[15] In this setting, his notorious preference for the music of Pan rather than Apollo suggests a way of thinking about value, judgment, and the appraisal of works of art that imitate classical models. Nashe frames his text with quotations from Ovid's poetry that appear to support his claim that Sidney not only equaled the poetic achievement of the ancients but also surpassed it. At the opening of the letter, "*Tempus adest plausus, aurea pompa venit*" (Now is the time for cheering, the golden procession comes), a line from the *Amores*, heralds Sidney's entrance onto the literary stage, following the vernacular poets whom Nashe describes as a "scene of idiots," presumably from a time after the ancients but before Surrey and Wyatt (3.2.44; A3r).[16] Another Ovidian passage brings the letter to a close. Nashe's phrase in the final paragraph, "Such is the golden age wherein we live," appears to be a translation of a line from the *Ars amatoria* – "*Aurea nunc vere sunt saecula*" (2.277). As best I can tell, this is the first reference by an English writer to the English Renaissance as a golden age.

Read alongside the favorable comparisons that Nashe makes between Sidney and Apollo, Mercury, and Orpheus, the implications of these Ovidian passages seem obvious. But Nashe was too good a classicist not to notice that in their original contexts, the lines that he culls from Ovid solicit very different interpretations from the ones that the letter seems to give them. In the second poem of the third book of the *Amores*, for example, the phrase "golden procession" (*aurea pompa*) refers to the exhibition of images of the pagan gods that occurred at the beginning of ancient chariot races. The setting may be appropriate to the rivalry that Nashe establishes between Sidney and his poetic predecessors, but the impulse behind these lines, far from being religious fervor, is erotic passion. A moment later, Ovid's speaker is passing off a sexual overture as pious regard for ceremonial decorum: "While I'm talking, some dirt has gotten on your white dress. Nasty dirt, get off that snow-white body!" (2.41–2). In the *Ars amatoria*, reflecting on the general disdain in which gifts from suitors are held, Ovid discourages aspiring lovers from sending poems to the objects of their desires: "Regrettably, a poem isn't worth that much. I Poems are praised, but it's the expensive gift they want. I As long as he's rich, even the barbarian pleases. I *Now it truly is the golden age*: the greater part of honor I sells for gold; love is bought for gold. I Though you yourself should come, Homer, and all Muses with you, I if you don't bring anything, you'll be shown the door" (2.273–8; italics mine). If the quotation from Ovid's *Amores* signals, in a general way, that things in Nashe's letter about Sidney are not what they seem to be, the translated passage from the *Ars amatoria* points to a more specific crisis in meaning that preoccupied Nashe and other Renaissance writers, such as Spenser and Jonson. Given an economy in which poets must depend upon patrons for a living, the value of poetry, and the judgments that poems articulate, cannot be held separate from the fungibility of poetic art as a commodity.[17]

As Nashe probes the depths of this problem in the course of praising Sidney's verses, words connoting "the highest value" and "the ideal condition" sprout from the forest-floor of his densely allusive text. The letter is only four short pages long, but the word "gold" or "golden" occurs six times, in Latin as well as English – more often than any other metaphor for worth. It is as if Nashe, by sheer force of repetition, is trying to foreclose the ambiguities that "gold" evidently opened up for classical and Renaissance writers; and in so doing, to temper this aureate language into an unalloyed discourse of criticism. From another perspective, however, the definition of "gold" remains malleable in Nashe's text. Never meaning the same thing twice, it is in fact associated with a range of other metaphors for value and non-value, from the brightness of the sun to the worthlessness of painted rocks. The extreme ambiguity of "gold" in this encomium of Sidney's writing is only the most conspicuous symptom of the complicated way that Nashe appears to think about authority and judgment in relation to the appraisal of works of art. Despite the certitude with which he commends Sidney's verses to the reader as the very best writing, and despite his confidence in the superiority of his own critical acumen, Nashe asks: If a poem's value is not self-evident – or, more fundamentally, if the value of poetic composition is not intrinsic to the activity itself

– who shall determine what it's worth? The poet? The models that he imitates? The subject of the poem? The poet's patron? A critic? The reader? Which reader?

It seems that for Nashe none of these agents may be described as sovereign in matters of textual interpretation or aesthetic appraisal, though they all make claims to sovereignty. And thus, a radical idea about the nature of meaning issues from this encounter with Sidney's art: Nashe appears to hold that in the context of interpretation and appraisal, no judgment can ever be sovereign in the sense of being necessary, universal, and inerrant. This is the terrain, in between vernacular composition, its literary models, and its audience, that Midas may be said to occupy. Here, we are in a position to appreciate the significance of Midas for Nashe's criticism and to make sense of two other, apparently unrelated motifs: "ear" and "ass." In this text, Midas, his golden touch, his ass's ears, his infamous desires and choices, and his tenuous claim on his own throne are all symbolic correlatives for a certain attitude toward the literary authority of ancient writers and the "modern" enterprise of imitating them.

Nashe alludes to Midas three times in his text. At the beginning of the letter, he commends the melancholy feeling of *Astrophel and Stella* to the admiration of "idle eares" (A3r). "Idle" is not a term of reproach, because Nashe is speaking to the discerning reader whose judgment fell into disuse during "the scene of idiots," a time when nothing worthwhile was written and his "eares were deafned with the eccho of Fames brasen towres." The same paragraph contrasts the perceptive but "idle ears" of the capable reader with the ears of "a number of *Midasses*." Since the word "asses" is obvious in the unusual locution "*Midasses*," Nashe is likely referring to asinine readers who "have seene *Pan* sitting in his bower of delights" and, because they themselves are unable to distinguish between good and bad compositions, come to "admire [the] miserable hornepipes" on which he plays those blaring imitations of Antiquity's monumental achievements in poetic art.

The next passage that links the ear and the ass, however, makes a claim about judgment that is antithetical to the distinction between competent and incompetent appraisal on which Nashe insists in an earlier part of the letter. When called upon to defend the elliptical style of his own prose, Nashe takes refuge in the argument that all judgments about writing are equally valid expressions of individual taste – or as he puts it, paraphrasing Cicero, "every man as he likes."[18] "To explain it by a more familiar example," writes Nashe, "an Asse is no great stateman in the beastes common-wealth, though he weare his eares *upsevant muffe*, after the Muscovy fashion, ... yet of many, he is deemed a very vertuous member, and one of the honestest sort of men that are; So that our opinion ... gives the name of good or ill to every thing" (A4v). Because Midas presumes to be the equal of the gods in judging them, and because he is a king who hides his ass's ears inside a scarf in order to remain in high esteem among his subjects, he may be said to provide a figurative context for the argument once again – though in this case, Midas is a parody of Nashe rather than the writers and critics whom Nashe earlier portrayed as "a number of *Midasses*," sharply differentiating them from Sidney, the perceptive reader, and himself.

In a final reference to "ass" and Midas at the end of the letter, an even more oblique reference than the others, Nashe associates the aureate quality of "this golden age wherein we live" with the creatures that inhabit it: "golden Asses of all sortes." This inscrutable figure of speech refers with equal plausibility to the writers whom Nashe admires for their fecund imaginations and to poetasters whom he deplores for their incontinence: "Such is this golden age wherein in we live, and so replenisht with golden Asses of all sortes, that if learning had lost it selfe in a grove of Genealogies, we neede doe no more but sette an olde goose over halfe a dozen pottle-pots, ... and we shall have such a breede of bookes within a little while after, as will fill all the world with the wilde fowle of good wits ..." (A4v). If the phrase "golden Asses" does refer to Midas, he would appear to symbolize not only a kind of writing that is divided in its authorization between priceless ancient authors and the authority of a patron's purse; but also the kind of reading that a passage like this one solicits – a process of inter-pretation, as generative as it is asinine, that is so intent on determining the value of ambiguous textual details that it cannot hear what texts may be saying about their meaning as whole compositions. And so it is among the "golden Asses" that bring the letter to a close that Nashe's most assiduous reader inevitably finds an equivocal portrait of himself.[19]

Etymologically speaking, neither "assiduous" and "asinine," nor *aurum* and *auris* (the Latin words for "gold" and "ear"), are connected to each other. Acoustically, their resemblance is striking, but it is only through the lens of the Midas myth that one may bring these playful associa-tions into focus as meaningful relationships and begin to clarify the way that Nashe (or Lyly) uses them in order to imagine the importance of the classical tradition for his vernacular art. It may be that the importance of this tradition is more difficult for us to grasp now than it used to be. That difficulty is due, in part, to a tendency to portray the late-sixteenth century as the beginning of the modern era; and in part to a reluctance among scholars working in the late phases of the New Historicism to address Renaissance vernacular writing from the perspective of contexts and traditions that are conventionally associated with "high" or "elite" culture and its desires.[20] These developments have only intensified the perception that during the late-sixteenth century the arrival of modernity in every cultural domain was anticipated by a change, necessarily much more limited in scope, in the way that Antiquity exercised its authority in the realm of vernacular poetic style and composition. Hans-Georg Gadamer, for example, linking the onset of modernity to the decline of ancient literature's "exemplariness," argues that whereas "the ars critica" of early humanist philology "unreflectively presupposed the exemplariness of classical antiquity, which it helped to hand down," the humanism of the late-sixteenth century, standing on the threshold of an epochal transformation, "had to change its nature when there was no longer any clear relation of model to copy between classical antiquity and the present. ... This problem resulted in the development of historical reflection, which finally demolished classical antiquity's claim to be normative."[21] Gadamer's argument gave rise, in turn, to Robert Weimann's claim that during the "early modern" period it was textuality itself that generated modernity, announcing the arrival of the future as a new sense of authority-in-representation.[22] A more detailed discussion of this influential model of cultural change lies beyond the scope of my essay, but in turning now to Lyly's *Midas* (1591), I would like to suggest that it would be equally plausible to argue that neither ancient literature nor its authority were ever monolithic or "normative" in the ways that currently we assume that they once must have been. Indeed, one might want to say that it was precisely the heterogeneity of Greek and Roman writing that gave rise to its irresistible authority over the vernacular writers on whom its shadow fell. In the eyes of an earlier criticism, ancient literature was "a traditional and international gold reserve," a precious vein in which any Renaissance poet might tap "the infinite poetic value of a malleable body of myth."[23]

Lyly

Academic readers and editors of Lyly's *Midas* have largely ignored the implications of its Ovidian source and described the text as a simple political allegory, "a product of the enthusiastic nationalism which swept over England in the period immediately following the defeat of the Spanish Armada in 1588." "[T]hrough his central character," it is said, "Lyly satirizes the ambitions, defeats, folly, and cruelty of Philip II of Spain. Phrygia represents Spain, and the island of Lesbos, which Midas is so determined to conquer, England. Midas' golden touch is the wealth flowing into Spain from gold mines in the new worlds of both East and West."[24] My interpretation of the play is also allegorical, though it focuses on Lyly's literary, rather than his political, concerns. For our purposes here, it is therefore important to grasp that in the myth that bears his name, Midas is not only a king and a judge; he is also an artist of sorts. Ovid raises this possibility at the beginning of the story, when he links Midas to Apollo and the Muses, and also at the end, when Midas comes physically to resemble Pan, the artist whose music he preferred to Apollo's. On these grounds alone he may have appealed to Renaissance writers as a symbol of their imitative art.

From its opening lines, Lyly's play is congenial to the argument that Midas is an imitator and that the play itself is an allegory about the authority and influence of ancient authors and the consequences of trying to become like them. In the first scene, in what is arguably a representation of the promise that the classical tradition extends to vernacular writers, the value of the gift that Bacchus grants to Midas (in return for his hospitality to Silenus, the god's companion), is the prospect of extraordinary augmentation that it opens up – in other words, the possibility that Midas might become a god, more like the giver of the gift (Bacchus) than its recipient (himself). Midas summons three councilors in order to decide how he should use this opportunity. The consequential nature of the discussion, and its relevance to the kind of writing that Lyly is attempting in relation to Ovid's *Metamorphoses* (imitation), is marked by the analogy that Midas makes between himself and Icarus and Phaeton, who were annihilated in their attempts to imitate their fathers – the one, a wonder-working artist and inventor (Daedalus); the other, the god of all the arts and father of the Muses (Apollo). "Give me leave to consult," says Midas to Bacchus in his first line, and the play's first explicit allusion to the classical text that it engages, "lest desiring things above my reach I be fired with Phaeton, or against nature and be drowned with Icarus, and so perishing, the world shall both laugh and wonder, crying, *Magnis tamen excidit ausis*" (He perished, nevertheless, from great boldness) (the Latin line is Ovid's, referring to Phaeton at *Met.* 2.328).

The first councilor, Eristus, advises Midas to wish for love; the second, Martius, for absolute power; and the third, Mellacrites, for infinite wealth in the form of a golden touch. Mellacrites carries the day when he reasons that love and power are implicit in the possession of gold. Indeed it appears to him, as shortly it will to Midas, that having a limitless supply of gold is tantamount to being a god: "In this word 'gold' are all the powers of the gods, the desires of men, the wonders of the world, the miracles of nature, the looseness of fortune, and triumphs of time" (1.1.46–9). As he dilates upon this theme, Mellacrites quotes five Latin sentences in which gold seems less like a precious metal (*aurum*), a type of money (*nummus*), or material wealth in general (*pecunia*) than it does a form of magic or an influence from the heavens that changes everything over which it extends itself. The first passage, taken from Juvenal's *Satires* (3.143–4), argues that each man is esteemed in proportion to his wealth, rather than his merit ("*Quantum quisque sua nummorum servat in arca, tantum habet et fidei*" [1.1.52–3]). Along the same lines, the second quotes Horace's *Epistles* (1.53–4): Money should be sought first, virtue after money ("*Quaerenda pecunia primum est, virtus post nummos*" [1.1.54–5]). Drawn from a different Horatian letter (1.6.37), the third passage reasons that Queen Wealth, rather than Mother Nature, gives good birth and beauty ("*Et genus et formam regina pecunia donat*" [1.1.57]). The fourth passage, from Ovid's *Ars Amatoria* (2.277–8), is familiar to us as readers of Nashe: Now it truly is the golden age: the greater part of honor sells for gold; love is bought for gold ("*Aurea sunt vero nunc saecula, plurimus auro venit honos, auro conciliatur amor*" [1.1.61–2]). Somewhat more ambiguous in its meaning than the other *sententiae*, the final passage is Virgilian (*Aen.* 3.56–7): What does the sacred [or the accursed] hunger for gold not drive men to do? ("*Quid non mortalia pectora cogit auri sacra fames*" [1.1.66–7]).

At the level of discourse, the argument exemplifies the metamorphic properties that Mellacrites attributes to gold. By the time that the councilor stops talking, these aureate *sententiae*, drawn from the treasury of ancient literature, have changed from premises into proofs. At the same time, the incantatory references to "gold" in the oration work a change in Midas himself. "Wish gold, Midas," exhorts Mellacrites, "or wish not to be Midas" (1.1.70–1). A moment later, Midas no longer appears to be the person that he was: a self constituted by the interplay of several different inclinations (toward generosity, piety, and gratitude as well as love, power, and wealth). Instead, in keeping with the logic of his councilor's imperative, all of his different impulses have become the same desire. Midas, by his own reckoning, is now identical to his lust for gold, and in this new state of being, he anticipates a time when everything else, having been turned into gold by his touch, will reflect himself to himself: "Cease you to dispute; I am determined. It is gold, Bacchus, that Midas desireth; let everything that Midas toucheth be turned to gold; so shalt thou bless thy guest and manifest thy godhead. Let in be gold, Bacchus" (1.1.103–6).

The god grants his wish; Midas tests his new power on a stone and a stick near to hand; and suddenly it appears, just as he would have it, that all is Midas and all is gold: "Fortunate Midas! It is gold Mella-crites, gold! It is gold! ... Gold, Mellacrites! My sweet boy, all is gold!" (1.1.109–11). "Thus," says Midas expansively of himself, "Midas shall be monarch of the world, the darer of fortune, the commander of love" (1.1.124–5). As he goes about determining that he is the same as his desire for gold, and as he wishes for the golden touch, Midas plots a path to a kind of self-fulfillment. But it is far from clear that in making these choices, he becomes "more" than he was earlier, when his mind was undetermined, when his subjectivity was as different from his desires as they were from each other, and when every possibility lay open before him. The matter is difficult to clarify since, at this point, the golden touch still holds out the promise of fulfilling Midas's desire – which far from being "determined" is evidently limitless. One thing, however, is certain: By the end of the scene, Midas is no longer pious. In contrast to the first lines that he utters, the last mark a conspicuous change in his attitude toward his benefactor. Referring to Bacchus, now departed to his revels, Midas scoffs at his authority: "Tush, he is a drunken god, else he would not have given so great a gift. Now it is done, I care not for anything he can do" (1.1.130–1). Another way to grasp the change that has taken place is to recognize that Midas no longer stands outside the *Metamorphoses*, as a reader who compares himself critically to characters such as Phaeton and Icarus. At the end of the scene, he stands (if you will) within Ovid's text as one of many tales about the perils of imitation and over-reaching.

In this sense, Midas's change from piety to impiety, from tractability to ambition, and from reader into text, are all symptoms of another movement that is taking place, as it were between Lyly's play and Ovid's poem: a movement from differentiation to assimilation. Ironic-ally, it is Midas's impiety and ambition that inscribe him, ever more definitively, within the *Metamorphoses*, rather than signaling that Lyly's text has itself departed from its Ovidian source and become something different. Another way to grasp the dynamics of Lyly's complicated med-itation on imitative writing is to ask whether it is the golden touch that changes Midas, or whether a change has occurred in him already, the consequence of being exposed to the anthology of golden sentences that Mellacrites culls from Latin verse. If we say that Bacchus embodies the authority and metamorphic potential of classical literature, then the ability to make a golden world that he grants to Midas might represent ancient poetry's godlike powers of transformation. In this scene, which depicts Midas's metamorphosis from a reader of Ovid into one of his characters, Lyly raises the possibility that this is a power over which he himself, as an imitator of classical poetry, has little or no authorial control.

The changes that Midas undergoes in the presence of the classical tradition are like rocks dropped into a pond: Their consequences extend in ripples to every point within the diameter of the world in which he lives. In this context, it is worth considering the play's unusual temporality. Just before Midas makes his wish, at a moment when it seems inevitable that he will choose the golden touch, Mellacrites remarks that the "iron world is run out, the golden is now come" (1.1.91–2). The grammar of his claim suggests that time is flowing toward the future along its customary channels. However, according to the mythology that the Renaissance inherited from Antiquity, the golden age comes before the iron age, not after it, and thus the implication of these lines must be that time is also running in reverse, even though the action of the play moves inexorably forward to the scene of writing in Renaissance England. Whether time runs backwards or forwards, the results are notably the same. As it flows in reverse, time approaches the origins of all things, as Ovid imagined them in the *Metamorphoses*: a primordial moment, prior to the most elementary distinctions, "before there was sea and land and sky hanging over all," when "Nature's face was all the same, a globe without features, what men call Chaos," "a crude, undigested heap, a lifeless mass of clashing seeds yoked in discord" (*Met.* 1.1.7–9). On the other hand, the prologue to Lyly's play similarly describes the modern period as undifferentiated. "Time hath confounded our minds, our minds the matter," writes Lyly of his era's decline from Antiquity, "but all cometh to this pass, that what heretofore hath been served in several dishes for a feast is now minced in a charger for a gallimaufrey." Referring to his own composition as "a mingle-mangle," he begs to be excused on the grounds that through its insatiable desire for change, "the whole world is become an hodgepodge" (Prol. 17–22). Here again, one might suppose that the nature and consequences of imitation are at issue, in the sense that imitation is a means of compressing time and of making the past and the present present to each other. As a fusion and confusion of old and new, imitative writing is hostile to the very idea of distinction. As with the golden touch, so with imitation: *Le plus ça change.*

What are the consequences of the general collapse of distinction that follows from the golden touch? Contrary to Midas's expectations in act one, scene one, his authority is not enhanced, nor is his wealth increased, by becoming godlike. By the same token, Lyly would appear to suggest that he himself has not succeeded in conferring upon his play the authority and value of Ovid's poem, though he makes a point of tracing the origins of his own composition back to the opening lines of the *Metamorphoses* and its influential myth of creation. The assimilation of Midas to his desire for gold, and of Lyly's play to its aureate Ovidian source (through imitation), invalidates the differential logic on which concepts such as authority and value, as Lyly understands them, finally depend. At the beginning of act two – when it is evident that the golden touch is not a blessing but a curse – the councilor Martius observes that the "greediness of Mellacrites ... hath made Midas a lump of earth, that should be a god on earth" (2.1.61–3). Partly he is saying that in a world where everything can be turned into gold, gold ceases to be precious. But if there is no difference between a clod and a god, then the consequences of the loss of distinction, for which the golden touch is both a cause and a metaphor, clearly extend well beyond the sphere of economics.

In the following scene, the effects of this loss become evident in signification itself. Asking whether Lydia is not "a golden world" (one might detect an ironic nod to Philip Sidney's assertion that Nature's "world is brasen, Poets only deliver a golden"[25]) Licio (a page to the daughter of Mellacrites) begins to play a language game with Petulus (a page to Mellacrites himself), in which they take turns proving that there is "no difference between an egg and gold" (2.2.1–56). The extreme fluidity of definition in this game is as thrilling as any metamorphosis in Ovid's poem (or so, presumably, Lyly intends it to be). But in displaying the extraordinary richness and variety of language, as well as its capacity to change one thing into another, the players come close to demonstrating that words have no value, make no discrimination, and mean nothing at all – the world "gold" in particular. In this regard, the play appears to anticipate Hannah Arendt's remarkably Ovidian vision of modernity: "Authority, resting on a foundation in the past as its unshaken cornerstone, gave the world the permanence and durability which human beings need precisely because they are mortals – the most unstable and futile beings we know of. Its loss is tantamount to the loss of the groundwork of the world, which indeed since then has begun to shift, to change and transform itself with ever-increasing rapidity from one shape into another, as though we were living and struggling with a Protean universe where everything at any moment can become almost anything else."[26] In Robert Weimann's reading of Lyly's prologue, the mutability that Arendt attributes to the modern age is rather more benign in its effects. Referring to "a new kind of heterogeneity in the social and aesthetic uses and effects of representation," Weimann points, in Lyly's text, to "the crumbling foundations of classical authority in poetics," an "irretrievable" loss that gives rise to "a "new historical departure in poetics": the possibility of self-authorization as a writer.[27]

I have been reading Lyly's play as though it were a parable about Renaissance art, in which Midas represents the imitator of classical litera-ture and his golden touch, imitation itself. In this context, imitation seems to be a process that creates an obstacle to its own fulfillment. As it unifies the ancient and the modern and turns them into the same thing, imitation erases the very differences that make the ancient desirable as a model for new compositions. When ancient and modern cannot be dis-tinguished, the ancient is no longer valuable as such. This is the claim that Lyly is making when Licio reflects that in the golden world that Midas has created, "[g]old is but the earth's garbage" and "the very rub-bish of barren ground" (2.2.5–6). It is also possible to state this idea in a slightly different way by saying that when imitation, which is stimulated by the recognition of authority in another writer, text, or tradition, is motivated by ambition, it tends to violate the authority of its models in such a way that it may not simply be usurped or transferred to the imita-tor's own compositions. Thus Sophronia (Midas's daugter), discussing the consequences of the golden touch with the councilors, associates Midas's ambition to climb higher than his place with the decline of his authority, and the decline of his authority with an imminent loss of life:

> Though I know love to grow to such looseness, and hoarding to such misery, that I may rather grieve at both than remedy either, yet thy animating my father to continual arms, to conquer crowns, hath only brought him into imminent danger of his own head. The love he hath followed, I fear unnatural, the riches he hath got, I know unmeasurable, the wars he hath levied, I doubt lawful, hath drawn his body with gray hairs to the grave's mouth, and his mind with eating cares to desperate determinations. (2.1.91–9)

The word "determinations" in this speech is a reminder of Midas's announcement, at the beginning of act one, that he is "determined" to wish for godlike powers. Completing the acoustical circuit, it makes something evident about Lyly's point of view: For him (as for Ovid), desire is associated with death and imitation with annihilation. At the same time, the word "determination" points to a different connection that Lyly draws between limitation and authority (or if you prefer, between their opposites: license and impotence). Presumably, it is in the context of these associations that Weimann's claim about the modern "self-authorization" of Renaissance writing must be scrutinized.

Prompted by an oracle from Bacchus, "pithy and pitiful" – "In Pactolus go bathe thy wish and thee; | Thy wish the waves shall have, and thou be free" – Midas sets off for the river, flowing north from Mount Tmolus, in the currents of which he hopes to find the means to restore distinction to his chaotic realm, regain his own authority, and save his life (2.2.57–9). "I will to the river," he says, "where if I be rid of this intolerable disease of gold, I will next shake off that untemperate desire of government, and measure my territories, not by the greatness of my mind, but by the right of my succession" (3.1.65–9). A moment later, rebuking Martius for his insatiable lust for conquest, Midas clarifies a distinction between legitimate and illegitimate methods for gaining authority. "Every little king is a king, and the title consisteth not in the compass of ground but in the right of inheritance," he says (3.1.80–1). This is a new discrimination in the play, and it signals an important shift in the way that Lyly represents the activity of imitation and the influence of the classical tradition. In the first part of the text, as we have seen, Lyly associates imitation with ambition, impiety, presumption, and a will to dominate others, and in this way he describes it as a violent act that returns upon the imitator in the form of self-loss: "[U]nhappy Midas," says Midas of himself, "who by the same means perisheth himself that he thought to conquer others, being now become a shame to the world, a scorn to that petty prince, and to thyself a consumption" (3.1.52–6). In the second part of the text, however, Lyly will come to associate imitation with a different set of impulses – circumspection, humility, obedience, and piety – and on this basis, theorize that imitation is a form self-authorization that leaves the authority of the writers or traditions from which it springs honored and intact. Thus Midas's journey to the Pactolus would appear to be the first scene in a new play about imitation and its consequences. The very fact that Midas must bathe in the river in order to restore his legitimacy as a sovereign suggests, *contra* Weimann, that classical literature has not lost its any of its authority for Lyly. As a natural boundary between "this place" and "that place," the Pactolus is not only a representation of the new limits that Midas has set upon himself; it is also image of the influential ancient sources of the play. And so it would appear that for Lyly the classical tradition is both the source and solution for the problems that imitation poses to vernacular composition.

Midas consigns his powers to the waves offstage, but the effects of these ablutions are immediately apparent in the play. There are several indications in the scenes that follow act three, scene one that through the king's humility, balance and distinction have been restored in Lydia. In act three, scene two, for example, we learn that gold has become precious again when Licio and Petulus compete with Motto, a barber, for ownership of a golden beard. In the next act, when Licio ponders the barber's skillfulness in cozening the pages of the prize, he links the new scarcity of gold (and thus its value) with an increase of ingenuity and wit: "The world will grow full of wiles, seeing Midas hath lost his golden wish" (4.4.74–5). In act three, scene three, in a reprisal of the debate between the royal councilors at the opening of the play, Sophronia's ladies dispute whether it is better to spend time talking of love, telling tales, singing, or dancing. Far from collapsing into one impulse or another, the distinctions between these different desires remain intact at the scene's conclusion, when Sophronia determines that "everyone, using her own delight, shall have no cause to be discontent" (3.3.86–7). Just then, a messenger arrives and reports that Bacchus has absolved Midas of his golden touch. In the third usage of an important word for Lyly, the messenger also explains that the king is absent from court because, "overjoyed with [his] good fortune," he "*determined* to use some solace in the woods" (3.3.105–6; italics mine). There is a latent contradiction here between Midas's determination and his superflux of joy. The simple mention of Midas's desires in the context of a limitation is sufficient to create new confusions, and in the scene's final lines, Sophronia anticipates the events that are to come when she remarks of the woods that "[w]ild beasts make no difference between a king and a clown, nor hunters in the heat of their pastime fear no more the fierceness of the boar than the fearfulness of the hare" (3.3.113–16).

At the beginning of act four, just steps ahead of Midas, we find Apollo and Pan on the slopes of Mount Tmolus. Readers of Ovid's *Metamorphoses* will expect that each is disputing the other's claim to be the better musician, but in Lyly's play it is the legitimacy of disputation itself that preoccupies the gods. It appears that moments before the scene began, Pan suggested to Apollo that they compare their skills. For Apollo, however, the question of musical excellence is of much less interest than Pan's insubordination in challenging his inherently superior place in the hierarchy of being. He sets the terms of their conversation, and of the scene, when he expresses amazement that while even Orpheus, Arion, and Amphion acknowledge their inferiority to him, "[o]nly Pan, with his harsh whistle ... seeks to compare with Apollo" (4.1.6–8). Pan replies by arguing that they are both gods, therefore that "[c]omparisons cannot be odious where the deities are equal" – an idea that he develops by comparing Apollo's love for Daphne to his own love for Syrinx, passions that resulted in both nymphs becoming the emblems of their suitor's art: Daphne the laurel, Syrinx the panpipe (4.1.9–10). As the debate continues, Apollo reveals that he concluded that Pan's music is "barb'rous," "savage," and "rude" not because of its aesthetic qualities, but because Pan himself is "but the god of beasts, of woods, and hills, excluded from heaven and in earth not honored" (4.1.20, 27, 62, 24–6). Pan's ambition rises with every degradation until, no longer content to suggest that he is the equal to Apollo, he declares, "I told thee before that Pan was a god, I tell thee now again, as great a god as Apollo. I had almost said, a greater, and because thou shalt know I care not to tell my thoughts, I say, a greater" (4.1.30–3). In a final act of insubordination, Pan plays on his own name, observing that "Pan is all, Apollo but one" (4.1.59–60).

When they reach this impasse, the gods determine to let several nymphs decide who has "sovereignty in music," and at this point, Midas arrives on the scene, bemoaning his recent misfortunes (4.1.79). Apollo, ever sensitive to the place and status of those around him, remarks that "[t]o be a king is next to being a god" (presumably he means "just below") (4.1.72). Midas explains his lament by confessing that it was his folly "[t]o abuse a god" (4.1.74). Apollo agrees that this was a serious mistake, but Midas's error does not prevent the god from pressing him into service as a judge for the contest. "Seeing [the contention] happens in earth," Apollo reasons, "we must be judged of those on earth, in which there are none more worthy than kings and nymphs" (4.1.79–81). When he is ordered by Apollo to take his place alongside the nymphs (4.1.77–8), Midas reacts in a way that suggests what the shape of his verdict will be: "If gods you be, although I dare wish nothing of gods, being so deeply wounded with wishing, yet let my judgment prevail before these nymphs, if we agree not, because I am a king" (4.1.83–6). The request seems to indicate that Midas, fresh from the scene of absolution, is as circumspect about his place as he was at the beginning of the play, when he was intent on not becoming Phaeton or Icarus. In fact, it is the expression of his ambition, still unabsolved, to be like the Olympian gods themselves. Finding it intolerable to be compared to the nymphs, and arguing for the superiority of his own place above them, Midas falls to imitating exactly the stance that Apollo took with Pan in the earlier part of the scene.

More presumptions follow, with dire consequences for Midas and his kingdom. Formally speaking, Apollo's performance differs from Pan's only in the sense that he plays the lute and sings his song at the same time, whereas Pan must play his pipes first and then sing. It may be surprising that Lyly declines the opportunity that Ovid gives him to compare classical and vernacular literary forms in this scene (Apollo and Pan are ripe as symbols for these different kinds of poetry), but the conspicuous similarity of the two compositions ensures that our attention is focused on Midas's judgment, the real object of Lyly's concern. In each case, when he is asked to give his opinion about the music, Midas seems determined to differentiate himself from the nymphs by contradicting what they have already said. At the conclusion of Apollo's song, for example, Erato explodes with accolades, "O divine Apollo! O sweet consent!" But to Thia's question, "If the god of music should not be above our reach, who should?," Midas responds by saying bluntly, "I like it not" (4.1.102 5). At the conclusion of Pan's performance, the positions are reversed. Erato speaks first, for all of the nymphs, when she says that "Apollo hath showed himself both a god and of music the god" and "to [him] we give the prize and reverence," while "Pan [showed] himself a rude satyr, neither keeping measure nor time, his piping as far out of tune as his body out of form." Midas, however, takes the contrarian position that "there's more sweetness in the pipe of Pan than Apollo's lute." In terms whose noteworthy impropriety is intended to suggest how inappropriate and out of place his judgment is, Midas rules for Pan, saying, "What a shrillness came into mine ears out of that pipe, and what a goodly noise it made!" (4.1.128–38). Not long after that, the gods and nymphs vanish, leaving Midas "but the two last letters of thy name, to be [his] whole name" (4.1.146–7). Crowned with ass's ears, the king who mistook himself for a god discovers that he is now much less than a man, and scarcely more than a beast. The fact that Pan escapes without any punishment at all only serves to underscore that for Lyly, as for Ovid, Midas's transgression is more serious, an idea that Renaissance emblem writing made proverbial: "Presumptuous PAN, did strive APOLLOS skill to passe: | But Midas gave the palme to Pan: wherefore the eares of an asse | APOLLO gave the Judge: which doth all Judges teache; | To judge with knowledge, and advise, in matters paste their reache" (Figure 2.2).[28] Ripa's *Iconologia* (1603) makes ass's ears synonymous with

218   *Peruerſa iudicia.*

Ouid. Metam.   P RESVMPTVOVS PAN, did ſtriue APOLLOS ſkill to paſſe :
lib. 11.   But MIDAS gaue the palme to PAN: wherefore the eares of aſſe
APOLLO gaue the Iudge: which doth all Iudges teache ;
To iudge with knowledge, and aduiſe, in matters paſte their reache ?

Figure 2.2   Geffrey Whitney, *"Perversa iudicia"* in *A choice of emblemes and other devises* (1586)
Photo credit: By Permission of the Folger Shakespeare Library

over-reaching when he uses them to crown the figure of Arroganza, whom he describes as "attributing to herself what she does not possess" (Figure 2.3).[29]

For the second time in the play, then, the determination that Midas reaches in his own thought is tantamount to an ambition to occupy a higher place than fate has assigned him. Immediately, the boundaries of his own identity begin to lose their definition, as they did earlier, when the subject and the object of Midas's desire were merged together in the golden touch. In a soliloquy that concludes this scene, Midas finds himself in an intermediate position between existence and non-existence: "Ah. Midas, why was not thy whole body metamorphosed, that there might have been no part left of Midas?" (4.1.168–9). The next scenes establish that numerous disorders follow from this onto-logical confusion in the king. In act four, scene two, a conversation between shepherds reveals that the legitimacy of Midas's authority is once again in question. Openly, they say, his subjects regard him as a "tyrant" and "usurper" (4.1.8–13). In act four, scene three, a huntsman objects to the presence of Licio and Petulus in the royal park, arguing that "[h]unting is for kings, not peasants"; but he is powerless to remove

Figure 2.3   Cesare Ripa, "Arroganza" in *Nova iconologia* (1618)
Photo credit: By Permission of the Folger Shakespeare Library

them (4.3.4–5). The huntsman also complains about the indiscriminate way that the pages mingle the argots of different aristocratic sports: "Treason, to two brave sports, hawking and hunting. Thou should'st say, start a hare, rouse the deer, spring the patridge" (4.3.47–8). Linguistic indecorum spreads like wildfire. In act four, scene four, the councilor Eristus observes that Midas has grown "melancholy" since returning from the woods; a short time later, "melancholy" has migrated out of the court and into the streets, where Licio and Petulus dispute with Motto, who has used the word in reference to himself, whether a barber should be allowed to "encroach upon our courtly terms" (5.2.109). They are also astonished that Motto has acquired some Latin, barbarous (and barberous) though it be.[30] All of these linguistic transgressions bespeak a blurring of the social boundaries that give each person in Lydia a certain place. Accordingly, Martius worries that "[d]uty is not regarded," while Eristus, when he hears that Midas has ass's ears, declares, "This is monstrous, and either portends some mischief to the king or unto the state of confusion" (4.4.43, 63).

When Sophronia describes her father's melancholy, she says that what makes her "most both to sorrow and wonder is that music, a mithridate for melancholy, should make him mad, crying still, *Uno namque modo Pan et Apollo nocent* (Pan and Apollo inflict harm in the same way)" (4.4.49–52). Midas's inability to distinguish Pan from Apollo is another noteworthy confusion in the play. Let me suggest that instead of "Pan," Midas might also have said "Bacchus," the Olympian deity with whom artists, ancient and modern, frequently associated him.[31] During Antiquity and the Renaissance, Bacchus and Apollo were both perceived to be poetic deities and leaders of the Muses – Bacchus achieving this distinction through his association with intoxication and divine madness and so with poetic furor.[32] The fact that the myth of Midas is framed and punctuated by the interventions of these gods, whom Nietzsche taught us to regard as opposed but complementary aspects of Greek civilization, suggests that in Lyly's play they symbolize two different imperatives for Renaissance imitation, both arising from the heterogeneity of the classical tradition. In this context, it is apparent that Bacchus might represent the limitless choice of ideas, forms, and content that ancient literature offered to Renaissance writers, and that Apollo, in contrast to Bacchus, the constraints that are implicit in the very concept of ancient literary authority. I think, however, that it would be slightly more accurate to say that for Lyly, Bacchus (or Pan) and Apollo symbolize two different kinds of freedom that issue from ancient literature: on the one hand, a license that leads to chaos and the dissipation of the poetic self in the solvent of its own desires; on the other, a liberty, informed by modesty and circumspection, that creates an order in which the selfhood of each individual imitator has definitude and meaning.

The final act of the play provides some evidence for this suggestion. Seeing Midas's bestial ears for the first time, Sophronia reveals the deep logic on which the whole play has been turning: "The gods dally with men; kings are no more. They disgrace kings lest they should be thought gods" (5.1.13–15). Her insight is the catalyst for her father's last, and most important, epiphany. "I will to Apollo," says Midas, "whose oracle must be my doom and, I fear me, my dishonor, because my doom was his, if kings may disgrace gods; and gods they disgrace when they forget their duties" (5.1.27–30). Here, at long last, Midas grasps the concept that his ambition is antithetical to the authority that he seeks for himself – or in other words, that total surrender to a higher power is the only way for him to acquire that authority. Asked what he is saying by an incredulous Mellacrites, Midas replies, "Nothing, but that Apollo must determine all or Midas see ruin of all" (5.1.32–3). This brief line is a crucial passage in the development of Lyly's thought about imitation and the subjectivity of the imitating poet. For the first time in the play, Midas presents himself as the object of the verb "to determine," rather than its subject, and this shift in grammatical person signals the new order that is coming into being at the end of the text. In act five, scene three, arriving at Apollo's oracle in Delphi, Midas makes a confession of all the mistakes that he has made since bathing in the river Pactolus, conceding his brain's "weakness" and the "thickness" of his ears in preferring Pan's "harsh noise" to Apollo's "sweet stroke," as well as the "justice" of Apollo's anger against him (5.3.51–3). He admits that his "ambition [has been] above measure" and promises, in all piety, to "yield myself to Bacchus, and acknowledge my wish to be vanity; to Apollo, and confess my judgment to be foolish; to Mars, and say my wars are unjust; to Diana, and tell my affection has been unnatural" (5.3.61–5). He also makes it clear that he now knows that it is only by yielding everything to the gods that he may be something in and of himself: "I doubt not, what a god hath done to make me know myself, all the gods will help to undo, that I may come to myself" (5.3.65–7). The oracle speaks. Apollo accepts Midas's "submission," enjoining him to a life of peace, justice, and moderation within the limits of his kingdom (5.3.80). Midas foreswears his conquests; his ass's ears fall from his head; and with that, he "is restored" (5.3.122). No such event occurs in Ovid's version of the Midas myth, and as the play concludes with a song of worship for Apollo, these changes point to the final disposition of Lyly's text in relation to the *Metamorphoses*. The moment when Midas accepts his distinctive but subordinate place below Apollo, and the moment when Lyly unequivocally differentiates his text from its source, are one and the same.

While some details remain unclear, the broad stokes of Lyly's theory of imitation are not difficult to discern. They amount to an ethical claim that imitation should be more like surrender than conquest, more like obedience than ambition, and (if you will) more like being the object than the subject of a transformation. It is only when Midas admits that he is inferior to the gods that he regains his throne and rises higher than every other mortal in the play. Presumably, this paradoxical thinking is the way that Lyly imagines a creative process through which English imitators will one day ascend to the lofty authority of ancient poets. Nevertheless, I cannot help but reflect on what Midas has lost in the process of gaining his position as a legitimate king and a competent judge. In the final moments of the play, Midas experiences nothing comparable to the undiluted joy of discovering, for the first time, that he had the power of the golden touch, that the world was conformable to his desires. By the same token, the rustic music that once consoled him for his troubles is now a torment, an indelible reminder of his asinine judgment and its shame. These thoughts obviously run against the grain of Lyly's own thinking, but were it to be interpreted as an allegory for the slow and humiliating process through which critical faculties come to perfection, this play might lead one to conclude that the price that Midas pays for establishing his authority as a judge of works of art is too great, for it is his pleasure and poetic license.

Notes

I am grateful to Paula Blank and Cathy Nicholson for reading this essay and for offering criticism that changed the course of its development.

1. Thomas Warton, *The History of English Poetry, from the Close of the Eleventh to the Commencement of the Eighteenth Century* (London, 1774–81), 3: 490.
2. I say "English professors" since it is still customary in Spanish departments to use the term "Golden Age" when referring to the Renaissance/Early Modern period.
3. C. S. Lewis, *English Literature in the Sixteenth Century, Excluding Drama* (Oxford, 1944), 64–5, 318.
4. Richard Hurd, *Moral and Political Dialogues: Being the Substance of Several Conversations between Divers Eminent Persons of the Past and Present Age* (Dublin, 1760), 141–2.

5. Note, however, the argument of Joseph Addison, another speaker in the dialogue, that the sphere of Elizabeth's authority may not have been fully coextensive with the authority of classical literature, in relation to which the Queen's subjects were apt to experience a kind of subjectivity that came into conflict with the authority of the monarch. "The passion for LETTERS," says Addison of the Renaissance, "was extreme. The novelty of these studies, the artifices that had been used to keep men from them, their apparent uses, and, perhaps, some confused notion of a certain diviner virtue, than really belongs to them; these causes concurred to excite a curiosity in all ... " It is the opinion of some of the speakers in Hurd's dialogue, that Elizabeth's golden reign brings about a "RESTORATION OF LETTERS" that introduces the Reformation to England and in this way becomes one of the "proper sources" of the "fidelity of [the Queen's] good subjects" (142). But in restoring ancient learning to public view, says Addison, the age stirred a curiosity that many Elizabethans would likely have regarded as disruptive to a subject's contentment with his place in a hierarchical society. "A sort of enthusiasm had fired every man with the ambition of exerting the full strength of his faculties, which way soever they pointed ..." (146).

6. On the golden age as an instance of Renaissance nostalgia and utopian thinking, see Harry Levin, *The Myth of the Golden Age in the Renaissance* (New York: Oxford University Press, 1969).

7. For a brief survey of Renaissance perceptions of progress and decline in relation to classical Antiquity, see Russell Fraser, "The Dark Ages and the Age of Gold," *College English* 28.2 (1966): 136–40, 145–9. In a resonant passage, William Wimsatt and Cleanth Brooks contend that "[t]he medieval and early Renaissance ages of criticism looked on literary norms as very safely fixed and enduring and on the history of literature – like that of civilization in general – as a decline from a Golden Age." *Literary Criticism: A Short History* (New York: Vintage, 1967), 523.

8. On Spenser, see David Landreth, "At Home with Mammon: Matter, Money, and Memory in Book II of the Faerie Queene," *English Literary History* 73.1 (2006): 245–74.

9. Geffrey Whitney, *A Choice of Emblemes and Other Devises* (Leiden, 1586), 202. Whitney's emblem is an elaboration of Erasmus, *Adagia* 2.4.25.

10. James VI and I, *Ane Schort Treatise Conteining Some Reulis and Cautelis to be Observit and Eschewit in Scottis Poesie*, in *Elizabeth an Critical Essays*, ed. G. Gregory Smith, 2 vols. (Oxford, 1904), 2: 209. See also Francis Bacon's related argument that "[T]rue antiquity should mean the oldness and great age of the world, which should be attributed to our time, not to a younger period of the world such the ancients. ... We expect from an old man greater knowledge of things human and a more mature judgment than from a young man." Francis Bacon, *The New Organon*, ed. Lisa Jardine and trans. Michael Silverthorne (Cambridge: Cambridge University Press, 2000), 68 (I.84).

11. For all these senses of the golden age, as well as supporting literary and academic bibliographies, see Levin, *The Myth of the Golden Age*. For Elizabeth I's adaptation of the golden age as a metaphor for her own reign, see Frances Yates, *Astraea: The Imperial Theme in the Sixteenth Century* (London: Routledge & Kegan Paul, 1975).

12. According to Horace, "Thrace was always the Siberia of the ancients" (*Odes* 1.25.11). Lydia, by contrast, was renowned for immoderate pleasures more familiar to Roman civilization, "luxury and voluptuousness" (1.8.1).

13. For information about Lydia and the mythographer Konon, I am grateful to David Sullivan. See *The Narratives of Konon*, ed. Malcolm Brown (Leipzig: K. G. Saur, 2002), 49–57.

14. I am grateful to Willa Rohrer for stimulating conversation about Meier's engraving, without which I would not have seen the image in quite this light.

15. *Sir P.S. his Astrophel and Stella Wherein the excellence of sweete poesie is concluded* (London: Thomas Newman, 1591).

16. Elsewhere in the letter, Nashe dilates upon this theme, insisting on the difference between the darkness of the Middle Ages and the light of the present time: "Long hath *Astrophel* (Englands Sunne) withheld the beames of his spirite, from the common veiw of our darke sence, and night hath hovered over the gardens of the nine Sisters, while *Ignis fatuus* and grosse fatty flames ... have tooke occasion ... [to] leade men up and downe in a circle of absurditie a whole weeke, and never know where they are. But nowe that cloude of sorrow is dissolved which fierie Love, exhaled from his dewie haire ... ; the night hath resigned her jettie throne unto *Lucifer*, and cleete daylight possesseth the skie that was dimmed ..." (A3v).

17. See, for example, the debate concerning "praise" and "price" in the October eclogue of *The Shepheardes Calender*; and also the poems that Jonson published as *The Forrest*, in which he acknowledges the bond between himself and his patrons but insists on the independence of his judgment, his immunity to the charge of flattery.

18. Nashe's Latin tag, "*Mens cuiusque is est quisque,*" appears to be taken from Cicero, *De re publica* 6.24.26.

19. Presumably, the phrase "golden Asses" may refer to Apuleius's *Golden Ass*, but that it not a possibility that I consider here.

20. On this point, see Nicholas Moschovakis, "Review of Charles Martindale and A. B. Taylor, eds. Shakespeare and the Classics." *Early Modern Literary Studies* 12.2 (September 2006): 15.1–11. http://purl.oclc.org/emls/12-2/revmart.htm.

21. Hans Georg Gadamer, *Truth and Method*, trans. Joel Weinsheimer and Donald G. Marshall, 2nd rev. edn. (London: Continuum, 2004), 178.

22. Robert Weimann, *Authority and Representation in Early Modern Discourse*, ed. David Hillman (Baltimore: Johns Hopkins University Press, 1996), 5.

23. Douglas Bush, *Classical Influences in Renaissance Literature*, Martin Classical Lectures, vol. 13. (Cambridge: Harvard University Press, 1952), 23, 40.

24. John Lyly, *Gallathea and Midas*, ed. Anne Begor Lancashire (Lincoln: University of Nebraska, 1969), xxii. All quotations from the play are taken from this edition. A more recent edition of the text, edited by George Hunter and David Bevington, has been published in *The Revels Plays* series (Manchester: Manchester University Press, 2000).

25. Philip Sidney, "An Apology for Poetry," in *Elizabethan Critical Essays*, ed. G. Gregory Smith (Oxford: Oxford University Press, 1904), 1: 156.33.

26. Hannah Arendt, "What is Authority?," in *Between Past and Future* (New York: Penguin, 1993), 93–5.

27. Robert Weimann, "History and the Issue of Authority in Representation: The Elizabethan Theatre and the Reformation," *New Literary History* 17.3 (1986): 462, 464.

28. Whitney, *"Perversa iudicia,"* in *A Choice of Emblemes*, 218.

29. Cesare Ripa, *Iconologia*, ed. Piero Buscaroli (Milan: TEA, S.A, 1992), 27–8.

30. Presumably this exchange is an echo and a parody of Apollo's argument his claim that such as "love" should not enter "the barb'rous mouth of Pan": "Let not love enter into those savage lips, a word for Jove, for Apollo, for the heavenly gods, whose thoughts are gods, and gods are all love" (4.1.20, 27–9).

31. Malcom Bull, *The Mirror of the Gods: Classical Mythology in Renaissance Art* (London: Penguin Books, 2006), 238.

32. Ibid., 258, 230.

3
Translating for Queen Anne: John Florio's *Decameron*

Michael Wyatt

With the accession to the English throne of King James VI of Scotland in 1603, the Italo-English language teacher, lexicographer, and translator John Florio found himself in a conspicuously more advantageous position than he had enjoyed in the preceding Elizabethan decades. A number of Florio's earlier patrons exercised considerable influence in the formative period of the first Stuart court – the dedicatory material to a different pair of English noble ladies preceding each of the three books of Florio's translation of Montaigne's *Essais*, published just as Elizabeth was dying in 1603, manifestly chart these patronage relationships – and Florio came to his position in Queen Anne of Denmark's circle as "Reader in Italian and Groom of the Privy Chamber" through them. The most striking aspect of Florio's arrival at court, however, is not so much that he had finally managed to realize a long-standing ambition, but rather that it would, in the end, prove to be of such little import. The greater part of Florio's influential yeomanship in the transmission of Renaissance and early modern Italian cultures had by this time already been accomplished; excepting the revised edition of his Italian-English dictionary in 1611, the most consequential work that he would produce in these final decades of his life would be an English translation of the *Decameron*, published in 1620 following the death of Queen Anne and the disappearance of the court in which she had provided him such a hard-won place. In this essay I posit a previously unconsidered explanation for Florio's effective invisibility on the public stage of the Stuart world, one for which Florio's version of Boccaccio's collection of *novelle* provides a number of suggestive clues. I focus in particular on the third story of the second day (*Decameron* II.3).

The male protagonist of this *novella*, Alessandro, is the nephew of a trio of profligate Florentine brothers. Though he brilliantly manages their commercial affairs in London, the Agolanti brothers rapidly spend the revenue. When a war breaks out between the English king and his second son, the money and property in Alessandro's control is frozen. Cut off from their only source of income, the brothers are imprisoned in Florence for failing to meet their obligations, and Alessandro, despairing after several years that peace would ever come to England, eventually sets off to return home. After crossing to the continent, leaving Bruges he meets an abbot traveling with a large party, including two knights (both related to the English king) who recognize him. Alessandro learns from them that the abbot, a relative of theirs, has recently been elected to head one of the largest monasteries in England, but as he is under-age they are traveling to Rome to see the Pope "che nel difetto della troppa giovane età dispensi con lui, e appresso nella dignità il confermi" (in order that the young man might be dispensed from the defect of his age and confirmed in his office).[1] They hasten to add, however, that the matter must be kept a secret. As the party prepares to continue on, the abbot shows an animated interest in Alessandro, invites him to travel to Italy with the group, and delegates to him the arrangements to be made wherever they stop for the night. One evening after settling the abbot into a comfortable inn, Alessandro realizes that he has not yet found a bed for himself, and the innkeeper suggests that, as there are no other places available, he might consider sleeping in one of the grain storage cupboards in the abbot's room. Overhearing the exchange, however, the abbot forms a different idea, and once the young man retires "con sommessa voce ... gli disse che appresso lui si coricasse; il quale, dopo molte disdette spogliatosi, vi si coricò" (in a subdued voice ... he told [Alessandro] to lie down beside him; and after many protestations to the contrary, Alessandro undressed and obliged; 98). Almost immediately, however, wandering hands have Alessandro concerned that the prelate has been moved by some "disonesto amore" (dishonest passion; 96), but acting quickly to dispel this anxiety the abbot says to him, "caccia via il tuo sciocco pensiero, e cercando qui, conosci quello che io nascondo" (chase away the silly thought, and searching here know that which I am hiding; 98), revealing himself to be a young woman by placing Alessandro's hand on her breast. She goes on to explain the real purpose of her journey to Rome: to seek permission from the Pope for her impending arranged marriage. Having now fallen in love with Alessandro, however, she tells him that he must either marry her or leave at once. Though as of yet he has no idea of her identity, Alessandro nevertheless recognizes the young woman to be "nobile e ricca, e bellissima ... [e] senza troppo lungo pensiero, rispose che, se questa a lei piacea, a lui era molto a grado" (noble, rich, and lovely ... (and) without giving it too much thought, he responded that if it were such that she wished, so did he; 99). Placing a ring on his finger, "gli si fece sposare" (she married herself to him) under an image of Christ hanging on the wall, after which "insieme abbracciatasi, con gran piacere di ciascuna delle parti, quanto di quella notte restava, si sollazzarono" (embracing each other with great pleasure in all of their parts, what remained of that night was enjoyed to the hilt; 99). Soon after arriving in Rome, the party goes to meet with the pope, and after making "la debita reverenza" (the customary curtsey; 99), the abbot (still dressed as such) reveals to the pope that he is, in fact, the daughter of the king of England and has fled to Rome to escape the marriage her father had arranged with the king of Scotland, a suitor she rejects, she says, not for his advanced age, but because of her (ambiguously expressed) fear that "per la fragilità della mia giovanezza, se a lui maritata fosse, cosa che fosse contra le divine leggi e contra l'onore del mio padre" (given my youthful vulnerability, were I to be married to him something counter to both the divine law and my father's honor; 100) might occur. She goes on to assert her marriage to Alessandro, boldly asking that the Pope himself formally recognize "quello che a Dio e a me è piaciuto" (that which has pleased both God and me; 100). Alessandro is as stunned and delighted to learn that his new wife is the daughter of the English king as the Pope is astonished "dello abito della donna e della sua elezione" (by the lady's attire and by her so choosing a husband; 100). Despite the evident rage of her attendant relatives, the pontiff acknowledges that what is done is done and, granting the couple his blessing, arranges a solemn wedding and ceremonial banquet to mark the marriage. After leaving Rome, the couple travel first to Florence in order to free Alessandro's uncles from prison and redeem the fortunes of his family; then on to France, where they are feted by the king, and finally arriving back in England, preceded by the two knights first encountered in Bruges, who, mollified by the pope, have in turn been able to calm the English king's anger. Alessandro proves to be a pacifier himself in settling the war between his new father- and brother-in-law, and he is rewarded for these efforts with the earldom of "Cornovaglia" (101). The *novella* concludes by relating that "il conte poi con la sua donna gloriosamente visse" (the earl lived gloriously with his lady), and that, as his culminating achievement, "col suo senno e valore e l'aiuto del suocero" (through his good sense and excellence, and with his father-in-law's assistance) Alessandro subsequently "conquistò la Scozia e funne re coronato" (conquered Scotland and there was crowned king; 101).

In Boccaccio's hands, the story revolves around several intertwined axes, including the seductive but potentially corrupting force of money, political uncertainties, sexual attraction, and unstable gender roles. The skill with which the *novella* is organized makes it one of the *Decameron's* most satisfying narratives. The two political issues in the story – the war between the English king and his son, and the marriage of the same king's daughter to the king of Scotland that was originally to be confirmed by the pope – both take their cues from the actual conflict that had erupted in the middle of the twelfth century between the English King Henry II and his second son, Henry, the so-called Young King, and the marriage the elder Henry had contracted between this second son and the daughter of the French King Louis VII, with the acquiescence of the weakened Pope Alexander III. There is a further historical referent in the *novella*, the collapse of the Florentine Bardi and Peruzzi banking interests in England in the early 1340s. Like Boccaccio's Agolanti brothers, the Bardi and Peruzzi families established a significant financial presence in England in the early fourteenth century, such that by the 1330s they were making loans to King Edward III to finance his wars in Scotland and France. By the early 1340s, Edward's obligations to the Florentines had become so enormous, and his resources so exhausted, that he defaulted on his loans. This, in tandem with similar moves by the kings of Naples and France, contributed to the massive economic depression that struck Europe just prior to the Black Plague's arrival in 1348, the *Decameron's* occasion and narrative frame.[2] Boccaccio resolves this recent history in the idealized figure of Alessandro, whose economic eye determines his various savvy choices, including his acceptance of the young lady's proposal of marriage, where the narrator notes that he sees her as "nobile e ricca" before he recognizes her as "bellissima."

The lady is an even more forceful and calculating presence in the *novella*, though her lack of a name ultimately signals the limits of her actual power. It is she, still in the guise of the abbot, who brings the reluctant Alessandro to her bed, proposes marriage, gives him a ring, and compels him to marry her. In Rome, she bullies the Pope into accepting what she alone has, in fact, effected (the image of Christ presiding over the nuptials notwithstanding). Obviously, no Florentine or English woman of the fourteenth century would have been in a position to behave with such brazen self-determination, but the imaginative space of the *Decameron* enables the breakdown of otherwise circumscribed hierarchies and social roles, and Boccaccio plays with his reader's expectations by manipulating the inherent unruliness of sexual, economic, and political practices.

Boccaccio's play with hierarchies suggestively frames the reception of his text's reception in England. A number of the *novelle* that make up the *Decameron* had been translated into English in the later sixteenth and earlier seventeenth centuries, and versions of the stories in French (on which many of the English translations were based) also enjoyed a wide circulation among the literate English public. In the 1580s, the London publisher of Italian books John Wolfe had intended to bring out a new edition of Boccaccio's Italian text as a response to the censored Florentine versions issued by Vincenzo Borghini in 1573 and Leonardo Salviati in 1582, as indicated in the preface to his 1584 edition of Aretino's *Prima parte de' ragionamenti*. There, Barbagrigia Stampatore (the *nom de plume* of Wolfe's likely editor, Giacomo Castelvetro) writes that "un giorno spero di darvi a leggere così compiute, come egli le compose, & non lacerate, come hoggi i vostri Fiorentini ve le danno a leggere, con mille ciancie, per farvi credere d'haverle ritornate a la loro forma originale" (one day I hope to give the [*Decameron*] to you to read in its entirety, as Boccaccio wrote it and not as it has been lacerated by your contemporary Florentines, who with a thousand ludicrous explanations try to make you believe that they have restored the *novelle* to their original form).[3] Wolfe was licensed by the Stationer's Company to publish the book, but for some reason it never appeared. It might seem surprising that, although the book had powerfully marked the elaboration of English Renaissance literary culture, a complete (or near complete) translation of Boccaccio's *novelle* did not find its way into English until 1620. The fact that even then two of the stories, III.10 and VI.6, were excluded from Florio's book – evidently due to their suspect sexual and religious content – suggests why the *Decameron* took so long to be realized in English.[4] Pressures of religious conformity were increasingly felt in Jacobean England under its theologically vigilant king. Both James and Anne were susceptible to criticism of their extravagant habits. And the mix of religious zealotry, authoritarianism (at least in theory), indolence, and homosociality in the king may have rendered a text such as the *Decameron* – occupied as it is with such topical fodder – legible as a potentially volatile commentary on Stuart actuality.

This is certainly how the translator of the 1620 *Decameron, containing an hundred pleasant novels. Wittily discoursed, betweene seaven honourable ladies and three noble men*, read the signs of the times, for he issued this important translation anonymously. Herbert Wright convincingly established Florio's authorship through a careful philological analysis of the translation's lexical and rhetorical patterns, reading it against Florio's other published work and that of the very few other possible candidates active as translators in England at the time.[5] Even though Wright never quite manages to square the overwhelmingly moralistic drift of the Florio *Decameron* with its author's preceding career in England, he does trace a number of the translator's more intrusive interventions in Boccaccio's narrative to the variously problematic Salviati edition utilized by Florio, a book published in 1582 to satisfy the demand of the Tuscan Grand Duke that one of the foundational texts of Florentine culture be rescued from the papal Index of Forbidden Books. Given the considerable circulation of Italian manuscripts and books in early modern England as well as Florio's privileged position at court, it is hard to imagine that none of the earlier Italian editions of Boccaccio's collection would have been available to the translator should he have wished to use them, and so the choice of Salviati's expurgated text must have been a deliberate one.[6]

In Florio's version of *Decameron* II.3, many of Boccaccio's carefully crafted narrative coordinates are blurred, and in several instances entirely rewritten.[7] In the nocturnal scene in the inn, Florio has Alessandro sleeping in a space "next adioyning to my Lord Abbots Chamber" (not, as in Salviati, in it), but when Alessandro is persuaded to join the abbot in bed – not after "molto disdette", but "some few faint excuses" – Florio represents him as "being not a little prowde of so gracious a favour."[8] Already Alessandro is portrayed as a more active participant in this aspect of the narrative, notably vitiating the calibrated build-up to this tantalizingly ambiguous moment in the original. Once the abbot begins to "imbrace and hugge him; even as amorous friends (provoked by earnest affection) use to doe ... Alessandro verie much mervayling, and being an Italian himselfe, fearing lest this folly in the Abbot would convert to foule and dishonest action, shrunke modestly from him" (35v). Whatever "being Italian himselfe" might mean in this context, the tone and direction of Florio's English version of the scene turns Alessandro first into an opportunist and then a shrinking violet. Once Alessandro's hand is placed on her breast, the young woman tells him to "let all bad thoughts of bestiall abuse be farre off from thee, and feele here, to resolve thee from all such feare," but when he goes to kiss her, "shee somewhat rudely repuls(ed) him" (36r). The economic opportunity Alessandro sees in the lady's offer of marriage in Boccaccio's *novella* is amplified in Florio's version: "his owne fortunes stood out of future expectation by his kinsmens overthrow, and his great losses in England; wherefore upon an opportunity so fairely offered, hee held it no wisdome to returne refusall, but accepted her gracious motion, and referred all to her disposing" (36r).

This greater calculation on Alessandro's part corresponds to a diminishment of the young woman's role, given that the succession of subsequent actions through which Boccaccio establishes her powerful manipulation of *fortuna* are reversed in Florio, who says that "she faithfully espoused him, refusing all the World, to be onely his" (36r), where in the original the emphasis is entirely on the lady's unambiguous agency ("gli si fece sposare"). To further adjust Boccaccio's sexual politics, Florio's English version has the marriage "confirmed solemnely, by an holy Vow, and chaste kisses; shee commanded him backe to his Chamber, and shee returned to her bed againe, sufficiently satisfied with her Loves acceptation" (36r). The lady has here been transformed from Boccaccio's self-determined English Amazon into a chaste and chastening paragon of virtue.

In terms of the contemporary political implications of this Englished *novella*, the most telling alteration in Boccaccio's narrative is the fact that when "the supposed Abbot" (36r) reveals her true identity to the pope, she tells him that she has been contracted to "the King of North Wales, an aged, impotent, and sickly man," and that she fears, in marrying him, that "lewd and dishonest desires might make me to wander, by breaking the divine Lawes of wedlocke, and abusing the royall blood of my Father" (36v). Florio resolves the ambiguity of the passage's original sense by stabilizing the potential transgression here as her adultery. It seems likely, however, that he read the original passage as implying that sodomy was the act evoked in Boccaccio's Italian ("cosa che fosse contro le divine leggi"), and lest too close a coincidence be implied between the original Scottish king – potentially forcing his young wife to indulge *his* "lewd and dishonest desires" – and James I, the translator turned a Scots monarch into a Welsh one. At the end of the story in English, ignoring the narrative connection in the original between Alessandro's marriage to a woman earlier engaged to the Scottish king and his later conquest of Scotland, Florio lets his reader know that this Italian "Earle of Cornewall ... proving to be so absolute in wisdome, and so famous a Soldier; that (as some report) by assistance of his Father in law, he conquered the Realm of Ireland, and was crowned King thereof" (37r). In an England dominated by an incipient Scots dynasty that was, in the wake of Queen Anne's death, indifferent to the kind of Italian influence that Florio represented, and with a king whose publicly-displayed affective preferences raised the specter of privately unnatural practices, no fiction could be allowed to end with the conquest of Scotland by an Italian son-in-law to the king of England. The substitution of Ireland is striking, not only because there had there been Italians involved in England's colonization of Ireland from early on in Elizabethan efforts there,[9] but also because the rapidly accelerating impulse to spread newly-minted English cultural politics abroad was perhaps the most decisive factor in the diminishing returns of the Italian Renaissance linguistic culture John Florio represented in early modern England.

Florio's position in Queen Anne of Denmark's court in England provides one possible explanation for the conflicted affective and political parameters of the *Decameron* translation as I have been tracing them. Florio was born in London in 1553, the son of one of the earliest of a succession of Italian Protestant refugees to play a crucial role in the development of English cultural politics during the reign of Edward VI. After his family's flight from England following the accession of Mary Tudor and his early life spent in the Italian-speaking mountains of the Swiss Grigione, Florio returned to England as a young man in the second decade of Elizabeth's reign, the heir to a proud tradition of Italian Protestant cultural arbitration which he was determined to exploit for his own professional and social advancement. That this recognition came with the arrival of the Stuarts in England is marked, however, by two significant incongruities. To the degree that any foreign vernacular operated in James I's humanistic and theological sensibility it came filtered through the French culture the Scots king had inherited from his mother. Second, Queen Anne had become a Catholic several years before arriving in England,[10] and was apparently allowed to practice her faith discreetly at the relatively safe distance of Greenwich, where Florio was among her principal daily interlocutors.

The second edition of Florio's dictionary, *Queen Anna's New World of Words* (1611), bears the queen's influence in more than merely its new title (the first edition of 1598 was entitled *A Worlde of Wordes*), for 16 of the 272 works Florio consulted during the compilation of his Italian-English vocabulary are Catholic devotional and hagiographical texts, many of them published in the years immediately preceding Florio's arrival in Anne's circle, and coinciding with his dictionary revisions. The majority of these titles have little or no obvious philological value, and though their presence in Florio's library alongside texts more easily identified with his Italian Protestant heritage is startling, the chronology of their appearance – none of these Catholic books appears in the 1598 edition – is not. The trajectory of Florio's career, as I suggested above, reached its intended goal with his arrival in the Stuart world, but it would be a mistake to identify the more or less independent court Anne established at Greenwich with any of the major initiatives of James I's reign. Florio's absence from the reopening of English relations with Venice in the early decades of the seventeenth century, and his lack of involvement in the cloak-and-dagger publication in London of either the original or the English translation of Fra Paolo Sarpi's *Storia del Concilio di Trento* (in 1619 and 1620 respectively) are the most conspicuous signs of Florio's marginality to Stuart cultural politics. The turn in Florio's work of this period toward the practice of translation into English on a large scale was a maneuver that to a very great extent rendered mute his earlier advocacy of learning foreign languages in order to negotiate the cultures they represented. Correspondingly, the choice for his English translation of the *Decameron* of an edition sanctioned by the Roman Inquisition is a striking sign of the distance Florio had traveled from his Italian Protestant roots. His further modification of the text's potential political relevance that we have seen in the story of Alessandro and the abbot represents an inevitably failed effort to placate the Scots king whose favor he had never really enjoyed.

That *novella* opens with a brief disquisition on Fortune that I cite here in Florio's translation as an epitaph to a career that in attempting to accomodate itself to mutable cultural forces effectively wrote its demise:

> Ladies of great respect, the more we conferre on the accidents of Fortune, so much the more remaineth to consider on her mutabilities, wherein there is no need of wonder, if discreetly we observe that all such things as we fondly tearme to be our owne, are in her power, and so (consequently) change from one to another, without any stay or arrest (according to her concealed iudgement) or setled order (at least) that bee knowne to us. (p. 34r)

Just as the *novella*'s movement back and forth between England and Italy – a mirror of Fortune's downward and upward turns in the course of Boccaccio's narrative – concludes in England, the community of Italians active there in the Tudor period had by the late years of James's reign become so assimilated to its dominant culture that it is difficult to identify as Italian most of the names that continue to appear in the census records that tracked the 'stranger' presence in early modern England. Florio's own daughter, Aurelia, having married the surgeon, James Molins, took his name and assumed the mantle of English respectability, and her case was probably typical.[11] As long as Italy remained a distant and largely inaccessible destination, its vastly more developed vernacular culture could provide an imaginative space of experimentation for a still nascent English cultural politics. But once Italy turned into a more known quantity, as it increasingly was in the early decades of the seventeenth century when it became more common for the English connected class to travel there, its gravitational pull was rapidly moving away from the linguistic and literary coordinates on which Florio's utility depended, as it assumed a more decidedly material form, whether through the appropriation of Italian art and architecture or through the conquest of Mediterranean economic markets previously dominated by the Italian city-states. That John Florio's last significant project should have been an anonymously attributed translation into English from the Italian language he had spent his life promoting is an unmistakable sign that the philological cultural politics to which he had dedicated his life were passing out of fashion.

Notes

1. Giovanni Boccaccio, *Decameron*, ed. Cesare Segre (Milan: Mursia, 1987), 97. Page numbers in this edition are cited hereafter in brackets after my English translations.
2. Earlier accounts of the failure of the Bardi and Peruzzi tended to overstate the English role in the wider European crisis; see Edward S. Hunt, "A New Look at the Dealings of the Bardi and Peruzzi with Edward III," *Journal of Economic History* 50:1 (March 1990), 149–62.
3. Pietro Aretino, *La prima parte de ragionamenti* (London: John Wolfe, 1584), A2r-v.
4. Though it is difficult to see why either of these stories would have been considered any more scandalous than any number of others. In III.10, a young Muslim woman, Alibech, travels into the Saharan desert to learn what Christianity might have to offer her; there she meets up with a hermit, Rustico, who teaches her how to "rimettere il diavolo in inferno" (put the devil back in hell) and thus instructed meets and marries a suitable husband, who then takes her back to the city where she inherits a great fortune. In VI.6, an apparently innocuous story about the pronounced ugliness of the Florentine Baronci family, the creative powers of God are called into question by suggesting that the Baronci must have been the earliest Florentines, the Creator not having yet worked out all the kinks in that particular race.
5. See Herbert G. Wright, *The First English Translation of the "Decameron" (1620)* (Upsala: A. B. Lundequistaka Bokhandeln, 1953), 129–64.
6. Wright, 165–88 and 266–70, also determined that Florio had utilized the considerably more faithful French translation of the *Decameron* prepared by Antoine le Maçon for Marguerite de Navarre, first published in 1545 and repeatedly reprinted through 1614.
7. In this *novella*, however, Florio restores the designation "abbot" for the disguised young woman that Salviati – attentive to the ecclesiastical censors – had turned into "Consigliere"; all other changes noted in what follows originated with the translator.
8. Giovanni Boccaccio, *The Decameron containing an Hundred Pleasant Novels*, trans. John Florio (London: Isaac Jaggard, 1620), 35v. All subsequent citations are given in brackets.
9. Lodowick Bryskett, who worked closely with Edmund Spenser in Ireland, was the most visible of the colonizing Anglo-Italians, but Florio himself might

have had something to do with English colonialist ambitions there, as a document in the Irish State Papers from 1609 suggests. A sum of 500 pounds was bestowed on Florio by King James, money that had been forfeited to the king by Sir Cayre O'Dogherty, after he had attacked the town of Derry, killed its governor and others who resisted him and his force, pillaged and then burned the town to the ground. Given the significant differences in the exchange rate of currencies, Florio was eventually supposed to receive 200 pounds, but it is not clear whether he ever did. As Arundell del Re notes in "References to Florio in the *State Papers of Ireland*," *Review of English Studies* 12 (April, 1936), p. 197: "it would be of considerable interest to ascertain why so large a sum had been bestowed upon Florio by the King ... [but] so far as I have been able to discover, no record has come to light specifically authorizing such a payment, which suggests that it may have been entered under some special secret fund, possibly used for the payment of 'intelligencers', but this is no more than a supposition." Non-payment might well have been the most likely outcome of this episode, if James's failure to ever pay Florio's pension after Anne's death is any measure; see Frances Yates, *John Florio: An Italian in Shakespeare's England* (Cambridge: Cambridge University Press, 1934), 292–300.

10. On the evidence for Anne's conversion, see Peter Davidson and Peter McCoog, SJ, "Fr. Robert's Convert: The Private Catholicism of Anne of Denmark," *Times Literary Supplement*, Nov. 24, (2000), 16–17; and for a useful consideration of how Anne may have squared her religious convictions with the prevailing Protestant culture of both her husband and the English nation, see Peter E. McCullough, *Sermons at Court, Politics and Religion in Elizabethan and Jacobean Preaching* (Cambridge: Cambridge University Press, 1998), 169–82.

11. See Yates, *John Florio*, 318–19.

4

The First Reader of *Shake-speares Sonnets*

Margreta de Grazia

One of the great outrages in the annals of publishing history is the edition in which Shakespeare's Sonnets circulated for the better part of the seventeenth and eighteenth centuries: *Poems: Written by Wil. Shakespeare. Gent.*, published in 1640. In this edition, the Sonnets as we know them are muddled almost beyond recognition. From two to five sonnets are combined to form new poetic units, each with its own generic title. Poems from another collection, *The Passionate Pilgrim* (1612), are shuffled into the volume. To add insult to injury, pronouns are altered so that poems addressed to a man appear to be written to a woman. Finally a mendacious prefatory address guarantees the easy comprehension of the poems, assuring readers that they will find them, "[s]eren, cleere and elegantly plaine, such gentle straines as shall recreate and not perplexe your braine, no intricate or cloudy stuffe to puzzell intellect."[1] Who is responsible for such flagrant corruption and deceit? The publisher, John Benson. And what lies behind it? Fraud. First he stole the copy of *Shake-speares Sonnets* from Thomas Thorpe, the publisher of the 1609 Quarto; then he completely overhauled it in order to conceal his theft from both the Stationers' Company and his readership. That the object of Benson's injury should have been the Sonnets, the only writing we have in Shakespeare's own voice and person, has made the offense all the more reprehensible.

This account of Benson's 1640 *Poems* is based on the detailed analysis by one of the last century's greatest editors of Renaissance verse, Hyder Edward Rollins, in his two-volume 1944 New Variorum edition of the Sonnets. Here is his melodramatic summary: "Benson pirated Thorpe's text, but took such pains to conceal his piracy that he has deceived many modern scholars, just as apparently he hoodwinked the wardens of the Stationers' Company."[2] A version of this account has been reproduced in almost every subsequent edition of the Sonnets: by Stephen Booth (Yale, 1976), John Kerrigan (Penguin, 1986), G. Blakemore-Evans (Cambridge, 1986), and Katherine Duncan-Jones (Arden, 1997).[3] The piracy narrative does more than enliven an obligatory textual history. It explains an otherwise inexplicably corrupted text. Why else would a publisher deliberately jumble and mangle an edition of the Sonnets? It could only be, as Rollins concludes, "to hide his tracks." Indeed, Rollins invents a crime in order to account for the violation. Benson broke no laws, much less customs or practices of the printing trade, by printing a text that had been out of print for over thirty years.

The value of Hyder Edward Rollins' work on Renaissance texts is inestimable: his editions of two monumental variorums, Shakespeare's *Sonnets* and Shakespeare's *Poems*, as well as of numerous early modern miscellanies and ballad collections, remain unsurpassed.[4] And yet it is important to recognize how a scholar of his expertise can be badly mistaken about a text, not only in matters of detail but in respect to something as fundamental as its identity. In his Variorum Sonnets, Rollins' first error is to identify the 1640 *Poems ... by Wil. Shake-speare* as an edition of the 1609 *Shake-speares Sonnets*. If it were that, it would indeed be an unconscionable travesty, and there would be reason to impute unethical if not criminal intentions to its perpetrator. But Benson published an edition not of Shakespeare's *Sonnets* but of, as his title page announces, Shakespeare's *Poems*. Indeed, at a time before the editor's function had been named, defined, or performed, what he published cannot properly be called an *edition* of any text. Rollins' condemnation of the 1640 *Poems* as an edition of the 1609 *Sonnets* has blinded us to what it is: a record, and the closest one we have to Shakespeare, of how the 1609 Quarto was read. John Benson is the first reader on record of *Shake-speares Sonnets*.

I

By Rollins' light, the title of Benson's volume is in keeping with his scheme to conceal his appropriation of the *Sonnets*. But the new title is no decoy: it describes what the volume contains, *Poems ... by Wil. Shake-speare*. As the dedicatory sonnet by John Warren makes clear, Benson's intention was to gather Shakespeare's scattered poems in one volume. The sonnet compares the publisher to Asclepius, who collected the dismembered pieces of Hippolytus and reassembled him as *Virbius* ("twice a man"). Benson, too, was in the business of collecting dispersed remains: he gathered the far-flung pieces of Shakespeare's poetic corpus and gave them a second life in his octavo, as *Poems*: "What, lofty *Shakespeare*, art againe reviv'd? I And *Virbius* like now show'st thy selfe twise liv'd"? There was, of course, a great precedent for collecting literary remains between the bound covers of a volume: the 1623 Folio *Mr. William Shakespeares Comedies, Histories, & Tragedies*. Benson followed the 1632 Folio, printed by Thomas Cotes, the same skilled printer who printed Benson's *Poems*.[5] Heminge and Condell, the supervisors of the Folio, maintain several times in their preliminaries that their function was to gather into their massive volume the disparate "remains" or "seuerall parts" of the dramatist's corpus.[6] Instead of a massive folio, Benson's tome was a modest octavo, the fashionable Caroline format for verse, but the Shakespeare Folio was clearly his model. Like the Folio, the octavo opened to a portrait of Shakespeare, obviously copied from Droeshout's engraving in the Folio. Beneath the octavo portrait is an inscription taken from Jonson's encomium in the Folio; the octavo reproduces other verses introduced in the 1632 Folio: an augmented version of Leonard Digges' dedicatory verse, as well as elegies to Shakespeare by both John Milton and William Basse. Both Folio and octavo contain an address to the reader establishing the connections of the volume's content to Shakespeare, as well as attesting to the integrity of its compilers. In sum, Benson's octavo is designed to canonize Shakespeare's poems by replicating the bibliographic formatting of the volume that had canonized the plays. It is likely that Benson conceived of the poetic octavo as a little companion to the big dramatic Folio; by purchasing the two volumes a reader for the first time could possess both the collected plays and the collected poems of England's great author.

In collecting Shakespeare's scattered poems, Benson had first to identify them and he used the most reliable criterion available to an early modern publisher after an author's decease: ascriptions on printed title-pages. (The same criterion would be used as late as 1664 when the Folio was enlarged to include five plays published with title-page attributions to Shakespeare and two to W. S.) Most of the verses attributed to Shakespeare in the 1640 *Poems* are printed from two publications ascribed to him, *Shake-speares Sonnets* (1609) published by Thomas Thorpe and *The Passionate Pilgrim or Certaine Amorous Sonnets ... By W. Shakespere* (1612) published by William Jaggard. Benson's claim that he was breathing second life into the poems was perfectly accurate: neither text had been reprinted. But there were other of Shakespeare's poems that had never died. In 1640, *Lucrece* was in its eighth edition and *Venus and Adonis* in its sixteenth, and their copyrights were tightly held. This was no minor disadvantage for Benson, for Shakespeare's reputation as a poet depended from the very start on those two narrative poems from classical sources. In his catalogue of England's poets in *Palladis Tamia* (1598), Francis Meres hails Shakespeare as the English Ovid, the poet who had received the "sweet witty soul of Ovid," as if by metempsychosis; *Venus and Adonis* had been infused by *Metamorphoses* and *Lucrece* by *Fasti*. To capitalize on that classicizing connection, Jaggard transferred nine Ovidian epistles translated from Ovid's *Heroides* from his publication of Thomas Heywood's *Troia Britannica* to his third edition of *The Passionate Pilgrim* (1612) attributed to Shakespeare. For Benson, too, these epistles substituted for the unobtainable Latinate centerpieces. Jaggard knew they were not by Shakespeare, and Thomas Heywood made the misattribution public in his *Apology for Actors*.[7] But Benson, we must assume, had only the authority of the 1612 title-page to go on. He did not, then, indiscriminately bulk out the 1609 *Sonnets* to render them unrecognizable; he compiled a miscellany of Shakespeare's poems.

At the start of his own culminating contribution to the Variorum tradition, Rollins regrets having to refer to the 1640 *Poems* as "a second edition" of the Sonnets. A stolen and manhandled text does not deserve to be called an "edition." But it is misleading to call it an edition, not because it is too bad to be one, but because it is not an edition at all. In order to have an edition, an editor is needed, and properly speaking, there are no editors in the seventeenth century. Nor are there any publishers, according to the *OED*, until 1740. Yet there is much to be gained by retaining the term, as does Zachary Lesser, to refer to the stationer who is involved in the acquisition, production, and sale of a text.[8] In his important book on the publication of seventeenth-century playtexts, Lesser has demonstrated how the publisher read texts with an eye to his readership in order to best determine how to cater to its interests. A publisher's allegiances, therefore, were less to the deceased author than to an active reading public. Benson's volume aimed to produce a readerly text rather than an authoritative or authorized one. And this required a different kind of textual preparation. His project was not to bring the text in alignment with what the author wrote; but rather to refashion the poems in order to capture a readership. He quite literally was invested in making Shakespeare *Virbius*. This is not to say that he was not motivated by self-interest, for as Lesser argues, you cannot make profit off a book unless it makes sense. Vendibility requires legibility. Benson's textual interventions all work to counter the obscurity of the poems, above all of the sonnets. His notorious promise, therefore, is not disingenuous: His *Poems* attempted to make Shakespeare's verses appear "cleere and elegantly plaine" with nothing to "perplexe your braine

... puzzell intellect." He took Thomas Thorpe's 1609 Quarto and transformed it into a volume that promised to make sense to its projected readership: his groupings and titles were intended as indices to how the verses were to be read in printed form, three decades after they had first been published.

II

When Benson is charged with theft, the assumption is that he stole an object of value. But the *Shake-speares Sonnets* he obtained in 1640 was not the Sonnets we have today: the priceless centerpiece of the Shakespearean canon. All evidence suggests that the Sonnets were not much appreciated between the publication of Thorpe's 1609 Quarto and Benson's 1640 octavo. Thorpe published the *Sonnets* only once, before he ceased publishing altogether in 1624.[9] That as many as thirteen copies of the 1609 Quarto have survived from an estimated print run of 500–800, suggests that, like a pristine library book, the 1609 Quarto was not much read. Indeed we have no certain evidence that it was read at all. Francis Meres' reference in *Palladis Tamia* (1598) to Shakespeare's "sugred Sonnets among his priuate friends" clearly references the sonnets circulating in manuscript, though there is no telling how many; we cannot even be certain they were among those printed in 1609.[10] Eleven of the 1609 Sonnets have been discovered in surviving verse manuscripts, a relatively low number compared to the verse of other poets.[11] One reference might be to the 1609 *Sonnets*, though it seems to be attesting to their obscurity rather than popularity: Leonard Digges jots in a flyleaf to Lope de Vega's *Rimas* (1613) that de Vega is as admired for his sonnets by Spaniards as Shakespeare should be in England.[12] There is a record that Edward Alleyn, the famous actor and theatrical entrepreneur, purchased *Shake-speares Sonnets* in 1609, but the note may well be a forgery.[13] Several lines from the Sonnets have been identified in Sir John Suckling's play *Brennoralt, or the Discontented Colonel*, but published in 1642, they may have been lifted from Benson.[14] For whatever reason, the Sonnets enjoyed nothing of the popularity of Shakespeare's other works, either of the plays, which by 1640 had already been published twice in grand folio form (1623 and 1632), or of the wildly popular narrative poems. The rights to copy the plays and the two narrative poems were valuable commodities; the right to copy the *Sonnets* was, it appears, quite worthless.

In 1640, a publisher could count on the name 'Shakespeare' to sell books but the sonnet form had no such appeal. The Elizabethan or early Jacobean sonnet collections were long out of print. Even in 1609, the sonnet vogue of the 1590s was on the wane, not to be revived until the end of the eighteenth century, when not coincidentally the Sonnets were reinstated in their 1609 form. What then could be done with a volume titled *Sonnets* and consisting of a relentless series of 154 quatorzains? After sonnets had lost their generic niche, how was the 1609 Quarto to be read? As Colin Burrow has noted, the Quarto is a "radically ambiguous thing."[15] The verses have no titles, only numerals. They are framed at one end by a mysterious dedication to Mr. W. H. from the printer T. T. and at the other by a long complaint poem. In 1640 the verses in between would have appeared uninvitingly outdated, monotonous, and inscrutable – just the kind of "intricate cloudy stuff" to perplex the brain and puzzle the intellect that Benson knew to spare his readers.

By conflating the poems of the *Sonnets* with the varied verse forms of the *Pilgrim*, by combining sonnets, and by ascribing descriptive titles to all the verse units, Benson demystified Shakespeare's sonnets and integrated them into a more familiar miscellany form. This is how he gave them a second life, and he preserved it in a new bibliographic repository, exchanging a format that was rarely bound, the quarto, for the octavo – portable, sturdier, easy to bind, and the most popular mid-century form for published verse.[16] The collection is emphatically a posthumous one. It concludes with three elegies to Shakespeare, followed by poems by a string of cavalier poets, among them Robert Herrick, William Cartwright, Thomas Carew, and William Strode. The cavalier poems are clearly set off from the rest of the volume with a separate title, *Additional Poems ... by other Gentlemen*, and Benson had duly entered the supplement into the Stationers' Register: "An Addition of some excellent Poems to Shakespeares Poems by other Gentlemen."[17] For Benson, canonizing Shakespeare involved collecting not only Shakespeare's poems, but also post-Shakespearean poems, as if to establish the continuing vitality of English amatory verse. There is no evidence that the 1640 *Poems* was reprinted in the seventeenth century, though *Mr. Shakspere's Poems* does rank in the 1658 *Catalogue of the Most Vendible Books in England*.[18] It was widely reprinted, however, in the eighteenth century multi-volumed editions of Shakespeare. Nicholas Rowe's 1714 edition was the first to combine Shakespeare's plays with his poems: with *Venus and Adonis*, *Lucrece*, and Benson's *Poems* (without the "Addition" and retitled *Poems on Several Occasions*). It was the first edition, therefore, that could correctly call itself *The Works of Mr. William Shakespear*. Benson's *Poems* filled out the canon of seven other editions of the *Works* or *Plays and Poems* in the eighteenth century. Until Malone's supplement in 1780, Benson's text accomplished his canonizing mission of keeping Shakespeare's poems alive.

III

Benson reduced the number of discrete sonnets in the 1609 Quarto from 154 to 72 by regrouping them; eight were omitted, presumably by accident. His intention, however, could not have been to phase out the telltale sonnet form, as the piracy theory maintains, or he would not have left twenty-seven sonnets intact; nor would he have prefaced the volume with a dedicatory sonnet. His regrouping had a different motivation: it materialized affiliations among the individual sonnets. That many of the sonnets couple or cluster with sonnets around them continues to be recognized by modern editors and critics, for example, the Oxford editor, Colin Burrow: "Readers of the poems in their [1609] sequence are invited to weld separate sonnets together ... to make sequences of time, of sound, of sense, of narrative, and of argument."[19] Many editors flag such "waves of consonance," though not always the same ones, and claim that their presence argues for Shakespeare's having ordered the sequence.

In their recent overview of the Sonnets, Paul Edmondson and Stanley Wells provide a table identifying thirty-six groups of from two to eight sonnets within the collection that are united either by a "keyword" or a "theme."[20] Allowing that their groupings are "subjectively inflected," they are open to alternatives. They do not look for them, however, in the text they describe as "a deliberately fraudulent volume, carefully designed to pull the wool over the eyes of the officials of the Stationers' Company."[21] Yet a number of their groupings in 2004 correspond to Benson's in 1640. For example, like Benson they group sonnets 27 and 28 together, Benson under the heading "A disconsolation," they under "Insomnia." Both combine sonnets 33 and 34, he under the rubric "Love's Releefe," and they under "Weather and relationship" (though Benson extends the run to 35, as do a number of modern editors). Both conjoin sonnets 44 and 45, Benson as "Melancholy Thoughts" and Edmondson/ Wells as "The four elements." Both cluster together the three attempts to cope with separation from the beloved in sonnets 97 to 99, Benson with the descriptive "Complaint for his Love's absence" and Edmondson/ Wells with the less apposite "Season."[22] Modern editors and critics of the sonnets, then, have responded to such waves or clusters, identifying various principles of coherence. When Benson saw affinities between or among the sonnets, he did something more radical than note or discuss them: he collapsed the space separating them so they ran together as a single poem; he retained Thorpe's indentation of the couplet, however, so that it functioned to signal either a new verse paragraph or the end of a sonnet.

There are limits to what Benson will conjoin: he never combines any of the sonnets from the 1609 Quarto with sonnets from the 1612 *Pilgrim*, much less with other verse forms. Nor does he force sonnets that resist adjoining. In a number of cases, when a sonnet will not readily coalesce with others, he leaves it alone. Several of them are sonnets that have since found their way into anthologies precisely because of their self-containment, for example, sonnet 129, "Th' expense of spirit in a waste of shame" (Benson's "Immoderate Lust"); sonnet 146, "Poor soul, the centre of my sinful earth" ("A Consideration of death"); and sonnet 116, "Let me not to the marriage of true minds | Admit impediments" ("The Picture of true love").[23] Others remain single because they are too *sui generis* to pair: for example, Benson labels sonnet 143, in which the poet likens his desire for his mistress, who desires another, to a babe crying after its mother who is chasing a chicken, with the non-committal "An Allusion."

While he does not conjoin any of the *Pilgrim* poems, he does resituate them so as to invite the same kind of clustered or serial readings. For example, he takes *A Lover's Complaint*, the narrative poem at the end of the 1609 *Sonnets*, and places it between poems (now attributed to Heywood) relating to the Trojan War. The poem preceding it, "*Achilles* his concealment of his sex in the court of *Lycomedes*," is based on the lubricious legend, originating in Statius' *Achilleid*, of Achilles' transvestism.[24] The nymph Thetis, upon learning that her son was destined to die in the Trojan War, sent him to the court of Lycodemus in Scyros disguised as a woman; so disguised, Achilles has easy access to the King's eight daughters and succeeds in bedding and impregnating one of them, Delademea. "Thus Lady-like he with a Lady lay." The poem ends with a playful deliberation of whether Delademea could have been forced, when she after the fact pleads for more, "What force (*Delademea*) call you this?" The poems following *A Complaint* comprise an exchange of epistles just prior to Helen of Troy's abduction, "The amorous Epistle of Paris to Hellen" and "Hellen to Paris." In the first, Paris declares his intent to have Helen, with or without her consent; in the second, Helen coyly responds with both resistance and encouragement. So flanked, the *Complaint* looks quite different. Has its maiden been raped or seduced? Has she resisted or yielded? In this context, *A Complaint* stimulates the same kind of questions around rape and consent that are deliberated in *Lucrece*; as in *Lucrece*, too, where rape leads to the overthrow of monarchy, the poems might invite political reflection. In 1640, constitutional change was more than the theoretical notion it was in 1594. In a volume in which poems by Shakespeare are followed by those of twelve cavalier poets, one might expect a royalist bias: an endorsement of monarchical power as the will of the people. Delademea, the maiden, and Helen in the end appear not only satisfied with what has been forced upon them, but desirous of more of the same.

IV

This is not to say that all of Benson's groupings and juxtapositions can be explained. It may even be that some of them are unmotivated, perhaps because Benson could not discover any linkages, perhaps because he wanted to leave the challenge open for the reader. For the most part, however, the groupings are based on some principle of coherence that is often highlighted by the title. The titles have been largely ignored by modern readers, however, and disparaged as generic, banal, and commonplace. And that is exactly what they are. They are headings intended to stress what a general readership would find widely relevant. Familiar and inclusive, the titles appeal to the *consentium gentium* of the readers' world rather the unique thoughts and feelings of the singular author. Nor was there anything irregular about the assignment of titles by a hand other than the author's. While Shakespeare is not known to have titled any lyric poem, compilers of verse manuscripts did so routinely. Arthur F. Marotti has described the practice by which readers would typically give titles to verses when transcribing them from either a manuscript or a printed source.[25] The titles were a way of personalizing verse (perhaps effecting a kind of informal entitlement) as well as of preparing it for classification and later retrieval. Benson foregrounds the implement key to this practice when he titles sonnet 122, "Upon the receipt of A Table Booke from his Mistris." It is in such a portable bound volume of pages that verses were copied before being inscribed under commonplace headings in a more permanent and stationary volume.

Twenty-five manuscript versions of Shakespeare's sonnets have survived and most have been given titles by the owners of the manuscript book in which they were copied.[26] Of those twenty-five, thirteen transcribe sonnet 2 ("When forty winters shall besiege thy brow") in which the addressee is urged to beget a "fair child." In all but one of these manuscripts, the sonnet has been titled, suggesting how it was read. Although

sonnet 2 contains no gendered pronouns, two versions direct it specifically to a woman: one title suggests courtship, "A Lover to his Mistres,"
while another (recurring in five manuscripts), appeals to a hopelessly dedicated virgin, "To one that would die a maid." The other manuscript titles
are epicene. One title introduces an encomium to marriage, "Benefitt
of Mariage." Another (repeated in three manuscripts) is an appeal to
dynasty, *Spes Altera,* the epithet Virgil applies to Rome's future hope,
Aeneas' son Ascanius (*Aeneid* 12.168), and another adds a musical setting
to that promise, "Spes Altera A song." Benson performs a similar service
when he assigns a sententious title to the group in which sonnet 2 appears
(sonnets 1 to 3), "Loves crueltie," a transposition of sonnet 1's charge that
the addressee's refusal to increase is destructive to both self and world. As
these six examples suggest, titles can be a highly abbreviated form of literary criticism that extrapolates meaning, function, or circumstance from
texts. The titles give the reader an interpretative threshold from which to
enter the poem; like an introductory head note, they point the way in. In
Benson's practice, they often epitomize the common denominator of the
conjoined sonnets.

Designed for readers of poetry, Benson's titles are the result of careful,
imaginative and even literary readings. Three of the titles are Latin tags,
compressing the sonnet into epigrammatic form: *Sat fuisse* ('To have
sufficed') suggests the satisfaction that the poet finds in sonnet 62 when
he sees himself reflected in his beloved, perhaps implying a contrast with
the insatiable Narcissus.[27] *Nil magnis Invidia* ('Envy is nothing to the
great') is an apt title for sonnet 70's repudiation of invidious slander.
Patiens Armatus ('The sufferer in arms') is the poet in sonnet 61, patiently
suffering as defenseless "watchman" to his beloved's infidelity. A number
of other titles depend on the Latin roots of a word. "Unanimitie" preserves the Latin *animus* when entitling two sonnets of soul-sharing, the
"undivided love" of sonnet 36 and the engrafted love of sonnet 37.
"Quicke prevention" (sonnet 7) draws on the Latin *pre-venire,* to come
before, in urging its addressee to reproduce *before* decline sets in; it also
inflects the root with the emergent sense of to avert or preclude. "Hap-
pinesse in content" (sonnet 25) picks up the pun in *content* (also present
in the Latin *continere*) in a sonnet that finds *contentment* in the love it *contains,* which unlike princely favor or military glory, cannot be removed.
The ambiguous title "Melancholy thoughts" is given to sonnets 44 and
45; *melancholy* refers to both the subject of his thoughts (he is thinking
about his own melancholy) as well as their effect (they make him melancholy). The one title that is itself a commonplace, "Familiaritie breeds
contempt," might be read as an indictment of the entire commonplace

tradition; the sonnet it entitles (sonnet 52) confirms its corollary: unfamiliarity breeds enjoyment (in the form of the beloved's infrequent appearances, holidays, special robes, unlocked treasure). And there is levity, too, in Benson's title for sonnet 128, "Upon her playing on the Virginalls," which reveals what kind of keyboard the poet has in mind when he wishes himself the keys moving up and down to his mistress' fingering.

Benson's titles often modernize familiar formulations, giving them new rings or spins. Nascent terms or uses surface in titles like "Valediction," the rubric for sonnets 71, 72, and 74; the term is Donne's recent anglicization, and applies just as well to these sonnets of leave-taking, which like Donne's suffer separation as an anticipation of death. "A conceit" refers to the ingenious notion of sonnet 22 that the aging poet will see himself young as long as he identifies with the youth ("My glass shall not persuade me I am old"); but it exploits a newly available ambiguity in "conceit" (*OED* 1605), a narcissistic opinion of oneself: the sonnet is a conceit, then, of self-conceit. "A master-piece" is the title given sonnet 24 that advertises the portrait hanging in the poet's bosom; *master-piece*, originally designating a piece of work by which a craftsman gained entrance to a guild and the title master, had only recently been applied to a work of art. Similarly "Magazine of beautie" (sonnets 4 to 6) introduces a word of Arabic origin, anglicized in the late sixteenth century to refer to a place where valuable things are stored; it is an apt title for three sonnets identifying the youth with "beauty's legacy," "summer's distillation," and "beauty's treasure" respectively; and it might be extended to cover the store house or treasury that is the poetic miscellany itself, anticipating its adaptation in the eighteenth century as the title of the periodical, *Gentleman's Magazine*.

These examples should suffice to demonstrate the considerable literary and semantic sophistication of Benson's titles. This is not, however, to say that the titles were intended to be definitive. As Sasha Roberts has established, it was quite routine for the owner of a printed miscellany to cross out the titles and assign new ones, as if aware that they were no more than one reader's interpretation.[28] Some of Benson's titles seem calculated to provoke revision. For example, he terms sonnet 129 "Immoderate Lust," but surely a stronger adjective is in order.

The Folger Library has several copies of the 1640 *Poems* with the owner's markings, including one in which the seventeenth-century owner scored out Benson's printed titles and penned in his or her own.[29] This reader's most extensive revision is of Benson's grouping of the first seventeen sonnets.[30] Benson either did not recognize their kinship or else thought the series too long for a single unit, so he divided them into six units: "Loves crueltie," "Magazine of beautie," "Quicke prevention," "An invitation to Marriage," "Youthfull glory," and "Good Admonition." One owner apparently disagreed: in one of the Folger Library's copies, the reader has scratched out all six rubrics and penned in his or her rendering, retitling the first group (sonnets 1 to 3), "Motives to procreation as the way to outliue Time"; the second (sonnets 13 to15), "On yet same subject," the third (sonnet 16 to 17), "On ye subject before," the fourth (sonnet 7), "On ye same subject," the fifth (sonnets 4 to 6), "On same subject," and the sixth (sonnets 8 to12), "On ye foregoing subject." As in our discipline, critical readings do not foreclose further readings; they precipitate and proliferate new ones – or recycle the old.

V

Modern editors since 1780 have agreed with the Folger reader that the first seventeen sonnets belong together. The so-called procreation sonnets work toward the same end of persuading the youth to marry and propagate. What editors rarely or barely mention, however, is the degree to which all of them draw on an epistle by Erasmus, the great translator and generator of commonplaces, urging a young gentleman to marry. The epistle, published in 1518 as *Encomium Matrimonii*, circulated widely in translation, in Richard Taverner's *A ryght frutefull epistle ... in laude and pryse of matrimony* (1536), and especially in Thomas Wilson's *An epistle to persuade a young Gentleman to marriage*, included in his influential *The Arte of Rhetoric* (1553). Precepts and figures proliferate in the course of the persuasion, as if the very subject matter of conjugal propagation itself generated rhetorical supply. But as Jennifer Jahner has observed, the epistle evoked another institution besides marriage.[31] Commonplaces circulated in the Tudor schoolroom as boys learned how language might be varied, amplified, and reduced by copying tropes and arguments from collections like Erasmus' *Parabolae*. As Jahner notes, "The language of marriage and pedagogy share an inseparable investment in profitable reproduction, one instantiated, moreover, in the act of copying commonplaces." As numerous scholars have pointed out, the commonplace was the central pedagogical tool for teaching elite males how to reproduce themselves in language.[32] The very first line of the 1609 *Sonnets* is a clear formulation of the epistle's ethos: "From fairest creatures we desire increase." Virtually every figure or argument that Shakespeare deploys has been drawn from the Erasmian thesaurus: from husbandry, music, mirrors, book-keeping, astronomy, mathematics, distillation, mimesis, and the law. Thus at the very threshold of the 1609 *Sonnets* the reader is met with an ostentatious invocation of the Erasmian commonplace tradition at the heart of the system that reproduced young men through the rhetorical generation of axioms urging their own reproduction. It appears no accident that one of the procreation sonnets, sonnet 2, as we have seen, was reproduced in more than half of the manuscripts that have survived. Also significant is that the most sustained early reading of Benson attempts to reassemble these seventeen sonnets. The sonnets themselves register an exchange of the apparatus at the heart of the commonplacing tradition. What might it mean to give someone a tablebook, as the poet has in sonnet 77? What might it mean to give away the gift of a tablebook, as the poet has in sonnet 122?[33]

That editors of the sonnets have either ignored or understated the significance of Erasmus' epistle to the first seventeen sonnet is not surprising.[34] Situating the sonnets in relation to commonplaces is, like assigning them generic titles, something of an affront to the lyrics associated with aesthetic novelty, the invention of poetic subjectivity, previously unprobed emotional depths, and unprecedented linguistic complexity. And yet what Jahner terms the "Erasmian uncanny" makes itself felt even when not named. Though she never mentions Erasmus in her edition of the sonnets, Helen Vendler obviously feels his commonplacing presence when she maintains that only after sonnet 17 can Shakespeare's "imagination come fully into play."[35] The authorship of sonnets 152 and 153, has often been questioned precisely because, as translations of a Greek epigram, they cannot be original. Colin Burrow nicely summarizes the sonnets' unique status, "The sequence rather seems to be sourced in itself."[36] And yet we are slowly coming to accept the centrality of commonplacing to Shakespeare's writing and reading. Roger Chartier and Peter Stallybrass have recently demonstrated that Shakespeare emerges as a canonical English poet not through his plays or poems, but rather through individual "sentences" or *sententiae* of ten to twenty syllables, extracted from his works and organized under topical headings.[37] The canonization of English literature might be said to begin when commonplace compilations like *Bel-vedere, or, The Garden of the Muses* consisted of commonplaces from "Moderne and extant Poets" rather than ancient Greek and Latin ones. In this context, the repeated references to Shakespeare as "Honie tong'd", "mellifluous", and "sweet" take on a new specificity. The bee is the most common figure for a reader, who ranges in the gardens of others extracting nectar from their flowers. As Chartier and

Stallybrass cleverly discern, these epithets attached themselves to Shakespeare because he "knew how to suck the nectar out of other [men's] books." As corollary, it might be added: he also knew how to prepare his own work for sucking, including in his sonnets, and beyond their procreational threshold. Here is a sampling of the most obvious ones:

> Roses have thorns, and silver fountains mud. (35)
> Clouds and eclipses stain both moon and sun. (35)
> [L] oathsome canker lives in sweetest bud. (35)
> Lillies that fester smell far worse than weeds. (94)
> To hear with eyes belongs to love's fine wit. (23)
> Sweets with Sweets war not. (8)
> Slander's mark was ever yet the fair. (70)
> In many's looks the false heart's history | Is writ. (93)
> The hardest knife ill-used doth lose its edge. (95)
> Sweets grown common lose their dear delight. (102)
> Among a number, one is reckoned none. (136)
> Love's best habit is in seeming trust. (138)
> Desire is death. (147)
> The sun itself sees not till heaven clear. (148)
> Love's fire heats water; water cools not love. (154)

Benson's commonplacing of the sonnets may be closer to Shakespeare's literary practices than the arbitrations of the Variorum editor.

VI

Nothing could be more antithetical to the Variorum project than commonplacing. The Variorum editions are designed to establish first what the author wrote, and second, what individual editors and commentators have contributed. In the case of the sonnets, Rollins returns to the 1609 Quarto and collates one copy against the twelve other extant ones. The emendations of the various editors appear in the stemma under each sonnet, the glosses of the various commentators appear after that. Longer comments appear in a separate section, "Appendixes to Shakespeare's Sonnets." Whether in the stemma, the glosses, or the commentary, the Variorum principle is to acknowledge the source of the contribution. The same standard of accuracy applies to reproducing each contribution as it does to the text itself. The very layout of the Variorum page demarcates the three divisions of textual labor: the author, the editor, the commentator are ranked on the page, their labors separated by a bold line. If the same word appears in the sonnet, the emendations, and the gloss, it is given a different type-face in each: Will, *Will*], Will].[38] It is then no wonder that Rollins should vilify Benson when his *Poems* at every stage play fast and loose with Rollins' rules of proprietary dispensation. He steals Thorpe's property, attributes to Shakespeare poems by other authors, slips in titles and emendations as if they were Shakespeare's own. But Benson belongs to the commonplacing regime in which texts are routinely altered in reproduction, and attributions, even to Shakespeare, are often omitted. In theory as well as practice, there is no source for a commonplace, no one either to credit or to defraud.

So strong is Rollins' scorn for Benson that it compromises his own "all-but-infallible" standard of accuracy.[39] He is so convinced of Benson's fraudulence that he misdescribes the bibliographic particulars of his *Poems*. His account would lead a reader to believe that Benson had muddled together Shakespeare, the writers of elegies to Shakespeare, and the Caroline poets:

> What Benson did, then, was to jumble together in a new unauthorized, and deceptive order all but eight of the sonnets ... with the *L[over's] C[omplaint]*, the entire contents of the 1612 *P[assionate] P[ilgrim]*, the *P[hoenix] & T[urtle]*, and various poems by miscellaneous authors – Milton, William Basse, Beaumont, Herrick, Thomas Carew, William Strode, Thomas Carey, William Cartwright, and others yet unidentified.[40]

But Benson did not "jumble" them together. The *Poems* attributed to Shakespeare conclude with FINIS. They are followed by three elegies on Shakespeare, which are in turn followed by a clearly marked division of later poets, *Addition by other Gentlemen*.[41] Rollins' description of Benson's publications is also skewed. He gives only the reference numbers from Edward Arber's *A Transcript of the Registers of the Company of Stationers of London* for Benson's publications, and leaves the impression that he was "chiefly a publisher of ballads and broadsides."[42] Yet had he given the titles referenced by those numbers, he would have revealed that Benson was more interested in everlasting works than ephemera. In 1640, he also published two octavos of Jonson's poetry, *Ben Jonson's Execration against Vulcan. With divers Epigrams* and *Q. Horatius Flaccus: His Art of Poetry ... with other Works of the Author*. In the latter volume, Benson may have been the first to introduce to vernacular text one of the marks of a classic: line numbers set against a text. Finally, Rollins suppresses the fact that some twenty of Benson's emendations have been retained by modern editors. Indeed it must have pained him to credit Benson in the stemma, followed by a series of conscientious editors, as if Benson stood at the beginning of their tradition, its *fons et origo*.

VII

If Benson is the great villain of the sonnets, then Edmond Malone is their great hero. He was the first to discredit Benson's *Poems* as of "no authority or value" and to reinstate the 1609 *Sonnets*, encased in a full editorial apparatus, first in 1780 as a supplement to the 1778 *Shakespeare's Plays and Poems* and then in 1790 as an integral part of the his eight-volume edition.[43] He was also the first to center the sonnets on the author, precisely what Benson's impersonal titles had precluded, and to divide the sonnets between two addressees at sonnet 126, one of the sonnets Benson happened to drop. The guiding light of his editorial project was *authenticity*. All of his editorial projects were driven by the same goal of reinstating what was closest to the author: the authentic text, the authentic life, the authentic portrait. He claimed to have established without "the smallest doubt" the authenticity of the 1609 Quarto. Benson reached for the same word in "To the reader," but not to assert his text's proximity to the author. The authenticity he seeks stands with his readers: he hopes his *Poems* will be greeted by their "authentick approbation."

Malone reads the sonnets for what they reveal about Shakespeare. Editing them entails affixing them to Shakespeare in as many ways as possible, starting with the identification of the "I" of the sonnets with the name on the title page; and followed by the identification of the second person of sonnets 1 through 126 with the Mr. W. H. of the dedication, which in turn leads to a sifting through of the documents for a nobleman of Shakespeare's acquaintance. His footnotes strengthened the connection between Shakespeare and the first person by drawing parallels between the sonnets and Shakespeare's biography, his times, and his other works. Once the authentic materials were in place, Malone could allow himself to speculate beyond the documents about what Shakespeare must have thought or felt; in one remarkable note that extends across five pages, he glosses the simile of sonnet 93, "So shall I live, supposing thou art true, | Like a *deceivèd husband*" (italics added). The combined strength of documents (Shakespeare's will), anecdotes (reports of Shakespeare's dalliance with a vintner's wife), as well as four plays from the canon that pivot on jealousy (*Merry Wives of Windsor, Othello, Cymbeline,* and *Winter's Tale*) gave Malone grounds for suspecting "that the author ... had himself been perplexed with doubts, though not perhaps in the extreme." The materials for such parallels – the first factual biography and the first chronology – were conveniently stored in the very same multi-volumed edition into which the sonnets were first incorporated. By cross-referencing them with the plays and narrative poems, he knitted them firmly into the canonical fabric.

Malone's task was to establish a text faithful to its author; Benson attempted to produce a text attractive to his readership. One used authentic texts and documents centered on the author. The other attempted to gauge the interests of his readership. This is not to say that Benson was indifferent to Shakespeare's authorship. Indeed he was heavily invested in his "everliving Workes" and the prospect that readers would want to possess them, *all* of them, the octavo *Poems* as well as the Folio *Comedies, Histories, & Tragedies*. In his desire to give permanent bibliographic form to the great English poet, he was not so different from Malone, retrieving Shakespeare through reading practices rather than Malone's "researches." It might be said that Malone had the easier task. By the end of the eighteenth century, the sonnet form had begun to regain popularity.[44] And in the newly organized print trade, in his clearly defined capacity of editor, his sole task was the preparation of the text. Business considerations were now in the hands of the publisher, who for Malone's 1790 edition took the form of a syndicate of thirty-five individuals. Out of this newly configured book trade, the Variorum edition emerged with its format of attribution.[45] Malone's edition of *The Plays and Poems of William Shakspeare* "with corrections and illustrations of the various commentators" (*cum notis variorum*) met the challenge of how to reproduce what properly belongs to Shakespeare as well as to those who have devoted their labors to reproducing him.

VIII

But what about the publisher who first prepared the sonnets for the press? Until recently, Thomas Thorpe belonged to the same rogue gallery as Benson: and his alleged offense, too, was both legal and textual. He was accused of having surreptitiously acquired the sonnets and then arranged and printed them without Shakespeare's authorization. In some accounts, he was blamed for the anomalous presence of both the Anacreontic sonnets 153 and 154 and *A Lover's Complaint*. But in recent decades, Thorpe's reputation has been on the rise; so, too, has that of the 1609 Quarto. Editors are more confident of its ordering of the sonnets, even to the point of assigning numerological significance to the numbering. For *A Complaint,* this has meant a complete reversal of critical fortune. After generations of exclusion from editions of the sonnets, as either spurious, or if by Shakespeare, not as part of the sonnets, the majority of editors from Kerrigan in 1986 to Burrow in 2003 have been admitting it as Shakespeare's fitting conclusion to the sonnets.

The reversal stems largely from the recognition that when 152 sonnets are followed by the Anacreontics and *A Complaint,* the 1609 *Sonnets* would fall into the same tripartite structure introduced in 1592 by Samuel Daniel's *Delia* and deployed by numerous other sonneteers, Thomas Lodge, Giles Fletcher, Richard Barnfield, Edmund Spenser among them. Shakespeare, it is assumed, fashioned his own belated sonnets to conform to the printed convention. But isn't it much more likely that the tripartite schema is Thorpe's contribution: his attempt to read (and have his readers read) Shakespeare's sonnets in the context of the earlier printed collections?[46] His interest in the Quarto is emphatic, registered not only at the foot of its title page, as is customary, but also in the dedication, usually signed by the author. The dedication reminds us that it is he who as "adventurer" has put up the capital with the risk of no returns. Might the tripartite structure have been his way of converting sonnets in manuscript for knowing "priuate friends" into sonnets in print for an otherwise clueless public? If it *is* his tripartite schema, then Thorpe is the first reader of Shakespeare's 154 sonnets, in whatever manuscript form he acquired them. By the time Benson laid eyes on the result, the 1609 *Shake-speares Sonnets,* the tripartite structure had faded into oblivion; he had to read them anew in preparation for a new generation of readers, and the 1640 *Poems* is the result. In 1780 Malone lights upon a new way of making the *Sonnets* readable: as first-person lyrics directed to a fair friend and to a dark mistress. His reading has proven so fruitful that we are still under its sway.[47] But what if the division at 126 were another attempt by Thorpe to organize the collection? We would then have been reading not Shakespeare's sonnets but rather *Shake-speares Sonnets* according to Thorpe.

Notes

1. *Poems: Written by Wil. Shake-speare* (London, 1640), "To the Reader."
2. Hyder Edward Rollins, ed., *New Variorum Edition of Shakespeare: The Sonnets,* 2 vols. (Philadelphia and London: J. B. Lippincott Company, 1944), 2: 18.
3. Two editors have resisted the narrative. Stephen Orgel passes no judgment on Benson's effort, though he does term it "pirated edition" (*The Sonnets* [Penguin Books: New York, London, etc. 2001], xliii). Colin Burrow terms the 1640 a "second edition of the Sonnets," and regards it as a revamping of the 1609 *Sonnets* (*The Complete Sonnets and Poems* [Oxford: Oxford University Press, 2002], 95, 94).

4. For an account of Rollins' remarkable work in the field, see Herschell Baker, *Hyder Edward Rollins, A Bibliography* (Cambridge, MA: Harvard University Press, 1960).

5. On the 1632 Folio as the model for Benson's *Poems*, see Margreta de Grazia, *Shakespeare Verbatim* (Oxford: Oxford University Press, 1991), 166–8.

6. On the 1623 Folio's project of gathering the scattered remains of the corpus, see de Grazia, *Shakespeare Verbatim*, 30–3.

7. On Jaggard's 1612 *The Passionate Pilgrim*, Heywood's protest against the attribution of his poems to Shakespeare, and the speculation that the original titlepage was replaced by one with no attribution, see David Scott Kastan, *Shakespeare and the Book* (Cambridge: Cambridge University Press, 2001), 55–61.

8. Zachary Lesser, *Renaissance Drama and the Politics of Publication: Readings in the English Book Trade* (Cambridge: Cambridge University Press, 2004), 27–30.

9. See Rollins (ed.), *Sonnets*, 2: 5, 18.

10. Francis Meres, *Palladis Tamia. Wits Treasury* (London, 1598), 282.

11. On the "relative paucity" of the sonnets' circulation in manuscript, see Arthur F. Marotti, "Shakespeare's Sonnets and the Manuscript Circulation of Texts in Early Modern England," in *A Companion to Shakespeare's Sonnets*, ed. Michael Schoenfeldt (Malden, MA: Blackwell, 2007), 186–7.

12. Katherine Duncan-Jones cites Digges' note commending "this Booke of Sonets which with Spaniards here is accounted of their Lope de Vega as in Englande we shoulde of our Will Shakespeare," and interprets it to mean that Shakespeare's sonnets should be esteemed more than they are. See Katherine Duncan-Jones, ed., *Shakespeare's Sonnets*, Arden Shakespeare, Third Series (London: Thomas Nelson, 1998), 71–2.

13. "[The note] is almost certainly a forgery by John Payne Collier," concludes Duncan-Jones, *Sonnets*, 7.

14. Suckling's liftings from Shakespeare sonnets are given in C. M. Ingleby, L. Toulmin Smith, and F. J. Furnivall, *The Shakespeare Allusion-Book* (London: Oxford University Press, 1932).

15. Burrow (ed.), *Sonnets*, 98.

16. On the durability of the octavo format compared to the quarto, see T. A. Birrell, "The Influence of Seventeenth-Century Publishers on the Presentation of English Literature," in *Historical & Editorial Studies in Medieval & Early Modern English*, ed. Mary-Jo Arn and Hanneke Wirtjes (Groningen: Wolters-Noordhoof, 1985), 166.

17. For the Stationers' Register entry, see Rollins (ed.), *Sonnets*, 2: 23.

18. William London, ed., *A Catalogue of the Most Vendible Books in England* (1658), as cited by Sasha Roberts, *Reading Shakespeare's Poems in Early Modern England* (Basingstoke and New York: Palgrave, 2003), 7.

19. Burrow (ed.), *Sonnets*, 108.

20. Paul Edmondson and Stanley Wells, *Shakespeare's Sonnets* (Oxford: Oxford University Press, 2004), 33.

21. Ibid., 118.

22. Also correspondent are their groupings of 109 and 110 "A Lover's excuse for his long absence" and "Contradiction of constancy and falsity" and 112–13 "A Complaint" and "Pity."

23. All references to the Sonnets are keyed to Colin Burrow's edition.
24. *Poems*, G5r–G6v. For the Achilles legend, see P. J. Heslin, *The Transvestite Achilles: Gender and Genre in Statius' "Achilleid"* (Cambridge: Cambridge University Press, 2005).
25. See Marotti, "Manuscript Circulation," 187–96.
26. See Burrow (ed.), *Sonnets*, 106, and Peter Beal, *Index of English Literary Manuscripts*, 5 vols. (London: Mansell; New York: R. R. Bowker, 1980–), 1: 452–4.
27. Burrow glosses "Making a famine where abundance lies" (sonnet 1.7) with "Narcissus's cry 'inopem me copia fecit'" ("My very abundance (of contact with what I love) make me poor")" and notes that it was one of the most frequently quoted phrases from the *Metamorphoses* (*Sonnets*, 382, n. 7).
28. See Roberts, *Reading Shakespeare's Poems*, 168–9.
29. For an analysis of two of the Folger's marked up copies of Benson, see Roberts, *Reading Shakespeare's Poems*, 167–9.
30. Rollins transcribes the corrections to this copy of Benson (Folger STC22344 copy 2), and assumes that the reviser got too "disgusted" with Benson to get beyond B7, where the revisions stop (*Sonnets*, 2: 22).
31. Jennifer Jahner, "Commonplace Shakespeare: Novelty, Generation, and Invention in the Sonnets to the Young Man," unpublished paper. I remain indebted to this paper for its striking insights into the meanings of "increase" in the procreation sonnets.
32. On the importance of Erasmus in the early modern classroom, see T. W. Baldwin, *Shakespeare's Small Latine & Lesse Greeke*, 2 vols. (Urbana: University of Illinois Press, 1944), 1: 179–95; on the reproduction of elite young men through the education system, see Richard Halpern, *The Poetics of Primitive Accumulation: English Renaissance Culture and the Genealogy of Capital* (Ithaca and London: Cornell University Press, 1991), 21–60
33. On the importance of these books "as the collection point of verse in the system of manuscript transmission of poetry" and their relevance to the circulation of Shakespeare's sonnets, see Arthur Marotti, "Shakespeare's Sonnets as Literary Property," in *Soliciting Interpretation: Literary Theory and Seventeenth-Century English Poetry*, ed. Elizabeth D. Harvey and Katharine Eisaman Maus (Chicago and London: University of Chicago Press, 1990), 147–8.
34. A notable exception is Barbara A. Mowat and Paul Werstine, eds., *Shakespeare's Sonnets* (New York, London, etc.: Washington Square Press, 2004), which prints excerpts from Wilson's translation of Erasmus' epistle in an appendix, 346–52. See, also, the discussion of sonnets 1 to 17 in Katherine M. Wilson, *Shakespeare's Sugared Sonnets* (New York: Barnes and Noble, 1974), 146–71.
35. Helen Vendler, ed., *The Art of Shakespeare's Sonnets* (Cambridge, MA: Harvard University Press, 1997).
36. Burrow (ed.), *Sonnets*, 116.
37. Roger Chartier and Peter Stallybrass, "Reading and Authorship: The Circulation of Shakespeare 1590–1619," in *A Concise Companion to Shakespeare and the Text*, ed. Andrew Murphy (Oxford: Blackwell, 2007).
38. Sonnet 57 in Rollins (ed.), *Sonnets*, 1: 154.
39. Burrow (ed.), *Sonnets*, 74, n. 2.

40. Rollins (ed.), *Sonnets*, 2: 20.
41. For a refutation of another of Rollins' fallacious characterizations of Benson – that in *Poems* "the man friend was in many cases disguised as a woman" – see de Grazia, "The Scandal of Shakespeare's Sonnets," in *Shakespeare's Sonnets: Critical Essays*, ed. James Schiffer (New York and London: Garland, 2000), 89–91.
42. Rollins is quoting from H. R. Plomer's *Dictionary of the Printers and Booksellers*, 2: 20.
43. For Malone's edition of the sonnets, see de Grazia, *Shakespeare Verbatim*, 152–62.
44. On the return of the sonnet form in the later eighteenth century, see Stuart Curran, *Poetic Form and British Romanticism* (New York and Oxford: Oxford University Press, 1986), 30–55.
45. For a brief history of the Shakespeare Variorum editions, beginning with that of Samuel Johnson in 1765, see de Grazia, *Shakespeare Verbatim*, 209–14.
46. For the argument that the sonnets sequence was a highly standardized print genre between 1590 and 1619, see Marcy L. North, "The Sonnets and Book History," in *A Companion to Shakespeare's Sonnets*, ed. Michael Schoenfeldt (Malden, MA: Blackwell, 2007), 204–21.
47. Bernard Lintott in 1711 and George Steevens in 1766 printed the 1609 *Sonnets*, but because neither provided an apparatus, neither can be remembered as readers. Lintott's title, *One Hundred and Fifty Four Sonnets, all of them in Praise of his Mistress*, also gives one pause.

Part II

Desire and the Disorganized Body

5

The Play of Wanton Parts

Jonathan Goldberg

> ... everything can be born from deviation.
>
> Michel Serres

As the description of Spenser's Garden of Adonis draws to its close, something happens which a very long tradition of interpreting *The Faerie Queene* would deny could be there at all. After the stanzas in which Venus and Adonis are described, a concluding stanza presents Adonis living "in everlasting joy" (III.vi.49.1).[1] One might presume that Spenser simply repeats himself; the previous stanza, after all, had opened almost identically, describing Adonis "in eternall blis, | Joying his goddesse, and of her enjoyed" (48.1–2). Indeed, repeating would seem all that might be possible given the extent to which Venus and Adonis are so firmly encircled one within each other, possessed and possessor, subject and object, as if excluding any other relationship. Stanza 49 opens echoing and seemingly repeating the initial line of the previous stanza, but this time Adonis is "with many of the Gods in company, | Which thither haunt, and with the winged boy | Sporting himselfe in safe felicity" (49.2–3). Adonis appears now to be paired with a boy. Moreover, the "safe felicity" of this relationship may be in question by the stanza's end. For, elaborating on the role of Cupid, it seems that he "with faire Adonis plays his wanton parts" (49.9). A piece of this conclusion is echoed in the opening of the next stanza; Adonis is no longer the subject, and Cupid remains: "And his true love faire Psyche with him playes" (50.1). Psyche now plays the part of Adonis.

What is at stake – and denied in the criticism – in this repositioning of Adonis as playmate of Cupid – is caught in the echo of "playes" against "playes" as it is understood conventionally. We can take the footnote to "playes" in 50.1 in the 2000 *Norton Anthology of English Literature* as a convenient guide: "'Playes' suggests, as well, sexual play."[2] Inviting the reader to find sexual meaning in the line about Cupid and Psyche, but presumably not in the unglossed line before, the Norton note implies that "playes" in 49.9, when used to describe the wanton relationship of Adonis and Cupid is somehow not sexual as it is additionally ("as well") only here, with Psyche. The reader, it seems, should infer that only the play between Cupid and Psyche could have that meaning and should not suppose what I have been implying: that the relationship of Adonis and Cupid might be identical to the relationship of Adonis to Venus insofar as both are sexual relations.

Not to hear the echo, not to see the parallel, and to insist that the same word means two entirely different things, depends upon a critical tradition that goes back to C. S. Lewis's 1936 *The Allegory of Love*, which drew the Garden of Adonis into pointed contrast with the Bower of Bliss: "The one is artifice, sterility, death: the other, nature, fecundity, life."[3] (It is of interest to note that Lewis offered his thesis precisely to counter critics who were unable to distinguish one place from the other – precisely the thesis I wish to revive in these pages.) Lewis's terms could easily translate into homo/hetero difference, and it is by now commonplace to add to his observations about the supposed sterile relationship between Verdant and Acrasia reminders about the representations of "naked boyes" (II.12.60.6) in the fountain in the Bower, or to recall the "lascivious boyes" (72.8) who join in the celebration of the "wanton joyes" (72.6) of Acrasia and her latest lover. It is under the aegis of such a division that the wanton boy in the company of Adonis fails to register.

Lewis was not explicitly drawing a homo/hetero comparison, and he urged moreover against misunderstanding the contrast he made to be between "lawless, that is, unwedded, love, as opposed to lawful love. It is a picture," he insisted, "one of the most powerful ever painted, of the whole sexual nature in disease. There is not a kiss or an embrace in the island: only male prurience and female provocation."[4] These terms are amenable of course to invidious distinctions between homo- and heterosexuality, but Lewis appears only to know about the latter, and the difference he points is between titillation and actual performance. Hence, for him, "the good Venus" of the Garden "is a picture of fruition," while Acrasia is anything but. Oddly enough, when one looks at the descriptions of these two scenes of coupling, one sees almost the same picture: Verdant is "sleeping by" Acrasia (II.12.79.1), while Adonis is said first to "ly, | Lapped in flowres and precious spycery" beside Venus (III.6.46.4–5). Lewis somehow misses the clear fact that the scene with

Acrasia is postcoital – i.e., that there is (or has been) sex in the Bower. Later critics have seen that, but they have not so much abandoned Lewis's thesis as retooled it for the heteronormative purposes that can be seen in the strange note in the Norton, which grants sexual meaning to the same word in a hetero context that it denies in a homoerotic one.

Later criticism has refashioned Lewis further, in fact to distinguish the lawful from the lawless, the point that he insisted he was not drawing. Stephen Greenblatt, for example, in his influential discussion of the destruction of the Bower of Bliss in *Renaissance Self-Fashioning*, certainly acknowledges that there is sexual activity in the Bower; for him, unlike Lewis, the Bower is not a site of perversion and disease, but of a beauty that threatens to be excessive and without purpose; it is therefore to be contrasted with a sexuality that leads to virtuous action "and ultimately, with the sanctification of marriage, in the generation of offspring."[5] Greenblatt does not name the Garden of Adonis as the site of such a realization; but, remarkably, his echo of Lewis invokes the lawless/lawful, unmarried/married distinction that Lewis declared beside the point. That is, sexuality is drawn by Greenblatt into the orbit of social reproduction; rather than being viewed potentially as a separate and separable domain, Spenser is said to consider that potential a reprehensible one, congruent with the art that he is willing to sacrifice on the altar of ideology.

Greenblatt implicitly depends on a reading of the kind that Harry Berger offered in his 1961 essay "*The Faerie Queene*, Book III: A General Description." Berger claimed there that the trajectory of book III was "married love," its aim to eliminate "confusion and ambiguity" ("confusion" is a code word critics regularly use to avoid any further specification of non-normative forms of sexuality, although Berger does say that the non-acceptable forms include the "auto-erotic and homosexual" as well as masculinized women).[6] "Normal" is his word for what book III wants, and in that respect he too echoes Lewis, contrasting the perverse with the healthy. Berger's attachment of all that is normal to the institution of marriage continues to echo in Spenser criticism, even where one would least expect to find it; thus Katherine Eggert summarizes and endorses the arguments of Maureen Quilligan and Lauren Silberman, who, she reports, read the Garden of Adonis "as a privileged site of feminine production – of earthly forms, of chaste love and marital fecundity, and of a female reader's access to understanding."[7] Likewise Mario di Gangi, in *The Homoerotics of Early Modern Drama*, in some remarks on book III, finds Spenser also to support a norm – one in which homosexuality threatens marriage.[8] And David Lee Miller, in his Lacanian account, finds that the ideality of the Garden is nothing less than a paean to heterosexuality: "orgasm and insemination cohabit like spring and harvest meeting at one time." "The Garden of Adonis idealizes wedded love," he concludes.[9]

This chorus of readings, spanning some seventy years and a variety of methodologies that would seem far from C. S. Lewis, is an extraordinary one; nonetheless, that his distinctions continue to provide the ground bass for readings of the paired cantos can be seen succinctly in a note to III.6.43 to be found in the 1993 Norton Critical edition of Spenser's poetry where we find this summary sentence: "The Garden's healthy fruitfulness contrasts with the Bower's infertile voyeurism and artifice."[10] What is most extraordinary here is the fact that it is impossible to figure out what in Spenser motivates it. Are Venus and Adonis married? Since the answer obviously is no, in what sense does their sex represent marriage? And, since they have no children either, in what sense does their coupling represent procreation? Granted, there are babies in the Garden, but they are not made by this couple; moreover, they are not actually babies, but baby forms of existence, "the 'seed principles' of natural life," as the Norton critical edition usefully glosses them.[11] Spenser, it is true, uses images of procreation to suggest processes of creation, but these just don't happen to be invested in human beings or in human sex (the closest to that in the canto is the impregnation of Crysogone; she is penetrated by the sun and bears Amoret and Belphoebe as a result).

Moreover, when we look at Venus and Adonis, it's not only that they look remarkably like Acrasia and Verdant; but, as I began by remarking, they are in a *ménage à trois* that repeats the feature of the Bower, its lascivious boys, that, in the critical tradition descending from Lewis, necessarily proves its sterility. While it is not quite the case, as I suggested earlier, that the possibility of a pederastic relationship between Adonis and Cupid has been totally ignored, the few critics who even have seen what the Norton note invites its readers not to see have managed to offer readings in line with the critical tradition that extends back to Lewis. In other words, they have found ways of denying the relationship of Cupid and Adonis that are congruent with the Norton footnote and with the critical view that insists that book III of *The Faerie Queene* is an endorsement of marital sex as the only sanctioned form of sexual desire. Richard Neuse, for instance, claims that whatever Adonis is doing with Cupid it's necessarily not sexual, an extraordinary thing to say, but motivated by the belief that homoerotics just can't be sex, even if it involves a

male figure whose name happens to be Eros: "Adonis's playing is different from Psyche's, since hers is sexual and hence involves the (possible) motive of reproduction."[12] Jon Quitsland, on the other hand, is
willing to grant that Cupid and Adonis are having sex, but only because
"homoerotic pleasure keeps Venus's consort ready for her" – and for
marriage, he hastens to add.[13] Sex with Cupid warms up Adonis for the
real thing, sex with Venus. Remarkably, Quitsland's reading grants the
possibility that same-sex sex and heterosexual sex might not be regarded
as necessarily antithetical even as it tries to draw a distinction between
the two. But when the distinction is made in the name of marriage,
and in the supposition that the only point in having sex is procreation,
it flounders precisely when put beside the scene it parallels: the "play"
of Cupid and Psyche. Granted, this is procreative: they have a child
called Pleasure. This procreative act reverses the supposition that the
only point in having sex is to procreate by making the fruit of procreative sex Pleasure itself, thereby making pleasure the point of sex,
not procreation. Moreover, it's crucial to remember that the marriage
of Cupid and Psyche is not exactly a real human marriage: marriage
here is once again a metaphor, in this case a metaphor that brings
together mind/spirit and desire.

And finally, to throw into question the supposition that human purposiveness only is found in or matched by marriage – or that male
heroic activity in Spenser is tied to procreation – one might recall the
narrator's relation to Verdant, his loving lingering over the young man's
face and the bit of downy hair above his lip:

> A sweet regard, and amiable grace,
> Mixed with manly sternnesse did appeare
> Yet sleeping, in his well proportioned face,
> And on his tender lips the downy heare
> Did now but freshly spring, and silken blossomes beare.
> (II.12.79.5–9)

Or remember the scene of male bonding that follows – as Acrasia is tied
up and sent on her way, and Verdant is released and sent on his with
the blessings of the Palmer and Guyon. Indeed, in this context it might
be worth recalling an earlier moment in book II when the Palmer discovers the moribund Guyon with "a faire young man l Of wondrous
beautie" (viii.5.1–2) beside him. This figure resembles Verdant, for
he too is "of freshest yeares" (5.2), newly blossoming. Spiritualizing
readers no doubt will want to call this winged figure an angel, but

Spenser does not. Rather, he takes a stanza to compare him explicitly with Cupid, conjuring up a scene of his "wanton play" (6.7) that beguiles Venus to sleep, placing her in a state comparable to Guyon's. This is only to say that in the purposive conclusion to the Bower, as in the coupling of Adonis and Cupid, or in Guyon's rescue by a beautiful boy, male–male attraction is acknowledged. If it is safe sex, its safety, I would argue, does not mean that it is not sex.[14] Rather, it just might be that marital sex is not where one finds sexuality in *The Faerie Queene*, but rather in couples, whether of the same sex or not, whose sex is not bound to the institutional form (marriage) that supposedly makes sex valid.

* * *

To provide some further terms to connect the Garden of Adonis to the Bower of Bliss I would follow the lead provided by Anthony Esolen in two essays on the role of Lucretius in *The Faerie Queene* (these appeared about a decade ago, at about the same time that Esolen was completing an English translation of *De rerum natura*).[15] Esolen points to a connection in Lucretius that underlies both episodes. This connection is arguably consequential for an understanding of the poem well beyond these moments. It is a remarkable fact, duly noted in the first footnote of the Loeb *De rerum natura*, for example, and recorded, of course, in the Variorum (Upton was the first to spot it) that Spenser translates the invocation to Venus in the opening lines of Lucretius' poem with some fidelity in the Temple of Venus (IV.10. 44–7). These lines, especially the relationship of Venus and Mars in them, Esolen argues, also subtend the representation of Venus and Adonis as well as of Verdant and Acrasia. That is to say, Spenser quite overtly associates the erotic system of his poem with Lucretius.

Esolen aims to further a reading of Spenser first proposed by Edwin Greenlaw in 1920: "Greenlaw's thesis that Lucretius exercised a profound influence on Spenser deserves new consideration," he writes.[16] Greenlaw's essay is indeed a remarkable one. After noting the virtual translation of the opening lines of *De rerum natura* in the Temple of Venus, Greenlaw proceeds to detail echoes of Lucretius in the Garden of Adonis and the Mutability Cantos. Greenlaw looks especially closely at stanzas 30 to 40 of the Garden – the stanzas that detail the complex movement from "the first seminarie | Of all things" (III.6.30.4–5) out into the world and back again, a movement of seeds out from the Garden and back that seeks to explain how the forms of things constantly change and mutate (and thereby how individual created beings come into existence and pass out of it) even as "that substance is eterne, and bideth so" (37.6). As Greenlaw notes, while these stanzas might most immediately recall the allegory of Er in Plato's *Republic* (it is among the sources duly noted in the Norton critical edition of Spenser), what is remarkable – and remarkably Lucretian – about the Garden is its resolute materialism. "Spenser ... alters in extraordinary fashion the Platonic and Christian idea of souls coming from a spiritual realm to inhabit mortal bodies to a conception as materialistic as that of Lucretius himself," Greenlaw declares.[17] It is not merely "as materialistic as," but offered even in the same terms. For, however much the circulation of the Garden resembles Plato's account of the movement of the soul, the "soul" of which Spenser writes, is metaphorized as flowers, seeds, babes, flowers. It only has material form, and the forms in which it is represented echo the terms Lucretius uses for the atom (a word not in his vocabulary – but, like "soul" for him, an invisible and nonetheless material principle of being, of mortal life). Rather than a movement from spirit to flesh and back to spirit again, Spenser writes of "a wheele ... from old to new" (33.9), a metamorphosing circulation of matter that his scheme shares with or derives from Lucretius.

In writing of the source of "first being" (III.6.37.1), Spenser would seem to be translating a crucial term in Lucretius – *primordia* – a term attached to metaphorizations that match Spenser's; the *primordia* are regularly represented as *semina* (seeds) and *materia*, even *corpora*, the substance and body that Spenser continually invokes. Indeed, Spenser goes so far as to imagine that even more primordial than the Garden of Adonis there is a Chaos of inchoate matter, the unformed mere matter – in Lucretius these are the atoms – that provides the basis for the forms (that is, for formed matter) that circulate in and out of the world. Each is always itself and yet each can become anything else as it wheels back, after decay and death, to resume its inchoate material being. Greenlaw works through these stanzas providing point after point of comparison in thought and terminology between Spenser and Lucretius, remarking what will come to be so remarkable for later critics as to need to be denied, that Spenser "gets away from supernaturalism as completely as Lucretius himself."[18] Moving to the union of Venus and Adonis, Greenlaw sees there the Lucretian principle of the permanence of matter and the persistence of differentiated species despite the decay and death of individual lives. Next to the lines in the Garden on the eternal life of Adonis, "All be he subject to mortalitie, | Yet is eterne in mutabilitie, | And by succession made perpetuall" (47.4–6), Greenlaw aptly cites the lines from book one of *De rerum natura* (1.225 ff.) on the process of nature that Lucretius calls Venus, the ability constantly to renew life out of death, the assurance that matter is conserved as the source of this renewal.

Claiming to want to revive Greenlaw, Esolen's detailing of Lucretian influence in Spenser extends beyond the passages that Greenlaw explored to encompass several other crucial episodes in the poem; most notably for the argument at hand, Esolen links the Temple of Venus in Book IV to the Bower of Bliss. Yet ultimately his point is more in line with those critics who argued against Greenlaw, so effectively, in fact, that the Norton critical edition of Spenser, replete as it is with various classical allusions in the Garden, never cites Lucretius even as it-affirms that the Garden offers an "account of the life process," where "life" there must mean spiritual life, precisely what Lucretius argues cannot be thought of except as a material principle.[19] Esolen invokes Lucretius and details his wide influence on *The Faerie Queene* only somehow to deny what he demonstrates. He presents the similarity between the Temple of Venus and the Bower of Bliss only to insist on their difference. The "lusty bowres" of the Temple (IV.10.45.4), he writes (of these two supposedly parallel episodes), "unlike the Bower of Bliss, bring about a refreshing, muscular action, and in fact seem to turn the world into one great lusty bower."[20] And this despite the fact that Esolen had claimed just a few pages earlier that the Genius of the Bower (a most unmasculine figure, Esolen will insist) is presented in a line that echoes Lucretius, indeed that echoes the line in which Lucretius proclaims Venus as the great maternal principle whom Spenser invokes.[21]

A partial explanation of these procedures can be offered by turning to the opening pages of Esolen's essay on the Bower of Bliss in *English Literary Renaissance*, for, not surprisingly, he situates his own reading in the critical tradition that, I have been suggesting, serves as the inevitable matrix for readings of this episode. Greenblatt is commended for taking seriously the "disease of the soul" depicted in the Bower, although also taken to task: "no doubt Greenblatt overstates the beauty of the Bower."[22] "No doubt": in other words, Lewis was right. Greenblatt, it turns out, also errs in making a colonial connection in his reading. We do not need, it seems, to historicize an eternal human problem in this way (Esolen is willing to admit that the poem may be inflected by Spenser's social world and its demands for hierarchy, law and order). This is the world Esolen endorses when the Temple of Venus (dedicated to a goddess notable for not having a consort and not needing one, even though she is the source of life) is said to sponsor masculine muscularity. How might Spenser nonetheless be Lucretian? The answer that Esolen seems to offer is, by being anti-Lucretian. Acrasia and Verdant are, he writes, "perversions" of Venus and Adonis.[23] This despite the uncanny identity between them, a point with which we began, and a point which is furthered by Esolen's persuasive insistence that we see the Venus and Mars invoked in the opening lines of *De rerum natura* as the model for these and other Spenserian couples.

When a critic starts discriminating couples as perverse or not, we can be sure that a juridical model of gender and sexuality that one cannot find in Lucretius is in play. Thus Esolen underpins his reading of the Bower of Bliss by likening Guyon's destruction of the Bower to a scene from 2-Kings in which wrath is unleashed on those who break the Judaic law.[24] The passage is rhetorically parallel, but since it otherwise fails to support the argument Esolen wishes to make, he finds another scene (from 1 Kings), which lacks verbal echoes with the Bower but does feature some sodomites. Then, a stray remark of David Lee Miller's describing the action of Acrasia's hungry gaze as a form of fellatio is invoked, and in rapid succession Esolen's plot falls into place: Verdant is declared effeminate, Genius unmanly, and when boys in the Bower are spotted in several widely dispersed lines, now cited one after the other, the point implicit in Lewis is delivered: sterile Acrasia and Verdant might just as well be a pair of sodomites, so "perverse" is their unproductive union. And yet: as Esolen also shows, this perverse couple is modeled on the Lucretian pair that opens *De rerum natura*. Venus is invoked there to join with Mars "who often casts himself upon your lap wholly vanquished by the ever-living wound of love, and thus looking upward, with shapely neck thrown back, feeds his eager eyes with love, gaping upon you, goddess, and, as he lies back, his breath hangs upon your lips" (1.31–7).[25] Spenser could be translating Lucretius when he presents Acrasia and Verdant, "wanton Ladies, with her lover lose, | Whose sleepie head she in her lap did soft dispose" (II.12.76.8–9). When the Palmer and Guyon throw a net over Acrasia they continue the allusion, for this is how Vulcan traps Venus and Mars.

What is Lucretius doing in Spenser? Esolen's conclusion is anything but Greenlaw's: "Spenser depicts the elevation of nature to deity as unnatural and idolatrous, and the Lucretian Venus as ungenerative unless Christianized – that is, re-masculinized."[26] Insisting on the Protestant masculinity of Spenser's poem, Esolen fails to note that Spenser opens *The Faerie Queene* by putting Elizabeth in the position of Venus, and asking for Mars to submit to the yoke of love. In the opening lines of *The Faerie Queene*, Spenser first assays a translation of the invocation to Venus in *De rerum natura*. The scene of Mars subjected to Venus in

Lucretius is characteristically recast, moreover, as it is in the Garden of Adonis, as a *ménage à trois*:

> And thou most dreaded impe of highest Jove,
> Faire Venus sonne, that with thy cruell dart
> At that good knight so cunningly did rove,
> That glorious fire it kindled in his hart,
> Lay now thy deadly Heben bow apart,
> And with thy mother milde come to mine ayde:
> Come both, and with you bring triumphant Mart,
> In loves and gentle jollities arrayd,
> After his murdrous spoiles and bloudy rage allayd.
> (I.Proem.3)

Unnatural, ungenerative: Esolen insists on reading couples as couples, and only a proper marriage of man and woman could possibly be what Spenser sanctions. Greenlaw lights upon Venus and Adonis not to make them a married couple (they aren't) but to see them as allegorical figures for the union of form and matter (strikingly, Greenlaw sees Adonis as matter, Venus as form, refusing the gender hierarchy upon which Esolen insists). For Esolen, the Garden of Adonis is an "allegory of physical generation" and since the union of Venus and Adonis can't quite be claimed as a marriage, Esolen turns it into a version of the eschaton; earlier in his essay he had invoked "the marriage of heavenly and earthly seeds" as a way of describing creation in Lucretius; he completes his translation when Venus and Adonis become figures for the redemption of the world at the end of time: "In Lucretius the earth is only partly repaired, and so dwindles to nothing; in Spenser the incompleteness of the repair is what will lead to the eschaton."[27]

The real task for criticism seeking to understand the relationship of Spenser to Lucretius would be to link Greenlaw's materialist reading of Spenser – a reading that has nothing to say about sexuality, to Esolen's recognition that the Venus of Lucretius lies behind Spenser's sexual representations. How to read sexuality and materiality together and outside of the spirtualized, masculinized, Christian, marital, juridical framework that Esolen supplies? Even here Esolen helps, for he has a candidate for the real Lucretian Venus in book II: Alma, whose name is the adjective Lucretius gives to Venus at the opening of his poem. Alma is a multilingual pun. She is the soul, and she is also, as Esolen insists, a principle of alimentation – the body is fed with food and thought in the House of Alma.[28] The body is the house of Alma. Alma is, at once, a principle of material life and the very spirit that inhabits the body as its "soul." Alma might be said to solve the philosophical problem that Ernst Cassirer identified as central to Renaissance thought, the subject–object problem. This is the philosophical question central to the Garden of Adonis, and the terms that Spenser mobilizes there join a materialist vocabulary to sexual representation.

I mention Cassirer here insofar as he complicates the question of Spenser's intellectual contexts by insisting that the early modern period plays a part in the history of philosophy (Greenlaw almost writes as if nothing comes between Spenser and Lucretius; so, too, Esolen in a similar history of ideas approach, treats Spenser as a subscriber to a universal Christianity that always will solve all issues). Cassirer's historicism has its limits, of course; his neo-Kantian bias makes Renaissance philosophy valuable only insofar as it anticipates Kant. Nonetheless, he does show that Renaissance philosophy features its own peculiar working out of problems posed by classical and medieval thought. The subject–object problem can be understood in a variety of ways – as the relation of mind to matter or of spirit to substance (or perhaps of one person to another; this is not an issue that Cassirer raises, but it is ultimately consequential for Spenser, since we must always keep in mind how the cosmic vision of the Garden of Adonis might relate to the human relations that seem central to book III). Cassirer insists that in the Renaissance "matter is no longer conceived of as the mere opposite of form ... ; instead, matter is that with which all activity of the form must begin and through which the form must realize itself."[29] Form forms, and therefore must be understood as a material principle. Or, rather, Cassirer argues, the period sees a debate between those who would subordinate matter to spirit and those who would reduce spirit to matter. Cassirer's solution to this dilemma is to speak of a coordination of matter and spirit and to find it glimpsed not so much in philosophical thought as in science and art. The coordination that he finds matches the "laws" of nature to the actions of the mind. *Mens* echoes *mensura*: the mind is the measure of all things because all things are themselves measured. Although Cassirer's solution is not purely mentalist, it remains idealist. Yet, it aims at the *invisibilia*, the laws that nonetheless explain matter – matter, moreover, that is not inert, but in motion. Strikingly, Cassirer ignores Lucretius even though one could say that the Epicurean poet's poetic/philosophical system anticipates the solution that Cassirer finds in Leonardo or Galileo, both of whom in fact Michel Serres has connected to Lucretius.

It is of course commonplace to remark a relationship between ancient Epicurean atomism and the scientific thought that follows upon the

Copernican revolution. In this context, however, it is worth recalling that Epicurean thought – and Lucretius specifically – played a role in Italian Renaissance philosophy, literature and art, especially after the early sixteenth-century rediscovery of *De rerum natura* by Poggio Bracciolini. George Hadzsits provided a standard survey of this topic in his 1935 study, and Spenser comes into the story he tells. First claiming that the imitation of Lucretius in the Temple of Venus does not suggest that Spenser was an "intellectual disciple," a page later Hadzsits revises his opinion: "Earthly Love assuredly is not antagonistic to Heavenly Love; and sensuous love is not condemned in consequence of Biblical or Platonic teaching. Perhaps in this there is a deep communion of spirit between Spenser and Lucretius, both of whom, also, were haunted by the thought of the mutability of things earthly and the brevity of human life."[30] If Spenser departs from Lucretius in any respect, Hadzsits avers, it is only by being more epicurean (in the ordinary sense of the word) than his predecessor. As evidence for this claim, he instances the Garden of Adonis, and the figures of Cupid, Psyche, and Pleasure that appear there.

Voluptas, as Edgar Wind suggested some time ago, is a significant term in the philosophical vocabulary of the period, and precisely for those thinkers who sought spiritual solutions to the subject–object problem.[31] As Cassirer mentions often, coition is a favored figure for the act of cognition that would overcome the distance between subject and object, and the philosophy of love is the site for some of the most significant workings out of this dilemma. Spenser has often been understood in this context, and not incorrectly, once neoplatonism is understood in the widely syncretic manner in which it functioned (here, in various ways, Cassirer, Wind, and Charles Dempsey all are illuminating).[32] More typically, ever since Josephine Waters Bennett supposedly answered Greenlaw definitively by clubbing his materialism with neoplatonism, readings of Spenser as a neoplatonist have turned him into a dualistic Platonist.[33] The Christian despair that Hadzsits felt allied Spenser to Lucretius has been taken just as often as a sign of Spenser's resolute otherworldliness. To read the Garden of Adonis in Lucretian terms is thus to notice that it can find terms for the life of the world that coincide with sexual fulfillment. It is to notice that the marriage of Cupid and Psyche allegorizes the meeting of mind and desire, that is, unites principles of spirit and matter in a form that is emphatically material, and in an end that perfectly answers Cassirer's call for a coordination of subject and object. What kind of pleasure is *voluptas*, of mind or of body? Is Spenser's Pleasure a figure for a mistaken Epicureanism or a proper one? To have come this far means, at the very least, to have revised the ending of book II. For the Garden of Adonis is the same place as the Bower of Bliss seen differently; it is what comes after and is made possible by an askesis that demands an ever-watchful war against desire as a force within the self that threatens to derail and unmaster it (this is what Acrasia means, as Esolen usefully notes a shared ethical imperative in Spenser and Lucretius). The question is the proper use of pleasure. I deliberately echo the title of one of Foucault's final volumes in his history of sexuality only to gesture to a body of work that could be of paramount importance to understanding Spenser.[34] As I have suggested, such propriety does not mandate marital coupling as its only realization.

The Garden of Adonis, like the surprise ending of book I of *The Faerie Queene* (the surprise that the apocalyptic plot of dragon slaying doesn't solve the dilemma of the sexual relationship of the Red Crosse knight and Una), suggests that sexuality in Spenser is not to be reduced to just saying no, nor to collapsing desire into its most normative forms. Saying yes is the more difficult task, and even the Bower of Bliss suggests this: Acrasia is chained up, not destroyed, what unmasters is mastered, and Verdant, looked at with desire, is allowed to go free. What follows, as Spenser's version of the solution to the subject–object problem, is the coordination of mastery with the submission to the forces of life that are embodied in Venus and Cupid. This is why we last see Adonis in a *ménage à trois*. And why pleasure is the difficult object of the quest.

* * *

The cosmic consciousness of the Garden of Adonis, and its attempt to coordinate an allegory of human desire (of proper human desire, the virtue Spenser calls chastity) with an explanation of the world as a site of continual recreation – of procreation without human sex – suggests how *The Faerie Queene*'s aim to fashion a gentleman could be read as a kind of spiritual exercise. This is a term that Foucault uses, borrowing it from Pierre Hadot, who devotes an essay to the subject in *Philosophy as a Way of Life*, and Hadot is significant in the Foucauldian context that I have just suggested as a further horizon for the concerns of this essay. Indeed the current interest in Hadot owes something to Foucault: Arnold Davidson reports in the opening sentence of his introduction to *Philosophy as a Way of Life* that he believes "it was in 1982, that Michel Foucault first mentioned Pierre Hadot to me."[35] Moreover, Hadot reviews *The Use of Pleasure* and *The Care of the Self* in a brief essay in *Philosophy as a Way of Life*. I pause over Hadot's essay here to suggest that some of the dilemmas that I have been identifying in literary criticism around

Spenser also haunt the theoretical/philosophical matrix in which I would seek to situate him.

Although Hadot concurs with Foucault's reading of ancient practices of the self insofar as they involve exercises of self-mastery and self-scrutiny, he also finds that Foucault slights what Hadot insists is the point of these exercises, a rising above the self or an inhabitation of an aspect of the self that is also selfless since it links the self to cosmic forces, to the world, to nature, to universal reason. Foucault's working upon the self, Hadot decides, is *"too* aesthetic" and constitutes "a new form of Dandyism, late twentieth-century style."[36] The danger here, quite obviously I think, is that Hadot has a sense of the aim of the practices he calls "spiritual" which carries its own sexual normativity; hence, the selflessness and universalization of the subject that is to arise from these practices must not be attached either to a personal form of stylization or to any non-normative (what Esolen has no trouble calling "perverse") form of human social or sexual arrangement.[37] This attempt to subordinate/eliminate forms of the sexual in the name of the spiritual resonates with the kinds of philosophical solutions that Cassirer offered as well: the mathematical laws of nature which he espouses inevitably are tilted in favor of activities of the mind that only mime the possibility of submission to matter since they depend upon the "discovery" that the laws of mind and matter are one and the same. Sameness here is the refusal of difference: whether it is gendered difference or differences in forms of sexual behavior that do not subscribe to the mandates of heteronormative reproduction as the law of desire.

This point is worth raising because Davidson is not only a leading advocate of Hadot's work to the Anglophone philosophical community but also because he seems poised to assume the same position for Foucault and especially for Foucault's work in the history of sexuality. In his introduction to *Philosophy as a Way of Life,* Davidson echoes Hadot, writing that Foucault's construal of the ethical was too narrow, and that "by not attending to that aspect of the care of the self that places the self within a cosmic dimension, whereby the self, in becoming aware of its belonging to the cosmic Whole, thus transforms itself, Foucault was not able to see the full scope of spiritual exercises," the aim of which is to transform oneself into "a philosopher, a lover of wisdom."[38] In Davidson's account there is then a shortcircuiting of the particular forms of self-concern and of sociality into a cosmic dissolve that also delivers a proper form of love, the love of wisdom that characterizes the philosopher. In other words, there is also implicitly a separation of private life and self-concern (and of sexuality as a proper site for these) from the more valued transformation of the individual into a depersonalized, public form of being.

Hadot, marshaled as someone who would set Foucault straight, can stand alongside the conservatism of literary study as it is presently practiced, and especially in the field of Spenser studies that has been writing footnotes to C. S. Lewis for so many years now. Part of my desire to recall Cassirer's work, which appeared initially in German in 1927, or Greenlaw's 1920 essay, is to suggest that there are other resources in the past that might be tapped. Of course, I am not suggesting that it is wrong to turn to Hadot's work – Foucault himself did that, and, as I've suggested, I believe that the notion of spiritual exercise could significantly extend our understanding of *The Faerie Queene*. For me, one of the most memorable moments in Hadot is a demonstration which he performed depending on someone else's supposedly authoritative scholarly demonstration (but who knows?) that a phrase attributed to or paraphrasing St Paul (but not, according to Hadot, corresponding to Paul's authentic thought) was attributed by St Augustine to Paul and thereby became Paul. Out of what Hadot calls "a purely material conjunction"[39] – by which he seems to mean a *merely* material conjunction – Augustine mistakenly taking a set of non-Pauline words as Paul – arises a significant moment in the history of the understanding of the self that links Augustine to Husserl, or so Hadot claims.

Telling in this account are several things, above all the fact that Hadot is depending on someone else for the "truth" here even as he traces a path in which something becomes true on the basis of what he nonetheless seeks to call an error. I like this especially because, as I hope this essay has shown, saying that Spenser is Lucretian has not meant one thing, as the example of Greenlaw and Esolen, both of whom are more than qualified to say, demonstrates. What Lucretian means remains in question. This moment in Hadot I cherish because it is so textually specific – we have the citation from Augustine – and yet so refuses the protocols of knowledge that Hadot demands. That is, it is an entirely aleatory moment, one therefore akin to the Epicurean materialism that I have been associating in this essay with Spenser, and with the reading practices his all but unreadable text demands. The play of wanton parts.

I would close by suggesting that we are here on the margin of an expansive field. I would locate Spenser within the broad matrix of a revised Epicureanism and reading of Lucretius that begins in Italy and is attached there to philosophical and humanist inquiry, but also to figures as diverse as Leonardo (as Cassirer all but shows), or Botticelli (as Dempsey demonstrates) or Giorgione (as Stephen Campbell argues), and ultimately to scientific thought of the seventeenth century and beyond.[40] That *beyond* encompasses the multiple materialisms of the seventeenth century that includes figures otherwise as diverse as Margaret Cavendish, Lucy Hutchinson, Marvell, Milton, and Hobbes, and with them a philosophical tradition that extends from Spinoza to the phenomenon of the new Spinoza (as Warren Montag and Ted Stulze have dubbed it), a theoretical current that includes the work of Gilles Deleuze or Michel Serres on Lucretius.[41] Perhaps this current goes back to the Christian materialism with which Esolen would associate Spenser. When he cites Augustine to the effect that the injunction to increase and multiply, when applied to humans, can't mean what it does when applied to cattle, he takes Augustine to divide animal sex from a humanity that rises above the sexual.[42] Just as plausibly, however, Augustine could be taken to suggest that the spiritual activity that distinguishes human behavior is covered by the command that applies to sex.

Notes

My thanks to Meredith Evans for her research assistance, and to Michael Moon for reading this essay in draft.

1. Edmund Spenser, *The Works, A Variorum Edition*, 11 vols. (Baltimore: Johns Hopkins University Press, 1932–45). Subsequent citations to Spenser are to this edition.
2. *The Norton Anthology of English Literature*, 2 vols. (New York: W. W. Norton, 2000), 1: 838n8.
3. C. S. Lewis, *The Allegory of Love* (New York: Oxford University Press, 1958), 326.
4. Ibid., 332.
5. Stephen Greenblatt, *Renaissance Self-Fashioning* (Chicago: University of Chicago Press, 1980), 176.
6. Harry Berger, Jr. *"The Faerie Queene*, Book III: A General Description," as reprinted in Berger, *Revisionary Play* (Berkeley: University of California Press, 1988), 98, 95.
7. Katherine Eggert, *Showing Like a Queen* (Philadelphia: University of Pennsylvania Press, 2000), 32.
8. Mario DiGangi, *The Homoerotics of Early Modern Drama* (Cambridge: Cambridge University Press, 1997), 32.
9. David Lee Miller, *The Poem's Two Bodies* (Princeton: Princeton University Press, 1988), 277, 281.
10. Hugh Maclean and Anne Lake Prescott, eds., *Edmund Spenser's Poetry* (New York: W. W. Norton, 1993), 316n3.
11. Ibid., 314n3.
12. Richard T. Neuse, "Planting Words in the Soul: Spenser's Socratic Garden of Adonis," *Spenser Studies* 8 (1990): 79–100, at 94. A similar collapse of sex and procreation can be found in Ronald A. Horton, "The Argument of Spenser's

Garden of Adonis," in *Love and Death in the Renaissance,* ed. K. R. Bartlett (Ottawa: Dovehouse, 1991). The safety of male–male sex, he argues, "renders service to sexual purity" (69), a view matched by Quitsland.

13. Jon A. Quitsland, *Spenser's Supreme Fiction* (Toronto: University of Toronto Press, 2001), 208.

14. It may support Stephen Orgel's emphasis throughout *Impersonations* (Cambridge: Cambridge University Press, 1996) on the anxiety of heterosexual relations, and draw his example of a painting of Venus and Adonis by Cornelis van Harlaam where "the same model was used for both" (95) – a male model, I assume – into the orbit of this discussion.

15. Anthony Esolen, "Spenser's 'Alma Venus': Energy and Economics in The Bower of Bliss," *English Literary Renaissance* 23.2 (1993): 267–86; Esolen, "Spenserian Chaos: Lucretius in *The Faerie Queene,"* *Spenser Studies* 11 (1994): 31–51; Lucretius, *On the Nature of Things,* ed. and trans. Anthony M. Esolen (Baltimore: Johns Hopkins University Press, 1995).

16. Esolen, "Spenser's 'Alma Venus'" 279n13. In "Spenserian Chaos," 49n1, Esolen details the "small war waged over the question of Lucretian influence on Spenser," a narrative also offered in appendix III in volume 3 of the Spenser Variorum. Basically, Greenlaw's thesis was denied by critics in the 1930s, who found the philosophic system more Platonic or simply unsystematic.

17. Edwin Greenlaw, "Spenser and Lucretius," *Studies in Philology* 17 (1920): 439–64, at 445.

18. Ibid., 447.

19. Maclean and Prescott (eds.), *Spenser's Poetry,* 313n8.

20. Esolen, "Spenserian Chaos," 42.

21. Ibid., 39.

22. Esolen, "Spenser's 'Alma Venus,'" 268.

23. Ibid., 275.

24. Ibid., 269–70.

25. Lucretius, *On the Nature of Things,* trans. W. H. D. Rouse, rev. Martin F. Smith, Loeb Classical Library 181 (Cambridge: Harvard University Press, 1992).

26. Esolen, "Spenser's 'Alma Venus,'" 285.

27. Esolen, "Spenserian Chaos," 46, 38, 48.

28. Esolen, "Spenser's 'Alma Venus,'" 282.

29. Ernst Cassirer, *The Individual and the Cosmos in Renaissance Philosophy,* trans. Mario Domandi (Philadelphia: University of Pennsylvania Press, 1963), 133.

30. George Depue Hadszits, *Lucretius and His Influence* (New York: Longmans, Green and Co., 1935), 275, 276.

31. Edgar Wind, *Pagan Mysteries in the Renaissance* (New York: W. W. Norton, 1968).

32. Charles Dempsey, *The Portrayal of Love* (Princeton: Princeton University Press, 1992.)

33. Josephine Waters Bennett, "Spenser's Garden of Adonis," *PMLA* 47.1 (March 1932): 46–80.

34. Michel Foucault, *The Use of Pleasure,* trans. Robert Hurley (New York: Pantheon, 1985); Foucault, *The Care of the Self,* trans. Robert Hurley (New York: Pantheon, 1986).

35. Pierre Hadot, *Philosophy as a Way of Life,* ed. Arnold I. Davidson, trans. Michael Chase (Oxford: Blackwell, 1995), 1.

36. Ibid., 211.
37. This can be seen as well in Hadot's *Plotinus or The Simplicity of Vision*, trans. Michael Chase (Chicago: University of Chicago Press, 1993), where, after mooting the question "whether or not Plato himself disapproved of homosexual love," and offering the reader the assurance that either way "Platonic love was certainly masculine in tone" (52), he turns with obvious relief to Plotinus where one cannot find "any trace of equivocal sentiments" (53). In the introduction that Davidson provided for this book, he too underlines this point, arguing that Julia Kristeva errs in finding autoeroticism in Plotinus when she draws on an essay by Hadot on the figure of Narcissus in Plotinus that Davidson insists she misreads (12).
38. Hadot, *Philosophy as a Way of Life*, 25.
39. Ibid., 66.
40. Stephen J. Campbell, "Giorgione's *Tempest, Studiolo* Culture, and the Renaissance Lucretius," *Renaissance Quarterly* 56.2 (2003): 299–332.
41. Warren Montag and Ted Stolze, eds., *The New Spinoza* (Minneapolis: University of Minnesota Press, 1997); Gilles Deleuze, "Lucretius and the Simulacrum," in *The Logic of Sense*, trans. Mark Lester (New York: Columbia University Press, 1990); Michel Serres, *The Birth of Physics*, trans. Jack Hawkes (Manchester: Clinamen, 2000).
42. Esolen, "Spenserian Chaos," 48.

6
Shakespeare's Narcissus, Sonnet's Echo

Bradin Cormack

This essay tracks a melancholic dynamic that Shakespeare develops in *Romeo and Juliet* and in the sonnets, as he engages the question of how repetition might structure a subject's relation to the object of desire. For that analysis, I argue, he looked centrally to Ovid's myth of Narcissus and Echo, a story that lays out the split between repetition and reciprocation through which someone caught by desire might remain attached to even the object he or she acknowledges as mis-taken.

1. Sonic affects

Things in Verona happen fast, as though through repetition: speech, action, the emergence of allegiances or versions of a name that may be identity or not – in *Romeo and Juliet* all these can seem to compress time retrospectively into iteration. Benvolio and Juliet's Nurse are, differently, the figures against which this organization of time is measured. Benvolio is the play's historian, and on different occasions repeats what he has witnessed: his meeting with Capulet's servants and Tybalt (1.1.105–14), Romeo's melancholy (1.1.117–29), the death of Mercutio at Tybalt's hand (3.1.151–74). Oriented towards the "cause" and "truth" (1.1.142; 3.1.174) of what he reports, his speech instrumentally reshapes the messier action that the play presents as, in fact, an always unpredictable scene of violence or desire.[1] On the other hand, the Nurse's speech – her digressive recovery of Juliet's age (1.3.16–57), her digressive insistence that Romeo be honorable toward Juliet (2.4.158–74), the quick turn of her allegiance from Romeo to Paris (3.5.214–27), even her wailing at Juliet's dying (4.5.49–54) – unfolds as a pleasure in the efficacy of speaking itself, ahead of the thought that seems to motivate it, though never ahead of itself. She is, with similar exemplary force to Benvolio, the play's anti-historian:

both her memories and her projections are polemical for the present, the time of pleasure (including the pleasure of remembering) or grief, always of doing.

Here the Nurse gestures towards the Mercutio of the Queen Mab speech (1.4.53–95) and the speech of conjuration to recall Romeo to himself and his friends (2.1.6–21). Like the Nurse, Mercutio is the agent of language that catches and propels him on. But where the Nurse's practical chat is oriented to the resolution of the particular crisis that presents itself, Mercutio's fantastic, potentially endless talk pursues – in response to Romeo's words or presence or absence – the unreachable object of desire.[2] In a scene that opens with the question "Where the devil should this Romeo be?" (2.4.1), and in immediate response to Benvolio's elated "Here comes Romeo! here comes Romeo!" (2.4.36), Mercutio counters the thought that Romeo is localizable by saying of his friend, "Now he is for the numbers that Petrarch flowed in" (2.4.38–9). This thought that poetic flow might index a state of being – one that is also always running after itself – describes Mercutio's desire as much as Romeo's. Through the twinned force of his subject matter and the prodigiously flowing discursive mode fitted to it, Mercutio emerges as historian and anti-historian both, caught by and in a language that properly indexes an amatory reality, but which does so by escaping a strict historical logic of cause and effect.[3] Like the play's protagonists, Mercutio's tragedy is to be caught in the "misadventure[s]" of desire and the "fearful passage" of "death-marked love" (Pro.7, 9). So it is exemplary that, in a play in which as go-between the friar causes the demise of the lovers he means to help, Mercutio's death should be effected by Romeo's intrusion as medium into a scene whose object he rather was. Having drawn for Romeo against Tybalt, Mercutio ends by asking, "Why the devil came you *between* us?" "I thought all for the best," Romeo answers (3.1.101–3, emphasis added), befuddled by his role in a love plot that has issued in violence for no good reason, but only through compelling accident. Dead by the misadventured "arithmetic" (3.1.101) of Romeo's swordplay, Mercutio's demise reminds the audience that Petrarch's memorable "numbers" for Laura began with death as much as ended there. In the sublimation of Merutio's desire (as measured against Benvolio's drive to historical reckoning and the Nurse's conversion of love into a practical calculus of the present), Shakespeare bids a failed love poet farewell.

As instanced in Mercutio, poetic speech – the speech whose making (Gr. *poieîn*) is also a primary content – is a medium in which desire tries to catch up with itself. In that erotic economy, Ovidian dynamics help describe the physics of Petrarchan flow. When, on the first night after meeting Romeo, Juliet laments that, though she must whisper into the garden where he lingers, she would rather "tear the cave where Echo lies I And make her airy tongue more hoarse than mine I With repetition of my Romeo's name. Romeo!" (2.2.162–4), she figures her desire as a relation of call and response in excess of a strict division of subject and object. For in the allusion, she is Narcissus hearing Echo's reply, but as repeater she is also Echo, in waiting for speech that can engender the speech she is compelled to utter, such that to Romeo/Narcissus's returning whisper (2.2.165–7) she might again speak the sound that matters most to her: "Romeo!" (2.2.168). What she cannot hear is that her apt Ovidian allusion (to a world where bodies flow into one another or into versions of themselves) is also dire prediction of Ovidian violence, an intertextual guarantee that this Rome-an love must end, too, in dissolution.

Juliet's echoes relate to the broader Petrarchan "discourse of repetition" that Heather Dubrow rightly associates with the "habits of recurrence that lie behind so many of the most misguided actions in the play," and which make *Romeo and Juliet* a "tragedy of repetition."[4] The melancholy reality of Juliet's echoing of Romeo's name is that repetition suggests a reciprocation with which, however, it is not logically identical. One way the play tests the relation between those two forms is through a microtextual analysis of the grammar governing the erotic field. To Benvolio's question in relation to Rosaline, "In love?" Romeo answers, "Out":

> *Benvolio*: Of love?
> *Romeo*: Out of her favor where I am in love (1.1.164–7)

Which is to say that he is not strictly in love, a dynamic that the Chorus, now in relation to Juliet, describes as a syntactic enclosure of reciprocal feeling in time: "Now Romeo is beloved and loves again" (2.Cho.5). Here, a chiastic circuit of affect – in which the adverb *now* is mirrored by *again*, and the indicative *loves* similarly doubles what is already a shuttling of affect internal to the past participle *beloved* – appears to charge repetition atemporally as reciprocation. This is what love feels like.

And yet the promise turns out to be illusory: cognate with the play's inter-familial violence, which is repetitively engendered by a rivalry manifestly empty of any relation other than the repetition itself, the play dramatizes the mistake of supposing that repetition must point beyond itself. We can note here the plot mechanics through which, in the last act, the protagonists' deaths repeat one another, but exactly apart, in an off-rhythm. Conversely, desire in the play seems driven towards the kind of closure for which lyric stands, as though it too were in search of a rhyme. This is true in a literal sense. In their first scene together, the protagonists jointly compose an English sonnet that, preventing Romeo's access to Juliet's hand, invents instead the possibility of their lips touching (1.5.94–107). Significantly, the lovers are in equal part responsible for the concluding couplet that expresses their desire. And, as Paul Edmondson and Stanley Wells note, the couplet thereby opens the way to a second sonnet, since Romeo's concluding thought and kiss (line 14 of his and Juliet's first sonnet) pivots on itself to become the first move (as line 1 of a second sonnet) in a further exchange:[5]

> *Juliet*: Saints do not move, though grant for prayers' sake. [13]
> *Romeo*: Then move not while my prayers' effect I take. [14]
> Thus, from my lips, by thine my sin is purged. [1]
> *Juliet*: Then have my lips the sin that they have took.
> *Romeo*: Sin from my lips? O trespass sweetly urged. (1.5.106–10)

The lovers discover in the poem a potential in their desire, as in the sonnet form, to generate a sequence or endless repetition. As Petrarch's sonnets themselves suggest, however, sequentiality is no guarantee of reciprocation. This is a point Juliet formulates in terms of the couplet's (and English sonnet's) most prominent technology. When she laments that it must be a "Prodigious" love that binds "me" to a "loathèd enemy" (1.5.141–2), and the Nurse asks, "What's tis? what's tis?" Juliet answers by comparing the eruption of erotic feeling in her to a poem's way of unfolding and resolving in time: it is, she says, "A rhyme I learnt even now | Of one I danced withal" (1.5.143–4). Although rhyme's repetition points to the reciprocity toward which the play insistently gestures, her particular rhyme, the binding of a "me" to an "enemy," emblematizes the gap between those forms, a gap that constitutes the tragic plot. In sum, the play uses the sonic experience of poetry to stage desire's disruption of subject and object as an erotic potential across time. Where desire so opens the Petrarchan lover onto a world "sweetly" apprehended as repetition, the sweet promise of reciprocation encounters an instability in the very positions that might secure repetition as that other form.[6]

2. Hearing Narcissus

Like *Romeo and Juliet*, Ovid's myth of Echo and Narcissus is a story less of particular objects and subjects than of relation and the tragicomic suddenness of its claim. Before considering the myth's implications for Shakespeare's sonnets, and in order to substantiate my sense of Shakespeare's Ovidianism as found in *Romeo and Juliet*, I want to describe what I take to be the main force of Ovid's analysis of Narcissus's desire by reflecting on Freud's important mischaracterization of the story.

In an influential essay, Michael Warner demolishes the absurd conflation of homosexuality and narcissism and the psychoanalytic arguments, originating in Freud, that have sustained it.[7] Underlying the conflation is a cultural logic, he argues, that reduces all difference to gender alterity. That logical move, the "*a priori* opposition of the genders as subject and Other," enables Freud to construe homosexuality as an arrested stage in the "normal development [that] leads from autoerotics to narcissism to heterosexuality," without raising the obvious question of how heterosexuality would "transcend its sources in narcissism more than homosexuality does."[8] Heterosexuality, Warner argues, can thus be understood as the "discursive organization of sex that treats gender difference as difference in general"; correspondingly, the reduction of homosexuality to narcissism allows the normative culture "to disguise from itself its own ego erotics" by locating "those ego erotics only in the person of the homosexual, apparently bereft of the master trope of difference."[9] This identification of narcissism and homosexuality is all the more striking, given that "[t]hrough most of Western history, erotics among men in particular have been understood precisely along axes of difference," a point that David Halperin has extensively documented.[10]

Like Halperin's work, Warner's essay challenges historians to engage the past by reading past the discursive organization of sex that is heterosexuality. So how, we might ask, did Narcissus mean before his queerness got fixed? After Foucault, this is almost too familiar a question, reminding us that, as Mario DiGangi notes, "early moderns could [hardly] understand the Narcissus myth as a parable of 'homosexuality,' since the idea of distinct sexual orientations emerged from nineteenth-century discourses."[11] But the question suggests as well a different historical complexity, such that reading Ovid's story might, as Steven Bruhm posits, unfold in Narcissus "something more than narcissism."[12] Getting Ovid's story straight matters in two ways. First, as Warner points out, it is sloppy reading that partly underlies Freud's discursive conflation: "The homosexual, after all, is by definition interested in others in a way that is not true of the narcissist in general. Ovid tells us that Narcissus rejects not just the girls who love him, but also the boys. Those boys, then, have an interest in other persons, if not in the other gender, and the myth of

Narcissus does not collapse the two."[13] Second, however, I would argue that a phrase like Warner's "the narcissist in general" does not itself do justice to the story Ovid tells. What we think we know is the story of a boy stunned by desire for his own reflection. As Gayatri Spivak has argued, what we forget in giving the story this ethical cast is Ovid's narrative frame and, in particular, Echo, returning to Narcissus, as her own, the fragments of his speech.[14] This forgetting makes Narcissus available as an emblem of enclosed personhood, hypostatizing Ovid's story of desire to a different something that happens at the pool's edge.

One consequence of a denarrativized reading is to de-eroticize Narcissus's fate into a story of vanity, of a self grown so large as to leave no room for desire, but only for an attitude that mistakes itself for desire. And yet, of course, the boy falls not for himself, but for an image, which means there is alterity in the structure of Narcissus's longing. A more responsive reading of Ovid might allow for the erotic dimension but pathologize Narcissus's gaze as misrecognition, a substitution of image for Other.[15] But in Ovid, although Narcissus comes to recognize something about his image he has not understood, the emphasis is not on the mistake, but rather on the fact that knowledge of the error should make a difference and doesn't. Narcissus recognizes just what he wants, both when he first "admires all that for which he is admired [*cunctaque miratur, quibus est mirabilis ipse*]" and when, after discovering his error, he becomes even more inflamed: "'*remane nec me, crudelis, amantem | desere!' clamavit; 'liceat, quod tangere non est, | adspicere et misero praebere alimenta furori!*' ['Stay, cruel one,' he cried, 'and do not desert me, who love you. May it be permitted to look on that which may not be touched, and to feed my sad passion']."[16]

For Ovid's account of Narcissus's desire, Echo is important because the structure of the boy's terrible longing replicates hers, and because her desire in turn unfolds aspects of his desire not captured by the drama at the pool's edge. In forgetting Echo, we are apt to de-eroticize the Narcissus complex by making self and Other more contained than they are in Ovid. We thereby separate the self's desire for its image from other scenes of desire, which, following Warner's logic, now become representable to themselves as fully interested in the Other. But Ovid is more generous to Narcissus than we are now inclined to be. His story is structured around a series of doublings, through which Narcissus's fate can encode a justice, at once poetic and divine, that gives him what he has given. As Leonard Barkan has emphasized, along with the image that doubles his features, Narcissus mirrors and is mirrored by Echo, her voice answering his, his sight answering her voice, her disembodiment answering his liquefaction, the fate of his desire answering hers.[17] Desiring

Narcissus, Echo is unable to call to him; instead, as Ovid says in a
curiously doubled formulation, she readies herself to be ready: "*illa parata
est | exspectare sonos, ad quos sua verba remittat* [She is ready to await the
sounds to which she may give back her own words]" (ll. 377–8). As Ovid
has it, Echo's desire is the state of waiting to be called. We can gauge the
importance of this figuration by noting that Narcissus's desire, when it
arrives, exactly replicates hers. For as Narcissus longingly addresses his
image, it is his invocation of voice that clears his vision, allowing him,
with a shocking suddenness, to see the object of his desire for what it is:
"*et, quantum motu formosi suspicior oris, | verba refers aures non pervenientia
nostras! | iste ego sum* [And, as I surmise from the movement of your beau-
tiful mouth, you send back my words to ears they do not reach. I am that
one]" (ll. 461–3). In this spell-breaking articulation, Narcissus's longing is,
like Echo's, the state of waiting to be called. And in both cases, Ovid fuses
the language of speaking and hearing to that of sight: speaking, Narcissus
sees only the trace of words he waits to hear; conversely, through an
etymological quibble on "*exspectare sonos*," Echo's awaiting becomes, in
an image only retroactively mobilized, a matter of peering, as Narcissus
does, for the sounds that will give her speaking self back to her.

Echo changes Narcissus's story by insisting on the relation between
voice and desire, by giving voice back to a desire that thus cannot locate
itself only in the seeing and seen body. Forgetting Echo, we make the
autonomy of the desired subject dependent on the body, and in so doing
transform Narcissus's desire for his image into a static and therefore only
illusory engagement. The point is not that Ovidian desire is plural, but
that it is diffuse. As such, desire is best imagined as the narrative produced
by the possible relations between subject and object, seen now not as
fully realized self and fully imaged Other, but as incomplete self and
other, subjects rendered incomplete by the scene of desire, at the same
time as desire produces those relations of incompleteness. The tension
between Echo and Narcissus that identically constitutes their respective
desires as an expectant looking for sound subordinates the individual
actors to the scene in which they play out the imperfections of their fate
and so imperfectly produce desire.

This formulation puts us in a position to see the relation between the
two discursive moves that have structured the reception of Ovid's Narcissus: on the one hand, the reduction of all difference to gender alterity
and, on the other, the collapse of desire and subjectivity into the visually
imagined body, at the expense of voice. As Warner notes, in the love of
the "*iuvenes*" for Narcissus (l. 353) Ovid allows for a distinction between
gender alterity and difference in general. It would be wrong, however, to

infer from this that Ovid's story has no stake in marking gender difference. In relating desire to a tension between voice and body, the story in fact depends for its charge on gender difference. As Echo waits to be called, to take in Narcissus's words and return them to him, the distinction between "*sonos*" and "*sua verba*" (l. 378), the sounds of Narcissus and the words Echo makes of them, is pointedly ungendered; and part of the erotic charge is that the male voice can be returned to itself as the female, just as the female voice can constitute itself through the male. This is a possibility in Ovid because gender is not based on aural distinctions, but on visual ones. Apart from the fact that it is clear to Narcissus that the beloved image is male, Ovid makes a point of saying that, at sixteen, Narcissus "*poteratque puer iuvenisque videri*" (l. 352). The syntax allows for two possibilities, that Narcissus was seen as "both boy and youth" or as "either boy or youth." The conditional auxiliary *poterat* further emphasizes that the distinction is being made from outside, both by means of a narrowing of gender possibilities and as a matter of seeing ("*videri*").

Since the Roman male youth was an object of erotic attention equally for men and women, the implicit gendering of "*iuvenis*" is to the point, even though it also amplifies the point that gender is hardly the only axis of difference to structure erotic attachment.[18] Difference in age is as important as that between male and female, not least because Ovid disrupts the already liminal category of *youth* through its visual confusion with boyhood. Ovid's story neither collapses all difference into gender alterity nor erases the possibility that gender difference might matter. Conceiving desire in relation both to body and voice suspends desire as the realizable, constituting it as the potentiality that, following Giorgio Agamben's account of Aristotle's theory of act, "never disappears into actuality," but instead "preserves itself as such in actuality."[19] This is desire known less along the axes of absolute difference than through what any given object only ever half discloses.

This potential in desire also opens its subjects to the tragedy of a mismatch between repetition and reciprocation. Ovid gives two versions of the point, according to the aural and visual hermeneutics structuring the tale. Echo's pathos, and part of her punishment, resides in her mistaking repetition for the possibility of reciprocity, an error that Narcissus is quick to articulate for her: "*ille fugit fugiensque 'manus complexibus aufer! | ante' ait 'emoriar, quam sit tibi copia nostri'*[He flees her and, fleeing, says, 'Lay off your hands from any embrace. May I die before giving you access to me']" (ll. 390–1).[20] Then, at the pool (and now in the visual regime), the repetition of a reflected image opens Narcissus himself to the same error, which the silence of his reflection articulates, in turn, for him. Echo and

Narcissus are figures for a repetition that withholds its own promise of reciprocation. The non-identity of Narcissus and his image is central to that dynamic, a structural gap that is re-measured as the disjunction within Echo's voicing of herself through the object of desire. In Echo, Ovid converts a structural fantasy of reciprocation into narrative time, whose surface makes evident as a stitch in time the difference between that reciprocity and the repetition it fatally resembles.

The two critical threats to Ovid's meaning – the exaggerated emphasis on gender difference and on the body – are complementary. On the one hand, when all difference is reduced to gender difference, there is room only for seeing, a seeing that blinds itself to the possibility that gender difference might be moot under a different erotic regime. On the other, when the autonomy of the other is made dependent on the body alone, when desire is figured as a looking only and not a waiting to be called, there is no room for the possibility of gender ambivalence that is also at the heart of Ovid's conception of desire. This complex of confusion suggests that the differences that charge the erotic scene and seem even to generate desire are in an alternative logical relation to it. In Ovid, no difference can claim to be prior to desire itself, a desire that uses the particular difference, as it might have used some other, in the game of its own realization. Not coincidentally, the two moves that threaten Ovid's story also structure Freud's conflation of narcissism and homosexuality, according to which desiring a particularly gendered other and desiring an image rather than a body are construed as desire structured by a difference that, parsed out, is no difference at all. The two moves are cognate, and it is possible to extract the homosexual from this logic without extracting Narcissus only by forgetting that the one narrowing brings the other along with it. For Ovid, for whom desire is sustained in all its complexity by the tension between eye and ear, Narcissus's desire for his image cannot be distinguished from Echo's desire for him. This is the source of the poem's generosity toward the boy. If Narcissus is credulous (l. 432), held to the pool by "*error*" (l. 431), infatuated with a "*quod*" (l. 433), a something that turns out to have no substance of its own ("*nil habet ista sui*" [l. 435]), this does not in itself pathologize his desire, since desire only ever catches the subject in that same narrative incompletion.

3. Seeing Echo

When Shakespeare invokes Ovid's story in *Romeo and Juliet* and in the sonnets he imports neither a de-eroticized narcissism of pride nor a pathologized narcissism of self-unknowing, but, as a whole, the charged scene of incompletion in which Narcissus and Echo fatefully play their roles. Juliet's and, in particular, Romeo's attractiveness (as witnessed by other characters' pursuit of him and by their echoing repetition of his name) drives the play forward as the promise of the protagonists' mutual regard and as the tragic certainty that their scene is already one of Ovidian loss. On first glance, Shakespeare's sonnets seem to present a different Narcissus, especially since the poems to the young man do thematize both his and the speaker's self-love, in apparent sync with Freud's conflation of the auto- and homoerotic.[21] I will suggest, however, that Shakespeare's engagement with Ovid in the sonnets exposes instead the poverty of that allegorization and of any allegory of desire that freezes an erotic dynamic into emblem by abstracting it from the narrative scene in which it is embedded.

In Petrarch and in earlier English sonnet sequences, speaker and beloved were both figured conventionally as Narcissus, the beloved for her disregard of the speaker and the speaker for his attachment ultimately to the image not of the beloved but of his own desire.[22] In Shakespeare's poems, lover and beloved are so implicated. It is a critical truism to say that Shakespeare's young man is narcissistic, and indeed sonnet 1 stages the young man's refusal to reproduce as a version of Narcissus's caught fascination at the pool: "But thou contracted to thine owne bright eyes, | Feed'st thy lights flame with selfe substantiall fewell, | Making a famine where aboundance lies, | Thy selfe thy foe, to thy sweet selfe too cruell" (11.5–8).[23] It is equally a truism to say, turning to sonnet 62, that Shakespeare's speaker acknowledges the same self-love in himself: "Sinne of selfe-loue possesseth al mine eie, | And all my soule, and al my euery part" (ll.1–2). Working from these conventional associations, however, the poems disrupt conventional expectations. Thus the "[s]inne of self-loue" in sonnet 62 turns out to have everything to do with love of the other: "T'is thee (my selfe) that for my selfe I praise, | Painting my age with beauty of thy daies" (ll.13–14). In the case of the young man, the allusion to Narcissus is more complicated. As Stephen Spender and Jane Hedley argue, procreation, the apparent answer to the youth's self-regard, turns out not to disrupt it at all.[24] Since sonnet 3 figures the child as an image of the young man more lasting than his mirror image (ll.1–2), reproductive sex turns out not to end self-regard, but rather to extend it, now as an integral part of erotic relation: "Make thee an other selfe for loue of me, | That beauty still may liue in thine or thee" (10.13–14).

Following such turns in the sonnets' use of Narcissus, one could see the sequence as an argument for the narcissistic basis of all desire. I want to argue instead that Echo's presence in the poems changes what we can make of Shakespeare's Narcissus, allowing us to see that the speaker and young man are occupying positions in an erotic scene that is in effect its own protagonist. This subordination of those-who-are-related to the scene of relation itself seems to me a principal source of the poems' Ovidian sadness at the inevitability of erotic failure. True to her Ovidian nature, Echo appears in the sonnets faintly, less as an allusion than as the lingering suggestion of one. In the remaining pages of this essay, I outline how the pairing of Echo and Narcissus works in sonnets 49, 125, and 126, so as to suggest some of the erotic implications of their double presence for Shakespeare's representation of desire and of the failed promise of the love that through repetition might be thought to emerge from desire's incompleteness.

In sonnet 49, the speaker imagines a time when the beloved will reject him, in order to say that the rejection will be just. Against the fantasy that the young man's waning love "[s]hall reasons finde of setled grauitie" for the turn of his affections, the speaker perversely defends himself by becoming advocate for the decision that will hurt him: "Against that time do I insconce me here | Within the knowledge of mine owne desart, | And this my hand, against my selfe vpreare, | To guard the lawfull reasons on thy part" (ll.8, 9–12). Shakespeare casts this dynamic, in which the speaker's rationalizing self-fortification answers the beloved's rationalizing self-enclosure, in Ovidian terms, by figuring the relation between lover and beloved as that pertaining between Echo and Narcissus. At work is an etymological pun in the opening quatrain, which contracts the Ovidian story into a single line encapsulating the moment when Echo disastrously emerges from the forest in response to Narcissus's call:

> Against that time (if euer that time come)
> When I shall see thee frowne on my defects,
> When as thy loue hath cast his vtmost summe,
> Cauld to that audite by aduis'd respects ...
>
> (ll.1–4)

Following Stephen Booth and Stephen Orgel, who gloss "aduis'd respects" to mean "judicious considerations" and "carefully considered reasoning," we can paraphrase line 4 to mean "summoned to that account-taking by judicious considerations."[25] Narcissus gives us a further way into the line, which masterfully takes on Ovid in his own terms, doubling the doubles that structure the story.[26] An audit is so called because the person whose accounts are under scrutiny is heard (Lat. *audire*) by the auditor. In the first half of the line, the one summoned to the audit is, like Echo, waiting to be called in order to be heard and in order to hear himself. Narcissus occupies the second half of the line, which yokes together the roots for "see" (Lat. *videre*) and "look" (Lat. *spectare*) and so figures in the adjectival phrase "aduis'd respects" a looking *toward* that is answered by a looking *back*.[27] Addressed in order to be heard, the one audited emerges as Echo responding to the call of a Narcissus whose gaze is answered only by itself: "Cauld to that audite by aduis'd respects."

In using the myth of Narcissus to diagnose syntactically the pull within desire between self-surrender and self-protection or self-enclosure, the poem conflates the players who might occupy the different positions in Ovid's story. As Booth points out, "thy loue" in line 3 can refer either to the young man's affection or to the speaker himself.[28] Correspondingly, in the first case, the young man in line 4 is both Echo and Narcissus, closed off by sound and by vision from the possibility of, or desire for, reciprocation. In the second case, the speaker, having himself "cast his vtmost summe," imagines he will be called, like Echo, by a one whose "respect" looks back only at itself. Even though that gaze contains a look returned, it is exactly counter to the specular reciprocation promised in sonnet 36, in which the speaker asserts that "[i]n our two loues there is but one respect" (l.5). As a repetition that withholds reciprocal gazing, indeed, the "respect" of sonnet 49 instead resembles the "vnrespected" view of sonnet 43.2 or the unanswered gaze of the "unwoo'd" roses that "vnrespected fade" (54.10). Like these unanswered gazes, this is a looking whose repetition evades reciprocation.

In Shakespeare's play with Ovid, the scene of desire defines fungible roles in which lover and beloved find themselves replicating the affective position and response of the other. In that context, we can note that sonnet 49 may be writing one more of Ovid's characters into its erotic grammar. When the speaker, in self-defense and self-accusation, says he will "this my hand, against my selfe vpreare" (l.11), he recalls the youth who, spurned by Narcissus, raises his hand to heaven and so brings about Narcissus's fate: "*inde manus aliquis despectus ad aethera tollens* | '*sic amet ipse licet, sic non potiatur amato!*' | *dixerat* [then one of the despised, raising his hands to heaven, said, 'so let him love and not attain the beloved']" (ll.404–6). In Shakespeare, however, this same despairing gesture effects the speaker's own self-enclosure as echo of the beloved's. In sum, sonnet 49 draws on Ovid to represent the punishing scene of desire in which self and other repetitively instantiate erotic claims that belong less to them than to the indifferent dynamic in which they are caught.

This same Ovidian dynamic finds expression in the final two sonnets in the group to the young man. Sonnet 126 takes leave of the beloved, while in sonnet 125 the speaker takes leave of his own desire for the beloved. The two poems thus relate to earlier instances of self-love in the sequence as the culminating moves in the subtextual renarration of the Narcissus myth. According to the generally received reading, sonnet 125 presents the speaker's reply to the accusation leveled against him by a disreputable third party, the paid *"Informer"* of line 13, that he has not given due honor to the beloved. In the first quatrain, the speaker protests that he cares nothing for mere ceremony, for the "canopy" and "great bases for eternity" that ultimately prove no match for time (ll.1–4). The next two quatrains, in which the Ovidian allusion first becomes apparent, lay out a comparison between the speaker and those who attend to others only by attending to form:

> Haue I not seene dwellers on forme and fauor
> Lose all, and more by paying too much rent
> For compound sweet; Forgoing simple sauor,
> Pittifull thriuors in their gazing spent.
>
> (ll.5–8)

The gaze of the thrivers, although outwardly directed, is self-absorbed and self-destructive. Line 8 thus returns us to sonnet 1, where the young man's refusal to have a child is similarly figured in terms both of his self-consuming gaze and his "making a famine where aboundance lies" (1.7). In its two parts, sonnet 125's eighth line calls up imagery crucial to Narcissus's story. The phrase "pitifull thriuors" suggests abundance and lack, and thereby, alongside sonnet 1.7, renders Ovid's *"inopem me copia fecit"* (1.466). "[I]n their gazing spent" suggests the Ovidian gaze that is satisfied only by extinction: *"spectat inexpleto mendacem lumine formam | perque oculos perit ipse suos* [He gazes with unsated eyes on the deceiving form, and perishes by his own eyes]" (ll.439–40).

In the third quatrain of 125, against these self-deceiving attendants, the speaker loudly insists on the authenticity and sincerity of his own attention:

> Noe, let me be obsequious in thy heart,
> And take thou my oblacion, poore but free,

>   Which is not mixt with seconds, knows no art,
>   But mutuall render, onely me for thee.
>   (ll. 9–12)

In these lines, Shakespeare puts the speaker in the position of Echo at
a point in the story, as was the case in sonnet 49, before her fate
has been sealed.[29] In Ovid, Narcissus's desire is represented as stasis, an
inability to depart from what he sees; thus, in a direct address, Ovid
warns the boy that his image "will leave when you do, if you can leave
[*tecum discedet, si tu discedere possis*]" (l.436). Echo's desire, on the other
hand, is represented as a movement through space, a point Ovid high-
lights through the repetition of a crucial verb: "*vidit et incaluit, sequitur
vestigia furtim | quoque magis sequitur, flamma propiore calescit*" (ll.371–2).
Arthur Golding's 1565 translation renders these lines with sticky materiality as:

>   She waxed warme, and step for step fast after him she hide,
>   The more she followed after him and neerer that she came,
>   The hotter euer did she wexe as neerer to hir flame.
>   (ll.462–4)[30]

So in sonnet 125's "Noe let me be obsequious in thy heart," it is Echo's
following (Lat. *sequor*) that the speaker pitches against the thrivers' (and
Narcissus's) gaze. The comparison of the true follower and the false attendants of lines 5–8 is double. The speaker is saying that, in opposition
to those who follow ceremony, he follows the beloved "internally, privately only."[31] Additionally, he insists that this private attention is following indeed, an erotic movement capable of producing the "mutuall
render, onely me for thee" of line 12, a phrase that indexes the speaker's
continuing attachment to the mutuality the poems withhold.

Sonnet 125 concludes as a struggle to detach from the dynamic
within desire that allows repetition to be misread as always already the
reciprocation the poem longs for. It does so, again, by punningly allud-
ing to the dynamics of Ovid's story:

>   Hence, thou subbornd *Informer*, a trew soule
>   When most impeacht, stands least in thy controule.
>   (ll.13–14)

These two lines make for a small interpretive crux in the poem, since
they swerve so sharply from what has preceded them. As all editors

note, they identify the paid informant whose accusation against the speaker turns out to have generated the defense raised in the first twelve lines. At the level of paraphrase, the speaker in the couplet answers the informant by declaring that a true soul is least subject to the informer's power when it is most impeached, that is, accused of wrongdoing. This paradox is a conventional enough defense of truth, even if it seems less like logic than bluster. Read in the context of the poem's earlier allusion to Narcissus and Echo, however, the lines' densities also take on a philosophical dimension. We can note first that when line 13 opposes true and false, a "trew soule" and an underhand "*Informer*," that opposition is charged by the conventional Aristotelian definition of the soul as the form of the body. To put the definition in an equally conventional way, the body could be said to be informed by the soul. So Shakespeare's line opposes not only true and false, and not only a true soul and an unlawful informer, but also a true form and an unlawful one. In cursing the suborned informer, the speaker expels a form that potentially overpowers the true soul, to the detriment of that primary form.

This pun points us back to Narcissus. In Ovid's story, *forma* is one of the words, alongside *imago* and *umbra*, that designate the boy's reflected image: "*spectat inexpleto mendacem lumine formam* [he stares on the deceiving form with unsated gaze]" (1.439). In addition, *forma* twice designates the shape of Narcissus's real body: his is a slender form inhabited by a hard pride ("*in tenera tam dura superbia forma*" [1.354]); and, according to what Narcissus says in the throes of desire, his body is a form meriting the attention of the image he adores: "*certe nec forma nec aetas | est mea, quam fugias* [Surely my form and age are not such that you should flee]" (ll.455–6). Like Ovid's story, Shakespeare's sonnets are invested in the capacity of certain words to figure both bodily matter and spiritual essence. *Substance* and *spirit* are two notorious instances, identifying both corporeal matter (flesh; semen) and the substantial or informing principle of that matter.[32] So, too, with *form*. In line 5 of sonnet 125, "forme" implies an external rather than internal reality. But in the procreation sonnets, as Burrow notes, where "form" means image or likeness, it carries too the Aristotelian implication of an internal determining principle.[33] Thus the young man is admonished that "The world wilbe thy widdow and still weepe, | That thou no forme of thee hast left behind" (9.5–6); and he is advised that his issue "your sweet forme should beare" (13.8). A notable usage occurs in sonnet 24, when the speaker says that his eye has "steeld, | Thy beauties forme in table of my heart" (ll.1–2), by which he refers both to the beloved's beauteous form and to the essence of that beauty or (to adopt the terms of sonnet 5) its distilled substance.

So form takes us right to the heart both of Ovid's story (in which Narcissus desires a form that is not substantially form, but rather form's reflected form or likeness) and of sonnet 125's reworking of Ovid through its intensification of the Aristotelian distinction between corporeal substratum and animating form. The "subbornd *Informer*" is the image in Narcissus's pool. And it is a false form, because, as a mere image of a substantial body, it cannot be form in the sense in which Narcissus speaks of his own shapeliness; and, second, because as determining principle it informs no body at all. Activating another pun responsive to Ovid's pool, we can say that, *suborned*, this form is a repetition that, rather than animating from within, falsely adorns from below, and which for that reason disastrously places the self outside the scene of reciprocation.[34]

To what or whom does this destructive and unlawful form in Shakespeare refer? A final allusion to Ovid suggests how the exorcism of these lines work to eject not so much the image that fascinates the beloved as the equally dangerous image that controls the speaker, namely the Petrarchan lover's desire for desire itself. The speaker declares that the unlawful *"Informer"* will exercise least control over his soul when the soul is "most impeacht." Impeachment has its proximate root in *empescher*, Old French for "block" or "restrain." In the legal sense in which it is here used, however, "impeachment" translated *impetitio*, which derives from *impeto*, Latin for "attack" and, in the legal context, "accuse." To be impeached in this sense was to stand *impetitus*, accused, sued or, most simply, aggressively pursued. This submerged root is interesting for the poem because pursuit is one category through which Ovid tropes Narcissus, as when Narcissus laments his unsuccessful pursuit of his image: *"quove petitus abis? certe nec forma nec aetas | est mea, quam fugias* [where do you go when I pursue you? surely my form and age are not such that you should flee]" (ll.455–6). If following pertains to Echo's desire, pursuing pertains to Narcissus's. And Ovid renders that pursuit pitiable by doubling it chiastically as *almost* the form of reciprocation – the dynamic that lovers most hope for, but which here turns out to be only the repetitive stasis of the boy's plight: *"dumque petit, petitur, pariterque accendit et ardet* [and as he pursues, he is himself pursued; equally, he ignites desire's flame and burns with it]" (l.426).

In this linguistic context, the Shakespearean sentiment that "a trew soule | When most impeacht, stands least in thy controule" functions as more than paradoxical bluster. If to be impeached is not only to stand accused but also, more simply, to be pursued, the lines offer a formulation for the mutuality Ovid withholds from Narcissus. As an image of pursuit, the soul's impeachment reaches back to the speaker's earlier obsequiousness, one movement of his desiring soul answering the other. The speaker's soul will stand least in control of the image of its own desire when it is most vigorously pursued: desire can be fully met only by being answered. So understood, the couplet that concludes sonnet 125 follows directly from the line preceding it, repeating from line 12 the image of bare reciprocity that is the fantasy ideal opposed to self-love: "But mutuall render, onely me for thee." The pursuit of line 14 is a self's pursuit of the other when it comes to be structured by the other's pursuit of the self. Even as the poem articulates reciprocal pursuit as the erotic dynamic that might overpower self-fascination, however, the Ovidian subtext marks this as fantasy, since in Ovid it is only Narcissus's failed desire for his image that is identified as pursuit. In accordance with Ovid's melancholic validation of the boy's desire, Shakespeare's punning allusion in this final couplet thus questions the very exorcism of Narcissus it attempts, refusing to order alternative desires, including those that hurt the speaker, as categorically different from the speaker's own.

Turning now to the second leave-taking, sonnet 126 opens with an address that again invokes Narcissus's beauty: "O thou my louely Boy" (l.1). As an argument about the inability of beauty to prevail over time, the sonnet explicitly looks back to the procreation sonnets. Like those poems, it warns the friend not to trust his loveliness just because Nature, to "disgrace" time, has thus far preserved him from "wrack" (ll.8, 5):

> Yet feare her O thou minnion of her pleasure,
> She may detaine, but not still keepe her tresure!
> Her *Audite* (though delayd) answer'd must be,
> And her *Quietus* is to render thee
> (   )
> (   )
> (ll.9–14)

According to the metaphor in these lines, Nature is borrowing against time to preserve the young man's beauty. But even she must pay her debt, which in a formal audit she will have to satisfy by rendering up the young man, "*Quietus*" being both the formal acquittance from a debt and the receipt given upon payment.

Sonnet 126 is remarkable for being in couplets rather than quatrains and, most of all, for the lack of a thirteenth and fourteenth line. Marked by printed parentheses, that absence tantalizingly suggests the young man's approaching demise, such that the typographical accident "create[s] the impression that *render* could be functioning as a transitive verb, of which the object is sliced away by the sickle hour of time, bracketed to oblivion."[35] Ovid's Narcissus points us to an alternative reading of the lacuna. With the pairing of *"Audite"* and "answer'd," line 11 recalls the terms in which Echo was etymologically figured in sonnet 49. Correspondingly, line 12 reinvokes Narcissus and, in "render," the characterization specifically of his death. Ovid's poem pairs the ways in which the two bodies disappear: responding to the fact that Echo's cares waste *("extenuant")* her body and cause all moisture to depart from it until only voice and bone remain, and then only voice (ll.396–8), Narcissus's body, wasted *("attenuatus")* by love, simply dissolves: *"sed ut intabescere flavae | igne levi cerae matutinaeque pruinae | sole tepente solent, sic attenuatus amore | liquitur et tecto paulatim carpitur igni"* (ll.487–90). Golding's translation makes this a passage about erotic dissolution:

> As lithe and supple waxe doth melt against the burning flame,
> Or morning dew against the sunne that glareth on the same:
> Euen so by peece-meale being spent and wasted through desire,
> Did he consume and melt away wyth Cupids sacred [secret] fire.
>
> (39r; ll.613–16)

In sonnet 126, in response to Ovid's (and Golding's) materialization of desire, Shakespeare's "render" translates *"liquitur."* Nature, in a horrid pun, will render up the boy by melting him, rendering him, as fat or tallow is rendered.

Although the *OED* provides from around 1375 a case in which molten lead is identified as "rendered," in the sixteenth and seventeenth centuries "render" and its cognates turn up in the sense of melting or clarifying only with reference to fat or tallow, and not in any more general sense of melting. In its conversion of the body to fatty matter, Shakespeare's usage is exceptional and grisly. We might note, however, that when Hamlet's ghost laments that "My hour is almost come | When I to sulphurous and tormenting flames | Must render up myself" (1.5.2–4), he may have his own melting in mind. And he may therefore be providing a frighteningly literal version of his son's metaphorical wish: "O that this too too sallied flesh would melt, | Thaw and resolve itself into a dew" (1.2.129–30), lines that perhaps themselves recall Narcissus's fate.[36] Allowing the pun on "render" at the end of sonnet 126, we can see that the poem closes off the group addressed to the young man with poignant Ovidian clarity. The melting in line 12 concludes the young man's story with Narcissus's particular fate. And it makes especially good sense of the poem's missing two lines, transforming the space enclosed by the parentheses into an emblem for the body's promised attenuation and even for the pool and element that the liquefied body must now join.

Most important, this melting suggests how Narcissus meant before he became an emblem only of self-involvement. Melting in the 1590s is a descriptive for sexual desire and, specifically, for the deranging experience of sex as that which opens the individual body onto another body and onto erotic relation itself. In Shakespeare's *Venus and Adonis*, the lovesick goddess tells Adonis that her "smooth moist hand, were it with thy hand felt, I Would in thy palm dissolve, or seem to melt" (ll.143–4).[37] Similarly, at the climax of *A Lover's Complaint*, the maid says that her unfaithful suitor's tears "[e]uen then resolu'd my reason into teares," this being a seductive prelude to that melting's sexual counterpart:

> There my white stole of chastity I daft,
> Shooke off my sober gardes, and ciuill feares,
> Appeare to him as he to me appeares:
> All melting, though our drops this diffrence bore,
> His poison'd me, and mine did him restore.
>
> (ll.295–301)[38]

The myth of Echo and Narcissus is one of the most important Ovidian sources for this erotically charged melting. Echo's voice partially dissolves the boundaries between her body and that of Narcissus. And even before Narcissus is dissolved into the pool, he desires a different version of that dissolution in the separation from his body that would allow him to attain the beloved: "*o utinam a nostro secedere corpore possem*" (l.467). Melting is a meeting of bodies in their incompletion. If the waiting that is Narcissus's desire is a waiting for the voice that will melt his boundaries, disrupting its limits without negating alterity, that waiting is a longing not just for the particular image, but exactly for the incompletion, constitutive of all desire, that the discontinuity between eye and ear produces and allegorizes.

The rendering with which Shakespeare concludes the sonnets to the young man construes the latter's unsteady affection in this way, even as it reduces his body to insubstantial silence. In the multiple narrative resolutions that Shakespeare discovers in sonnet 126, the final rendering that acknowledges the beloved's wandering desire is a melting that also acknowledges his (and Narcissus's) desire as authentic. In a poem of couplets, the typographical absence of a concluding couplet (which in *Romeo and Juliet* is, melancholically, the very promise of iterative mutuality) marks the sequence's failure to engender the relation of "mutuall render" it pursues elsewhere. For the rendered lines that conclude sonnet 126 make for quite another melting than that optimistic one. As a sadness that yet gestures to the promise of what it forgoes, this final rendering extracts from the beloved, and from the scene in which he and the speaker both move, the substantial form that, as echo and repetition, resides within longing as the source, but also the loss, of a love that might be said instead to belong.

Notes

For their helpful suggestions, I am grateful to Paul Edmondson, Jacqueline Goldsby, Sean Keilen, Sandra Macpherson, Carla Mazzio, Stephen Orgel, Joshua Scodel, Eric Slauter, Richard Strier, Goran Stanivukovic, Candace Vogler, Stanley Wells, and especially Lauren Berlant.

1. William Shakespeare, *Romeo and Juliet*, ed. Peter Holland, in *The Complete Works*, ed. Stephen Orgel and A. R. Braunmuller (Harmondsworth: Penguin, 2002). All subsequent parenthetical citations are to this edition.
2. On Mercutio's desire in relation to Romeo and Rosaline, see Jonathan Goldberg, "*Romeo and Juliet's* Open Rs," in *Queering the Renaissance*, ed. Jonathan Goldberg (Durham: Duke University Press, 1994): 218–35.
3. For law in relation to love's cases and love's jurisdiction, see Peter Goodrich, *The Laws of Love: A Brief Historical and Practical Manual* (Basingstoke: Palgrave Macmillan, 2006).
4. Heather Dubrow, *Echoes of Desire: English Petrarchism and its Counterdiscourses* (Ithaca: Cornell University Press, 1995), 265.
5. Paul Edmondson and Stanley Wells, *Shakespeare's Sonnets*, Oxford Shakespeare Topics (Oxford: Oxford University Press), 93–4.
6. On the implications of material sweetness for the circulation between bodies, see Jeffrey Masten, "Toward a Queer Address: The Taste of Letters and Early Modern Male Friendship," *GLQ* 10 (2004): 367–84.
7. Michael Warner, "Homo-Narcissism: Or, Heterosexuality," in *Engendering Men: The Question of Male Feminist Criticism*, ed. Joseph Boone and Michael Cadden (New York: Routledge, 1990), 190–206.
8. Ibid., 195.
9. Ibid., 202.
10. Ibid., 203. See David Halperin, *One Hundred Years of Homosexuality and Other Essays on Greek Love* (New York: Routledge, 1990); David Halperin, *How to Do the History of Homosexuality* (Chicago: Chicago University Press, 2002).
11. Mario DiGangi, "'Male Deformities': Narcissus and the Reformation of Courtly Manners in *Cynthia's Revels*," in *Ovid and the Renaissance Body*, ed. Goran Stanivukovic (Toronto: University of Toronto Press, 2001), 94–110, at 94. On the need for a non-teleological history of sexuality, see Jonathan Goldberg and Madhavi Menon, "Queering History," *PMLA* 120 (2005): 1608–17.

12. Steven Bruhm, *Reflecting Narcissus: A Queer Aesthetic* (Minneapolis: University of Minnesota Press, 2001), 12.

13. Warner, "Homo-Narcissism," 193.

14. Gayatri Chakravorty Spivak, "Echo," *New Literary History* 24 (1993): 17–43.

15. In Lacan, the narcissist experiences an erotic attraction to the specular image, whose wholeness stands in contrast with the subject's material body, thereby threatening the subject with fragmentation. That threat in turn engenders in the subject a "narcissistic suicidal aggression" that Narcissus' own dissolution emblematizes. See Jacques Lacan, "Propos sur la causalité psychique," in Lacan, *Écrits* (Paris: Seuil, 1966), 151–93.

16. Ovid, *Metamorphoses* 3.424; 477–9. Cited from *Metamorphoses I–VIII*, ed. Frank Justus Miller, rev. G. P. Goold, LCL (Cambridge MA: Harvard University Press, 1977). All subsequent references to Book 3 are to this edition, by line number. I have adapted the translation.

17. Leonard Barkan, *The Gods Made Flesh: Metamorphosis and the Pursuit of Paganism* (New Haven: Yale University Press, 1986), 46–52.

18. On axes of difference in Greek homoeroticism, see Halperin, *One Hundred Years*.

19. Giorgio Agamben, "On Potentiality," in Agamben, *Potentialities: Collected Essays in Philosophy*, trans. Daniel Heller-Roazen (Stanford: Stanford University Press, 1999), 183. In my reading, Ovidian desire already approaches the ethical scene described by Candace Vogler in her analysis of Derek Jarman's *The Angelic Conversation* as an attempt to produce, in conversation with Shakespeare, "a properly queer body politic," where "homosexual visual and tactile attachment mark turf without the specificity of normal cartography. Queer conscience works by holding time out of joint." See Vogler, "Fourteen Sonnets for an Epidemic: Derek Jarman's *The Angelic Conversation*," *Public Culture* 18.1 (2006): 23–51, at 50.

20. Narcissus's extraordinary use of "*copia*" against Echo is in tension with the more famous sentiment at the pool's edge: "*inopem me copia fecit*" (1.466). There, *copia* denotes a plenteous beauty, which, without the possibility of desire's reciprocation, is simultaneously poverty. In the earlier passage, "*copia*" denotes Echo's power of access to the object, but the operative genitive construction in "*copia nostri*" still evokes at the plenty Narcissus denies her, as though *copia* were mirroring in itself the dynamic erotics of being drawn towards an opening onto the fullness of the desired object.

21. Several critics have invoked the Freudian association to overturn heterosexist readings of the poems. See, for example, Joseph Pequigney, *Such Is My Love: A Study of Shakespeare's Sonnets* (Chicago: University of Chicago, 1985); Jane Hedley, "Since First Your Eye I Eyed: Shakespeare's Sonnets and the Poetics of Narcissism, *Style* 28 (1994): 1–30. For an account of the sonnets in which the Freudian conflation takes on a negative valence, see Paul Zweig, *The Heresy of Self Love* (1968; Princeton: Princeton University Press, 1980), 100–8. See also C. L. Barber, "Shakespeare in his Sonnets," *Massachusetts Review* 1 (1960): 648–72; William Flesch, "Personal Identity and Vicarious Experience," in *A Companion to Shakespeare's Sonnets*, ed. Michael Schoenfeldt (Malden MA: Blackwell, 2007), 383–401, at 384–5. The most delicate psychoanalytic reading of the poems is Joel Fineman, *Shakespeare's Perjured Eye: The Invention of Poetic Subjectivity in the Sonnets* (Berkeley: University of California Press, 1986).

Configuring the poems as it does in terms of a teleological arc toward the heteroerotic, Fineman's book does miss the erotic subtleties of the earlier poems in favor of the complexities of the late ones.

22. For an analysis of the figure of Narcissus in the sonnets in light of the earlier tradition, see A. D. Cousins, *Shakespeare's Sonnets and Narrative Poems* (London: Longman, 2000), chaps. 3–4. On Petrarchism generally (and Shakespeare's relation to the tradition), see Dubrow, *Echoes of Desire*, esp. chap. 4; Gordon Braden, *Petrarchan Love and the Continental Renaissance* (New Haven: Yale 1999); Gordon Braden, "Shakespeare's Petrarchism," in *Shakespeare's Sonnets: Critical Essays*, ed. James Schiffer (New York: Garland, 2000), 163–83. For a reading of Shakespeare's Petrarchism in light of the complexities of Petrarch's own sequence, see Richard Strier, "The Refusal to be Judged in Petrarch and Shakespeare," in Schoenfeldt (ed.), *Companion to Shakespeare's Sonnets*, 73–89. On Petrarch's importance for Shakespeare's engagement with Ovid, see Lynn Enterline, *The Rhetoric of the Body from Ovid to Shakespeare* (Cambridge: Cambridge University Press, 2000). On the plays' varied grappling with metamorphosis, see Barkan, *The Gods Made Flesh*, 243–88.

23. All references to the sonnets are to the 1609 Quarto, as printed in *Shakespeare's Sonnets*, ed. Stephen Booth (1977; New Haven: Yale University Press, 1978). I cite two other editions: William Shakespeare, *Complete Sonnets and Poems*, ed. Colin Burrow (Oxford: Oxford University Press, 2002); William Shakespeare, *The Sonnets,* ed. Stephen Orgel (New York: Penguin, 2001).

24. Stephen Spender, "The Alike and the Other," in *The Riddle of Shakespeare's Sonnets*, ed. Edward Hubler (London: Basic, 1962), 120–1; Hedley, "Since First Your Eye I Eyed," 3.

25. Booth (ed.), *Sonnets*, 213; Orgel (ed.), *Sonnets*, 52.

26. For Latin etymologies as a source of poetic and philosophical meaning in the sonnets, see Bradin Cormack, "Tender Distance: Latinity and Desire in Shakespeare's Sonnets," in Schoenfeldt (ed.), *Companion to Shakespeare's Sonnets*, 242–60.

27. On the semantic value of "re-" as a prefix for repetition and recursion in sonnet 45, see Fineman, *Shakespeare's Perjured Eye*, 229; Cormack, "Tender Distance," 250–1.

28. Booth (ed.), *Sonnets*, 212.

29. For a reading of "oblacion" in a religious context that links the beloved to Christ, see Margaret Healy, "'Making the quadrangle round': Alchemy's Protean Forms in Shakespeare's Sonnets and *A Lover's Complaint*," in Schoenfeldt (ed.), *Companion to Shakespeare's Sonnets*, 405–25, at 416.

30. Ovid, *The XV Bookes of P. Ouidius Naso, Entituled, Metamorphosis*, trans. Arthur Golding, *Ovid's Metamorphoses* (London, 1587), 37r. Subsequent parenthetical citation, including folio number, is to this edition. The line numbers are taken from the modern-spelling edition: *Ovid's Metamorphoses*, trans. Arthur Golding, ed. Madeleine Forey (Baltimore: Johns Hopkins University Press, 2002).

31. Burrow (ed.), *Complete Sonnets and Poems*, 630.

32. For substance's status at the boundary between material and immaterial, see Kenneth Burke, *A Grammar of Motives* (New York: Prentice-Hall, 1945), 21–58. On the play of matter and substance in the sonnets, see Michael Schoenfeldt, "The Matter of Inwardness: Shakespeare's Sonnets," in Schiffer (ed.), *Shakespeare's Sonnets*, 305–24; Cormack, "Tender Distance," 248–57.

33. Burrow (ed.), *Complete Sonnets and Poems*, 398.
34. For a reading of sonnet 125 as a poem of doublets, including the doubled play of Latin against English, see Helen Vendler, *The Art of Shakespeare's Sonnets* (Cambridge MA: Harvard University Press), 530–2.
35. Burrow (ed.), *Complete Sonnets and Poems*, 633. For the typographical and grammatical background to the parenthetical markers used in sonnet 126, see John Lennard, *But I Digress: The Exploitation of Parentheses in English Printed Verse* (Oxford: Clarendon Press, 1991), 10–51, at 41–3. For a nuanced reading of sonnet 126, and of its concluding couplet, as hourglass, see Rayna Kalas, "Fickle Glass," in Schoenfeldt (ed.), *Companion to Shakespeare's Sonnets*, 261–76.
36. William Shakespeare, *Hamlet*, ed. Ann Thompson and Neil Taylor, Arden Shakespeare (London: Thomson, 2006).
37. William Shakespeare, *Venus and Adonis*, in Burrow (ed.), *Complete Sonnets and Poems*, 182.
38. William Shakespeare, *A Lover's Complaint*, in Schoenfeldt (ed.), *Companion to Shakespeare's Sonnets*, 501. The line numbers are taken from the modernized text in Burrow (ed.), *Complete Sonnets and Poems*.

7

Coriolanus: The Rhythms and Remains of Excess

Peter Holland

Yo, i-o, ee-o, eye-o. Cor-yo-lanus, Cor-eye-o-lanus. At the center of the name Caius Martius acquires is a phonic ambiguity and I shall want to play with the implications of that imprecision as a lengthy preface to my argument. There is less ambiguity and more meaning elsewhere in the name. In 1924 Gordon Crosse, that inveterate playgoer, noted in his diary with relief, "I was glad to hear them pronounce Coriolahnus, not Coriolainus."[1] It was an avoidance tactic for the risks of speaking of the anus, one that would not penetrate critical writing about the play until much later, with Kenneth Burke's recognition about the end of the name Caius Martius acquires:

> in the light of Freudian theories concerning the fecal nature of invective, the last two syllables of the hero's name are so "right," people now often seek to dodge the issue by altering the traditional pronunciation (making the *a* broad instead of long).[2]

When Stanley Cavell turned to the question of invective in the play, it was only in the added postscript to his essay on the play when he reprinted it in *Disowning Knowledge* that, after considering orality and anality in *Coriolanus* with the latter defined as "less explicit," he turns to Burke as someone who has taken "the issue to be given full explicitness in the play's, and its hero's, name."[3] The word "issue" here is a strange choice when it is precisely what issues from the anus that is the issue. But Cavell is nervous about the topic, even while being unable to avoid both senses of the issue:

> Burke is immensely tactful in mentioning the subject, in his essay here and elsewhere, and while on the occasions of delivering versions of

my essays as talks I would allude to the fecal issue as something to be considered, I did not see how to consider it well in unprotected prose.[4]

No such anxiety inhibited Jonathan Goldberg in his fundamental exploration in "The Anus in *Coriolanus*."[5] In all three cases it is the polysemous and driven excess of language itself that constitutes the site of their investigation – for Goldberg linked it to the nature of the body's issues and the anal pleasures that Aufidius so powerfully invests in his dream relationship with Caius Martius. I shall want, later, to see different fields of excess operating across the name and across the play. For Cavell, however, the name becomes a kind of local joke about the uncontrollable doublenesses of language itself:

> Granted the intentionality of Shakespeare's play's attention to the name, he may in it be seeking a heavenly horselaugh at language's vengeance in distributing one and the same sound equally to a suffix that encodes a name's military honor and to the name of the shape of a sphincter; as if noting a kind of poetic justice.[6]

But I also want to note now another oddity in the name, a strangeness in its framing, for while Burke, Cavell, and Goldberg are right to be fascinated by the anality of Coriolanus's ending, I am surprised that they never explore the Latin heart of his name in the "Cor" that opens it, so that the name is framed by heart and sphincter, a name which, in its opening at its core, astonishingly appears to share this foregrounding of its heart in Shakespeare's works uniquely with, of all people, Cordelia – unless the implication is really also there in *As You Like It*'s Corin and *King Lear*'s Duke of Cornwall.

Whatever significance there may be at bottom in ending with the sound of *-anus*, the name's form defines another vital doubleness in the play, a space of a refusal to clarify. As someone whose Latin primer in the equivalent of fourth grade at school was called *Civis Romanus Sum*, I am well aware that Coriolanus is both an *agnomen*, the "addition" granted Caius Martius by Cominius "For what he did before Corioles,"[7] and, more provocatively, the standard word to define a citizen of the Volscian town of Corioli. A male inhabitant of Rome is *Romanus* and a male inhabitant of Corioli is *Coriolanus*.

But consider for a moment the experience of a playgoer who, like many, perhaps most, early modern playgoers, did not know her Plutarch. She would have known the play's title. So there must be a major character called Coriolanus. But when Caius Martius first comes onto the stage there is no hint that his name might be Coriolanus. Instead, as with Hamlet, there has been plenty of talk about this character before he makes his first entry: the First Citizen identifies "Caius Martius" as "chief enemy to the people" (1.1.7–8) Only after Menenius has calmed the crowd down, does "noble Martius" (160) enter and the audience would presumably have recognized Burbage (if, as is likely, he played the role).

If Burbage is playing Caius Martius, what about Coriolanus? Where is he? In the next scene, the Volsces have to defend one of their cities against the Roman forces, a town named Corioles: "Noble Aufidius, I Take your commission, hie you to your bands. I Let us alone to guard Corioles" (1.2.25–7). So *Coriolanus* must be a play about one of this city's male inhabitants. All the audience has to do is to wait to see who is playing that citizen of Corioles, the Coriolanus of the play's title, not Burbage as star this time but someone else.

They would have had a long wait. They would have heard the city's name in the dialogue again (at 1.3.101–2 and at 1.7.37, for instance). But only at the moment of victory, hundreds of lines into the play, as Cominius praises Caius Martius' deeds, does he rename Caius: "For what he did before Corioles, call him, I With all th'applause and clamour of the host, I Martius Caius Coriolanus!" and the army thunders back, how loudly depending on how many extras the production can afford, "Martius Caius Coriolanus" (1.10.63–7). This act of renaming is remarkable. Technically it is the addition of an *agnomen*, a special title of victory that becomes a permanent part of the name, like Lawrence of Arabia or Montgomery of Alamein. For all Shakespeare's frequent delay in the act of naming (and Volumnia will not be named in the play's dialogue until Act 5 when Menenius names her in valuing her: "This Volumnia I Is worth of consuls, senators, patricians, I A city full; of tribunes such as you, I A sea and land full" [5.4.52–5]), here is a Shakespeare character new baptized before our ears, the play's title-character created as we listen, formed out of his deeds, not his family. It is a unique effect, comparable only to the way in which the title of a play like *The Tragedy of King Richard III* tells us what Richard, Duke of Gloucester will become. But the oddity of this process of naming, of making a person, of creating in the name the process of the tragedy is striking.

Coriolanus is, of course, always potentially an inhabitant of the Volscian town. If "To his surname 'Coriolanus' 'longs more pride I Than pity to our prayers" (5.3.171–2), then he is also a "fellow" who "had a Volscian to his mother; I His wife is in Corioles" (179–80), as is only right for one of its citizens. The honour of the title of victory permanently added to his name is the beginning of turning Caius Martius, the quintessential Roman, into someone of increasingly ambiguous and contentious citizenship, entering a limbo of statelessness, just as Aufidius will create for him a denial of maturity, returning him, impossibly, to the class of "boy" (5.6.103). I shall come back to this ambivalence of state soon.

Playing with the resonances of the language of names is always tempting but the problematic vowel sound between "cor-" and "-lanus" is not simply a matter of playfulness. Actors need to know what the sound is but the sound refuses to stay fixed. For Lee Bliss, in her excellent edition of the play, the word is "usually compressed to four syllables (the *rio* sounding like that in *chariot*)."[8] But in 1817 John Philip Kemble was sure that the center was an emphatic dissyllable – Cor-eye-o-lan-us[9] – and in this he was followed by Sir Peter Hall in his second production (at the National Theatre in 1984). For Aufidius' extraordinary taunt something like that is necessary: "Dost thou think | I'll grace thee with that robbery, thy stol'n name | 'Coriolanus,' in Corioles?" (5.6.90–2). Helge Kökeritz, still our traditional guide to Shakespearean pronunciation, asserts the name of the town, whether three syllables or four, "is always stressed on the second syllable": "'Cor*i*olanus,' in 'Corioles' as well as 'Holding Cor*io*les in the name of Rome'" (1.7.37).[10]

The syllabic count for Coriolanus plainly varies, four on some occasions and five elsewhere. If Shakespeare and Wilkins changed the name of the Prince of Tyre from Apollonius, his usual name, to Pericles primarily because the latter scanned better, it may have been after the awkward experience of trying to make the word Coriolanus work in verse lines. The first time we hear the word at all it is part of a line whose rhythm seems trochaic: "call him, | ... Martius Caius Coriolanus!" (1.10.63–5) – four trochees in a row, surely. But the word at other points can be stressed differently: the Herald greets him "Welcome to Rome, renowned Coriolanus" (2.1.162) but does he welcome Córiolánus or Coríolánus? And what does Volumnia say in greeting? "My gentle Martius, worthy Caius, | And, by deed-achieving honour newly named – | What is it? – 'Córiolánus' must I call thee?" (168–70) or does she call him "Coríolánus" here? Perhaps Volumnia is unsure how to pronounce the word, letting it come awkwardly from her mouth as she tries out her son's glorious new "addition."

All this is by way of being a phonic preface about the name's central ambiguity of rhythm to my real concern which has to do with fascinating rhythms and excessive possibilities but not with names at all. I will want, in a moment, to turn from the rhythmic sound at the heart of the name to the equally ambivalent structural rhythms at the center of the play. But I need first to explicate briefly the underlying and hereafter implicit polemical thrust of one of my concerns here. Put on a production of a play, any play, whether by Shakespeare or not, and a central search during the rehearsal process is the quest for the rhythms of the drama, its balances and structures, its echoes and connections, its variations of pace and speed from beat to beat, its articulation, in a myriad ways, of its dramatic form. The more complex the drama, the more subtle and demanding the task of comprehension of that multi-layered form by the entire production team will be and the more difficult its communication to the audience will become. This intense awareness for all theater workers that the shape of the drama is there if only one could find it isn't quite what Ira Gershwin had in mind but the opening lines of the verse to "Fascinating Rhythm" seem right:

> Got a little rhythm, a rhythm, a rhythm
> That pit-a-pats through my brain;
> So darn persistent
> The day isn't distant
> When it'll drive me insane.

We know how excitingly the repetition of a word or a pattern of blocking, of a gesture or a lighting state, of a prop or a costume, can function as a part of the definition of that formal structure. As we see or hear something again or see or hear something transformed from its previous state so we can learn the movement of the play's argument, its meaning shaped by its forms. This is obvious to all of us with any interest in theater and we will all have favorite examples of Shakespeare using the devices of theater to make a play's form and meaning intertwine. My favorite example is the decision to bring the corpses of Goneril and Regan onstage at the end of *King Lear*, a remarkable choice given both how difficult it is to carry dead bodies on and off stage and how carefully Shakespeare elsewhere avoids the difficulty. Those few productions prepared to do what Shakespeare asks for here give their spectators the sight, for the first time since the opening scene, of Lear and his three daughters onstage together, a rhyming across the expanse of the play that is a visual marker of the distance of the drama's journeyings.

Now look in the work currently being done in Shakespeare studies for articles or books investigating such structural or formal concerns and you will be surprisingly hard pressed to find examples. Of course there are some but it seems largely to be the case that investigation of dramatic form by major scholars and critics is now almost entirely restricted to the writing of introductions to editions of the plays, a place where, often with a pedagogic rather than peer-group purpose in mind, an account of the shape of the play is not only desirable but necessary. There is little in Shakespeare journals concerned with such matters. Of the dozens of critical studies reviewed over the last few years for *Shakespeare Survey* by Michael Taylor, only one, Simon Palfrey's *Doing Shakespeare*, is interested in such things and the book is avowedly written as a course-text for undergraduates.[11]

Our sustained and energetic interest in contextual work, in the immense success of the project of cultural studies, seems to have suggested that, while we might have to teach our students about dramatic structures, we have nothing more to tell each other. To want to speak of structures and shapes, of forms and articulations is somehow to appear old-fashioned and reactionary in the discipline. To want to read and see and hear more precisely by working inwards rather than outwards has come to seem mistaken, even if that move in is driven by a profound awareness of contextual issues. Shakespeare studies are apparently not yet ready to accept the move or catch up with the move made in other areas of literary or performance study to redefine what close reading might be, a move that is in no sense retrogressive – I think here for instance of the kinds of investigation of the performance of poetry typified by the exhilarating essays in Charles Bernstein's collection *Close Listening* (Oxford: Oxford University Press, 1998), published nearly a decade ago. If the study of what we can loosely call dramatic form or structure has a place in the classroom – and I doubt that many would deny that to be the case – then it surely cannot be the case that we are ready to say that the problems of analyzing form are solved, that there is nothing new to be said, that we know all there is to know about the matter. Directors and actors, as well as set, costume and lighting designers, would say to us that they find new things about the shapes and structures of Shakespeare plays every time and that those rhythms are as fascinating as they are fluid.

I return to the heart of *Coriolanus*, not to the sound of *i* and *o* but to a structural ambivalence in the sequence that follows the decision to banish Coriolanus, the moment when the aedile can say, triumphantly or wonderingly, "The people's enemy is gone, is gone" (3.3.137). The sense of release of the dynamic of many minutes of playing time is immense, indeed the verbal echo by the aedile of the First Citizen's line at the very start of the play's first scene, "First, you know Caius Martius is chief enemy to the people" (1.1.5), means the moment seems to end everything that has occurred since the opening of the play. The release is palpable in a wonderful energized physical action: "The Citizens all shout, and throw up their caps" (136.1), a moment that reminds me of the end of commencement ceremonies where a similar release is apparent.

F1, our only copy for the play, marks the end of Act 3 here. Peter Hall's 1984 production had difficulties with the moment in preview. As Kristina Bedford notes of the first preview, "The entrance in 4.1 [that is of Coriolanus and his family, Menenius, Cominius 'with the young nobility of Rome' for the scene of leave-taking] comes hard on the heels of the banishment scene to prevent the audience thinking it the interval."[12] But it didn't work; by the third preview she is noting "Audience again thought it was the interval after the end of 3.3" and the confused playgoers, reaching for their bags and preparing for the stampede to the bars and restrooms, were unsettled for the next two scenes.[13] You can hardly blame them. Rhythmically it seems the moment for a decisive break and the two scenes that follow, the leave-taking and the encounter of Volumnia and Virgilia with the tribunes, which Hall ran seamlessly together, are a quieter coda to the terrifying energies that precede them.

When we reach the third scene of Act 4, we are clearly aware of a break, for the scene has all the rhythmic hallmarks of an expository scene marking a deliberate break and restarting in the play's articulation of its form. This scene, usually and far too often cut in performance, for example by Hall in 1984 or the Royal Shakespeare Company production by David Farr in 2002, is a brilliant achievement. Two figures we have probably never seen before meet somewhere. The vagueness is beautifully articulated. The Roman recognizes the Volscian but the latter takes a moment or two to identify Nicanor who has to ask "Know you me yet?" (4.3.5). The line and the process are of course proleptic: two scenes later the unrecognizable Coriolanus will ask Aufidius "Know'st thou me yet?" (4.5.64) and he might make a similar gesture at this moment, throwing back the hood of his cloak for instance so that the face is now seen, as in the RSC's 1977 production. The scene, of course, stands as a stage along the road – it might well be taking place on a road – that Caius himself is taking, its time marking his journey time from Rome to Antium. It is, as it were, at that mid-point on the journey between Rome and Antium, a mid-point that is geographically defined as Corioles, a town almost exactly equidistant from each, only a mere 15 miles away, a reminder to us that this is a play of cities, Shakespeare's drama of the polis, not an account of Rome as the center of empire. *Coriolanus*, a tale of three cities if ever there was one, is aware of Corioles as its crucial border point, the town that changes statehood as the play progresses (Volscian-Roman-Volscian), the marking of the fluidity of the liminality defined by ownership in the condition of permanent conflict the play records. I am not suggesting that this scene takes place at or near Corioles but rather that it identifies the blurring of the opposition of citizen identity that the activities of spying necessarily dictates. Is a Roman traitor really a Volscian? How does a Volscian spy seem Roman? How, in effect, is the contrast between the two city-states manifest in performance? I am painfully aware that many productions have placed conventionally be-toga-ed Romans against Volscians who seem like a cross between Mongol hordes and Aztecs.

If Coriolanus begins as a word that can only mean a citizen of Corioles and becomes the triumphalizing onomastic possession of the man who conquered it, then this scene marks the beginnings of the return of the word to its previous separation, one in which Coriolanus can no longer be a Roman's agnomen. The 1964 Berliner Ensemble production of Brecht's version of the play visibly collapsed the three cities into two and the gates of the two cities, a towering white stone archway for Rome and a rougher brown wooden stockade serving for both Corioles and Antium, were placed on the revolve, the Roman one moving to unmask the other as the stage space was redefined. The effect was to elide difference, to see one city as implicit in, barely a mask for, the other. The design made clear what Brecht – and to some extent Shakespeare – sought to create: that all cities are potentially the same city.

Modern productions, played with a single intermission, define the overall shape of the play as a two-act form. This is crucial to our understanding of the performance rhythm: in a production with one intermission, no members of the audience other than Shakespeare editors have the faintest idea which of F1's five acts the play is in; it is simply before or after the intermission. And most productions place their intermission, like Hall, after the play leaves Rome for its journey to Antium. Emrys Jones, identifying sensitively the two-part structure of Shakespeare's plays, is a little over-emphatic here: "Coriolanus is first a Roman among the Romans, and then a Roman among the Volscians." But he notes that "the Folio act-division does what it can to obscure this clear contrast, for the sequence of Coriolanus' banishment ends in [4.2], after which there is a marked break." "It would," he asserts, "clarify the design if the fourth act were to begin with...[4.3]."[14] Well, it certainly would, but clarifying the design in such sharp-edged ways is exactly what the play refuses to do. The blurred unevenness here of the act-division is part of the effect, the move out of Rome in the farewell scene at or near the city-gates through the awareness of a Rome without Coriolanus through the encounter of a non-Roman and a non-Volscian to the sight of a Coriolanus alone on stage, "in mean apparel, disguised and muffled" (4.4.0.1–2), a Coriolanus visibly unlike himself and often, for a while, unidentifiable by the audience, a Coriolanus who is neither Roman nor Volscian and whose state of belonging in Antium is impossible yet to fix.

There is a good case for considering *Coriolanus* to be Shakespeare's first play written with the Blackfriars in mind[15] and, if that is so, then the question of act-division becomes part of its first performance and not an editorial restructuring. If the play was written after the freezing of the Thames in the winter of 1607–8, and perhaps quite late in 1608, or even perhaps not finished until 1609, then this was certainly close to or after the date when Burbage took back control of the Blackfriars theater and reopened it as the King's Men's by the summer of 1608, only to have it closed because of plague probably from August 1608 and perhaps continuously until November 1609. Shakespeare is most likely to have finished writing *Coriolanus* during the frustrating period when the King's Men owned the Blackfriars but, because of plague, could not play there. The Folio text of *Coriolanus* undoubtedly points to performance in an indoor playhouse, not least if the assumption is correct that the cornets which sound four times in the play (another articulation of form by sound in this noisest of Shakespeare's plays) were only used at theaters like the Blackfriars and never at the Globe.[16] At the very least it is reasonable to assume that the text we have is derived from a manuscript marked up in part for indoor performance.

If act-divisions were marked in performance in King's Men's productions at the Blackfriars, perhaps, though not necessarily, by music as the boys' companies had done, then Shakespeare could well have written the play with an awareness of five-act form as performance practice, experimenting with its potential to mark the articulation of the action in performance perhaps for the first time ever or at the very least for the first time since *Henry V* (depending on when you believe the choruses to *Henry V*, absent in Q1 and present only in F1, were written – and I am not yet quite convinced that they were in place in 1599 when the play was first performed). Where Jones confidently defined the two-part structure by labeling them, in relation to Caius, "a Roman among the Romans, and then a Roman among the Volscians," the five-act shape is similarly amenable to such overly neat definition of its structural form. Charlotte Porter and Helen Clarke, the only two women ever to have edited Shakespeare's complete works, identified each act, in their fascinating *Shakespeare Study Program* (1914):

Coriolanus as Soldier, Coriolanus as Candidate, Coriolanus as "A Foe to the Public Weale," Coriolanus the Avenger, and, finally, Coriolanus as Human.[17] Performance practices, of course, may want to label smaller units: Trevor Nunn's 1972 RSC production divides the play into 44 units, up to four per scene, each "block" named in the promptbook: "The home truth, the overthrow of the consul, the Banished man, the argument for war" and so on, within a two-part structure either side of the interval.[18]

Of course it could be that Shakespeare wrote the play with continuous performance at the Globe in mind and that the act-division, reflecting Blackfriars performance, was created by a playhouse employee later and that we should blame someone for the awkwardness of the division between Acts 3 and 4 rather than congratulating Shakespeare on the brilliance with which the transition is managed. In other words, we can complain of someone else's ineptness – or indeed Shakespeare's own failure with an unfamiliar mode of dramatic form – or we can praise him for the brilliance with which he recognized that a play of three cities, in two parts, shaped in five acts was a mathematical problem incapable of comfortable solution, that two into five won't go and that the unevenness, the inexactitude, the sense of fascinatingly disrupted rhythms, of something as syncopated as Gershwin ever imagined, is a central element in the way the play argues for the imprecision, the impossibility of Coriolanus being either a Roman or a Volscian and/or both at once, the equal impossibility of the inversion of the city in Caius' being able to say "I banish you," of the spatial movement across the play's fictive spaces being articulated in this transitional passage in ways that depend on a formal structure of act-break which the action cannot and should not comfortably accommodate. The problem of pre-fractional mathematics – two goes into five with the answer two, remainder one – is then exactly the point. This is the play of remainders, of what is left over when divisions are made, of the social difficulties of superfluity and inequitable division, of the class and wealth basis structured into Roman society that leaves most people as the remainder, the "musty chaff" Coriolanus sees the population of Rome being.

Before pursuing the specific ways in which the play's form articulates its remains, I want to push at the problem of excess and superfluity. If my first move has been to be concerned with a certain ambiguity of formal structures, a deliberate insecurity in the ways in which form is to be observed, then there is also a kind of doubleness in the play's explorations of early modern forms of excess.

In the crucial tension at the heart of the concept of excess lies a distinction between, on the one hand, a desirable fullness, that which is more than needed, yet wanted and enjoyed, and, on the other, a wasteful over-plus, the fullness that is not only not necessary but also to be dispelled and reduced back into a form of moderation, a normal, normative, controllable range of values. If the former is continually to be aligned with an early modern valuation of, praise of, and desire for *copia* – that extravagance that denotes fertility, a copiousness, the delights of the cornucopian text that so fascinated Terence Cave[19] – then it is found at its fullest, the fullest state of its own fullness, within Shakespeare's language, an expanse of signification that is so often multiple in its valencies and possibilities but whose *copia* is, in the inventiveness of our engagement with it, never a waste, an over-plus, an excess in need of reduction, but instead and always a site of expanding meanings, semantic fields which we analytically reconnect with the texts within which their valencies may speak. We deny, in the self-satisfied way in which we perform the revelation of such excesses and opulencies, the possibility of their wastefulness; they are what we find them to be: that is, meanings needed by us, for, having identified their excess beyond the required, we work with, not against, the revelations of their multiplicity, reveling proudly precisely in that fullness that is more than the minimally required meanings. Superfluous to the narrow communicative adequacies of the processes of quasi-realist discourse, their excesses are a, perhaps *the*, site of poetic language, an enjoyment of and desire for excess within the local, not a superfluity of superabundance of extent, but a pleasurable excess within the tightly defined claustrophobia of language that can often look superficially to be also merely adequate but which we know to be excessively, delightfully more than that.

Excess as a quality of the *un*necessary within the discourse registers of Shakespearean speech is located within extent of time, not the crucial poetic delights of compaction. That Italian-German definition which so delighted Ezra Pound, dichten = condensare, is in opposition to some kind of temporal dynamic of expansiveness (temporal in performative dramatic language, if spatial in its visible print manifestation). So Caius Martius Coriolanus, a character whose name has excessive extent, a 50% excess beyond the normative Roman forms elsewhere in the play, is someone whom I often hear to be speaking at too great a length, speaking too much, excessive in the extents of his discourse at moments. But, in the passage I want to focus on (and which also concerned Goldberg[20]), Caius Martius is excessive only in the compacted way in which the meanings generated are those he wishes for or those which we may posit as being within his desires (as opposed to those meanings which in other subtextual spaces we posit as undesired, opposite to desire, an excess that denies, works against, the fields of valencies that are wished for), speaking language, that is, that is as clever as the speaker, not only as clever as the playwright.

I am intrigued, then, by a small passage from *Coriolanus*, Caius Martius' reaction in the first scene to the news that the Volsces are in arms: "Then we shall ha' means to vent I Our musty superfluity" (1.1.223–4). Shakespeare has chosen so potently to transform what he found in North's Plutarch, where war was a patrician device to solve a genuine food crisis as well as an equally genuine political threat:

> So the wise men of Rome beganne to thincke ... howe by this occasion it was very mete in so great a scarsitie of vittailes, to disburden Rome of a great number of cittizens: and by this meanes as well to take awaye this newe sedition, and utterly to ryd it out of the cittie, as also to cleare the same of many mutinous and seditious persones, being the superfluous ill humours that grevously fedde this disease.[21]

With the news of the war comes the possibility of getting rid of people now redefined as precisely the mouldy corn, the "musty chaff" (5.1.26) which, at the other end of the play, Cominius will report Coriolanus describing the population of Rome as being, as if the equivalence of people and corn were a recurrent motif in his discourse. We can hear a tension in Caius Martius' phrase between "means" and "superfluity," the former not only a sign of resource and possibility but also of "the mean," the desired parameters of adequacies against which the superfluity functions: eliminate the superfluous (people, corn) and what remains is within the mean, defines itself as mean, not now mean as meagre but as appropriately sufficient, the size of population that, on the one hand, Rome can profitably feed and that on the other it can control. If "musty" is the sign of the uselessness of the corn/people, for mouldy corn is precisely the substandard produce that one would rather eliminate, dispose of, waste for its excess to use, its wasteful uselessness, ideally by selling (venting in that sense current for Shakespeare) and leaving to others to decide how or whether to consume, then "musty" is also a space of the citizen desire that Caius Martius rejects: these people are the ones who voice what they *must* have, they are must-y in that sense, not a sense the *OED* identifies as current in early modern speech but which we can, I believe, still choose to find hovering behind the word. The superfluous to the organization of the state are those who voice a will, speak what they must have (here, food) and who refuse their silence (in a play whose action will depend on a silent act, Shakespeare's only stage-direction for silence, "He holds her by the hand, silent" [5.3.183]).

As such, the space of voiced will is a part of the play's exploration of what it means to "vent." The sound has already been heard twice in the scene: Menenius has prefaced the tale of the belly with the comment that "It may be you have heard it, I But since it serves my purpose, I will *vent*ure I To stale't a little more" (87–9) and Martius has, just a few lines before, described how the citizens "With these shreds I ... *vent*ed their complainings" (205–6). Menenius dares to make his tale yet more stale (a sense which, like "musty," suggests goods become waste, needing to be disposed of, that second sense of excess) and the people release the air of their voices from their bodies, expelling the sound, giving the pent-up pressure within the closed container of the body corporal and politic a venting, an outlet that is good for it, getting rid of the body's gases, as the Volscian servants will describe war as "full of vent" (4.5.228).

Elsewhere what comes out, forced out of the body through the desire to vent, is something more highly valued in its formulation than complainings. One vents or gives vent to one's emotions, as Menenius will later describe as a kind of compulsion within Caius Martius, "His heart's his mouth. I What his breast forges, that his tongue must vent" (3.1.259–60). If to vent here is to sell, to speak, to utter forth, it is also something whose choice of bodily aperture can be contrary. "Vent" can mean to fart, to shit or to piss (and the last will then link back to Menenius's use of "stale" which is also urine, as if he is pissing in telling the story again). So Stephano will wonder whether Trinculo has been shat out of Caliban: "How cam'st thou to be the siege [*sc.* turd] of this moon-calf? can he vent Trinculos?" (*The Tempest*, 2.2.106–8).

As Goldberg recognizes, in Menenius' fable of the belly, what is left after the patricians' supposedly generous distribution of everything that is good and nourishing and useful is "bran," the waste that is the unusable excess in the economies of the production of corn: "the belly," he writes, "assumes the position of the anus, receiving what is normally expelled; a closed economy is imagined in which waste is consumed."[22] In this vision of a hyper-efficient system there is no waste to be disposed of, no excess to the consumption, no outside to which the waste is turned for a different kind of recycling that has so fascinated Shakespeare in for example the progress of Alexander in *Hamlet*. There is no need here for the services of waste management, of sewerage, of the ways in which the modern state deals with its forms of socially wasteful excess, the moment at which goods become only and irrevocably garbage, land-fill rather than city-fill; indeed, the sense of the belly as "the sink o'th'body" (119) might now, in a presentist methodology, lead us to "sink estates," those urban sites of the disposal of socially useless individuals, a semi-expulsion.

But in the irruption into the play of another location, the imma-nence of the Volscians provides the opportunity for expulsion, evacu-ation, venting. The *OED*, not quoting this passage under any of its senses of *vent*, offers only one example for its obscure usage of the verb to mean "to rid (a kingdom) of people" and only one for the similarly unusual usage to "eject or expel (people) *out of* a country," both usages appearing within a mere four years of the date of *Coriolanus*.[23] Both surely hover here as well: the closed walls of Rome will be opened to release its superfluity and rid the state of their presence, turning them from people to corpses through the state's use of this musty corn as cannon-fodder. Where murder as garbage disposal has for us paro-dically become a practice of mafia gangsterism (in the operations of New Jersey Waste Management), here it is a function of the state's self-regulation through expulsion. We can, of course, see similar practices of waste and value operating throughout the play's battle-scenes, the ones that will earn Caius Martius the play's name, in the onstage opening and closing of the gates of Corioli, ingesting and expelling Volsces, Caius Martius, and the Romans, as if we are watching the bodily processes of the city beyond the feeding cycles that Menenius had described.

Yet this first scene has also an especial visual and aural concentration on its own excess, the first as the people who mark the superfluity, not an abstraction but a literal presence of the crowd, that group of citizens who, to Caius excessive in their demands, can be redefined as the city's excesses to be shat upon in the excesses of his language before being shat out. The King's Men, like most modern companies, cannot have repre-sented the excess of the crowd by sheer numbers. Recent experiments to achieve that have ranged from the embarrassing, like Peter Hall's use of audience members in his National Theatre production of 1984, unconvincingly clutching their handbags, briefcases, and shopping, to the spectacular, like Tim Supple's use, in his Chichester Festival Theatre production in 1992 starring Kenneth Branagh and Judi Dench, of local amateur actors, more than fifty of them, filling the stage excessively and defining exactly the quantity of which Rome had need to be vented.

If, though, *Coriolanus* is a Blackfriars play, then the sheer experi-mental and radical daring of *Coriolanus* is all the more apparent, of writing a play which depends so much on a sizeable crowd, in F's apparently authorial entry in the voices scene, no fewer than "seven or eight" (2.3.0.1), not as many as Jack Cade's entry "with infinite numbers" (*Henry VI Part 2*, 4.2.30.1), but more than any other play specifies. On the smaller Blackfriars stage, the crowd must have loomed larger, more threateningly, more significantly than at the Globe. This group of players – citizens or plebeians, a company, troop or rabble, a sequence of possible opposites established by the variants in entry markings – define rhythmic movements in the action simply through their presence, from their tumultuous entry as starving mutinous Romans, who may or may not be considered by the patricians to be "citizens" as equally as they are, to their extraordinary final entrance, no longer Romans but Volscians and no longer the object of Martius' contempt but the group of "commoners" who willingly and celebratingly accompany him on his last entry (5.6.70.1–2). Without names (except for the servant Cotus who works in Aufidius' house), randomly numbered, unspecified by gender, this amorphous group figure out one aspect of the dramatic rhythms through the mechanics of their entrances and exits.

If aural excess is conceived of in terms of volume, then Supple's Chichester crowd were magnificent in their excess, not a superfluity but an aural abundance as, for instance, in their thundering of their response to Sicinius, "True, | The people are the city" (3.1.200–1) – and the word "people" is spoken a simply astonishing 78 times in the play, a hammering away at the word, both revealing and breaking its meanings through excessive repetition. For a sense of the degree of excess that this repeated usage constitutes, compare the mere 11 occurrences in *Julius Caesar* or 15 in *Titus*, with the frequency in *Coriolanus* amounting to more than one-third of the occurrences across the entire corpus of Shakespeare's plays.

If aural excess is quantitative and temporal, then it is effectively Caius's own. Of the sixty-four lines from the moment of Caius's first entrance to the lines that are so obsessing me, Caius speaks an astonishing 56 of them, an apparently limitless vomiting of language as invective that was, of course, a spur to Cavell's concerns. I would want to see this excess of speech as the inverse of the excess of scars, those signs of his wife's fear and of parental pride, each of the 27 lovingly counted and located as a bodily history of heroic fighting for Rome. In their operation, also, as political symbols of state service, of the longevity and commitment of his work for the city they are inscriptions of worthy candidature. These multivalent writings on the body are a location of voyeuristic desire, the aftermaths of wounds and death ("every gash was an enemy's grave" [2.1.151–2]) that are signs of shame that neither the citizens nor the spectators may see: "I have wounds to show you which shall be yours in private" (2.3.72–3). As we quickly desire the sight of the excess of bodily writing so we quickly turn from the site of the excess of the same body's speaking. As the theatre critic Kenneth Tynan once advised an over-energetic actor, "Don't just do something; stand there."

I have been articulating two contrary tensions of energy in *Coriolanus*: the insecurity of forms and the processes of excess. The prefractional maths of the former connects with the policing of superfluity in the latter, for both tensions are, in the end, concerned with remainders, with the nature of this waste. *Coriolanus* is a play that is fascinated by what remains. Quite unexpectedly, I find that *Coriolanus* turns out to share with *Cymbeline* by far the highest frequency of occurrence in Shake-speare's works of the word "remain" and its cognates, fourteen in *Coriolanus* and fifteen in *Cymbeline* with no other play reaching double figures.[24] The word suggests two senses in *Coriolanus*, a stasis and a sequence. On the one hand, Menenius images the complaint of the other members of the body against the belly in terms of remaining static: "That only like a gulf it did remain | I'th' midst o'th' body, idle and unactive" (1.1.95–6). Lartius calls on the troops to act to save Caius at Corioli "Let's fetch him off, or make remain alike" (1.5.35). On the other, it indicates what still has to be done, what the necessary next stage in a sequence of activity is to be. Here is Menenius working through the Senate's agenda:

> Having determined of the Volsces, and
> To send for Titus Lartius, it remains
> As the main point of this our after-meeting
> To gratify his noble service that hath
> Hath thus stood for his country.
> (2.2.35–9)

Later he twice tells Coriolanus the next steps towards becoming con-sul: "It then remains | That you do speak to the people" (133–4) and, after gaining the voices, "Remains | That, in th'official marks invested, you | Anon do meet the Senate" (2.3.135–7). The name Coriolanus itself becomes something that remains, a static sign of all that will survive, both in his own description of what Rome has done to recognize his service ("The painful service, | ... Shed for my thankless country, are requited | But with that surname ... | ... Only that name remains" [4.5.69–74]) and in Volumnia's of what the chronicles will say of Coriolanus as traitor:

> "The man was noble,
> But with his last attempt he wiped it out,

> Destroyed his country, and his name remains
> To th'ensuing age abhorred."
>
> (5.3.146–9)

But I am particularly interested in two of the three occurrences of *remain* in the play that are beyond the fourteen others, the three that do not read the same in F, where F's "manet," the action of remaining on stage, is always now translated by editors as "remain." For there is a striking aspect to the play's rhythm, especially through its first half. In every scene bar one in which the two tribunes of the people appear on stage, they are on stage at the end of the scene. In all of the first four scenes in which they appear, 1.1 and all three scenes of Act 2, and once again late in the play when the news comes of Coriolanus' invasion, they alone are left, two politicians reflecting on what has happened and determining what remains to be done. Their coda-like duologues vary immensely in length: 65 lines at the end of 2.1 including their being summoned to the capitol by a messenger, just six lines at the end of 2.2 and only four at the end of 4.6. Other scenes in which they are on stage at scene's end do not define their dual dominance of stage-space, especially in the greater chaos of the opposition to the election in Act 3, though they may well dominate the crowd in the celebrations of Coriolanus' banishment. In only one scene do they finally leave before the scene's end, chased from the stage by Volumnia's apocalyptic anger after her son's departure, a scene in which they repeatedly try to leave: "Let's not meet her ... Keep on your way ... Pray, let's go ... Well, well, we'll leave you. Why stay we to be baited | With one that wants her wits" (4.2.9–47). The disruption here of the drama's usual formal practice defines something of Volumnia's power and their entirely justifiable terror of her.

But the five scenes that end with the two onstage establish a repetitive rhythm of their presence, a marking of their significance in changing the play's course, a statement about their odd status in Rome. It is not only in computers and the early work of structuralist criticism that binary oppositions are dominant. We recognize how strongly in a drama like *Coriolanus*, the forms of the agon are defined in pairs: externally Romans and Volscians, Caius and Aufidius, Rome and Antium; internally as Forum versus Capitol, that spatial definition of the division in Roman society, with the capitol as the place of senators, nobility, patricians, political authority, and the forum as the space of the plebeians, citizens, the rabble (as Caius, his mother and the stage directions alone refer to them). For Caius Martius the institution of the tribunes is itself a superfluous action, a sign of patrician cowardice, and incidentally something that is marked by an excess of information beyond the processes of the play; the people are granted "five tribunes" but only two are named and present in the action, the other three conjured momentarily into existence and then ignored as excess and waste:

Menenius: What is granted them?
Martius: Five tribunes to defend their vulgar wisdoms,
Of their own choice. One's Junius Brutus,
Sicinius Velutus, and I know not. (1.1.211–14)

Where then do the tribunes of the people fit in this structure? Though they are the plebeians' representatives it does not mean that they are themselves plebeian. They share with Menenius the same word to the people as a greeting, "neighbours," he at his first entrance (1.1.59), they at the moment of basking in their greatest triumph (4.6.22, 26), as Volumnia will use it, perhaps ironically, of those among whom the women will die: "So, we will home to Rome I And die among our neighbours" (5.3.173–4). Like him, the tribunes' use of the word may define patronizing superiority masquerading as connection. Often now played as the middling sort, representatives of a Roman bourgeoisie separated both from their blue-collar neighbours and the unattainable heights of patrician power, Sicinius and Brutus, whatever their analogies to modern class structures, may signal their own extraneousness, their ambiguous status as what remains after the two dominant forces of Roman social structure are removed. They are unidentified in and unassimilated into the self-defined structure that Rome uses as its slogan: senatus populusque Romanus, the senate and the people of Rome. The tribunes may, more than any other division of characters in the play, be the site of excess, waste, remains.

Part of my concern, then, using *Coriolanus* as a test-case, has been to find the dramatic and performative location of excess in formal terms, the outward manifestations of excess, less excess of emotion than excess of language, less excess of feeling than excess in the number of characters, the form of a name, the density of semantic meaning. If the evidence has its own copiousness, its *copia*, then it also risks its own wastefulness, the excess of our analytic process. *Coriolanus* has come, for me, to be the great play of the closure of the city and the body, of the limits of containment and the meaning of the body/city's procedures with waste, its paralleling evacuations and expulsions. No wonder it was a play that so fascinated

Brecht. No wonder its taut politics have been so potent in France, perhaps even more often than in England. In the exiguous processes of its action, the dramatics of excess are perfectly revealed.

But I have also been concerned with the ways in which the awkard, tense, and often ambiguous ramifications of the rhythms of formal structures reveal themselves. Surely it is worth continuing to study such things, surely here is something the theater continues powerfully to teach academics. As Gershwin wrote,

> Fascinating Rhythm,
> You've got me on the go!
> Fascinating Rhythm,
> I'm all a-quiver.

But Ira's words don't quite match George's melody and the last word has a false accent, "all a-qui*ver*." Rhythms are fascinating precisely because of their refusal to fit the tunes we would wish them to have.

Notes

1. Gordon Crosse, Theatrical Diaries, 1924, MS in Birmingham Shakespeare Library, 24.
2. Kenneth Burke, *Language as Symbolic Action* (Berkeley: University of California Press, 1966), 96.
3. Stanley Cavell, *Disowning Knowledge in Six Plays of Shakespeare* (Cambridge: Cambridge University Press, 1987), 174.
4. Ibid., 174–5.
5. Jonathan Goldberg, "The Anus in *Coriolanus*" in *Historicism, Psychoanalysis, and Early Modern Culture*, ed. Carla Mazzio and Douglas Trevor (New York: Routledge, 2000), 260–71.
6. Cavell, *Disowning Knowledge*, 174.
7. All quotations from *Coriolanus* are taken from R. B. Parker's edition (Oxford: Clarendon Press, 1994), here at 1.9.63 and 66.
8. *Coriolanus*, ed. Lee Bliss (Cambridge: Cambridge University Press, 2000), 103.
9. John Ripley, *"Coriolanus" on Stage in England and America, 1609–1994* (Madison: Fairleight Dickinson University Press, 1994), 137.
10. Helge Kökeritz, *Shakespeare's Names: A Pronouncing Dictionary* (New Haven: Yale University Press, 1959), 45. I take it that the town's name here is something like "Cor-eye-lees."
11. Simon Palfrey, *Doing Shakespeare* (London: Arden Shakespeare, 2005).
12. Kristina Bedford, *"Coriolanus" at the National: "Th'Interpretation of the Time"* (Selinsgrove: Susquehanna University Press, 1992), 279 (also 109, 348 n.1).
13. Ibid., 292.
14. Emrys Jones, *Scenic Form in Shakespeare* (Oxford: Oxford University Press, 1971), 81.

15. See Parker (ed.), *Coriolanus*, 86–9.
16. There is no example of the use of cornets in a play-text unequivocally derived from the Globe or similar playhouses and a number of examples of their use in play-texts certainly derived from private theatres.
17. Charlotte Porter and Helen A. Clarke, *Shakespeare Study Programs: The Tragedies* (Boston: Richard G. Badger, 1914), 21–6.
18. See the production promptbook *ad loc.*, Shakespeare Centre Library.
19. Terence Cave, *The Cornucopian Text* (Oxford: Clarendon Press, 1979).
20. Goldberg, "The Anus in *Coriolanus*," 262.
21. Geoffrey Bullough, *Narrative and Dramatic Sources of Shakespeare. Volume 5: The Roman Plays* (London: Routledge, 1964), 516.
22. Goldberg, "The Anus in *Coriolanus*," 261.
23. *OED*, vent *v.*[2], 7.a and 7.b.
24. There are ten in *The Rape of Lucrece*.

8

The Joys of Martha Joyless: Queer Pedagogy and the (Early Modern) Production of Sexual Knowledge

Valerie Traub

I want to inspire queers to be more articulate about the world they have already made, with all its variations from the norm, with its ethical understanding of the importance of those variations, with its ethical refusal of shame or implicitly shaming standards of dignity, with its refusal of the tactful silences that preserve hetero privilege, and with the full range of play and waste and public activity that goes into making a world.

— Michael Warner, *The Trouble With Normal*[1]

Teachers and writers might better serve the claims of know-ledge if we were to resist not sex but the impulse to split off sex from knowledge.

— Jane Gallop, *Feminist Accused of Sexual Harrassment*[2]

1.   "A wanton maid once lay with me"

In Richard Brome's stage play, *The Antipodes*, a comedy first performed in 1638, a theme of sexual distress is introduced by a reference to two women lying in bed together. Martha Joyless, a countrywoman suffer-ing from a virgin's melancholy straight out of Robert Burton,[3] is dis-mayed that her marriage of three years has never been consummated; she reports to her new London acquaintance, Barbara, of her equally melancholic husband, Peregrine: "He ne'er put child, nor anything toward it yet I To me to making." At the same time, she expresses ignor-ance about the actual means of conceiving children: "For were I now to die, I cannot guess I What a man does in child-getting" (1.1.252–3).[4] Joyless and clueless as she is, however, she is not altogether without

170

sexual experiences, as becomes clear when she relates to Barbara this memory:

> I remember
> A wanton maid once lay with me, and kissed
> And clipped and clapped me strangely, and then wished
> That I had been a man to have got her with child.
> What must I then ha' done, or (good now, tell me)
> What has your husband done to you?
>
> (1.1.253–7)

In an aside, Barbara directs the audience's perceptions: "Was ever I Such a poor piece of innocence three years married!" She then asks Martha directly: "Does not your husband use to lie with you?" Martha's earnest answer further displays her ignorance:

> Yes, he does use to lie with me, but he does not
> Lie with me to use me as he should, I fear;
> Nor do I know to teach him. Will you tell me?
> I'll lie with you and practise, if you please.
> Pray take me for a night or two, or take
> My husband and instruct him but one night.
> Our country folks will say you London wives
> Do not lie every night with your own husbands.[5]
>
> (1.1.261–8)

Despite Martha's unwitting, if nonetheless thoroughly conventional, jab at the promiscuity of city wives, the dramatic focus throughout her request for erotic instruction is her astonishing "innocence." So eager for knowledge that she would place both herself and her husband in Barbara's bed, Martha's rural simplicity is posed against Barbara's urban sophistication. Clearly, Martha is the butt of this sexual joke. Yet, her lack of understanding of the mechanics of procreation is nonetheless accommodating to her fond recollection of a "wanton maid" who kissed, clipped, and clapped her. Modern editors gloss "clipped and clapped" as "embraced and fondled passionately," as well as "embraced and patted" – with the added suggestion that clapped "may imply something more firmly administered"; and one editor suggests that "'slap' is a recent equivalent" – still so used, I am told, in contemporary Ireland.[6] Apparently, this unnamed maid's behavior took the form of passionate, even forceful caresses that were not incompatible with her own desire to be penetrated and impregnated. Like Barbara's urbane sophistication, this maid's erotic desires and actions contrast comically to Martha's erotic ignorance and dependence on the knowledge of others.[7]

The play's thematization of Martha Joyless's sexual dilemma invites us to consider anew the historical production of sexual knowledge – by which I mean the conditions of collecting, creating, and disseminating information about sexuality, in the past as well as in the present.[8] Although the intent of Brome's play is to satirize Martha's "innocence" and to pity her marital lot, I want to resist its satiric pull long enough to consider the implications of the fact that she does articulate knowledge about sex, although not the kind her culture readily acknowledges. Of what does Martha's knowledge and ignorance consist?[9] On the one hand, she is inexperienced in the mechanics of sex with men – so much so that although she is, by her own admission, "past a child I My selfe to think [children] are found in parsley beds, I Strawberry banks or Rosemary bushes," she nonetheless confesses to "have sought and searched such places I Because I would fain had had one" (1.1.241–4). On the other hand, she *is* experienced, however briefly, in the erotic caresses of a woman; but other than realizing that this is *not* the way to procreate, she possesses little understanding of what such contact signifies. Indeed, given her incomprehension, one hesitates to call it knowledge at all.

Martha's asymmetrical position of knowing and not knowing (or more precisely, of having experienced something eccentric to the dominant discourse that is then overwritten as simplicity) introduces sexual knowledge as a problem of pedagogy: Martha seeks tutelage from Barbara because she has not been properly taught by her husband. At the same time, in its lack of accommodation to both dominant discourses of reproductive sexuality and to the counter-discourses generated by recent queer scholarship, Martha's situation forces us to confront, as an epistemological problem, the function of sexual knowledge as an analytical category within historiography. One only has to inquire whether the conceptual categories thus far made available by the history of sexuality help to elucidate Martha's erotic situation to see the difficulty, given the present state of our knowledge, of doing her analytical justice. Within the history of sexuality, debate has focused largely on whether same-sex sexualities in eras prior to the nineteenth century are best understood as connoting sexual identities or sexual acts.[10] Yet, neither the logic of sexual identities (that is, the self-perception or social ascription of being a "lesbian," "heterosexual," or even a "sapphist") nor the idiom of sexual acts (in which all non-reproductive contact is simply a form of carnal sin) adequately comprehends or describes the complex meanings of Martha's experience.

Nor are the analytical categories that have illuminated the relationship of modern homosexuality to knowledge of particular help here: this is not the "open secret" analyzed by D. A. Miller, nor is it precisely the "privilege of unknowing" anatomized by Eve Kosofsky Sedgwick – not only because the epistemology of the closet requires homosexuals, that is, sexual identities, in order to enact its discipline, but because Martha is so very *open* about what is *not* a secret.[11] Nor is it sufficient to fall back on the tired trope of inconceivability that has so dominated our understanding of lesbianism in the past; erotic acts between women are part of what is at stake, albeit comically, in Martha and Barbara's exchange, or the joke would lose its effectiveness. We are in undefined territory here, where the relations of knowledge to subjects, and both to eroticism, have yet to be charted.[12]

Indeed, to what extent is it possible to apprehend Martha's subjective *desire* at all? The passage from *The Antipodes* inscribes nothing of her possible pleasure, and is equally silent about her possible *dis*pleasure. Only Martha's ambiguous descriptors of the "wanton" maid and her "strange" behavior offer any clue – and both of these could signify approval, disapproval, or neither.[13] Other than her wish to learn what her husband must do to conceive a child, Martha gives us little access to her desire or interiority. Indeed, her indifference as to whether Barbara bed down with her or her husband underscores that nothing essential about the state of Martha's erotic subjectivity is revealed in her remembrance.[14]

Even when we broaden the analytical optic beyond the question of Martha's subjectivity to survey the wider implications of her recollection, its significance remains obscure. Indeed, the status of her erotic remembrance is a prime example of what Laurie Shannon, echoing Alan Bray, says of early modern sexuality more generally: that there is nothing fully dispositive about the power of eroticism to convey particular meanings; that erotic acts operate only unreliably as a trigger for articulation or as a mode of signification.[15] Is Martha's experience with her unnamed bedmate a transgressive act? Is her narrative a tale of misconduct? To the contrary: no repugnance on the part of other characters is generated by her story of clipping and clapping, nor is any stigma attached to it. Barbara's pity is explicitly directed toward the sorry state of Martha's marriage: "Poore heart I gesse her grief, and pitty her. | To keep a Maidenhead three years after Marriage, | Under wed-locke and key, insufferable! Monstrous, | It turns into a wolfe within the flesh" (1.1.202–4). Contrary to modern expectations, the homoerotic experience recalled by Martha is neither cause nor symptom of her illness; rather, it is the protracted keeping of her "maiden-head" that has given rise to her virgin's melancholy and obsession with child-getting. It is not just that Martha's ignorance is its own form of knowledge or that her knowledge is overwritten as a form of ignorance, but that her ill health is a result of her ignorance. It is from this position that her "virgin's melancholy" authorizes her quest for carnal knowledge.[16]

The play is quite clear about the need for Martha's marriage to be consummated, and it pursues this end via a medical discourse and therapeutic intervention that diagnoses Martha as "full of passion," "distracted," "mad for a child," and, my personal favorite, "*sick* of her virginity" (2.1.40, emphasis mine).[17] Under the dominant Galenic medical dispensation, the conventional treatment for virgin's melancholy was a wedding, the presumption being that legitimate sexual congress would bring about the orgasm that purges the sexually congested body of its built-up humors.[18] Absent regular vaginal intercourse, an alternative treatment prescribed in several medical textbooks was the manual manipulation of the genitals by a female midwife;[19] given that Martha's sexless marriage is diagnosed as the cause of her melancholy, it is significant that *The Antipodes* does not allude to this method of cure. To do so, of course, would be to call further attention to the same-sex contact that the play introduces only in order to forget. Instead, Martha's narration calls little attention to itself and is quickly passed over as the text focuses on the means of bringing Peregrine back to a state of mental health capable of the penetrative sexual performance demanded by the tight early modern linkage of marriage to reproduction.[20]

Despite the fact that Martha "presents" as both a melancholic and hysteric, and, in seeking Barbara's help, positions herself as a patient, it is Peregrine who is judged to be sicker than his wife, and it is he who holds the promise of the couple's return to sexual health. Peregrine's melancholy, initially caused by an overindulgence in reading travel literature, was exacerbated by his parents' refusal to allow him to travel the world; instead, seeking to bind him close to home – and in spite of his over-determined name – they married him off to Martha. Forbidden to travel, he is now "in travail" (1.1.175), his mind fully taken up in wandering "beyond himself" (1.1.149). His refusal to consummate his marriage apparently derives from an overly credulous reading of Mandeville's *Travels*, which includes a description of the "Gadlibriens" who employ other men to deflower their wives because of the risk of being stung by a serpent lodged within the female body.[21] There is much that could be said about Peregrine's resistance to marital sexuality and the specific form that his resistance takes. Motivated in part *by* the desire for travel,[22] his "Mandeville madness" (4.1.466) could also be motivated by other desires – homoerotic ones, perhaps – that would render this unhappy family multiply queer. Given that travel in this period offered Englishmen opportunities for a variety of sexual encounters – travel narratives are full of descriptions of both cross-sex and same-sex liaisons, whether fantasized or real, consensual or coercive – it would be a mistake to view Peregrine's resistance to marital sexuality as a rejection of sex altogether.

Nonetheless, the play enacts Brome's customary belief that the best way to remedy madness is by humoring delusions through metatheatrical fantasy. Under the direction of a doctor and a rather eccentric lord, Peregrine's family and a troupe of actors collude in convincing the patient that he has journeyed to the Antipodes (when he actually has been under the influence of a sleeping potion). Not surprisingly, the Antipodes, also called anti-London in the play, provides Brome with the opportunity for an extended dramatization of the world turned upside down, where lawyers are honest, servants govern their masters, and men are ducked as scolds.[23] The climax of this theatrical inversion therapy occurs when Peregrine, who, in good colonialist fashion, proclaims himself King of the realm, marries and takes to bed the Antipodean queen: Martha, thinly disguised.[24] Thus tricked into consummating his marriage by committing mock adultery, Peregrine is cured of his melancholy overnight. In fulfillment of the expectations of Galenic psychophysiology, coitus proves to be a potent restorative. The newly unified spouses emerge from their bedroom kissing, caressing, and cooing, to the obvious delight of the other characters that, throughout much of the stage action, have functioned as on-stage voyeurs.

The Antipodes is extremely canny about staging its interest in sex through metatheatrical means. Although the consummation of the Joyless marriage takes place off-stage, this does little to minimize its erotic interest;[25] indeed, the play's dramatization of on-stage voyeurs who are deeply invested in the success of the coital cure saturates the performance space with eroticism.[26] A subplot dramatizing the attempted seduction of another woman, Diana, by the fantastic lord, Letoy (who turns out to be her long-lost father), adds to the erotic effect.[27] In addition, roughly half of the vignettes staged to convince the delusional Peregrine that he has voyaged to the end of the earth concern sexual matters: courtiers who complain of being "jested" sodomitically from behind (4.6.8–14); old women who "Allow their youthful husbands other women ... And old men [who] give their young wives like license" (2.7.48–9); a maid who attempts to sexually assault a gentleman (4.2.16–45); and a tradesman who procures a gentleman to sexually pleasure his wife, to the acclaim of the gentleman's lady (2.7, 2.8, 3.9). With its sexual thematic and bawdy innuendo, with its treatment of voyeurism as entertainment and entertainment as cure, *The Antipodes* publicizes sex in such a way as to come very close to making sex public.

At issue, of course, is not only what Martha knows, but, given that this play was written for the stage, what the performers and audience know. What kind of sexual knowledge is being produced and exchanged, not only among the characters involved in this metatheatrical sex play, but also among the performers, and between them and the audience? Given the cultural context of the original production – wherein crossdressed boy actors played the female parts – some audience members may have experienced an additional homoerotic frisson. Yet, while transvestite boy actors may ironize Martha's assertion of erotic ignorance, their performance of femininity does not resolve the issues raised by it. Evidently, *The Antipodes* was designed to meet the needs of Beeston's company with its large numbers of children.[28] One might well ask, how did this play function pedagogically for these young players? Just what *was* it that they were learning? No less salient is the pervasive interpretation of Brome's drama which, based on the play's Jonsonian commitment to theater as comic therapy, submits that the "real patients" are those who are watching the play.[29] To what kind of "therapy" is the audience being subjected through *The Antipodes'* public discourse about sex?

To speak of public sexual discourse in the early modern era may seem odd, especially insofar as modern relations between public and private were only beginning to emerge.[30] Yet certain aspects of sexual life that we now tend to consider private were performed "publicly" in a variety of ways, including the sexual contact that arose, either consensually or through acts of violence, out of the practice of sharing beds (especially common among servants and between servants and masters); the sex unwittingly witnessed by travelers, both male and female, sleeping in communal inn rooms; and deliberate acts of group sex and voyeurism in taverns, fairs, and, later in the century, molly houses.[31] More conventionally, the early modern community was unabashedly concerned with the status of marital consummation. Until the urban elite started to separate themselves off from communal celebrations after the Restoration, wedding festivities across all status groups were accompanied by a good deal of sexual innuendo and erotic play, not least of which was the customary ritual of wedding guests escorting the bridal couple to bed, relieving them of the ribbons and laces that served as clothing fasteners, and "throwing the stocking" or relieving them of their hose.[32] As David Cressy notes, these actions were meant both "[t]o help them to their happiness, and to help establish plausible evidence of their consummation."[33] The public theater likewise promoted its own discourse of sex, in no small part through stage comedy's focus on physicality, bodily senses, domestic scenarios, and, more often than not, erotic desire. A traditional comedic plot device, the bed-trick, makes comic hay out of sexual knowledge relations. Temporarily inverting the usual patriarchal hierarchy in order to reintegrate the recalcitrant man into the reproductive community, the conventional Renaissance bed-trick dramatizes male ignorance about particular female bodies while asserting female knowingness over the duped male. *The Antipodes* trumps this convention by exploiting Peregrine's delusion and making Martha pose as a sexual fantasy, the Antipodean queen. Depending less on male ignorance and female duplicity than the collusion of an entire community, the bed-trick in Brome's play functions like the ritual festivities of the wedding night, forging ties of communal sexual knowledge through the approbation of marital consummation.

Within the play's context of marital dis-ease, theatrical sex therapy, publicity about sex, and communal investment in it, it is striking that Martha's narration of her prior homoerotic encounter with the "wanton maid" elicits no overt condemnation – indeed, it seems to exist in some field of discretion untouched by moral, medical, religious, or legal judgment. We would err in judging the application of this discretion to be a form of tolerance, for tolerance assumes recognition of the object of forbearance – precisely what is lacking here. Nor is such discretion explained by other conceptual safety nets that might seem to minimize the threat of female–female sex: that Martha's sexual experience is presented in the past tense; that she now is safely married. After all, she has just asked Barbara to repeat, if in a more pedagogical guise, the bedroom performance of the "wanton maid," and it is the miserable state of her marriage that has led her to look outside it for erotic instruction. We need only imagine the direction the plot might have taken if, in the adulterous mode of Restoration comedy, Barbara had capitalized on maximizing her own erotic pleasure and, in response to Martha's plea, bedded down with Peregrine, or Martha, or with both of them; the fact that the play entertains no such possibility for comic entanglement confronts us with the particular indifference with which Martha's reminiscence is met.

I am not suggesting that a patriarchal teleology or heterosexual privilege fail to organize the logic of Martha's situation: Martha's naiveté expresses an altogether conventional form of early modern femininity; her friend's embraces are positioned narratively as a precursor to marital intercourse; and her request for Barbara's tutelage likewise has the restoration of procreative sexuality as its end. Nonetheless, Martha's predicament forces us to acknowledge a decided disjunct between marriage and sex. Of what does Martha's marriage of three years consist? Whatever it is, it is not sex: and this absence of joy, of *jouissance*, is quite literally driving her mad. Even though Brome's play craftily brings about a three-years-delayed consummation to great communal fanfare and tendentiously maps erotic *jouissance* onto a reproductive imperative, the fact remains that Martha's journey to erotic satisfaction can hardly be called straight. And having turned to her friend Barbara for erotic instruction once, it is certainly conceivable, if we permit ourselves the intellectual indulgence of thinking outside the plot, that she might do so again. That, at least, is a conceit made possible by Martha's erotic remembrance, embedded as it is in a scene of erotic yearning – a yearning simultaneously for knowledge and sex – that the play both gestures toward and disavows.

2.   "What must I then ha' done, or ... What has your husband done to you?"

By raising marital sexuality to the status of a question and by posing that question by means of female–female eroticism, Brome's representation of the state of Martha's knowledge urges us to reconsider the state of *our* knowledge about early modern sex: not only what we know, but also how we know it. I thus turn away from the possible pleasures we might infer from Martha's fictional biography to pursue instead the knowledge relations that the representation of her ignorance performs. Within this inquiry, Martha functions less as a character or a subject – indeed, her flat characterization all but precludes that – than as a heuristic for accessing strategies of knowledge production. To treat her in this way no doubt accords to Brome's play more intellectual heft than it deserves. Nonetheless, this strategy propels our analysis further than does simply rehearsing the terms of early modern patriarchy or, alternatively, fantasizing an erotic elsewhere beyond patriarchy's frame.

To begin, then, with the current state of our knowledge. If, as I've begun to intimate, the historiography of sexuality fails to do justice to

Martha's situation, so too does the work of most feminist and social historians. Taking gender as its primary term of analysis, for instance, feminist scholars have tended to focus on sexuality as it pertains to women's so-called "life cycle" as maid, wife, mother, or widow.[34] The patriarchal "life cycle" likewise informs the work of most social historians, whose studies of marriage, gender identity, and social transitions generally are organized along the lines of wooing, wedding, birth, and maternity.[35] Were they to read *The Antipodes*, such scholars would likely emphasize Martha's obsession with child-getting, thereby implicitly privileging a reproductive imperative over sexual pleasure. Those scholars of sexuality who attempt to work outside the logic of the female reproductive life cycle tend to do so by deploying categories of deviance or transgression: premarital sex, bastardy, adultery, prostitution.[36] Whether the critical accent is on the disciplining of women's bodies or opportunities for female agency, transgression has functioned heretofore as the primary analytical means for conceptualizing erotic conduct that fails to conform to patriarchal mandates. Yet, because notions of norms and their transgression are structured by a binary of the licit and the illicit, they necessarily are indexed to the dominant social orthodoxy – even when the intention is to uncover the existence of those who would defy it.

But what of Martha's memory of kissing and clipping? Some forms of female eroticism are neither subsumed under marital exigencies nor defined in defiance of them; not primarily organized by the neat logic of a life cycle lived in compliance with patriarchal ideology *or* its transgression, they cannot adequately be comprehended within the licit/illicit divide.[37] Thus, simply adding female homoeroticism to a list of deviant acts or identities would fail to account for Martha's desire for marital sexuality and procreation *alongside* her experience of sex with a woman. Nor does this divide help us to map the complex relations inscribed in Martha's sexual history: casual sex with an unnamed woman; marriage utterly devoid of sex; request to a female acquaintance for erotic instruction; marital consummation with an unfaithful husband. Much less does it account for the erotic improvisation of Martha's anonymous bedmate, who passionately embraced and slapped her companion while expressing her own desire to conceive a child. Was she as ignorant about the means of procreation as Martha? How are we to understand the maid's desire to be impregnated by Martha and Martha's desire to learn how to conceive by having sex with Barbara? How do we account for the queer circuit whereby these characters' desires, frustrations, and hopes are represented?

The representation of Martha's sexual history urges a recognition that none of the bicameral rubrics through which we routinely process early modern sex – the licit and illicit, the homo and the hetero, erotic acts and erotic identities – provide us with much analytical purchase on the sexual and knowledge relations enacted in this play. Let us ask, then: What *are* the historical conditions of the production of erotic knowledge in the early modern period? To date, the most analytically generative method for approaching this question has been Michel Foucault's distinction between "two great procedures for producing the truth of sex": an *ars erotica*, supposedly pursued by premodern and non-Western cultures through practices of initiation, secrecy, and mastery; and a *scientia sexualis*, the distinctively modern, Western disciplinary apparatus, based on confession, which elicits and produces knowledge of sexuality in order to administrate it.[38] Yet, despite the therapeutic intent of Brome's play, Martha's homoerotic experience is not subject to any particular procedure for producing truth. Her request for erotic initiation, after all, is denied; and if the *ars erotica* proves unavailable to her, also unavailable is the disciplinary effect of confession. It is striking that Martha's confession is one that *no one wants to hear* – not Barbara, not the Doctor, perhaps not even Brome, so quickly does he pass over it. It would appear that Martha's problems, experiences, and queries exist outside of the nexus of knowledge, truth, and power that both the *ars erotica* and the *scientia sexualis*, however distinct their methods, tend to produce. Martha's tenuous and ambiguous relation to erotic knowledge thus calls for a mode of analysis eccentric to Foucault's opposition of initiation to discipline.

Although Brome denies Martha access to an *ars erotica*, some knowledge of continental Renaissance pornography seems to inform his approach to the relation between sexual knowledge and sexual pedagogy.[39] The enduring tropes of early modern literary obscenity were created in the sixteenth century by Italians such as Pietro Aretino: an older, experienced woman (generally a prostitute) initiates a young, "innocent" girl into the arts of love – first by talking, then by doing.[40] Her own desire for pleasure drawn forth from a homoerotic scene of instruction, the girl then seeks out more "mature" pleasures with men. This mode of initiation through imitation, considerably elaborated by the French later in the seventeenth century,[41] pursues its pedagogical intent by means of various narrative strategies: loquacious female speech; graphic nomination of body parts; sequential movement from sex talk to sex acts; a metaphoric inventiveness that mirrors the inventiveness of bodily postures and activities; the eroticization of narrative itself.

All of this inventiveness and loquaciousness is denied to Martha. On the one hand, as Laura Gowing remarks, "[t]his was a culture in which it was positively virtuous not to be able to describe sex" – particularly, one might note, for women.[42] Even within women's unofficial oral culture, marital status tended to regulate the circulation of knowledge about sexual matters: "The key rituals of the female body, those where knowledge was shared and experiences were public, were organized by and for married women. Being single meant exclusion from the exchanges of reproductive knowledge."[43] Having failed to be initiated into reproductive sex by her husband, Martha remains outside of this circuit of verbal instruction; her plea to another wife for information results not in the sharing of women's secrets, but the communal orchestration of her husband's sexual performance.

On the other hand, like so much else during the period prior to the Civil War, the representation of Martha's predicament sits on the cusp of two different public cultures. In the first four decades of the seventeenth century, sexual knowledge circulated primarily by means of gossip, bawdy ballads, chapbooks, jestbooks, and vernacular medical texts.[44] Bawdy verse was sung, recopied, and recorded in commonplace books; sexually suggestive libels and insults were pinned on posts and church doors, read or sung aloud to crowds. But "the widespread use of allusion and metaphor" in such materials, as Gowing notes, "served as a partial barrier to the participation of the young and the single."[45] Thus, to my earlier description of the public culture of sex, we need to factor in the ways that sexual knowledge and its expression were regulated according to gender, age, and status. Young women, in particular, might witness sexual acts but not have the language to describe what they saw; they might hear allusions to sexual conduct, but not know precisely what was implied.[46]

These barriers to knowledge and expression began to break down in the 1640s and 1650s, when a scurrilous political satire, arising out of social unrest and temporarily free from censorship, mined the sensational possibilities of conflating political with sexual slander, giving rise to far more explicit representations. So, too, vernacular medical texts, including ones directed toward women, became increasingly available and sexually explicit, read as much for their sexual advice as for their medical information.[47] Together, the languages of satire, medicine, and sexual advice reconfigured the terms of what could be said and written about sex in public. After the Restoration, the rise of a

courtly libertine culture, the increased availability of vernacular pornography, and the growth of molly houses all gave birth to what we might
call a nascent sexual public.

The extent of Brome's investment in dramatizing Martha's ignorance
is such that she enjoys no access to sexual discourse. Our recognition
of this prohibition gains critical traction beyond the obvious feminist
one once we note that Martha's articulation of her sexual past and her
request for tutelage generate the operations of a tacit knowledge (the
implied, supposedly self-evident, dominant discourse that "goes without saying"). As a result of these operations, her effort to satisfy her
desire is ignored, deflected, passed over. This "non-response" in the
face of her attempt at sexual agency enacts a process of disqualification
all too familiar to contemporary queers. So let us pause at the moment
of deflection and disqualification to ask: What goes (sexually) without
saying? What are the tacit processes by which certain sexual knowledges are rendered intelligible, legitimate, and enabling, while other
knowledges are rendered unintelligible, illegitimate, and disqualifying?
How do the relations between sexual knowledge and ignorance produce unpredicted knowledge like Martha's – consigned, on the one
hand, to irrelevance or insignificance, but which, on the other
hand, might hold within itself a future possibility of articulation and
power? How do irrelevant or insignificant knowledges become counter-
hegemonic and agential? And how does that possibility, then and now,
relate to publicity about sex, to public sexual cultures, indeed, to public
sex?

By raising such questions, I am suggesting that our emerging epistemology of early modern sex is not nearly as supple, nuanced, or
complex as its representations warrant. Eroticism in this period was
more "wanton" in its forms and more "strange" in its effects than
we tend to believe. Our reluctance to credit early modern sex with
sufficient diversity persists despite the explosion of interest among
literary critics in queering early modern texts – especially purportedly
heterosexual ones[48] – and despite the most important advance in queer
historiography: namely, the effort to articulate the extent to which
homoeroticism was embedded in a variety of early modern social
systems, such as domesticity, apprenticeship, authorship, patronage,
and politics.[49] The recognition that homoeroticism was one point in a
networked system of social relations has enhanced our understanding
of the meanings of sexuality to individuals and to social polities, as
well as our appreciation of sexuality's ideological utility, pliability, and
susceptibility to pressure.[50] Yet, despite the invocation of networked

relations, our scholarship generally does not make good on its promise of detailing processes of mutual constitutiveness; we tend to analyze relationality only from the angle of the social formation with which sexuality is imbricated. Conceived as a discrete, unified, bounded, and essentially passive object of inquiry, sexuality is *embedded in, deployed, made use of* by other discourses and systems.[51] Thus positioned, sexuality becomes an epiphenomenon of gender, rank, family, patronage, politics; it is to these domains, not eroticism, that social agency accrues.[52]

The Antipodes' enactment of a belabored, inefficient, *sick* marital sexuality invites us to consider whether eroticism is not only *embedded* in systems of knowledge (in this case, medical, domestic, theatrical), but itself is an *agent* of knowledge production. Rather than embodying an innate desire whose meaning is self-evident – something we all already know – sexuality in Brome's play is a question to be asked, an answer to be given, as well as a task to be learned and performed. "What must I then ha' done, or … What has your husband done to you?" queries Martha; and, with a cluelessness that is as provocative as it is disarming, she attempts to direct her own training: "I'll lay with you and practice, if you please." Insisting that sex is a matter of *doing something*, Martha introduces the practical approach toward sexual pedagogy enacted by others throughout the play. The fact that Martha's request for hands-on instruction is silently denied, and then deflected onto the therapeutic elicitation of Peregrine's desire – a desire that he quickly learns how to direct – renders no less significant the play's overall interest in what might be called "sex education." (This displacement merely reminds us that sex education tends to render intelligible and popularize only particular forms of sex.[53]) Indeed, the successful performance of sex in *The Antipodes* is, as I have noted, a communal effort; it requires the combined resources and diligent attention of family and neighbors, as well as the intervention of the medical and theatrical communities. If marital sexuality is figured by the end as a remedy for all that ails Martha and Peregrine, if procreative intercourse is therapeutically reinstalled as the only legitimate sexual practice, these nonetheless are revealed to be the result of a particular social production, a process of knowledge construction – one that draws its energy from seeking a friend's advice and, when that fails, submitting to the professional expertise of an early modern psychotherapist.

The play's intervention proceeds by a route more circuitous and more self-consciously metatheatrical than the shaming rituals that generally enforce early modern sexual and household discipline – the stocks, the cucking stool, the charivari. However, it is not as though the politics of shame are absent from the reception of Martha's reminiscence – either by the other characters or by literary critics. On the contrary. But rather than shame being directed primarily toward Martha's subjectivity, it is directed toward her inadequate grasp of tacit knowledge.[54] Having confounded, in the words of Mary Poovey, "what counts as acceptable knowledge about sex,"[55] Martha breaks, in the words of Michael Warner, her culture's "tacit rules about what can be acknowledged or said in public."[56] Those rules are not exactly ours, but they nonetheless work, as they do in the present, to privilege certain knowledges and to discredit, by means of condescension, pity, or shame, unofficial or dissident knowledges. As Warner remarks, "isolation and silence are among the most common conditions for the politics of sexual shame." Combating these conditions requires "the circulation and accessibility of sexual knowledge, along with the public elaboration of a social world."[57] Absent such circulation and such worlds, it is all too possible for the dominant culture to enforce a collective amnesia about the pervasiveness of erotic variation, routinely asking us, as Warner puts it, to "forget everything [we] know about sex."[58]

The belief that sexual pleasure is a source of knowledge motivates Warner's and others' exposé of the "geography of shame" and sexual paranoia that, through zoning laws and real estate transactions, has recently remapped the sexuality of New York city.[59] Their defenses of gay male cruising, of the importance and creativity of public spaces of and for sex, are part of a defense of the unpredictable exchanges that can take place – simultaneously public and intimate – in what Warner calls the "world-making project of queer life."[60] I want to draw out of Warner's defense of a queer ethos of public sex the importance of sexual pedagogy to such world-making projects:

> The naive belief that sex is simply an inborn instinct still exerts its power, but most gay men and lesbians know that the sex they have was not innate nor entirely of their own making, but *learned* – learned by participating, in scenes of talk as well as of fucking. One learns both the elaborated codes of a subculture, with its rituals and typologies ... but also simply the improvisational nature of unpredicated situations. As queers we do not always share the same tastes or practices, though often enough we learn new pleasures from others. What we do share is an ability to swap stories and learn from them, to enter new scenes not entirely of our own making, to know that in

these contexts it is taken for granted that people are different, that one can surprise oneself, that one's task in the face of unpredicted variations is to recognize the dignity in each person's way of surviving and playing and creating.[61]

Although there is a tendency here to idealize the nurturing aspects of queer culture, I agree that, because we bring to sexual activity a shared disqualification from the norm, a broadly empathic ethos of generosity tends to inform queer sex. Whatever ideological divisions and tensions around race, class, and gender fracture our political alliances and propel us to blame and shame one another, sexual variation tends to enjoy a policy of non-policing. In the erotic realm, at least, queers are apt to recognize as an axiom (and not merely a theoretical one) that, as Eve Kosofsky Sedgwick memorably put it, "People are different from each other."[62]

The ethics of queer sexual culture are derived in part from the ways that knowledge and disclosure are used by and against queers. What Martha Joyless's position vis-à-vis erotic knowledge shares with the epistemology of the closet is the extent to which that intersubjective space is constructed "by dominant assumptions about what goes without saying, what can be said without a breach of decorum, who shares the onus of disclosure, and who will bear the consequences of speech and silence."[63] Making sex public, insisting on the publicity of sex through a reasoned defense of the right to a public sexual culture, moves the consideration of sex beyond a matter of private appeals (for instance, Martha's request of Barbara) or sexual therapy (such as that deceptively enforced upon Peregrine). This movement beyond the private and the therapeutic challenges the presumptive onus of disclosure, and refigures public discourses of sex – both doing it and talking about it – as a question of sexual pedagogy.[64]

Eroticism isn't just something that people do (or, in the case of Peregrine, refuse to do); it is something that people learn; it requires initiation, experimentation, education – in Martha's words, practice. Erotic encounters, including discursive encounters about sex, teach particular skills, some of which have cultural capital (the simultaneous orgasm recommended in early modern prescriptive literature, for example); others of which do not (the clipping and kissing of women). Yet, the history of sexuality over the longue dureé suggests that under certain conditions, the information made available by doing, making, and talking about sex can translate into nascent forms of counter-knowledge, capable of dissident effects and future, and as yet unknown, possibilities.

How knowledge of and about sex becomes sexual dissidence,[65] how one might identify the precise mechanisms by which this occurs, are questions to which I don't, at this point, have an answer – although I believe any such answer will derive from the practices and insights of specific collectivities. What I do know is that we need to conceptualize erotic pedagogy more expansively and flexibly, and, even in the face of recurring sex panics, with less paranoia about the potential overlap of sex and words. Such self-protection is an understandable reaction to our current cultural situation: resurgent homophobia; moralistic redeployments of feminist critiques of sexual harassment, incest, and child molestation; and the sacrifice of sexual justice for political self-interest. Yet, we concede the terms of public discourse about sex at our peril. The contemporary US is a sex-obsessed yet sex-negative culture, one that is simultaneously seduced by sexual scandal and enamored of punitive measures that make people pay, sometimes tragically, for their sexual desires. It is a culture in which adolescents enjoy unprecedented access to sexual imagery, both hetero and homosexual, in the media, yet increasingly are denied basic information about sex itself. It is a culture in which the Surgeon General can be fired for suggesting that discussion of masturbation might be included in publicly-funded sex education. It is a culture in which sexual responsibility increasingly is defined as sexual abstinence before marriage, and where abstinence is the primary public health strategy for combating sexually transmitted diseases and unwanted pregnancy. Not surprisingly, it is a culture in which the transmission of HIV continues unabated, and the correlation between teen pregnancy and poverty high. Conservatives have been extraordinarily effective in using sex education as a forum in which to push their social agenda; they have succeeded in part by deploying a rhetoric that renders talk about sex, especially sexual speech, as sexual abuse.[66]

As the Right Wing equation of sexual language with sexual immorality makes clear, there are dangers to forging an intimate analytic connection between sex acts and sex talk.[67] Collapsing sexual speech with sexual behavior is, I believe, a category error, one which elides important differences between the incitement to discourse and the incitement of bodies.[68] The problems that can arise when talk about sex is interpreted as sexual behavior were vividly put in relief, for example, when Jane Gallop was accused of sexually harassing a female graduate student. Gallop's defense against the charge of sexual harassment hinged first, on a denial of having committed unwanted sexual acts; second, on a critique of sexual harassment policies that conflate sex ("harassment on the basis of sex") with sex ("sexual advances"), thereby confusing sexism with sexuality;[69] and third, on her contention that the "unprofessional, personal behavior that ran afoul of sexual harassment policy was in fact my application of feminist pedagogical methods."[70] Arguing that "[b]reaking down the barrier between the professional and the personal has been central in the feminist effort to expand the institution of knowledge to include what and how women know,"[71] Gallop maintains that it is in the overlapping zone of talk and sex, pedagogy and eroticism, that knowledge production is, for her, most "productive."[72] Whatever our own preferred bodily boundaries as learners and teachers, as well as our collective interest in preventing those abuses of power that can occur by means of sex, it is crucial to acknowledge how wide and hazy the overlap of sex and talk can be, and how much disservice we do to both eroticism and knowledge when we too quickly collude with the institutional policing of their strict separation. In the present social milieu, such policing not only provides an easy vehicle for political gain, but is often motivated more by fear of litigation than concerns about the abuse of power.[73] Rather than capitulate to these forces, then, we need to respond by refining our understandings of the relations between sexual speech and sexual pedagogy; analyze the different forums in which viewing sex and reading and talking about it might operate ethically; and publicly affirm our pedagogy as ethically motivated social action.

Several commitments impel my advocacy of a capaciously conceived sex education as a rich epistemological resource in the present and on behalf of the past.[74] In the tradition of Foucault and Sedgwick, I want to supplement the usual understanding of sex as power with an understanding of sex as a knowledge relation. This does not involve advocating a classroom pedagogy of personal confession or the development of a queer *ars erotica*. Nor am I attempting to add yet another chapter to the *scientia sexualis* through the further proliferation and visibility of modern erotic taxonomies.[75] Rather than use sex to produce the truth of the subject, I want to understand better the processes by which sex and sex talk function as forms of knowledge relations – by which I mean not only knowledge of or about sex, but knowledge through and by means of sex. Knowledge so conceived is less a set of sexual *contents* – for instance, greater historical knowledge about acts and identities, bodily positions and erotic rituals – than an intellectual disposition, a way of approaching sexual variation through the complex mediations of history.[76]

For instance, in posing the question of marital sexuality in the terms provided by Martha's seduction at the hands of a woman, *The*

Antipodes confronts us with the inadequacy of a dominant tenet of the history of sexuality which would position queer sexuality always in opposition to histories of the family and reproduction. I hope to have shown that this analytic is out of touch with the situation depicted in Brome's play – and, I would argue, with many aspects of early modern culture. Without subsuming the homo under the hetero or so extending the boundaries of the queer that it is emptied of all specificity, we need to ask more of queer studies than that it provide access to homoerotic subjects or enable the queering of heterosexuality. As queer theory has long maintained, a more capacious and flexible analytic would provide modes of understanding that exceed the current hegemonic discourse on erotic identity, pushing beyond the concerns of any identity-based constituency (L, G, B, or T). At the same time, it would maintain a political commitment to those constituencies – something too easily forgotten in the current academic drive to queer *everything*. In order to apprehend sexuality as a form of knowledge production, as an agent in the construction of knowledge, we need to analyze homoeroticism and heterosexuality, not just as theoretically imbricated and historically constitutive of one another,[77] not just as contingent and unstable, but as posing similar and interrelated epistemological and pedagogical problems. These problems, I hope to have shown, require the development of new analytical strategies.

In transiting from a feminist reading of Martha Joyless to contemporary discourses of public sex, I have implied, however obliquely, that a cultural phenomenon indicatively, if not exclusively, inflected as male might be useful for articulating the possibilities and stakes of female sexual knowledge and agency. Building on Sedgwick's Axiom 7 – "The paths of allo-identification are likely to be strange and recalcitrant"[78] – I have followed the contours of one such curving path.[79] The conjunction of public sexual knowledge – that which women, historically, have been denied – and the culture of public sex – which gay men, in particular, now seek to defend – may seem perverse. To read both of these through a feminist resistance to the misuse of sexual harassment discourses as they police sexual pedagogy may seem even more so. But it is only through such perverse affiliations across sex, gender, sexuality, and history that I have been able to explore how the production of sexual knowledge relies so heavily on an under-theorized process of making sex public – on a publicity, in other words, that is also a pedagogy.

What draws me on in forging these conjunctions is the historical elusiveness and epistemological opacity of sex. Despite the common assumption that we all know what sex is, I want to conclude by suggesting that there is much about sex that we *don't know*: of what acts sex consists, what pleasures it affords, what difficulties it encounters, and what inventiveness it engenders.[80] It just may be that Martha's cluelessness – reconceptualized as a precocious if unwitting eccentricity, an under-theorized resistance to tacit knowledge, a persistent curiosity about the yet-to-be-known – offers us clues about the disposition which we might adopt in order to more attentively interpret earlier – and current – sexual regimes.[81]

In appropriating Martha Joyless to raise questions about the conditions of knowledge production, in bringing the homo and the hetero, the cruising gay man and the unhappily married woman, into closer analytical contact, I have traversed diverse sites of sexual pedagogy: the early modern stage, the public spaces of gay intimacy, the contemporary classroom. I have done so in order to map an alternate route for bridging the historical divide separating the queer past from the queer present. In framing the historiographic issue as one of epistemology and pedagogy rather than identity, of knowledge and ignorance rather than transgression, of *how* we know as much as *what* we know, I have tried to gesture toward an ethics, and not merely a history, of sexuality. This is less because I feel confident about how to practice such an ethics than because Martha Joyless's dogged attempt to transform her joyless state has had an effect on me that can only be called pedagogical. Her naïve quest for knowledge – enacted through the exposure of ignorance, pursued in the name of joy, and revealing a life cross-cut by strange circuits of desire – invites us to consider what it might mean to develop an ethics, a pedagogy, adequate to the complexity of sex in history, as well as in contemporary culture.

Notes

I thank Michael Schoenfeldt, Patsy Yaeger, and Valerie Wayne for their thoughtful responses to an early draft of this essay. Members of audiences who have heard various formulations of this essay have been particularly helpful: David Halperin, Annamarie Jagose, Michael Warner, Anna Clark, Jean Howard, Mary Bly, Wendy Wall, Jeff Masten, Peter Stallybrass, Ania Loomba, Suvir Kaul, Joan DeJean, Barbara Bono, Jim Swan, Jim Holstun, Andy Stott, Chris Nagle, and Will Fisher all asked probing and productive questions. I am particularly grateful to Julie Crawford for her observation of an early draft that, in many ways, my argument thematizes my own pedagogical career. I also thank Laura Ambrose and Marjorie Rubright for their valuable research assistance.

1. Michael Warner, *The Trouble With Normal: Sex, Politics, and the Ethics of Queer Life* (Cambridge, MA: Harvard University Press, 1999), 192–3.
2. Jane Gallop, *Feminist Accused of Sexual Harassment* (Durham: Duke University Press, 1997), 100.
3. Robert Burton, *The Anatomy of Melancholy*, trans. F. D. Kessinger and P. J. S. Kessinger (Kila, MT: Kessinger: 1991). See also Jacques Ferrand, *De la maladie d'amour, ou mélancholie érotique* (*The Disease of Love, or Erotic Melancholy*) (1610/1623), trans. as *A Treatise on Lovesickness*, ed. Donald A. Beecher and Massimo Ciavolella (Syracuse NY; Syracuse University Press, 1990). Drawing heavily from André Du Laurens, *A Discourse of the Preservation of Sight: Of Melancholike Diseases* (1597), Ferrand's treatise was not translated into English until 1640; however, Du Laurens was translated into English in 1599 and Burton cites Ferrand in the 1632 edition of his *Anatomy of Melancholy*.
4. There are three modern editions: *The Antipodes*, ed. David Scott Kastan and Richard Proudfoot (London: Globe Education, Nick Hern Books, 2000); *The Antipodes*, ed. Ann Haaker (Lincoln: University of Nebraska Press, 1966); and *Three Renaissance Travel Plays*, ed. Anthony Parr (Manchester and New York: Manchester University Press, 1995). All citations are taken from the latter.
5. The only critic to discuss this passage, Claire Jowitt, *Voyage Drama and Gender Politics, 1589–1642: Real and Imagined Worlds* (Manchester and New York: Manchester University Press, 2003), emphasizes the patriarchal framing of this encounter: "The woman-to-woman sexual relationship described here is obviously not a celebration of same-sex desire, rather it is predicated on the need of a(n absent) man to father children and thus fulfil women's biological and social roles. Desire flickers here between Martha and the 'wanton maid' because of the absence of any available man" (218). This rather skewed causality – we have no indication that the encounter with the wanton maid occurred because of *anything*, much less the absence of a man – is replicated in Jowitt's assertion that Peregrine's disease is "a consequence rather than a cause of the moral malaise described in the text. The contagion, represented in Martha's case as same-sex desire, was already fully present prior to Peregrine's reading of travel accounts" (219). Linking this "contagion" to the supposed sexual eccentricities of Letoy and ultimately, Caroline London, Jowitt seeks to demonstrate the "pointlessness" of "the whole text" (222).
6. In *A Dictionary of Sexual Language and Imagery in Shakespearean and Stuart Literature* 3 vols. (London and Atlantic Highlands, NJ: Athlone, 1994), Gordon Williams defines "clip" as "sexual embrace," citing several examples from 1510 to 1676 (251). In *A Glossary of Shakespeare's Sexual Language* (London and Atlantic Highlands: Athlone, 1997), Williams defines "clip" as "embrace closely," citing *Coriolanus* and *Venus and Adonis* (71). In both works, he defines "clap" only in its noun form as a "sexual mishap," referring to gonorrhea or pregnancy (*Dictionary*, 246; *Glossary*, 70). In contemporary Irish, clap is defined as slap.
7. See my brief discussion of a textual/sexual crux in this play; Valerie Traub, *The Renaissance of Lesbianism in Early Modern England* (Cambridge: Cambridge University Press, 2002), 60–2.

8. As Barbara Johnson has remarked, ignorance should never be taken for granted. See Johnson, *A World of Difference* (Baltimore: Johns Hopkins University Press, 1987), 16.

9. Miranda Chaytor, "Husband(ry): Narratives of Rape in the Seventeenth Century," *Gender & History* 7.3 (1995): 378–407, exposes a peculiar double bind. In the context of rape accusations, women's "innocence was not a matter of behaviour but a condition of being; and a condition of being defined by absence – of sexual knowledge, intentions, desires. As such it was a difficult virtue for women themselves to invoke, for how could they lay claim to their innocence without laying claim to the knowledge which wasn't supposed to be there?" (399).

10. For a helpful overview of the debate, see Carla Freccero and Louise Fradenberg, *Premodern Sexualities* (London and New York: Routledge, 1996).

11. D. A. Miller, *The Novel and the Police* (Berkeley and Los Angeles: University of California Press, 1988); Eve Kosofsky Sedgwick, *Epistemology of the Closet* (Berkeley and Los Angeles: University of California Press, 1990).

12. Nor does Martha's story accord with recent accounts of the history of scientific knowledge and the role of secrets, particularly the "secrets of women," in medieval and early modern science and medicine. See William Eamon, *Science and the Secrets of Nature* (Princeton: Princeton University Press, 1994); Karma Lochrie, *Covert Operations: The Medieval Uses of Secrecy* (Ithaca: Cornell University Press, 1999); Monica Greene, "From 'Diseases of Women' to 'Secrets of Women': The Transformation of Gynecological Literature in the Later Middle Ages," *Journal of Medieval and Early Modern Studies* 30 (2000): 5–39; Katharine Park, *Secrets of Women: Gender, Generation, and the Origins of Human Dissection* (New York: Zone, 2006).

13. Among many other meanings, the *OED* defines "wanton" as "1) undisciplined, ungoverned; 2) lascivious, unchaste, lewd. Also, in a milder sense, given to amorous dalliance; 3) sportive, unrestrained in merriment; 6) capricious, frivolous, giddy; 8) unrestrained, extravagant." The many relevant meanings of "strange" include "1) foreign, alien; 7) unknown, unfamiliar; not known, met with, or experienced before. 8) Of a kind that is unfamiliar or rare; unusual, uncommon, exceptional, singular, out of the way; 9) extreme; 10) unfamiliar, abnormal, or exceptional to a degree that excites wonder or astonishment; difficult to take in or account for; queer, surprising, unaccountable; 12) unpracticed or unskilled at." That strangeness is a function of both knowledge and skill seems particularly relevant.

14. One might compare this to Alan Bray's reading of the sexual dreams and fantasies expressed in the diary of Michael Wigglesworth, which he uses to argue against the contemporary scholar's imposition of a modern concept of desire; such an internal, generative mechanism or drive is, according to Bray, alien to the psychic, emotional, and ideological landscape of early modern culture. See Bray, "The Curious Case of Michael Wigglesworth," in *A Queer World: The Center for Lesbian and Gay Studies Reader*, ed. Martin Duberman (New York and London: New York University Press, 1997), 205–15.

15. Laurie Shannon, "Queerly Philological Reading," for "Lesbianism in the Renaissance" seminar, Shakespeare Association of America, Minneapolis, 2001, and *Sovereign Amity: Figures of Friendship in Shakespearean Contexts* (Chicago: University of Chicago Press, 2002); Alan Bray, *Homosexuality in*

Renaissance England (London: Gay Men's Press, 1982); rpt. with a new After-word (New York: Columbia University Press, 1995); Alan Bray, *The Friend* (Chicago: Chicago University Press, 2003).

16. According to Carol Thomas Neely, "Lovesickness, Gender, and Subjectivity: *Twelfth Night* and *As You Like It*," in *A Feminist Companion to Shakespeare*, ed. Dympna Callaghan (Oxford: Blackwell, 2000), 276–98, the therapeutic dis-course of love melancholy was surprisingly ecumenical about the diversity of sexual practices: "In the discourse of lovesickness, gender is less polarized and sexuality less normalized than in many other early modern texts. Because the discourse is concerned primarily with the satisfaction of desires, only sec-ondarily with marriage, and not at all with reproduction, it includes without sharp distinction a wide and weird range of gender behaviors, erotic objects, and amorous styles" (279).

17. A similar malady afflicts the Jailor's Daughter in Shakespeare and Fletcher's *The Two Noble Kinsmen*, and in it, as well, female–female eroticism arises as a possibility in the context of thematizing female *hetero*sexual illness.

18. Virgin's melancholy, greensickness, womb hysteria, suffocation of the womb, and chlorosis were closely related diagnoses, all stemming from an imbalance of humors caused by a lack of the proper expulsion of seed. Womb fury, writes Ferrand, is "a raging or madness that comes from an excessive burning desire in the womb, or from a hot intemperature communicated to the brain and to the rest of the body through the channels in the spine, or from the biting vapors arising from the corrupted seed lying stagnant around the uterus" (*A Treatise on Lovesickness*, 263).

19. See Traub, *The Renaissance of Lesbianism*, 84.

20. Martha's request would enjoy what limited indemnity it possessed only so long as the Galenic medical model governed the intelligibility of bodies. By the mid-eighteenth century, any such request would face a more pro-nounced knowingness and, presumably, a more forcible resistance to the breach of bourgeois decorum and propriety. For the growing concern about propriety in sexual matters by the late seventeenth century, see Harriette Andreadis, *Sappho in Early Modern England: Female Same-Sex Literary Erotics 1550–1714* (Chicago: University of Chicago Press, 2001); Elizabeth Susan Wahl, *Invisible Relations: Representations of Female Intimacy in the Age of Enlightenment* (Stanford: Stanford University Press, 1999).

21. *The Travels of Sir John Mandeville* was reprinted five times between 1612 and 1639; although viewed as fraudulent by many, it continued to be appreci-ated as an entertaining mixture of fantasy and fact. See Julie Sanders, "The Politics of Escapism: Fantasies of Travel and Power in Richard Brome's *The Antipodes* and Ben Jonson's *The Alchemist*," in *Writing and Fantasy*, ed. Ceri Sullivan and Barbara White (London: Longman, 1999), 137–50.

22. There is much that could be said about the relations among travel, sex, and sexual dysfunction in Brome's play, including that both travel and sex function homeopathically – they are both problem and cure.

23. On the politics of inversion in this play, see Marina Leslie, "Antipodal Anxieties: Joseph Hall, Richard Brome, Margaret Cavendish and the Carto-graphies of Gender," *Genre* 30 (1997): 51–78.

24. The play seems devoid of anxiety about cross-cultural sex, and takes as a given that Peregrine would desire to wed the Antipodean queen.

25. Katherine Eisaman Maus argues that Renaissance playwrights "inevitably encounter a gap between their limited theatrical resources and the extravagant situations they dramatize. English Renaissance theatrical method is thus radically synecdochic, endlessly referring the spectators to events, objects, situations, landscapes that cannot be shown them. We are provided ... not with an actual sexual act but with the preliminaries or consequences of a sexual relationship ... . [T]he English Renaissance stage seems deliberately to foster theatergoers' capacity to use partial and limited presentations as a basis for conjecture about what is undisplayed or undisplayable." See Maus, *Inwardness and Theater in the English Renaissance* (Chicago: University of Chicago Press, 1995), 32.

26. In one sense, Martha's narration of her homoerotic encounter makes it more visible than the off-stage heterosexual consummation; in another sense, the lack of dramatization of the Joyless's sexual encounter leaves room for the reader's/spectator's possible fantasy of unconventional sex.

27. This feigned seduction is, not incidentally, another instance of pedagogy.

28. R. J. Kaufmann, *Richard Brome, Caroline Playwright* (Columbia University Press, 1961).

29. See, in addition to the introductions to the editions of the play, Martin Butler, *Theater and Crisis, 1632–64* (Cambridge: Cambridge University Press, 1984); Ira Clark, *Professional Playwrights: Massinger, Ford, Shirley, and Brome* (Lexington: University of Kentucky Press, 1992); Jackson I. Cope, "Richard Brome: The World as Antipodes," in *The Theater and the Drama: From Metaphor to Form in Renaissance Drama* (Baltimore: Johns Hopkins University Press, 1973); Ian Donaldson, "'Living Backward': The Antipodes," in *The World Turned Upside-Down: Comedy from Jonson to Fielding* (Oxford: Clarendon Press, 1970).

30. In particular, the notion of the public sphere as a realm of rational sociability separate from both the private realm and the sphere of public authority was just beginning to emerge in the 1640s, and gained ground after the Revolution. Nuancing, from a historical perspective, Jürgen Habermas's influential *The Structural Transformation of the Public Sphere: An Inquiry into a Category of Bourgeois Society* (trans. Thomas Burger and Frederick Lawrence [Cambridge MA: MIT Press, 1989]) are Sharon Achinstein, *Milton and the Revolutionary Reader* (Princeton: Princeton University Press, 1994); David Norbrook, *Writing the English Republic* (Cambridge: Cambridge University Press, 1999); Steve Pincus, "'Coffee Politicians Does Create': Coffeehouses and Restoration Political Culture," *Journal of Modern History* 67.4 (1995): 807–34.

31. See, for instance, Tim Hitchcock, *English Sexualities, 1700–1800* (New York: St. Martin's Press, 1997); Margaret Hunt, "The Sapphic Strain: English Lesbians in the Long Eighteenth Century," in *Singlewomen in the European Past, 1250–1800*, ed., Judith M. Bennett and Amy M. Froide (Philadelphia: University of Pennsylvania Press, 1999), 270–96.

32. David Cressy, *Birth, Marriage and Death: Ritual, Religion, and the Life-Cycle in Tudor and Stuart England* (Oxford: Oxford University Press, 1997), 350–76.

33. Cressy, *Birth, Marriage, and Death*, 374. Lack of consummation was one of the few grounds available for annulment of a marriage.

34. Two exceptions are Sara Mendelson and Patricia Crawford, *Women in Early Modern England, 1550–1720* (Oxford: Clarendon Press, 1998); and Patricia Crawford and Laura Gowing, *Women's Worlds in Seventeenth-Century England:*

A Sourcebook (New York and London: Routledge, 2000). These not only provide source materials for a richly diversified history of women, but reconcept-
ualize, in both the categories of the *Sourcebook* and in the analysis proffered
in the monograph, some of the primary terms by which women's lives are
defined. The categories in the *Sourcebook*'s chapter on "Sexual Experiences"
– "sex and single women; sex and marriage; sex between women; secrecy and
adultery; rape, assaults, and attempts" – usefully belie the life-cycle truism
as well as the licit/illicit binary. In addition to the monograph's chapter on
marriage, there is a chapter on relationships, which includes the wonderfully
ecumenical list, "neighbors, families, friends and lovers, animals and spirits."

35. Cressy, *Birth, Marriage and Death*; John Gillis, *For Better, For Worse: British
Marriages, 1600 to the Present* (Oxford: Oxford University Press, 1985); Anthony
Fletcher, *Gender, Sex, and Subordination in England, 1500–1800* (New Haven and
London: Yale University Press, 1995). Among these, Cressy is most able to
resist the subordination of sexual pleasure to the reproductive life cycle;
nonetheless, insofar as his study is structured by public ritual, it cannot resist
very far.

36. "Pre-marital" sex is an interesting case of the difficulty of construing "transgression," insofar as was often a customary phase of wooing and wedding;
according to Cressy, *Birth, Marriage, and Death*, some 20 percent of marriages were bridal pregnancies.

37. In this, my argument has something in common with Anna Clark, "Twilight
Moments," *Journal of the History of Sexuality* 14.1–2 (2005): 139–52.

38. Michel Foucault, *The History of Sexuality, Vol 1: An Introduction*, trans. Robert
Hurley (New York: Random House, 1978), 57. Recent scholarship suggests
the extent to which the Western/non-Western divide in Foucault is over-
drawn, particularly for cultures such as India and the Middle East, which
had their own highly elaborated sexual taxonomies. For a consideration of
the adequacy of Foucault's conceptualization of the *ars erotica*, see Valerie
Traub, "'The Past is a Foreign Country?': The Times and Spaces of Islamicate
Sexuality Studies," in *Islamicate Sexualities*, ed. Kathryn Babayan and Asfaneh
Najmabadi (Cambridge MA: Harvard University Press, 2008).

39. For the sexual advice embedded in medical texts, as well as a discussion of
English obscene texts in relation to female homoeroticism, see Traub, *The
Renaissance of Lesbianism*, 77–124.

40. See James Grantham Turner, *Schooling Sex: Libertine Literature and Erotic Education in Italy, France, and England, 1534–1685* (Oxford: Oxford University
Press, 2003), who analyzes the "educational fantasy in sexual writing" (10). On
the origins of obscenity, see David Foxon, *Libertine Literature in England,
1660–1745* (New Hyde Park, NY: University Books, 1965); Lynn Hunt, ed., *The
Invention of Pornography: Obscenity and the Origins of Modernity, 1500–1800*
(New York: Zone Books, 1993); Bette Talvacchia, *Taking Positions: On the Erotic
in Renaissance Culture* (Princeton NJ: Princeton University Press, 1999); Ian
Frederick Moulton, *Before Pornography: Erotic Writing in Early Modern England*
(Oxford: Oxford University Press, 2000).

41. Although she does not much discuss this model of initiation, Joan DeJean,
in *The Reinvention of Obscenity: Sex, Lies, and Tabloids in Early Modern France*
(Chicago and London: University of Chicago Press, 2002), provides a detailed
analysis of the French context.

42. Laura Gowing, *Common Bodies: Women, Touch and Power in Seventeenth-Century England* (New Haven and London: Yale University Press, 2003), 84. Like Gowing, Patricia Crawford argues that there existed separate male and female domains of sexual knowledge, constituted partially by different levels of literacy, as well as by the unofficial knowledge that circulated within female culture; "Sexual Knowledge in England, 1500–1750," in *Sexual Knowledge, Sexual Science: The History of Attitudes to Sexuality*, ed. Roy Porter and Mikulás Teich (Cambridge: Cambridge University Press, 1994), 82–106.
43. Gowing, *Common Bodies*, 70.
44. Stephen Orgel, "On Dildos and Fadings," *ANQ: A Quarterly Journal of Short Articles, Notes, and Reviews* 5.2–3 (1992): 106–11 contests the assumption that there was a large Elizabethan broadsheet literature featuring overt obscenity. He is no doubt correct. Nonetheless, far more work needs to be done on specific genres (ballads, broadsides, libels, jestbooks, commonplace books, medical texts, manuscript verse) in order to periodize the circulation of sexual knowledge confidently.
45. Gowing, *Common Bodies*, 84. See also Hitchcock, *English Sexualities*.
46. The extent to which sexual expression operates euphemistically during this period is made clear by Gowing's reading of women's testimonies about illicit sex and Garthine Walker's reading of rape testimonies in "Reading Rape and Sexual Violence in Early Modern England," *Gender and History* 10.1 (1998): 1–25.
47. Roy Porter, "The Literature of Sexual Advice before 1800," in Porter and Teich (eds.), *Sexual Knowledge, Sexual Science*, 134–57.
48. See, for instance, Jonathan Goldberg, "Margaret Cavendish, Scribe," *GLQ: A Journal of Lesbian and Gay Studies* 10.3 (2004): 433–52; Madhavi Menon, "Spurning Teleology in *Venus and Adonis*," *GLQ: A Journal of Lesbian and Gay Studies* 11.4 (2005): 491–519; Jonathan Goldberg and Madhavi Menon, "Queering History," *PMLA* 120.5 (October 2005): 1608–17; Karma Lochrie, *Heterosyncrasies: Female Sexuality When Normal Wasn't* (Minneapolis and London: University of Minnesota Press, 2005); Carla Freccero, *Queer/Early/Modern* (Durham and London: Duke University Press, 2006).
49. In addition to Bray's *Homosexuality in Renaissance England* and *The Friend*, see Jeffrey Masten, *Textual Intercourse: Collaboration, Authorship, and Sexualities in Renaissance Drama* (Cambridge: Cambridge University Press, 1997); Mario DiGangi, *The Homoerotics of Early Modern Drama* (Cambridge: Cambridge University Press, 1997); Julie Crawford, "The Homoerotics of Shakespeare's Elizabethan Comedies," in *A Companion to Shakespeare's Works, Vol 3: The Comedies*, ed., Richard Dutton and Jean Howard (Malden MA: Blackwell, 2003), 137–58.
50. Relational readings of homoeroticism run certain risks, one of which is conveniently represented by David Levine's blurb on the back cover of *Sexualities in History: A Reader*, ed. Kim M. Phillips and Barry Reay (London and New York: Routledge, 2002), which observes that, "sexual behaviors and mentalities are embedded in systems of power," but precedes this recognition with the claim: "Sex is, perhaps, the *least* interesting aspect of the history of sexuality" (emphasis mine). I don't mean to impugn the worth of this volume, which reprints some excellent essays from the 1990s; I do want to suggest that, in positioning sexuality as a relational system, scholars may find their work used to protect the study of sexuality from sex.

51. See, for example, Goldberg's description of Bray's "sense of the ways in which male–male intimacies *were furthered by* the power structures that organized households, schools, and patronage networks" (emphasis mine). See the Introduction to Jonathan Goldberg, ed., *Queering the Renaissance* (Durham: Duke University Press, 1994), 5. There are good reasons for so conceiving sexuality, including the need to define an object of inquiry and to bring it into conceptual focus by provisionally isolating its parameters and claiming for it a relatively independent social status.

52. To my knowledge, only one study has raised, as an explicit question, whether homoeroticism might have played a constitutive role, performing as an effective agent, in larger social relations, and it is focused on the eighteenth century: Susan Lanser, *The Sexuality of History: Sapphic Subjects and the Making of Modernity* (forthcoming).

53. See Janice M. Irvine, *Talk About Sex: The Battles over Sex Education in the United States* (Berkeley, Los Angeles, and London: University of California Press, 2002); Judith Levine, *Harmful to Minors: The Perils of Protecting Children from Sex* (Minneapolis: University of Minnesota Press, 2002).

54. Jowitt remarks, for example, that the "sex-starved and still virgin" Martha "meanders through scenes making embarrassing, misdirected sexual remarks as she tries to discover the secrets of married love," *Voyage Drama and Gender Politics*, 218.

55. Mary Poovey, "International Prohibition Against Sex in America," in *Intimacy*, ed. Lauren Berlant (Chicago: University of Chicago Press, 2000), 381.

56. Warner, *The Trouble With Normal*, 182.

57. Ibid., 171.

58. Ibid., 184.

59. Ibid., 192; Samuel R. Delany, *Times Square Red, Times Square Blue* (New York: New York University Press, 1999).

60. Warner, *The Trouble With Normal*, 139. See also Lee Edelman, "Tearooms and Sympathy or, The Epistemology of the Water Closet," *Homographesis: Essays in Gay Literary and Cultural Theory* (New York and London: Routledge, 1994), 148–70; Christopher Castiglia, "Sex Panics, Sex Publics, Sex Memories," *boundary 2* 27: 2 (2000): 149–75; and the essays in *Policing Public Sex: Queer Politics and the Future of AIDS Activism*, ed. Dangerous Bedfellows (Boston: South End Press, 1996).

61. Warner, *The Trouble With Normal*, 178. It could be argued that Warner collapses the mode of erotic production (sex acts) with their mode of circulation (teaching, ethics); however, that slippage is precisely what is provocative in his account. See also Philip Brian Harper, *Private Affairs: Critical Ventures in the Culture of Social Relations* (New York and London: New York University Press, 1999). Harper attempts to disrupt the clear conceptual boundaries between public and private that legislate sexual life by focusing on the conditions of visibility and modes of negotiation apparent in spaces of sexual encounter.

62. This is the first of Sedgwick's Axioms in *Epistemology of the Closet*, 22.

63. Warner, *The Trouble With Normal*, 180.

64. In the words of Michael Warner, "A public sexual culture changes the nature of sex, much as a public intellectual culture changes the nature of thought" (*The Trouble With Normal*, 178). See also Warner's reflections on

the meanings of public sex in "Queer World Making: Annamarie Jagose Interviews Michael Warner," *Genders* 31 (2000), n.p.

65. The term is from Jonathan Dollimore, *Sexual Dissidence: Augustine to Wilde, Freud to Foucault* (Oxford: Clarendon Press, 1991).

66. See Irvine, *Talk about Sex*, and Levine, *Harmful to Minors*.

67. See, for instance, Candace Vogler, "Sex and Talk," in Berlant (ed.), *Intimacy*, 48–85, who counters the pop-psych and philosophical equation of sex and conversation by linking sex and sex talk "non-expressively."

68. I would disagree with James Kincaid, for instance, when he says of the Clinton/Lewinsky affair: "Sex exists where we can find ways to talk about having sex. Where we can't do that, there is no sex." If this were true, there would have been no *ars erotica*, its independence from discourse precisely Foucault's point. See Kincaid, "It's Not About Sex," in *Our Monica, Ourselves: The Clinton Affair and the National Interest*, ed. Lauren Berlant and Lisa Duggan (New York: New York University Press, 2001), 73–85, citation 73.

69. Jane Gallop, *Anecdotal Theory* (Durham and London: Duke University Press, 2003), 44–7.

70. Ibid., 55.

71. Ibid., 55.

72. Ibid., 54. "Consensual amorous relations are included in my university's sexual harassment policy. Thus, although I had sexually harassed no one, I was nominally in violation of sexual harassment policy. The 'consensual amorous relation' in question was neither a sexual relation nor even a romantic, dating one; it was a teaching relation where both parties were interested in writing and talking about the erotic dynamics underpinning the student–teacher relation" (53). It is out of concern that "an entire stretch of experience [feminist academics' sexual relations with their teachers] was being denied, consigned to silence" that Gallop crosses a "discursive line in order to bring into theoretical discourse what is whispered in the social spaces of institutional life" (163). For a similar critique of policies that bar consensual sexual relations between students and faculty, see Afshan Jafar, "Consent or Coercion? Sexual Relationships Between College Faculty and Students," *Gender Issues* 21.1 (Winter 2003): 43–58.

73. On the complex erotics of queer pedagogy, see David Halperin, "Deviant Teaching," *Michigan Feminist Studies* 16 (2002): 1–29; Ellis Hanson, "Teaching Shame," in *Gay Shame*, ed. David Halperin and Valerie Traub (Chicago: Chicago University Press, 2008); Catherine Lord, "Minor Eruptions: Lesbian Accused of Promoting Pedophilia," *Radical Teacher* 66 (2003): 22–7.

74. My use of "epistemology," influenced by the field of feminist epistemology, is meant to invoke a general inquiry into the means of knowledge, rather than the traditional philosophical assumption of mental contents that align referentially with the world.

75. As Lee Edelman and Annamarie Jagose have argued, so embedded is the figure of "the homosexual" in symbolic systems of illegibility, that simply taking recourse in visibility will not solve the problem of homosexual representation. See Edelman, *Homographesis*; Annamarie Jagose, *Inconsequence: Lesbian Representation and the Logic of Sequence* (Ithaca: NY: Cornell University Press, 2002).

76. I also am not advocating a positivist mode of inquiry, in which data about embodied sex acts might be used to ground or secure our knowledge, and

whose accuracy in representing sexual practices (past or present) would be directed toward satisfying our hunger for enlightenment.

77. The dependence of the hetero on the homo has been given influential theoretical expression by Judith Butler, *Bodies That Matter: On the Discursive Limits of "Sex"* (London: Routledge, 1993). Recent historical studies that make an effort to demonstrate the historical mutual imbrication of the hetero and the homo include Mendelson and Crawford, *Women in Early Modern England*; Crawford and Gowing (eds.), *Women's Worlds in Seventeenth-Century England*; Hitchcock, *English Sexualities*; Randolph Trumbach, *Sex and the Gender Revolution, Vol. 1: Heterosexuality and the Third Gender in Enlightenment London* (Chicago: University of Chicago Press, 1998).

78. Sedgwick, *Epistemology of the Closet*, 59.

79. Many queer scholars have relied on Sedgwick's work to authorize a separation of sexuality from gender studies, and increasingly, to enact a skepticism regarding the applicability of feminist to gay male studies and vice versa. See, for instance, Richard Rambuss's review of Cynthia Herrup's *"A House in Gross Disorder": Sex, Law, and the 2nd Earl of Castlehaven*, in *Shakespeare Studies* 30: 274–81. I believe, to the contrary, that recognizing the potential utility of cross-gender identification, not merely as a form of generosity but as an analytical method, might help us move beyond accusations of inattention and exclusion and toward more productive modes of engagement across gender. For a more detailed articulation of the ways in which cross-identification affects gay/lesbian/queer scholarship, see the Introduction to Halperin and Traub (eds.), *Gay Shame*.

80. See, for example, Karma Lochrie's advocacy of "a hermeneutic of epistemological uncertainty regarding contemporary heterosexuality," in *Heterosyncrasies*, xvii; Annamarie Jagose's argument that orgasm is neither an act nor an identity in "'Critical Extasy': Orgasm and Sensibility in *Memoirs of a Woman of Pleasure*," *Signs* 32:2 (2007): 459–82; Douglas Crimp's reminder that the gay community invented safe sex practices (memorably encapsulated in his assertion that "it is our promiscuity that will save us"), in "How to Have Promiscuity in an Epidemic," *Melancholia and Moralism: Essays on AIDS and Queer Politics* (Cambridge MA: MIT Press, 2002), 64; Laura Kipnis's theorization of adultery as resistance to the labor of monogamy, in *Against Love: A Polemic* (New York: Pantheon, 2004); and Samuel Delany's advocacy of institutions for public heterosexual sex controlled by women, in *Times Square Red*, 197.

81. See Sedgwick's meditation on the need to "pluralize and specify" ignorance: "If ignorance is not – as it evidently is not – a single Manichaean, aboriginal maw of darkness from which the heroics of human cognition can occasionally wrestle facts, insights, freedoms, progress, perhaps there exists instead a plethora of *ignorances*, and we may begin to ask questions about the labor, erotics, and economics of their human production and distribution. Insofar as ignorance is ignorance *of* a knowledge – a knowledge that may itself, it goes without saying, be seen as either true or false under some other regime of truth – these ignorances, far from beings pieces of the originary dark, are produced by and correspond to particular knowledges and circulate as part of particular regimes of truth" (*Epistemology of the Closet*, 8).

Part III
Intimate Matters

9
Bearded Ladies in Shakespeare

A. R. Braunmuller

Once upon a time in America, it was said that an intellectual was a person who could hear Rossini's *William Tell* overture and not think of the Lone Ranger. Many readers – intellectuals all – will, notwithstanding their status, associate my title with Phineas T. Barnum and one of his most celebrated performers, Annie Jones, the so-called Bearded Lady. Shakespeare, too, offers bearded ladies, bearded and unbearded men, and boys, bearded and unbearded.

Uncompromisingly single, it seems, Beatrice sternly discriminates among varieties of beards, (un)beardedness, and masculinity:

> He that hath a beard is more than a youth, and he that hath no beard is less than a man; and he that is more than a youth is not for me, and he that is less than a man, I am not for him.[1]

Comically certain and comically self-contradictorily, Beatrice speaks an early modern English orthodoxy and creates a heterosexual dead-end. A beard marks male maturity, no beard, no man; a "youth" has no beard; he who has a beard is no youth; "youth" and "beard" are therefore mutually exclusive. She wants – or claims she wants – what her beard-system of masculinity forbids. Her certainties become fruitfully misty when we consider Barnum's and Shakespeare's bearded and unbearded ladies, men, and (especially) boys, an obvious omission from Beatrice's scheme.

Many of Barnum's stunts and shows were deceptions, tricks, cons, or jokes daring the audience to solve the deceit or to confess themselves dupes and rubes if they failed.[2] Annie Jones and such fellow Barnumites as Anna Swan (the "Nova Scotia Giantess"), Charles S. Stratton (a.k.a. General Tom Thumb), and Chang and Eng Bunker, the original "Siamese twins," were a different order of attraction altogether; these folk were all really truly as they and Barnum claimed: unusually tall, unusually short, joined at the sternum, and, yes, bearded. Or so the extensive photographic evidence strongly suggests.[3] A sucker may be born every minute and is assuredly not to be given an even break, but we condescend unjustly to W. C. Fields, Barnum, and their audiences if we dismiss Barnum's exhibitions' attractiveness as either or only an appeal to open-mouthed folly or to a repellent hankering after an abnormality that reassures viewers and customers of their own safe conformity.

Why take Barnum and his audiences and his bearded lady seriously and unapologetically? In a very different context, Stephen Orgel offers two reasons. One explanation is: "constructing gender and the nature of the desire engendered by it as a binary opposition ... has rendered the constructed quality of the subject – what is recognized as masculine and feminine, whether on stage or off – all but invisible." If we take a theatrical beard as a costume, as prosthesis, and I think we must, then we must also recognize "the dependence of gender on costume, and not on sexuality."[4] My essay is, then, about a few things others have not noticed nor yet found visible.

Both early modern and modern orthodoxy see paired categories: beard(ed)/not beard(ed), hairy/not hairy, male/female, masculine/ feminine, martial/effeminate, and so on to the end of dichotomy. I propose to dissolve this binary through the next stage of my argument and, I believe, the next move in early modern thinking: the beard as opprobium – a beard marks the shameless or outcast woman, the witch, the bawd, the whore. Equally opprobrious is the absence of beard: the unbearded male, also castigated as a "boy," who is ridiculed as an unworthy warrior and/or as an unlikely or incapable sexual partner and who – changing the terms of the argument – as actor plays both a woman and an old man on stage.

* * *

Barnum called the individuals I have named, and others, "living curiosities," and he charged admission to see them and other shows and exhibits in the grandiosely named American Museum in New York. The choice of "museum" may merely have been part of the semi-swindle: fine art in the Metropolitan Museum up-town, real life in the American Museum down-town.[5] And yet the word *museum* and even some of the contents Barnum provided hark back to a long trans-

Atlantic heritage of both itinerant showmen and the *Wunderkammer*, the cabinet, later to grow to the room, still later the rooms and then the buildings Europeans (and, still later, North Americans) filled with the exotic, the unusual, the mythical, the rare, and the abnormal.

I move closer to Shakespeare's plays and audiences, and to his and their likely experiences, by pausing over some early modern non-elite practices that long pre-date P. T. Barnum and his living curiosities. In July 1579, Queen Elizabeth formalized and regularized the provision of court entertainment, practices that had been evolving throughout the reigns of her father and grandfather, when she appointed Edmund Tilney Master of the Revels.[6] About eighteen months later (24 December 1581), a privy signet patent of commission specified the Master's control over a wide variety of entertainments, not just those destined for or commanded by the court, and similarly granted him very extensive powers to carry out his duties.[7] To wit: Tilney had the authority to employ "at competent wages" the following artisans: "painters, imbroderers, taylors, cappers, haberdashers, joyners, carders, glasiers, armorers, basketmakers, skinners, sadlers, waggen makers, plaisterers, fethermakers, as all other propertie makers and conninge artificers and laborers whatsover ..." He could "take at price reasonable ... any kinde or kindes of stuffe, ware or merchandise, woode or coale or other fewell, tymber, wainscott, boarde, lathe, nailes, brick, tile, leade, iron, wier, and all other necessaries ... as he shall thinke behoofefull and expedient ..." To achieve the "speedie workinge and fynisheinge of any exploit workmanshippe or peece of seruice that shall at any tyme ... belong to ... [the] office of the Revells," Tilney was empowered to arrest and imprison, to release from prison and hold safe from arrest any "partie or parties" he deemed necessary to carry out his duties, and he and his deputies were explicitly held immune "without any losse, penaltie, forfaiture or other damage" when carrying out their duties.

So much for the Master's responsibilities in originating and equipping entertainment for the monarch and her court. With an insouciant "And furthermore also," the commission then specifies the Master's virtually unlimited powers:

> to warne, commaunde, and appointe in all places within this our Realme of England, aswell within francheses and liberties as without, all and euery plaier or plaiers with their playmakers, either belonginge to any noble man or otherwise, bearinge the name or names of vsinge the facultie of playmakers or plaiers of Comedies, Tragedies, Enterludes or what other showes soever, from tyme to

> tyme and at all tymes to appeare before him with all suche plaies ... or
> showes as they shall haue in readines or meane to sett forth, and them
> to present and recite before [the Master] ... whom wee ... appointe and
> aucthorise ... of all suche showes, plaies, plaiers and playmakers,
> together with their playing spaces, to order and reforme, auctorise and
> put downe, as shalbe thought meete or vnmeete vnto himselfe ... .

The commission then ends by giving Tilney and his deputies the
power to imprison any one who resists or defies his authority and to
release such persons when the Master is satisfied that "the tyme of ...
ymprisonment [is] ... punishement sufficient."

Much of this document is Tudor legal boiler plate, and the Master's
powers in the real world (as opposed to the sometimes mildly fantastic
precincts of the royal court) depended upon judicious and steady
applications of his nominal authority mixed with equally judicious
moments of just plain looking the other way. In other words, it took a
good many years and a good many skirmishes and several Masters
before these delegated powers reached anything like the pervasive
control and surveillance the 1581 commission apparently envisages.[8]
From the point of view of both practical authority and the fees that
went with it, the pinnacle of the Master's control seems to have come
in the approximate period 1607–1630 or thereabouts, when the office
was first under the daily and later the official direction of Sir George
Buc and, then, from 1623 onwards, of Sir Henry Herbert.[9]

Students of Tudor–Stuart drama know of the Master's authority to
license plays for performance and eventually to license plays for printing (this latter power increased over time and was consolidated by
Buc); perhaps less well known is the Master's authority over the
"playing places" themselves, the celebrated amphitheatre and hall
locales, each of which had to be licensed and for the licensing of which
a weekly or monthly fee went to the Master from a quite early period.[10]
These are all what might be called the Master's metropolitan and high-
end responsibilities, the "museum" sort of show as opposed to the
Barnumesque raree-show, but the Master had – at least by Sir George
Buc's day – some nice earnings from entertainers who probably never
saw the inside of the Globe, much less the Blackfriars.[11] These entertainers were itinerant, traveling through the provinces constantly
rather than periodically as the major London theater companies, or
sub-groups of them, did.[12] Buc and, later, Herbert secured what Tilney
had only reached for: countrywide control over entertainments of
every sort.

Thus – this listing is just a sample – in 1622–3, the moment when Shakespeare's First Folio was being printed and published, Henry Herbert collected 10 shillings each for an annual license from:

> Thos. Barrell with one man his wife & children to toss a pike ...
> Marke Bradley with his wife to make shew of a Ramme with 4 horns ...
> William Reece & Thos. Gittins to make shewe of a strange Ratt ...

An unexpected moment of generosity or perhaps masterly curiosity appears when Herbert grants a free license "to Mr. John Williams with foure more to make showe of an Elephant for a yeare ... ."[13] Over the next several years Herbert licensed displays of many animals – a fish, a bird, "a Bay nag dancinge," "a live Beavr [sic] & a Racoon"[14] – as well as the "motions" and other "feates" that had earlier also filled his office-diary.[15]

Sprinkled among these entries are some other sadder, but also in a sense more familiar ones. For example:

> A license to Humfry Bromley & 3 assistants to show a childe with 3 heades ...
> A license granted to Lazarus an Italien to shew his brother Baptista that grows out of his navell & carrys him at his syde ...

In time, "Lazarus" Colloretti (or Colloredo) and his brother, Baptista, became famous enough to elicit a broadside, Martin [Parker], *The Two inseparable brothers* [with] *The second part* (1637), complete with woodcut.[16] These exhibited individuals might not have been what their entrepreneurial showmen claimed; the shows, or some of them, may well have been faked. True or false, and modern scholarship accepts Lazarus and Baptista as genuine, we are not far from P. T. Barnum's American Museum and its successors.

Finally, with this entry in Sir Henry Herbert's office-diary on 1 February 1632 we come closer to my specific interests:

> A license to Balthazer Ursty to shew Ann Christi a female childe of 70 yrs. of age overgrown with Heare from the face to the foote ...

Ann Christy seems a direct ancestor of Barnum's nineteenth-century "living curiosity," Annie Jones, though the perturbing phrase "a female childe of 70 yrs. of age" may possibly mean that Ann Christy was mentally deficient – *child* could have that meaning – while the nineteenth-century Ann Jones was anything but.

The three-headed child, the navel-growing brother, the female "over-grown with Heare from the face to the foote" have whatever historical reality and truth Herbert's licenses and other contemporary documents may be accorded. The plays of William Shakespeare and Benjamin Jonson, to go no further, attest, though they do not necessarily document historically, a still more extensive range of exhibited or desiderated curiosities – from Caliban, if Stephano could only get him to Naples (or London), to Lovewit's suspicion that the cozening trio of the *Alchemist* must have been displaying "a strange calf with five legs ... Or a huge lobster with six claws" or "The boy of six year old with the great thing" to have drawn such a crowd of aspiring dupes to the Blackfriars.[17]

Ann Christi/Christy in the seventeenth century and Annie Jones in the nineteenth achieved note as curiosities rather differently from the other unusual humans in Herbert's book and in Barnum's museum and circuses. Christy and Jones are unusual not because they exhibit distortions, extremes, or multiplications of what is usually and expectedly there, but because they display something – beards, extensive bodily hair – that is usually *not* there. Or rather, not there in persons *customarily regarded as female*. Difficult as early modern observers and modern scholars find this distinction to make and explain – and the ways both groups have done so has varied over time – the point is worth dwelling on. Historically, the relevant terminology included "wonder(s)," "curiosity," "monster(s)."[18] Many of Barnum's curiosities and those listed centuries before in Herbert's records were variations on an accepted, recognized and recognizable norm: very tall or very short, very fat or very thin, a man was a man, a woman, a woman; a ram, a ram however many horns it had; a "Ratt," a rat, however "strange," and so forth. The bearded woman, however, crosses analytic categories and from classical times onward has seemed to demand another sort of explanation. For early modern Europeans, the most telling examples requiring some other explanation might be those female saints who miraculously grew facial and/or bodily hair to thwart male lust and who – in the case of the most celebrated, Saint Wilgefortis or Ontcommer or Uncumber – achieved martyrdom through crucifixion.[19]

* * *

Social and cultural historians as well as literary critics have established that Tudor–Stuart popular and elite culture policed the boundaries between appropriate and inappropriate gendered behavior very carefully, though the most strident early modern attention typically fell upon female violations of cultural expectations rather than similar or analogous male transgressions. Thus we find elaborate categories – the mannish or "virile" woman, the virago, the Amazon, for example – erected to identify and stigmatize women thought to have usurped patterns of behavior acceptable and even requisite in men. A tidy example appears in the title of Thomas Dekker and Thomas Middleton's play about Mary ("Moll") Firth, a Jacobean woman-about-town who publicly wore a sword and some articles of traditionally male clothing, smoked tobacco, swore and drank excessively, and seems to have served as a combination Robin Hood and Jonathan Wild-like "finder" of stolen property. Dekker and Middleton called their 1611 play *The Roaring Girl*, a kind of oxymoron based upon the well-established Jacobean type, the "roaring boy," a swaggering, strutting, violent bully exemplified by Jonson's Kestril – the type the Restoration later called a "bravo."[20] "Roaring" a young man might be, and his public (mis-) behavior, while hardly condoned, seemed no more than an exaggeration of behavior both expected and accepted. "Roaring" a woman should not be, or if she was, as Mary Firth seems to have been, then both play title and actual behavior are oxymoronic.

The fragility of such discursive distinctions and the persistent male anxiety demanding their enforcement also produced parallel categories of men whose behavior was found effeminate. These parallel categories – women who are perceived as behaving as men and men who are perceived as behaving in some way or ways as do women – often employ the figurative and literal language of boys and boyishness, that is, the life-period and the practices preceding fledged, bearded, manhood – what Stephen Orgel calls "the common gender of childhood."[21] The frequency with which Shakespeare describes certain male characters through references to their "unrough" (unbearded) or "smooth" faces seems to me, in my hirsute pursuit, quite notable. Boys and their tertiary position will return later.

Mary Firth's transgressive apparel and actions seem to have been self-aware and -chosen. Annie Jones's and Ann Christy's appearance was not chosen, and yet their beards and extensive hair violate cultural assumptions or presumptions extending back beyond the middle ages to classical times: men were bearded, women were not. Before we plunge fully into the way bearded women function in early modern English cultural discourse, it must quickly be said that classical and early modern writers were thoroughly familiar with what most of us also recognize: the human body, especially the aging body, does not, and (it seems likely) never has, conformed to the tidy categorizations and divisions required by the language and practices of male/female, masculine/feminine distinctions. The classical proof-text here is *Epidemics* VI by the pseudo-Hippocrates. Here's the version in John Sadler's *The Sick Womans Private Looking-glass* (1636):

> *Phaetusa* ... being exiled by her husband *Pythea*, her termes were supprest, her voyce changed, and [she] had a beard, with a countenance like a man.[22]

There are several pertinent elements here. The changes are initiated by a male's action, the husband "exiling" his wife from the conjugal bed and home; the exiled wife's menstruation ("her termes") ceases; her voice changes (presumably it deepens, becoming what the author and his expected audience consider to be more "masculine"), as does her appearance. Note that the one detail supporting the claim that she has "a countenance like a man" is that she develops a beard. I will return to the further detail concerning the end of menstruation.

To some degree, pseudo-Hippocrates is describing changes that occur, or may occur, to any female body over time, and there are parallel, stereotypical changes that occur in the aging male body that steer that body across conventional male/female, masculine/feminine divisions in the other direction, as Jacques' description of the sixth age of man testifies:

> and his big manly voice,
> Turning again toward childish treble, pipes
> And whistles in his sound.[23]

More cruelly, in *A Wife* (1614) attributed to Sir Thomas Overbury, the character of "An Old Man" opens by claiming that an old man "Is a thing that hath been a man in his daies."[24] Francis Bacon also testifies that "Age loves to prattle and brag, and being desirous to doe least, is desirous to talke most."[25] Excessive, high-pitched "talke" was of course a common complaint about women of any age; as a man aged, then, he became more like a woman of whatever years, and so he inevitably and unavoidably confounded gender boundaries. At a psychological and moral rather than sheerly physical level, Aristotle in the *Nicomachean Ethics* and numerous early modern followers found "the vice of 'softness' (*mollities*)" in "woman, old men and those living in inclement climates."[26]

However common an aging woman's beard-like hair might have been or be, however commonly perceived and recorded by medical practitioners ancient and modern, a bearded woman violated some ingrained cultural assumptions and distinctions, so it is no surprise, though it may be unpleasant, to discover that Celestina, the procuress of the translated Tudor *Interlude of Calisto and Melebea* (c.1530), is triply damned. She is repeatedly called an "old hore" (406, 408), a "rybaud" (787), "Not only a baud, but a wych by her craft" (423) and an "old which" (818). "Old," "whore," and "witch" are evidently not vituperation enough because Celestina twice receives a further vilifying epithet: "that old berdyd hore" (395), or more elaborately, "Thow berdyd dame, shameles thou semest to be" (785).[27] The key idea linking whoredom, procuring, witchcraft, and the bearded, aged woman is shamelessness. Each of Celestina's imputed aspects violates a cultural protocol for female behavior, moving her from accepted shamefastness into shamelessness, moving her from institutional and social protection to institutional and social ostracism and persecution. The bawd's, the whore's, the witch's institutionally unacceptable sexuality are manifested physically: advanced age and beardedness. As Hamlet makes clear to Gertrude, even middle-age and sexual desire do not mix. Neither do women and beards. When sexuality, age, witchcraft, women, and beards all come together, the culture's normative expectations respond with the overdetermined name-calling in *Calisto and Melebea*.

Consider one final intersection of these ideas, this time not from a playtext but from documents having less obviously "imaginative" goals. Seeking to prepare English subjects for the planned Spanish invasion of summer 1588, the Roman Catholic and English Cardinal William Allen wrote a justification of both the invasion and Pius V's earlier bull, *Regnans in Excelsis* (1570) excommunicating Elizabeth I, upon which that invasion relied for legal and diplomatic sanction. Allen's *Admonition to the Nobility and People of England and Ireland concerninge the present warres* (Antwerp [?], 1588) was either smuggled into England or perhaps secretly printed there; it survives in a single complete copy plus three partial ones, probably because it was instantly proclaimed seditious and copies were hunted down and destroyed.[28] Allen stresses the various ways in which Elizabeth's sovereignty might be illegitimate, including her own supposed legal bastardy, the better claims on the throne of other persons, especially the late Mary Queen of Scots and dowager Queen of France, and so forth. Allen also attacks Elizabeth as morally defective and therefore unworthy her subjects' allegiance:

> ... she hathe abused her bodie, against Gods lawes, to the disgrace of princely maiestie & the whole nations reproche, by vnspeakable and incredible variety of luste, which modesty suffereth not to be remembred, neyther were it to chaste eares to be vttered how shamefully she hath defiled and inflamed her person and cuntry, and made her Courte as a trappe, by this damnable and detestable arte, to inta[n]gle in sinne and ouerthrowe the yonger sorte of the nobilitye and gentlemen of the lande, whereby she is become notorious to the worlde, & in other cuntryes a como[n] fable for this her turpitude, which in so highe degre namely in a woman and a Queene, deseruethe not onelie deposition, but all vengeaunce bothe of God and man ...[29]

Allen rings complex changes on the basic charge of sexual license. He apparently finds Elizabeth's alleged "luste" objectionable not so much in itself as for its "incredible variety" and for its effect upon "the yonger sorte" rather than upon – it seems – a jaded and imperturbable older sort. Sexism and snobbery neatly unite when Allen implies that Elizabeth's "turpitude" becomes worthy of deposition because she is "a woman and a Queene." Cardinal Allen's attack on Queen Elizabeth was among the more forceful, but it was by no means singular. There were other foreign and domestic ones along the same lines, and all tended to rely on a few basic assumptions about "proper" behavior in a woman and a queen: particularly, that she should marry and have children, and that her failure to do so made charges of sexual license more plausible.

Allen's attack helps explain a later, more outré piece of propaganda. This one appeared in the virulently anti-Catholic preface to a 1607 English translation of a French Protestant work ridiculing Catholic belief in various miracles and "wonders." Among such Catholic "lying reports," the translator mentions "That *Luthur* was begotten by an *Incubus,* and strangled by the devil. ... That *Bucer* renounced Christian religion at his death, and died a Iew. That *Beza* reconciled himselfe to the Church of *Rome,* and died a Catholike. ... That when *Campion* was drawne to the place of execution, the water in *Thames* stood still."[30] Each of these ridiculed claims is carefully documented in the margin with citations of printed texts, but interspersed is one that is credited only to "D List. ex rum. Ital." Here's the claim attributed – I suggest –

to the historical Dr Thomas Lister, SJ, and Italian rumor: "That Queene *Elizabeth* had a blacke beard."

Bizarre as this "wonder" might seem in isolation, we have seen a cultural context that makes it explicable and suggests how it might be effective political slander. For an Elizabethan or Jacobean audience, Elizabeth I's imaginary/imagined black beard might adumbrate or even epitomize her masculine, or at least unfeminine, sexual independence, her aggressive dominion, her witchiness, her shamelessness.

* * *

Elizabeth I probably didn't have a beard, black or otherwise, and if she did the medicine of her day and ours has quite unsensational explanations – including, today, anorexia – for it. So, Queen Elizabeth is unlikely to have been bearded.

Was Lady Macbeth? Straightforwardly, of course, the answer is simple: the play offers no evidence that the (boy?) actor performing Lady Macbeth originally appeared with a beard, real or theatrically false. Cultural predisposition or prejudice is another matter. To make a speculative case that the original audience would not be surprised at the question is relatively easy. According to Banquo, the play's three sisters have indeed a prime, though not an exclusive, witchy quality:

> Live you, or are you aught
> That man may question? You seem to understand me,
> By each at once her choppy finger laying
> Upon her skinny lips; you should be women,
> And yet your beards forbid me to interpret
> That you are so.
>
> $(1.3.40-5)^{31}$

Like Celestina and many other "witches" of the period, these sisters are bearded, though theatrical producers recognized sooner than literary critics that only Banquo's words attest the seeming "fact." Janet Adelman has persuasively charted the axes of anxiety that link the witches with Lady Macbeth with demonic possession with male fantasies of female, especially maternal, hostility.[32]

Asking questions about beards introduces another factor into the equation, and that arises from Lady Macbeth's extraordinary invocation of the "spirits | That tend on mortal thoughts" (1.5.38–9), when she especially pleads:

> make thick my blood,
> Stop up th'access and passage to remorse
> That no compunctious visitings of nature
> Shake my fell purpose nor keep peace between
> Th'effect and it. Come to my woman's breasts
> And take my milk for gall, you murd'ring ministers,
> Wherever in your sightless substances
> You wait on nature's mischief.
>
> (1.5.41–8)

Here Lady Macbeth invokes two "unnatural" conditions: stopping up the circulation (or in Jacobean scientific terms, the ebbing and flowing) of blood that makes her more compassionate ("compunctious") than a male, and ending her menstruation ("visitings of nature"), the shedding of blood that typified a female in contemporary English culture and marked her ability to bear children.[33]

Pierre Le Loyer's French treatise on fantasy, translated into English and published in 1605, about the time of *Macbeth*'s composition, discusses the unusual psychological state male doctors supposed a woman underwent when menstruation ceased:

> ... the blood of their monthly disease [i.e. unease, discomfort] being stopped from his course, through the ordinary passages and by the matrix dooth redound and beate backe again by the heart ... Then the same blood, not finding any passage, troubleth the braine in such sorte, that ... it causeth many of them to have idle fancies and fond conceipts, and tormenteth them with diverse imaginations of horrible specters, and fearefull sights ... with which being so afflicted, some of them doe seeke to throwe and cast themselves into wells or pittes, and others to destroy themselves by hanging, or some such miserable end.[34]

Like Le Loyer's normative amenorrheal woman, Lady Macbeth suffers "diverse imaginations of horrible specters, and fearefull sights" in Act 5, scene 1, when she seems to reimagine Duncan's murder. The play's most unreliable narrative moment claims Lady Macbeth destroyed herself "by hanging, or some such miserable end" (Le Loyer): the "fiend-like queen," Malcolm says, "as 'tis thought, by self and violent hands I Took off her life" (5.9.36–8).[35]

This same physical condition, or its absence, also linked women with witches. The valiantly skeptical Reginald Scot records medical scholars' claims that amenorrhea, the absence of menstruation that might mark menopause, also defines female witches, who constitute a sub-category of "melancholike" persons:

> Now, if the fansie of a melancholike person may be occupied in causes which are both false and impossible; why should an old witch be thought free from such fantasies, who (as the learned philosophers and physicians saie) upon the stopping of their mon-ethlie melancholike flux or issue of bloud, in their age must needs increase therein [i.e. in melancholy], as (through their weaknesse both of bodie and braine) the aptest persons to meete with such melancholik imaginations: with whome their imaginations remaine, even when their senses are gone.[36]

Shakespeare's earliest audiences might thus associate Lady Macbeth's invocation in Act 1, scene 5 with an aberrant desire to be both a fantast (a "melancholike") and a witch, a woman seeking to deny what her culture understood as a woman's defining "nature" – her bodily or physical ability to bear children – and a woman seeking to become what established doctrine most feared, a renegade or "wayward" woman, a witch or uncontrolled wife.[37]

Post-menopausal women – "some of them beyng a while frutefull, but after widowes, and for that suppressed of naturall course [menstruation]" – were also, according to the surgeon-anatomist John Banister, supposed to "have beardes ... being then [as widows and non-menstruating women] bearded, hearie [hairy], and chaunged in voyce."[38] The description may only hypothetically suit Lady Macbeth, but its most provocative claim – "bearded, hearie" – concerning women whose "naturall course" has been "suppressed" anticipates Banquo's first view of the sisters and thus adds one more cultural predisposition for an audience to at least entertain the question: Was Lady Macbeth a bearded lady?

* * *

As companions to Lady Macbeth, there could hardly be less likely sisters than two wives of Windsor. Critical consensus holds *The Merry Wives of Windsor* to be Shakespeare's most (or only) bourgeois comedy, the comedy most firmly tied to late-Elizabethan culture, local English geography, and even such precisely historical events as the Garter installation ceremony of 1597.[39] In ways, it is also Shakespeare's most Jonsonian comedy, though in other aspects *Measure for Measure* might share that distinction. Yet, like *Macbeth*, *The Merry Wives of Windsor* is about embarrassment and shame, particularly in the figures of Falstaff, Master Ford, and the Host of the Garter, and that shame and embarrassment are couched in terms of personal dignity, gender identity, class solidarity, and ethical, especially marital, confidence. Further, but not differently, *The Merry Wives of Windsor* concerns the war of the sexes, confusions of gender, and the permeability of assumedly secure gender boundaries. Of course, the plays appear very different: aristocratic, medieval, and Scottish; bourgeois, contemporary, and English, for example.

Macbeth and *Merry Wives* come closer to one another when we ask questions about women and men, witches, and beards. Before women, witches, and beards, however, consider women and men in *The Merry Wives of Windsor*. Mistress Page, reading Falstaff's arrogant letter inviting an assignation, is angered by his assumption that she is available for his exploitation and makes a root-and-branch homicidal proposal: "Why, I'll exhibit a bill in the parliament for the putting down of men" (2.1.26–7). Very soon, she discovers that Mistress Ford has received a nearly identical epistolary proposition when Mistress Ford claims "If I would go to hell for an eternal moment or so, I could be knighted" (2.1.44–5). Mistress Page makes a revealing, appropriate reply: "What? Thou liest! Sir Alice Ford? These knights will hack [fornicate], and so thou shouldst not alter the article of thy gentry."[40] Alice Ford, a commoner though a gentle woman, could not be knighted, could not become Sir Alice Ford, a titled man, but the fantasy and the comic misprision here will be repeated in a different key, when Sir John Falstaff is unknighted and made a woman. Later, Mistress Ford repulses Falstaff's sexual advances with a pun on the social and the gendered meanings of *lady*: "I your lady, Sir John? Alas, I should be a pitiful lady" (3.3.48–9). She would be a morally pitiable woman were she to succumb to Falstaff; she would be a traitor to her class and a pitiful, hypocritical, and unconvincing member of a class other than her own.

Where Mistress Ford momentarily speaks of being knighted, of receiving a title through receiving a knight's sexual overtures, her jealous husband has a different fantasy when he envies his wife's close relation with Mistress Page. She has arrived to visit her friend and asks if she is at home; he grumpily replies: "Ay, and as idle as she may hang together, for want of company. I think if your husbands were dead you two would marry" (3.2.11–13). Mistress Page momentarily diffuses the common male fantasy of a female friendship that is also sexual: "Be sure of that – two other husbands." The reassurance jabs again at Ford's jealousy: the two wives may perhaps not be lovers, but they will find new males to serve as *post mortem* objects of Ford's obsessive envy.[41] In the earlier scene, when Mistresses Ford and Page compare Falstaff's identical propositions, Mistress Page's indignant response, when she imagines what Falstaff thinks she might be, is also suggestive and threatening to male egotism and male sexual primacy: "I'll entertain myself like one that I am not acquainted withal" (2.1.79–80). The obvious meaning is that she rejects adultery, a self and a behavior she is unacquainted with, but the nearly so obvious possibility is that she, like Ford's fantasies of his wife, has fantasies of adultery. And a less obvious possibility in the words is that she will entertain herself without a man, perhaps with another woman, perhaps alone. "Madam with a dildo" (*Alchemist*, 5.5.42), perhaps?

Master Page, the loving, confident husband who in the play's joking sexual mathematics complements his friend, the jealous, suspicious Master Ford, does not escape the pervasive questioning of gender roles and sexual identities. Mistresses Ford, Page, and Quickly have evidently agreed (off-stage, when they exit together in Act 2, scene 1) to demand that Falstaff's page Robin be sent to Mistress Page to assist, as go-between, Falstaff's assault on Mistress Page, and soon Mistress Quickly – she who favors all the suitors of whomever, be it Mistress Ford, or Mistress Page, or Miss Anne Page – assures Falstaff that Master Page "has a marvellous infection to the little page" (2.2.108–9). Mistress Quickly's pervasive malapropism has already taught us to understand that she misplaces words, says things she should not say. On the play's comic verbal plane, her linguistically inept (or inapt) "infection," the editors tell us, is really to be understood as "affection."

Shakespeare's practice elsewhere, however, suggests her mistake is not mere verbal bumbling. This time, she might not have used the "wrong" word. Or at least her mistake, if it is one, has put into play an appropriate sexual possibility and an appropriate complement to the other sexual possibilities the play embraces. "Affection" may be too weak, and "infection" rather a strong, possibility here. When the tri-partite plot to fool Benedick into thinking Beatrice loves him succeeds,

Claudio gleefully cries, "He hath ta'en th'infection; hold it up!" (*Much Ado*, 2.3.122)[42] Mistress Quickly's "infection" might be a more sexual and physical a term than the anodyne gloss-substitution "affection" suggests. If she speaks true, then it is possible that Master Page has indeed a sexual, a loving, "infection" or "affection" for Robin. After all, in *The Taming of a Shrew* the Lord's page, Bartholomew, successfully bears "himself with honourable action | Such as he hath observed in noble ladies | Unto their lords,"[43] and it seems plausible that Robin might do the same for Master Page. Mistress Quickly supports this possibility by praising Mistress Page's freedom to "Do what she will, say what she will, take all, pay all, go to bed when she list, rise when she list, all is as she will" (2.2.111–13), an obvious hint to Falstaff that Mistress Page might like to do what she will with *him*, but an only slightly less obvious hint that Robin – "You must send her your page, no remedy" – may serve as a distraction or substitute for Master Page, that "honest man" (2.2.110).

So much, and too briefly, for men, women, and pages. What of women, boys, near-boys, and beards? Flute, assigned Thisbe's part in the mechanicals' play in *A Midsummer Night's Dream*, supposes that Thisbe is a "wandering knight"[44] – *Clyomon and Clamydes* might have predisposed him, and the audience, to this pseudo-Greek assumption.[45] Horrified, it seems, when he discovers that Thisbe "is the lady that Pyramus must love," Flute tries to reject the role, perhaps as a realistic objection, perhaps as a defense of his not yet quite having left puberty, perhaps as a defense against a suggestion of uncertain sexual preference. "Nay, faith, let me not play a woman. I have a beard coming" (1.2.41–2). Whether the physical actor's beard is coming or not yet arrived or all too luxuriant – directors typically have fun with this moment – the assumption that beardedness precludes playing a woman is as plain as the beard on or not yet on or never to be on Flute's face. Quince reassures him that the theater has a way to save the realism of the performance. "That's all one. You shall play it in a mask, and you may speak as small as you will" (1.2.43–4). The offer of a mask, a frequent disguise for aristocratic or bourgeois women attending the theatre, underlines the delightful confusion of realism and fantasy pervading the mechanicals' enterprise, but the working dramatic assumption that beard = masculine, no beard = feminine remains intact. When Bottom learns he is to play Pyramus, beards and theatrical disguise suddenly but not unexpectedly return. Appropriately, as "a most lovely, gentleman-like man" (1.2.78), Bottom's first question is about theatrical props:

"What beard were I best to play it in?" He offers a catalogue: "your straw-colour beard, your orange-tawny beard, your purple-in-grain beard, or your French-crown-colour beard, your perfect yellow" (1.2.80–6).[46]

The catalogue and the comic theatrical ignorance and equally knowing theatrical reflexivity recall an even blunter moment in *Sir Thomas More*, when the performance of an inner play, *The Marriage of Wit and Wisdom*, is derailed because an actor has trouble finding John Ogle, one of the men who supplied prop-beards for the London companies:

> We would desire your honour but to stay a little: one of my fellows is but run to Ogle's for a long beard for young Wit, and he'll be here presently.[47]

If we need confirmation of this particular *Dream*-like crossover of London reality and London fantasy, we may turn to the Master of the Revels' accounts in 1572–4 or Philip Henslowe's later accounts and there find a number of references to Ogle father and son and their supplying of theatrical beards, wigs, and other hairy props.[48]

Once more, of women, witches, and beards. According to one popular play, *The Honest Mans Fortune* (1613), "the women that I came to us, for disguises must weare beardes, I & thats they saie the token of a witch."[49] As we know from *Calisto and Melebea*, this "token" is an old one in English plays, but it required the later drama, with its almost compulsive self-consciousness, to move from the popular "token" still alive in Banquo's response to the three sisters to the nuance of women (or men or boys playing women) disguised with a theatrical beard as theatrical witches.

Following the buck-basket episode in *Merry Wives*, Falstaff must once again be found and not found in Master Ford's house, where Mistress Ford assures us, "Neither press, coffer, chest, trunk, vault" (4.2.53–4) will escape her husband's knowledgeable search, and the action soon shows us, as we expected, that Ford will not be fooled twice by the buck-basket, though we are doubly amused when he fails to find Falstaff in the basket, as we also expected, or should have if we remembered how comedy works. Mistresses Page and Ford recall the never-until-this-moment-mentioned "fat woman of Brentford," the imaginary aunt of Mistress Ford's maid, who has left, it suddenly appears, "a gown above" (4.2.66–7). Even more fortuitously, or fortunately, for Shakespeare's comic success, Mistress Ford knows her irascible husband's mind:

> I would my husband would meet him in this shape. He cannot abide the old woman of Brentford. He swears she's a witch, forbade her my house, and hath threatened to beat her. (4.2.75–8)

In a strikingly subtle piece of dramaturgy, Shakespeare soon has Mistress Page (who had, apparently, never until this moment known of the supposed maid's supposed aunt or of any supposed fat woman of Brentford) describe this woman as "the *witch* of Brentford" when she agrees that they should "dress" Falstaff "like the witch of Brentford" (4.2.88; my italics). She adopts, that is, not Mistress Ford's version of the woman, but Master Ford's, and thus advances both the comedy to come and the argument of witchcraft.

Master Ford arrives, surrounded by a skeptical group of friends. Page suggests that his friend should "be pinioned" (4.2.112) as a lunatic – and Ford validates their judgment (true enough in general but wrong in this instance) when he paws through the now Falstaff-less laundry basket. Master Page concludes, rightly and wrongly, that Falstaff and Mistress Ford's adultery is "nowhere else but in [Ford's] ... brain" (4.2.145).[50] To release Falstaff for his third and final humiliation at Hearne's Oak, Mistress Ford calls to Mistress Page to "bring the old woman down" and when Mistress Ford explains to her husband that the supposed "old woman" is "my maid's aunt of Brentford," Master Ford amalgamates many of the cultural assumptions and ideological issues I have discussed:

> A witch, a quean, an old cozening quean! Have I not forbid her my house? She comes of errands, does she? We are simple men; we do not know what's brought to pass under the profession of fortune-telling. She works by charms, by spells, by th'figure, and such daubery as this, beyond our element ... Come down, you witch, you hag, you! (4.2.157–64)

The "errands" a witch might run were often, in early modern belief, errands of love or sex. Master Ford probably and conventionally suspects the old woman of Brentford is delivering love-potions, or spells, to inhibit his sexual performance or enhance another man's.[51] As Master Ford beats Falstaff (or the witch of Brentford or the aunt of the maid or the Woman of Brentford) out the door, he cries: "Out of my door, you witch, you rag, you baggage, you polecat, you runnion! Out, out! I'll conjure you, I'll fortune-tell you!" (4.2.170–2). So much for the Witch of Brentford, or Mistress Ford's maid's aunt, or the disguised Falstaff, but Parson Evans has – as is a teacher's wont – the last Welsh-inflected word: "By yea and no, I think the 'oman is a witch indeed. I like not when a 'oman has a great peard. I spied a great peard under her muffler" (4.2.178–80). In the environs of Windsor, Falstaff is indeed a witch. He has a peard, and he has a peard in disguise as the aunt of Mistress Ford's maid or as the old fat woman of Brentford, and he has a peard because he is a p/bearded man.

By now in *Merry Wives* and by now in this exploration of bearded ladies in Shakespeare, we might conclude that by their beards ye shall know them, but who and what "they" are remain quite puzzling and ambiguous. "They" might be the sisters of Windsor, or even the Lady of *Macbeth*, or Flute in *A Midsummer Night's Dream*, or Falstaff in *The Merry Wives of Windsor*, or that transvestite page Bartholomew in *Taming of a Shrew*, or Robin the page and Master Ford, or even the Duke of Gloucester, "Goneril with a white beard."[52] Beards – real, the-atrical-prosthetic, or imagined – mark limits and crossings of limits, and those limits may be gender boundaries and within those bound-aries of appropriate from inappropriate gendered behavior, of shame and shamelessness, or those limits may be demarcations of sexual fecundity and sterility, or divisions of permissible from reprehended sexual unions, or the division between real life and imagined play, or the human from the demonic. Shakespeare's exploitation of his culture's beard-lore and beard-belief ranges from the initially unprob-lematic association of beards with witches and with old women to the much more complex possibilities of those associations themselves being fungible, open to manipulation by the dramatist or by his char-acters in their imagined situations or by the players in their always mysterious twilight of natural fictions.

With Falstaff the bearded lady, I return to where we began, to Phineas Barnum and Sir Henry Herbert, Master of the Revels, and I have not progressed to the lower beard, the pubic beard immortalized in Chaucer's *Miller's Tale* or Sir David Lindsay's *Thrie Estaitis*, and deli-cately alluded to when Viola answers a wish that she grow a beard: "I am almost sick for one, though I would not have it grow on my chin" (3.1.46). Some of the many links among women, sexuality, witches, and beards appear in a less delicate remark from *The Honest Whore*, Part I (1604): "for some women have beards; marry, they are half witches" (4.1.185–6), i.e. a woman's lower half is the witchy half.[53]

When Lucio slanders his Duke to his face as "a better woodman than thou tak'st him for," the offensive slang term (*woodman*) alludes to a sexual predator in the hairy nether forest, or what D'Urfey calls the "Beard below."[54] About these beards I have not written. Another time, I hope.

Notes

Earlier, less precise versions of this essay were spoken at the Folger Shakespeare Library and the Huntington Library, and a few paragraphs derive from the introduction to my New Cambridge Shakespeare edition of *Macbeth* (1997). For help and comment, I thank Claire Banchich, Rebecca Jaffe, Bill Phelan, and Sue Wiseman.

1. Shakespeare, *Much Ado about Nothing*, ed. Claire McEachern, Arden Shakespeare (London: Thomson, 2006), 2.1.30–4. Subsequent citation is parenthetical. Since this essay was composed, Mark Albert Johnston's "Bearded Women in Early Modern England," *Studies in English Literature* 47 (Winter 2007): 1–28 appeared. Johnston's central interests are "economic and erotic autonomy" and "deference to patriarchal primacy" (8); mine are not.
2. For a strong argument that Barnum's most flagrant, even admitted, deceptions could themselves attract customers, see Neil Harris, "The Operational Aesthetic," chapter 3 in Harris, *Humbug: The Art of P. T. Barnum* (Chicago: University of Chicago Press, 1973), 59–89.
3. The literature on Barnum and his enterprises is enormous. For relevant illustrations and many of the details that follow, see Philip B. Kunhardt et al., *P. T. Barnum: America's Greatest Showman* (New York: Knopf, 1995).
4. Stephen Orgel, *Impersonations: The Performance of Gender in Shakespeare's England* (Cambridge: Cambridge University Press, 1996), 9 and 33, respectively. On hair as prosthesis, see, briefly, Ann Rosalind Jones and Peter Stallybrass, *Renaissance Clothing and the Materials of Memory* (Cambridge: Cambridge University Press, 2000), 208; and, more elaborately, Will Fisher, "The Renaissance Beard: Masculinity in Early Modern England," *Renaissance Quarterly* 54 (2001): 155–87. Fisher (175 ff.) also stresses the boy/boy actor as a *tertium quid* in earlier male/female feminine/masculine binary arguments.
5. Incorporated in 1870, the Metropolitan Museum's first Central Park building opened in 1880 (see Calvin Tomkins, *Merchants and Masterpieces: The Story of the Metropolitan Museum of Art* [New York: Dutton, 1970], chap. 1). Barnum purchased the pre-existing American Museum in December 1841; numerous similarly named buildings followed.
6. Tilney's patent is reprinted in Albert Feuillerat, ed., *Documents Relating to the Office of the Revels in the Time of Queen Elizabeth* (Louvain: A. Uystpruyst, 1908), 55. Tilney probably oversaw the Revels from as early as February 1577/8: see W. R. Streitberger, "On Edmond Tyllney's Biography," *Review of English Studies*, n.s. 29 (1978): 11–35, esp. 20–1.

7. The commission is reprinted in E. K. Chambers, *The Elizabethan Stage*, 4 vols. (Oxford: Oxford University Press, 1923), 4: 285–7, from which I quote. On the immediate circumstances of this commission, see Streitberger, 21–2.

8. In this general point, I agree with Richard Dutton, *Mastering the Revels: The Regulation and Censorship of English Renaissance Drama* (London: Macmillan, 1991), 49.

9. Mark Eccles, "Sir George Buc, Master of the Revels" in C. J. Sisson, ed. *Thomas Lodge and Other Elizabethans* (Cambridge MA: Harvard University Press, 1933), 463–4 and Streitberger, 30–1 jointly demonstrate Buc's participation in the Revels Office *c*.1608 and his development of "licensing for the press as a source of income" (Streitberger, 31).

10. See, for example, Henslowe's payments for the Rose theatre in *Henslowe's Diary*, ed. R. A. Foakes and R. T. Rickert, 2nd edn. (Cambridge: Cambridge University Press, 2002), 15 (26 February 1591–14 June 1592).

11. Not that the public theaters were venues for plays and jigs alone; they often hosted other forms of entertainment – Henslowe's Rose saw "mr haslette" and his "valtinge" in November 1598, a month when "James cranwigge" also "playd his c[h]allenge in my howsse" (see *Henslowe's Diary*, 101) – but none so humble as those that follow here.

12. See, for example, David Bradley, *From Text to Performance* (Cambridge: Cambridge University Press, 1991) and Scott McMillin and Sally-Beth MacLean, *The Queen's Men and their Plays* (Cambridge: Cambridge University Press, 1998).

13. See N. W. Bawcutt, *The Control and Censorship of Caroline Drama: The Records of Sir Henry Herbert* (Oxford: Clarendon Press, 1996), entries 45, 46, 52, and 44, respectively. I have not reproduced Bawcutt's use of superscript letters nor his indications of inserted material.

14. Ibid., entries 107, 116, 164, and 237, respectively. Animal acts are documented in London "before 1572"; see Arthur Freeman, *Elizabeth's Misfits* (New York: Garland, 1978), 131, quoting Joseph Strutt, *Sports and Pastimes*, ed. William Hone (1876), 330, but almost certainly were a feature of medieval fairs centuries before; Richard Altick, *The Shows of London* (Cambridge MA: Harvard University Press, 1978), 7 records a 1578 display of a smith's skill in making miniature gear for trained fleas, but, again, such displays of surprising, "magical" skill must have been far older.

15. In general, see Bawcutt, 76–83.

16. See Bawcutt, entries 175 and 369, respectively, and, on the Colloretti brothers, Jan Bondeson, *The Two-headed Boy, and Other Medical Marvels* (Ithaca NY: Cornell University Press, 2000), vii–xv and his discussion of relevant sources, 285. Parker's broadside is preserved in the British Library, Roxborough Ballads, III.216–17.

17. Shakespeare, *The Tempest*, ed. Stephen Orgel (Oxford: Oxford University Press, 1987), 2.2.27–30; Jonson, *The Alchemist*, ed. Alvin B. Kernan (New Haven: Yale University Press, 1974), 5.1.8–9 and 24. Subsequent citation is parenthetical.

18. Explanations and their variations over time are well discussed by Lorraine Daston and Katherine Park in *Wonders and the Order of Nature, 1150–1750* (New York: Zone, 1998), *passim*, esp. 15–20 and chapter 5.

19. See the excellent and too-little cited study, Jan [Jean] Gessler, *La Légende de sainte Wilgeforte ou Ontcommer, la vierge miraculeusement barbue* (Brussels: Ed. Universelle, 1938).
20. In *The Alchemist*, Kestril has come for training in fashionably rude behaviour. The conceit is elaborately developed in Thomas Middleton and William Rowley, *A Fair Quarrel*, ed. R. V. Holdsworth, New Mermaids ed. (London: Ernest Benn, 1974), where instruction in "the mathematical science of roaring" is offered (4.1.23–4).
21. Orgel, *Impersonations*, 15.
22. John Sadler, *The Sick Womans Private Looking-glass* (1636), 17.
23. Shakespeare, *As You Like It*, ed. Michael Hattaway, New Cambridge Shakespeare (Cambridge: Cambridge University Press, 2000) 2.7.161–3.
24. *The Overburian Characters*, ed. W. J. Paylor (Oxford: Blackwell, 1936), 4.
25. Francis Bacon, *The History of Life and Death* (1638), excerpted in Thomas Cole and Mary Winkler, eds., *The Oxford Book of Aging* (Oxford: Oxford University Press, 1994), 35.
26. Ian Maclean, *The Renaissance Notion of Woman: A Study in the Fortunes of Scholasticism and Medical Science in European Intellectual Life* (Cambridge: Cambridge University Press, 1980), 51.
27. Quotations and parenthetical line numbers are from H. Warner Allen, ed. *Celestina, or the Tragi-comedy of Calisto and Melibea* (London: Routledge, 1908).
28. The single complete copy is today in the British Library, shelfmark G[renville] 6067, from which I quote.
29. Allen, *Admonition*, sig. B2. For discussion of a number of slanders, more native than foreign, of Elizabeth in the 1560s, '70s, and '80s, prompted at least in part by public desire for an heir to the throne, see Carole Levin, "Wanton and Whore," chapter 4 in Levin, *The Heart and Stomach of a King* (Philadelphia: University of Pennsylvania Press, 1994). Levin sees a greater degree of knee-jerk misogyny in these attacks than I do.
30. Henri Estienne, *A World of Wonders*, trans. R. C[arew?] (1607), sig. ¶4v–A1.
31. Shakespeare, *Macbeth*, ed. A. R. Braunmuller, New Cambridge Shakespeare (Cambridge: Cambridge University Press, 1997). Subsequent citation is parenthetical.
32. See Janet Adelman, *Suffocating Mothers: Fantasies of Maternal Origin in Shakespeare's Plays, Hamlet to The Tempest* (London: Routledge, 1992), 130–46.
33. See *Macbeth*, 1.5.41–2 n. and *OED* visit *n.* 4; Alice Fox, "Obstetrics and Gynecology in *Macbeth*," *Shakespeare Studies* 12 (1979): 127–41; Jenijoy La Belle, " 'A Strange Infirmity': Lady Macbeth's Amenorrhea," *Shakespeare Quarterly* 31 (1980): 381–6.
34. Pierre Le Loyer [Loier], *Treatise of Specters*, trans. Z. Jones (1605), ff. 110r–v. See Patricia Crawford, "Attitudes to Menstruation in Seventeenth-Century England," *Past & Present* 91 (1981), 47–73.
35. Malcolm's "as 'tis thought" is an extraordinary qualification, marking the narrative's unreliability and, perhaps, Malcolm's politically motivated effort to portray the previous régime as insane or despairing.
36. Reginald Scot, *The Discoverie of Witchcraft* (1584), ed. Brinsley Nicholson (London: E. Stock, 1886), 3.9.

37. "[T]he play [*Macbeth*] also offers, in the figure of Lady Macbeth, the drama's most vivid manifestation of the witch as a dangerous familiar and her witch-craft as 'malice domestic,' as an invasion of the household and its daily life" (Frances Dolan, *Dangerous Familiars* [Ithaca NY: Cornell University Press, 1994], 226).

38. John Banister, *The Historie of Man* (1578), sig. B2v. Banister is never very original and cites *Epidemics* VI here. On how hair might discriminate masculine from feminine historically, see Joan Cadden, *Meanings of Sex Difference in the Middle Ages* (Cambridge: Cambridge University Press, 1993), 181–3.

39. See Shakespeare, *Merry Wives of Windsor*, ed. T. W. Craik (Oxford: Oxford University Press, 1989), 1–13 for a skeptical account. Subsequent citation is parenthetical. Craik's edition is based on the Folio text; the quarto differs in many ways.

40. In Act 4, scene 1, the overheard and misunderstood declension *hic, haec, hoc* becomes, for the wives, "hick and hack," further evidence of male lust.

41. A wife's "chastity" (i.e. celibacy) after her first (or some subsequent) husband's death, her fidelity to a dead man, is an obsessive concern in early modern English drama, reflecting real world wills in which husbands disinherited their widows if they remarried. The most elaborate dramatic working out, and ridiculing, of this fearful concern is George Chapman's *The Widow's Tears* (c.1605); see, in part, Robert A. Fothergill, "The Perfect Image of Life: Counterfeit Death in the Plays of Shakespeare and his Contemporaries," *University of Toronto Quarterly* 52 (1982–83): 155–78.

42. See also, among many examples, Shakespeare, *Love's Labours Lost*, ed. G. R. Hibbard (Oxford: Oxford University Press, 1990), 2.1.228.

43. Shakespeare, *The Taming of the Shrew*, ed. Ann Thompson, New Cambridge Shakespeare, 2nd edn. (Cambridge: Cambridge University Press, 2003), Ind.1.106–8.

44. Shakespeare, *A Midsummer Night's Dream*, ed. Peter Holland (Oxford: Oxford University Press, 1995), 1.2.39. Subsequent citation is parenthetical.

45. The first printing of *Clyomon and Clamydes* is the 1599 quarto.

46. For providers of theatrical beards mentioned below, see Fisher (above, n. 4), 163–6.

47. Anthony Munday et al., *Sir Thomas More*, ed. Vittorio Gabrieli and Giorgio Melchiori, Revels Plays (Manchester: Manchester University Press, 1990), 3.2.139–41.

48. Feuillerat, 177 and 199. These payments also suggest there were conventionally shaped and possibly color-coded beards for different professions and occupations; see, briefly, Fisher, 159 and figures 1–5.

49. Francis Beaumont and John Fletcher, *The Honest Mans Fortune*, ed. Johann Gerritsen (Groningen: Wolters, 1952), 2.1.23–5.

50. This use of "brain" and Ford's earlier disguise as "Brooke" (a word obviously related to *-ford*) suggest that F's and Q's "Brainford" should not be editorially amended, as it almost always is, to the modern place-name's spelling, "Brentford". Retaining the older spelling, "Brainford," stresses the fact that the witch of *Brain*ford exists only in Ford's fantasy.

51. See Dolan, *Dangerous Familiars*, 215–17, among many others.

52. Shakespeare, *The Tragedy of King Lear*, ed. Stephen Orgel, in *Complete Works*, New Pelican Shakespeare (New York: Penguin, 2002), 4.5.96 (Folio text only).

53. Cited (in modernized spelling) from *The Dramatic Works of Thomas Dekker*, ed. Fredson Bowers, corr. edn., 4 vols. (Cambridge: Cambridge University Press, 1964–70), 2: 77.

54. Shakespeare, *Measure for Measure*, ed. Brian Gibbons, New Cambridge Shakespeare (Cambridge: Cambridge University Press, 1991), 4.3.152; Thomas D'Urfey, *Wit and Mirth, or Pills to Purge Melancholy*, 6 vols. (London, 1719–20), 4: 162: "I have also seen on a Woman's Chin I A hair or two to grow, I But, alas the Face, it is too cold a place! I Then look for a Beard below."

10
Shakespeare in Leather

Anston Bosman

William Shakespeare was born into leather. Biographers have noted as much since 1821, the year in which Edmond Malone's *Life of William Shakspeare* saw posthumous publication. The *Life* – which, on his deathbed a decade earlier, Malone had asked the younger Boswell to edit – was frankly revisionist in intent, and proceeded by identifying and correcting the errors of earlier scholars. Among those errors was the matter of Shakespeare's father's job. Whereas John Shakespeare had previously been identified as a butcher or a dealer in wool, Malone's scrupulous research yielded no evidence to support either claim.[1] Nor could the biographer at first shed any new light on the question, and his *Life* records that "after a very tedious and tiresome search" he "began to despair" of an advance – until, to his relief, he found in the Stratford archives a legal document from 1556 which "furnished me with the long-sought information, and ascertains that the trade of our great poet's father was that of a *glover*."[2] Malone went on to explain what a profitable business gloving was in Elizabethan England: gloves were ubiquitous articles, essential to fashion and ceremony, ranging in style from the serviceable to the elaborate. Though London was the center of the trade, Malone found at least five glovers were at work in late sixteenth-century Stratford, and he argued that their wares extended beyond gloves to such workaday items as "leathern hose, aprons, belts, points, jerkins, pouches, wallets, satchels and purses."[3] This information changed forever our picture of William Shakespeare's childhood, and in this respect as in many others the 1821 *Life* achieved "a quantum leap forward in Shakespeare studies."[4]

Yet Malone was also a man of his times, and this may explain why his scholarship consistently represents gloving as a trade rather than as a craft. Writing in the dawn of the Industrial Revolution, he always describes John Shakespeare engaged in "manufacture," never in manual labor.[5] So compelling was this view that biographers took a century to reaffirm, in balance with the commercial viability of the enterprise, the glover's artisanal skill. Only in 1930, by which time archivists had unearthed more records of Shakespeare's father as a glover and a "whittawer" or dresser of light-colored leather, was E. K. Chambers prepared to argue, in *William Shakespeare*, that John "combined these occupations" – that is, he not only made and sold gloves, but also "cured and whitened the soft skins which were the material of the glover's craft."[6] (Influentially, Chambers also reinstated the long-discredited claims of butchery and wool-dealing as "subordinate activities" to the gloving business.)[7] Once John Shakespeare had been reconceived as an artisan, moreover, biographers began to ask what influence his craftsmanship might have had on that of his son. Not a decade after Chambers, the Warwickshire antiquary Edgar Fripp devoted a chapter of his aptly named *Shakespeare: Man and Artist* to the question of "What Shakespeare learnt from his Father's Shop." But whereas Malone's nineteenth-century account of John's profession had cited Shakespeare's text only once (referring to the gloves Autolycus offers for sale in *The Winter's Tale*), Fripp crammed his few pages with nearly fifty footnoted references to the poems and plays. His work repays lengthy citation because it set at once the standard and the limit for all subsequent biographical accounts. I have stripped the following passage of its twenty-three original footnotes:

William Shakespeare refers to the hides of oxen and horses, to calf-skin, sheep-skin, lamb-skin, fox-skin, and dog-skin, deer-skin and cheveril. He knew that neats-leather was used for shoes, sheep's leather for a bridle. "Is not parchment," asks Hamlet, "made of sheep-skins?" Horatio replies, "Ay, my lord, and calf-skins too." The uniform of the serjeant-at-mace in *The Comedy of Errors*, and no doubt in Stratford town, was made of calf-skin. The poet was aware that horse-hair was used in bowstrings and "calves' guts" in fiddle-strings. He notices leathern aprons, jerkins, and bottles, the "sow-skin bowget" or bag carried by tinkers, and he comments humorously on the capacity of tanned leather to keep out water. He alludes to "flesh and fell," to the "greasy fells" of ewes, and, with evident pleasure, to the lamb's "white fleece." He knew that the deer's hide was the keeper's perquisite, and we may believe that his father made purchases from the keepers round Stratford. References to cheveril (kid-skin) are much to the point. On account of its softness and flexibility it was used in the making of finer qualities of gloves. Shakespeare speaks of "a wit of cheveril, that stretches from an inch narrow to an ell broad." This is technical language, borrowed from his father's business. [8]

With the brisk precision of a concordance, Fripp assembles Shakespeare's allusions to hides, skins, gloves, parchment and leather – but what is the point of the exercise? What relation does it assert between the life and the work? On the one hand, the relation itself appears "technical": Shakespeare's Ephesus is "borrowed" from his Stratford, and his depiction of Henry VI's age (in which the keeper retains the deerskin) from that of Elizabeth. On the other hand, the references are deployed "humorously," "with evident pleasure," and the quality of cheveril that draws Shakespeare is "flexibility." So more than technical borrowing is at play here after all. How shall we then describe the operation? Though Fripp doesn't pursue the question, his text strains against its own attempt to reduce Shakespeare's fictions to a single point of origin, to find a full explanation of the work in the knowable details of the life.

In this respect, moreover, Shakespearean biography has not come far since 1938. Even in our biographical age, when a new life of Shakespeare appears almost annually, writers are content with a version of Fripp's account. To be sure, we now know more about the Elizabethan glove trade and its place in the guild structure; about how John Shakespeare's gloving linked with his dealings in wool, barley, timber, and real estate; and about his puzzling signature marks (often construed as a pair of glover's compasses or a clamp on which leather was stretched and stitched). There have been lively reconstructions of Henley Street: Michael Wood depicts a "cottage industry" run by John and Mary "with outworkers, and with women in his outhouse doing the sewing," and Stanley Wells adds that "some of the family urine would have been put to practical use here, for softening the skins."[9] The trace of the workshop in Shakespeare's writing can surprise, as when Peter Ackroyd links the "smelly business" of tawing to a "pronounced aversion to unpleasant smells" in the drama.[10] But here, as almost everywhere, literary references to gloving are catalogued *pro forma*, culminating in Mistress Quickly's comparison of a "great round beard" to "a glover's paring-knife" (*The Merry Wives of Windsor* 1.4.18–19). At once specific and trivial, this example allows the biographer to close the subject and tackle more promising issues like religion or schooling. Fripp's assumption still holds: Shakespeare's allusions to his father's craft serve only to confirm what we already know.

Such biographical reductionism dulls even the most inventive recent life of Shakespeare, Stephen Greenblatt's *Will in the World*. For though Greenblatt sets out "to understand how Shakespeare used his imagination to transform his life into his art," and though he at times proceeds by enough conjecture to dismay scrupulous critics, his tale of Shakespeare in leather is the traditional one.[11] Like his predecessors, Greenblatt notes that "gloves, skins, and leather show up frequently in the plays, in ways that seem to reflect an easy intimacy with the trade," and the usual index ensues.[12] Yet *Will in the World* is not quite prepared to consign these references to local color: "For Shakespeare," Greenblatt muses, "leather was not only a means of providing vivid detail but also the stuff of metaphor; it evidently came readily to mind when he was putting together his world."[13] This would be an exciting claim if the instances Greenblatt goes on to cite were not proverbs older than Shakespeare himself; Mercutio's line about "a wit of cheveril, that stretches from an inch narrow to an ell broad" (*Romeo and Juliet* 2.3.79–80) fuses two such popular expressions. Here leather certainly is the "stuff of metaphor," but that metaphor cannot be explained, much less explained away, by the facts of biography.[14] If we are to ask what sheepskins really have to do with parchment, or the sale of gloves with the circulation of lies, or the twisting of language with the pliability of kidskin, then the settled certainties of most life-writing will not serve us well.

Leather, as Will Shakespeare knew well, is prepared skin – more precisely, the term describes the middle layer of a mammal's skin once it has been cleaned, worked, and preserved. The conversion of skin into leather is broadly referred to as tanning, a chemical process designed to render the pelt imputrescible while at the same time maintaining the natural fibrous structure from which the final product's strength and pliability are derived. To be sure, several types of prepared skin are not tanned, and today some experts do not consider them leathers, but in Shakespeare's time such demarcations were far from clear: a genealogy of the leather gilds reveals a dozen or so companies, dealing with every kind and preparation of skin, regrouping over time by acts of incorporation, union, or secession.[15] The Glovers, for instance, were first regulated in the fourteenth century, overlapped with the Leathersellers, split from them in 1479, joined with the Pursers in 1498, were again absorbed by the Leathersellers in 1502, and were granted their charter only in 1638.[16] In 1635, an ordinance was deemed necessary to distinguish the Leathersellers from the Fellmongers, Parchmentmakers, and Leatherdressers; the problem was that all these occupations could be pursued on the same premises by the same craftsmen.[17] So it is prudent to suspend modern distinctions and treat the ensemble of leather crafts as a family business, its members occasionally squabbling yet thoroughly interdependent.

How did the business work? All leather workers began with a heavy cattle hide or the skin of a smaller animal – a sheep, goat, calf or deer, even a dog. Once stripped of hoof and horn and washed, the raw hides or skins had their hair or wool and their remaining flesh removed; this was achieved by hanging in smoke or by soaking in lime, and then by scraping both sides with a knife. At this point, if the craftsman was a parchment maker, he would take the limed pelts and stretch them on frames using cords and pegs. During the drying process the skin was regularly splashed with water, re-tensioned by means of the pegs, treated with a chalky paste to remove fat, and scraped with a two-handled crescent-shaped knife. Finally, the dried parchment or vellum was shaved to a uniform thickness, cut from the frame and rubbed smooth with pumice. It was finally ready to be written on; to cover boxes and caskets and drums; and, in the heavy-duty form known as forel, to bind books.

By contrast, if the limed skin was to be used by a tanner or tawyer (*tan* and *taw* being Latin and Germanic verbs for related processes), additional preparation was required. The pelts would be further softened by soaking them in an alkaline bating of dog or bird droppings, and then the tanning processes could commence. Of these there were three: (a) oil tanning (or chamoising), where the skins were soaked in troughs of fish and whale oils; (b) mineral tanning (or tawing), where the skins were dressed with a mixture of alum, salt, and egg yolks; and (c) vegetable tanning, where the skins were soaked in infusions of oak bark for six months to two years.[18] After tanning, a hide would typically be dressed and finished by a currier and passed on to, say, a shoemaker. After tawing, on the other hand, a skin would be treated by a light leather craftsman such as a glover. Each craft employed special techniques: a glover, for instance, dampened and stretched the material, cut out the shape, pointed and stitched the parts, then ironed and polished the finished glove. Such a glove represented one end-point of a complex system of materials and procedures – a system with which a family like the Shakespeares would have been familiar.

Nor should the reach of that system be underestimated; for although Malone's biography may have neglected the skill required in gloving, his word "manufacture" grasped the scale of the operation. In early modern England, the leather industry was arguably more important than the metal crafts and second only to woolen cloth.[19] By the sixteenth century, midland towns like Leicester and Northampton were effectively specializing in leather and allied trades.[20] The product was ubiquitous, required in the streets as footwear and clothing; on the farm as boots, saddles, and horse collars; in industry as belts, buckets, and bellows to provide the blast in iron furnaces. Forceful advocates protected the interests of the trade. A 1629 petition to Parliament entitled "Leather: A Discourse" asserted the centrality of leather to a range of occupations, from the obvious "Shoomakers and Curriers" to an impressive list of "Booke binders, Sadlers, Upholsters, Budget-makers, Truncke-makers, Belt-makers, Case-makers, Woll-Card makers, Sheath makers, Hawkes-Hood-makers, Scabberd-makers, Box-makers, Cabinet makers, Bottle and Jacke makers, Girdlers, Glovers."[21] This survey shows leather to be indispensable at all levels of society from the "Courtier" to the "Clowne": both "the Merchant and the Mechanicke," notes the author of the "Discourse," "walke in Bootes."[22]

To identify leather as essential to the making of Renaissance gloves, clothes, objects, and books is to discern a material feature common to the institutions in which William Shakespeare lived and worked. Great as the differences were between the glove trade into which he was born and the businesses of theater and publishing in which he made his name, all three enterprises shared a reliance on the extraordinary attributes of hides and skins expertly prepared. Henslowe's playhouse inventories from 1598, for instance, show that the costumes of the early modern stage included such items as decorated gloves, leather jerkins in black or white or crimson, some skirted coats for antics, and a "yelow leather dublett for a clowne."[23] Henslowe lists several accessories either certainly or probably made of leather: in the first category are a "lether hatchete" and a bridle for Tamburlaine, while the second might include vizards, the skins of exotic animals such as lions, and perhaps a pair of wings for Mercury. To these should be added the percussion instruments – a drum and "tymbrells" – which were made of vellum stretched over a wooden frame. The inventories exclude workaday leather items, although these could be vital to dramatic effect; when Launce in *The Two Gentlemen of Verona* improvises a puppet-show of leaving his family, the surrogates he chooses for his mother and father are his own left and right shoes.

When the actor Richard Jones sold his share in theatrical property in 1598, he transferred to Edward Alleyn "All and singuler suche Share parte and porcion of playinge apparrells playe Bookes, Instruments, and other comodities whatsoeur belonging to the same."[24] While it is clear that leather was important to "playinge apparells," musical "Instruments," and "other [theatrical] commodities," what about "playe Bookes"? If by this term is meant only the playhouse manuscript that critics have traditionally called the promptbook, then it suffices to note that these folios, sewn or stabbed together, were enclosed in protective vellum wrappers.[25] But if we take "playe Bookes" to include dramatic texts printed, sold, and bound, then leather assumes a more complex role.[26] Book production relied on leather from the first stages of printing – pressmen used leather bands when casting letters, and leather balls when inking type – to the final phase of binding.[27] Depending on the book, seller, and buyer, binding might precede or follow sale; the covering material might be calf, sheep, goat or vellum; the leather might be kept plain or elaborately tooled and decorated. From the bookstall or the binder, printed volumes of plays might end up in a school or study – or, for that matter, in a dramatic representation, where books served as indispensable hand properties. Stage directions attest to the frequency with which education, magic, accountancy, and prayer were signaled by books; in the theater, moreover, audiences would have judged these books by their covers. When we consider illustrations of the early modern stage, we can now recognize book bindings as properties as much as jerkins and aprons, hats, boots, and gloves, and scabbards, globes, and drums. Together these leather items make up a skin in which performance is enveloped.

Leather, then, was a pervasive element of Shakespeare's material world, from his childhood home to the professional theatre and the increasingly lucrative book trade. But prepared skins and hides exercised an equally powerful influence over his poetic and dramatic imagination, and this influence cannot be reduced to his father's choice of occupation. Just as literary biographies of Shakespeare have mostly given short shrift to the artisanal practices and economic context of the early modern leather industry, so they have yet to recognize the wider philosophical and cultural domain from which the dramatist adopted leather as what Greenblatt felicitously termed "the stuff of metaphor." In fact, the broadest range of early modern writers found ingenious uses for leather, likening it in both positive and negative ways to the products of the creative mind.

In the beginning, God stretched the sky over the earth like a sheet of leather. This remarkable creation metaphor occurs in the Old Testament, most clearly in Psalm 104, and despite its apparent simplicity it has yielded several different interpretations. In the original Hebrew psalm the outstretched sky is figured as *yeri'ah*, a cloth of tanned skins used by the nomadic Israelites to make tents and especially to cover and protect the tabernacle. Yet the material specificity of the psalmist's metaphor was obscured when the word was translated into early modern English as "curtain": the version of Psalm 104:2 in the Geneva Bible, for instance, tells how God "covereth him self with light as with a garment, and spreadeth the heavens like a curtaine."[28] By contrast, the Vulgate insisted on the cloth's materiality, describing the Creator as *extendens caelos ut pellem*, that is, stretching out the heavens as a skin; this Latin rendering made possible a Continental tradition that construed God as a currier or tanner.[29] Exponents of that tradition notably included Erasmus, who was interested enough in the Psalms to publish some dozen commentaries on them, and later to invoke them in some surprising contexts.[30] Towards the end of *The Praise of Folly*, for example, Moria takes aim at the scriptural exegeses of self-certain theologians, and her charge is that the learned expositors usurp the leatherworking sovereignty of God.

At this point in Erasmus' text Moria is trying to recruit Saint Paul to the cause of Folly, but in doing so she must challenge authoritative readings of Paul's text. Suddenly she interrupts the exercise to protest: Why should she fret over her interpretation when other scholars blithely make of scripture whatever they will? Here are her words in Chaloner's 1549 translation:

> But whereabout goe I now? Shall I stand to one onely exemple in my defence, seyng all doctours take it commenly for theyr priuilege, to streche out heauen (that is to saie) holy writte lyke a cheuerell skynne?[31]

Coelum, hoc est, diuinam scripturam, ceu pellem extendere: Moria's allusion to Psalm 104 mocks theologians for manipulating scripture in the way God the Tanner stretched out the sky.[32] Might Erasmus have literal skins in mind here, that is to say, the parchment onto which the sacred books were copied in biblical times?[33] Whether or not this is so, Moria's jest shifts the symbolism of leather-work from the divine creation of a world to the human interpretation of a text, and in the process leather – that crafted material, flexible and protective – becomes a figure for figuration itself. Here leather is "the stuff of metaphor" not in the weak sense of facilitating a range of verbal images, but in the stronger sense of embodying the metaphoric process by which our minds shape experience into expression.

On the other hand, adds Moria skeptically, sometimes leather is just plain stuff, in which case efforts to extend or stretch its meaning reveal the ignorance of the interpreter. Unlike Paul, who rightly twisted the words of a pagan inscription at Athens in order to preach the Gospel (*torqueret in argumentum fidei Christianae*), modern theologians do wrong when they wrench scripture from its context. Such was the error of the preacher who took an Old Testament reference to military tents as a reference to an apostolic excoriation. At issue was Habakkuk 3:7, which reads in the Vulgate as *turbabuntur pelles terrae Madian*:

[An other doctour] interpretyng a place of Abacuc the prophet, where he saieth, *The skinnes of the lande of Madian shall be disparcled and torne asunder*: nothing consideryng that the Prophete spake of the *Madianistes lodgeynges or tentes for the fielde*, whiche were made of beastes skinnes, as aunciently men in warrefare vsed, writeth plainly, that Abacuc did prophecy there of the fleayng of Sainct Bartholomeus skynne. (114)

Moria deplores stretching skin – the word, the text, and the idea – as a gesture typical of "foolelosophers" who assert their wisdom by subtle definitions, analogies and inferences (10). Ridiculous as their interpretations may be, their deeper error is to lay claim to an authority that properly belongs to God. Instead, it is truly wise to admit that we and our readings are foolish. This is, of course, what Moria does from her dramatic opening lines, rising suddenly to address the crowded hall in what she calls "this so straunge an apparell" (7–8). Holbein's marginal illustrations depict her in foolscap and bells, but Moria never tells us what she is wearing – unless we take her literally when, turning her attention to Christian folly, she declares that "I have ones taken vpon me to plaie the doctresse, *putting on a Lyons hide*" (121). Presenting herself as the proverbial ass in lionskin, Moria wears her folly on her sleeve. In her earlier remarks on the *theatrum mundi*, she asserted that we are all players in costume, and that society could not function otherwise. Now it is not merely that skin provides a metaphor for life's necessary disguise; in addition, metaphor itself appears essential to the performance of speech. For Erasmus, metaphor is the skin of language: "a certaine veile or shadow, which taken awaie ones, the plaie can no more be plaied" (38).

Erasmus had already defined utility and obscurity as the twin qualities of proverbial discourse. The *Adages* begins by noting that ancient definitions of the proverb stress "either helpfulness in the conduct of life, or the outer covering of metaphor, and sometimes they join the two together."[34] Ideally, a proverb is an everyday saying, drawn from "common usage," which "wraps up" a valuable idea in "some kind of envelope" or "metaphorical disguise."[35] Now since the physical envelope we all have in common – our everyday outer covering – is our skin, it is hardly surprising that skins and hides should occur so widely throughout the Erasmian anthology. Like *The Praise of Folly*, the *Adages* returns obsessively to the Cumaean ass in lionskin, but it also cites proverbs on the skin of dogs, foxes, snakes, elephants, old people, thin people and liars. The entry on "Keep inside your own skin," for example, refers to military tents, a leather-seller in Aristophanes, a shoemaker in Martial, and the flaying of Marsyas. This proverb, Erasmus summarizes, "tells us not to forget our condition and attempt what is beyond our powers."[36] Skin is here a figure for our natural or proper limits; to stretch our skin, or to assume the skin of our superiors, is to court disaster. Ironically, however, proverbial discourse relies on just such distortion or misrepresentation, as Erasmus acknowledges when, searching for one trope "specially appropriate to adages as a class," he lights on the figure of hyperbole.[37] If an adage is an idea wrapped up in an envelope, then we may say (as we today describe the performance limits of an aircraft) that the envelope is always being pushed. A proverb is language straining at its own skin.

Even in England, where translations of Psalm 104 imprecisely likened the sky to a curtain, proverbs often used prepared skins as a model for processes of creation and manipulation, whether those processes were deemed sinister or benign. Some of these popular sayings – such as "to cut large thongs of other men's leather," meaning to be lavish with that which is another's – are also listed in the *Adages*, but others draw on materials and articles that were current in Shakespeare's day. Among these the kid-leather or cheveril glove was perhaps the most suggestive exemplar. Pliant kidskin was an intuitive analog for a personality compliant to the point of sycophancy: to call someone "as supple as a glove" in sixteenth-century England was not to deliver a compliment. Whereas stretching skins had once simply conveyed the idea of overreaching, the elasticity of cheveril could now imply mean-spiritedness as well as ambition. In a 1576 sermon on the apocalypse, Richard Curteys, bishop of Chichester, described the massed forces of evil as armored in kidskin, and extended the metaphor to his own time:

> the nature of Cheverel Leather is, that if a man take it up by the sides and pull it in breadth he may make a little Point as broad as both his hands. If he take it by the ends and pull it in length,

he may make it as small as a thread. Most men nowadays have Cheverel consciences, if the matter touch their own profit or pleasure: they make their consciences wide enough, and large enough. If it touch another man's profit, they make them as small as a thread.[38]

As the bodies of the devil's soldiers are clad in leather, so are the minds of fallen humans. Indeed, as Curteys may be assuming in this passage, the Bible presents leather production as an immediate consequence of the Fall itself. For whereas modern paleontologists suggest that a crude sort of tanning may have been mankind's first manufacturing process, carried out by hominids over a million years ago, Genesis declares the preparation of skins to be God's first act on behalf of the Original Sinners.[39] After eating the forbidden fruit, Adam and Eve sew themselves "breeches" of "fig tree leaves," but God clothes the pair in "coates of skinnes" before casting them out of Eden.[40] This biblical episode left early modern moralists with a dilemma: Was leather to be praised as a divine gift, a souvenir of paradise? Or should it be condemned as a legacy of our primordial disgrace?

We can see this deep ambivalence underlying Philip Stubbes's 1583 diatribe, *The Anatomie of Abuses*. Early in the first part of the *Anatomie*, two characters debate the vice of pride as manifested in clothing. When the first character asks "wherefore our apparel was given us, and by whom," his interlocutor replies that God so pitied Adam and Eve that he "gave them pelts, & fells of beasts to make them garments withal, to the end that their shameful parts might less appear."[41] So far, so good – except that "we have so perverted [those garments], as now they serve in stead of the devil's nets, to catch poor souls in" (C4v). At once the question arises whether we should curb vanity by returning to the fashions of Genesis:

> Did the Lord clothe our first parents in leather, as not having any thing more precious to attire them withal, or for that, it might be a permanent rule, or pattern unto us (his posterity) for ever, whereafter we are of force to make all our garments, so as it is not now lawful to go in richer array, without offending his majesty?

Neither of these alternatives turns out to be quite right. In fact, God (who could have used any material) chose leather for its "austerity and simplicity," and now we too (though we need not wear skins) must rigorously eschew "gorgeous attire." In sum, the skin-coats provided to

Adam and Eve were meant as a "sign, or pattern of mediocrity unto us" (C5v).

And yet the symbolic value of leather is curiously transformed as we pass from this volume of the *Anatomie* to its sequel, subtitled *The Display of Corruptions*. In this second part, which castigates vices in various Elizabethan institutions, Stubbes drops the notion of leather's primitive simplicity and instead associates it with forms of worldly perversion. The first reason for this shift is that the text zealously exposes abuses in the physical manufacture of leather and the economic regulation of the trade. Stubbes declares the craftsmen idle and corrupt: tanners, he says, skimp on time and chemicals, shoemakers on sealant and stitching, and everyone passes off inferior hides and skins for top quality.[42] Since leather itself has become synonymous with corruption, it is wholly apt that Stubbes also uses the material to denounce another profession – the law – in terms with which we have become familiar: "the lawyers have such cheveril consciences, that they can serve the devil better in no kind of calling than in that: ... law is turned almost topsie turnie, and therefore happy is he, that hath least to do with them" (C3v).

Matters are indeed topsy-turvy when biblical example runs across modern practice, when the utility of materials cannot easily be squared with the extravagance of metaphors. But it would be misguided to construe leather dualistically as either natural element or cultural product. A prepared skin, after all, must be at once organic and artificial, and its making is a figure for the process by which those qualities, if not reconciled, are softened and mutually infused.

In early modern England, then, leather was valuable as both artifact and discourse, and between those values lay an intimate and changeable relation. To separate leather-as-material from leather-as-metaphor would be to misinterpret this culture, in which prepared skins daily linked tanners to preachers, interlocking artisanal practice and educated rhetoric. The life of William Shakespeare, glover's son and grammar-school boy, registers the impact of both these forms of work. Since his plays deploy literary and theatrical expertise alike, they attest to leather's prominence in the objects and stories of his age. They also call our attention to three general properties of leather.

First, leather is *laborious*. As Shakespeare describes it, the surface of the natural world is leathery: strong, flexible, entire. Thus the forester in *As You Like It* sings of the slaughtered deer's "leather skin" (4.2.11); the rough-skinned russet apples that Davy offers to Bardolph in *Henry IV Part 2* are called "leather-coats" (5.3.41); and in *A Midsummer Night's*

Dream Titania dispatches some of her fairies to "war with rere-mice for their leathren wings" (2.2.4). Like fauna and flora, humans too appear encased in a prepared hide: Dromio of Ephesus in *A Comedy of Errors* likens his skin to "parchment" (3.1.13) and the gloomy poet of Sonnet 62 regards himself as "beated and chapped with tanned antiquity" (10). The passage from living tissue to leathered preservation is most clearly rendered in the Gravedigger's words to Hamlet: to the prince's question "How long will a man lie i'th' earth ere he rot?" the digger replies that "a tanner will last you nine year" since "his hide is so tanned with his trade that 'a will keep out water a great while. And your water is a sore decayer of your whoreson dead body" (5.1.163–72).

But to describe the world as leathery is already to see it as manufactured. An apple called a leather-coat is natural produce phrased as cultural product; similarly, Titania wants the "leathern" bat's wings to be harvested to "make [her] small elves coats." In the human realm, Shakespeare's tanned poet – aged by everyday sunburn – seems uncomfortably close to the tanner proper, steeped in the astringent solutions of his trade. Leather here becomes a figure for labor: specifically, the conversion of skin into parchment or costume suggests the transformation of the world into the materials of writing and performance. "Is not this a lamentable thing," says Cade to the Butcher in *Henry VI Part 2*, "that of the skin of an innocent lamb should be made parchment? That parchment, being scribbled o'er, should undo a man?" (4.2.80). The force of the verbal text invoked by Cade has its match in the performed action of *As You Like It*, where the hunters bring home their catch and vow to don its skin in a celebratory ritual. "What shall he have that killed the deer?" sings the forester, "His leather skin and horns to wear" (4.2.10–11). While critics differ over the precise effect of this behavior in the play – linking it variously to mummer's disguising, skimmington rides and the carnival shaming of cuckolds – most agree that it stages a demotic political transgression to which the deerskin is the essential accessory. From pelt to parchment, therefore, the work of Shakespeare's theater is accomplished through the skin.

Second, leather is *dimensional*. Separating the skin's middle layer from the hair and the flesh does not yield a flat surface. On the contrary, that layer consists of a fibrous network of protein embedded in a jelly-like ground substance. When an animal dies this network breaks down and putrefaction sets in. Tanning cleans up the skin structure, allows artificial cross-links to form, and then restores the ground substance. Depending on the raw material and the processes used, vellum or leather will be stiff or supple, stretchy or rigid, limp or springy. A desirable quality for a garment maker is the ability of a lightly tanned skin to stretch in one direction while remaining relatively elastic at right angles to the direction of the original pull; this quality is called "run" and is especially valuable in the manufacture of well-fitting gloves.

In Shakespeare's work, we can discern complex interest in the dimensionality of skins, whether on the slaughtered animal or the live one. In *As You Like It*, the First Lord famously describes the melancholy Jaques in the forest of Arden, reclining at the foot of a tree beside a stream:

> Today my Lord of Amiens and myself
> Did steal behind him as he lay along
> Under an oak, whose antic root peeps out
> Upon the brook that brawls along this wood;
> To the which place a poor sequestered stag,
> That from the hunter's aim had ta'en a hurt,
> Did come to languish; and indeed, my lord,
> The wretched animal heaved forth such groans
> That their discharge did stretch his leathern coat
> Almost to bursting, and the big round tears
> Coursed one another down his innocent nose
> In piteous chase.
>
> (2.1.29–40)

The passage has rightly been praised as an instance of bravura pictorialism in an intensely visual play, but Shakespeare achieves effects here that far exceed the Renaissance emblems to which the scene is routinely compared. For unlike an emblem (or the memorable illustrations of this moment by Blake and Constable) Shakespeare's picture of Jaques and the stag does not lie flat. Instead, the image is in constant motion, vibrating with prepositions – behind, along, under, out, upon, along, to, from, forth, down – and deploying verbs of elongation, throbbing, and swelling. The stag languishes and heaves, stretches and threatens to burst. It is puzzling that one recent critic calls this scene "static and distanced" and a second terms it "bookish pastoral ... more emblematic and mannered than dramatic," for if one begins with the stag's "leathern coat," an altogether different image takes shape – an image not merely vivid but visceral.[43] This is germane to the scene because Shakespeare is presenting an analogy between the stag's dis-

tress and Jaques's melancholy, and Burton's *Anatomy* defines the condition by not only the recumbent "stretch" posture (also captured in
images by Hilliard and Oliver) and "weeping for no reason," but also
distending, "groaning" and "much leaping of wind about in the skin";
"continual, sharp, and stinking belchings, as if the meat in their stom-
achs were putrefied."[44] As a manifestation of Jaques's symptoms, therefore, the stag seems as least as dramatic as it is emblematic; we might
say, in fact, that the passage offers its audience an anatomy theater of
melancholy.

If in *As You Like It* the stretching and swelling of leather figure the
distemper of the melancholic mind and body alike, then elsewhere
Shakespeare separates the two analogies, using leathery elasticity as a
model for hyperbolic extensions of language or performance. We are
more familiar with the first category, since it tropes upon proverbial
expressions: Feste in *Twelfth Night* calls a sentence "but a cheveril glove
to a good wit. How quickly the wrong side may be turned outward"
(3.1.12–13); and Mercutio, in a scene full of references to skins, teases
Romeo for his "wit of cheveril, that stretches from an inch narrow to
an ell broad" (2.4.83). If, following the *OED*, we take wit to be "that
quality of speech or writing which consists in the apt association of
thought and expression," then we may also note Shakespearean
instances of stretching at both poles: on the side of thought, Anne
Boleyn is encouraged by the old lady to accept Henry VIII by "[stretch-
ing]" her "soft cheveril conscience" (2.3.32); on the side of expression,
the poet of Sonnet 17 imagines his verses dismissed as "stretchèd metre
of an antique song" (12). Here wit is "strained beyond natural or
proper limits" (*OED*) into the realm of hyperbole, the figure Puttenham
gave the English name "the over-reacher."[45] It should not surprise,
therefore, that Shakespeare uses the language of stretching also in the
case of "immoderate excess" (Puttenham's phrase) of the performing
body. Best known here is the instance of the mechanicals' playlet,
which Philostrate advertises to Theseus as "extremely stretched and
conned with cruel pain" (5.1.80); the pain of performance is specified
in *Troilus and Cressida*, when Ajax enjoins the trumpeter to "Blow ...
Outswell the colic of puffed Aquilon. I Come, stretch thy chest, and let
thy eyes spout blood" (4.5.10). Indeed, *Troilus and Cressida* contains
perhaps the most remarkable instance of stretched enactment. An early
scene narrated by Ulysses depicts Patroclus and Achilles amusing themselves in their tent with a mirthful parody of Agamemnon. It would be
noteworthy enough that Patroclus "like a strutting player, whose
conceit I Lies in his hamstring, I doth think it rich I To hear the

wooden dialogue and sound I 'Twixt his stretched footing and the scaffoldage" (1.3.153–6); but it is all the more extraordinary that this vignette transposes into comedy one of the most wrenching similes in Homeric epic – the tug-of war over Patroclus's corpse in the seventeenth book of the *Iliad*, which the poet likens to a tanner's crew stretching out an enormous oxhide.[46] The dimensionality of leather – its capacity to be pulled in one direction, then another – suggests here not only the limits of word and action but the transformation of genre itself.

Third, leather is *synaesthetic*. "If this skin were parchment, and the blows were ink, I Your own handwriting would tell you what I think": so Dromio of Ephesus complains to the man he mistakes for his master Antipholus (3.1.13–14). This ingenious couplet fuses the skin's capacities for impression and expression, for receiving the disfiguring touch of the other and making that effect visible in its turn. The unfortunate Dromio, who earlier at the mart countered Antipholus of Syracuse's demand for a thousand marks by recalling "some marks of yours about my pate" (1.2.82), is once again wishing that those marks could be remarked. His couplet imagines his skin as a writing surface and his self not as a beaten slave, but as a bookmarked page. How else to call an end to this comedy of errata? His only other solution is to be tanned, stretched, and sewn up whole – this makes sense, he tells Adriana, if she continues to make sport with him:

> Am I so round with you as you with me,
> That like a football you do spurn me thus?
> You spurn me hence, and he will spurn me hither:
> If I last in this service, you must case me in leather.
>   (2.1.82–5)

From receptive parchment to resilient leather, Dromio's wordplay blends the tactile and visual qualities of prepared skins. These were not, to be sure, the only sensory charms of early modern leather. For example, while the workaday glove – for hawking, say – would be simply constructed, the ceremonial glove would be tawed and buffed to softness, richly embroidered and jeweled, and finally perfumed. Moreover, scents were not confined to aristocratic leathers: in *The Winter's Tale* Autolycus offers "gloves as sweet as damask roses" (4.4.221) from his peddler's pack. Still in a pastoral setting, Henry VI invokes the taste of leather when he soliloquizes on the "happy life" of a "homely swain" eschewing a prince's "golden cup" to take "his cold thin drink out of his leather bottle" (*Henry VI Part 3* 2.5.21–2; 52; 48). Mingled with the flavor of its wax, pitch or metal lining, the taste of oak-tanned cattle-hide would have been a ubiquitous accompaniment to early modern liquor, from cloister to tavern to the open field.

Finally, one can hear leather. Prepared skin has often helped to control or enhance sound and has long been an indispensable material in musical instruments. Soft, white tawed leather is used for organ bellows, the valves of brass instruments are bushed with leather, and the bass wind instrument called the serpent is made of leather-covered wood. But nowhere are skins more essential than in the class of percussion called membranophones, commonly known as drums. The most familiar of these in the early modern period was the side drum or tabor, which consisted of a cylindrical shell of wood covered at each end by heads of vellum (skins of sheep or calf, or even pig or goat). Leather often covered the ends of sticks used to beat the heads: in these cases, drumbeats were the sound of skin on skin. Originally a military instrument adopted by crusading armies from their Muslim foes, the side drum was a keynote of the Renaissance soundscape and an integral "speaking property" in the inventory of theater companies, traveling and resident alike.[47] Dramas liberally called for drums both offstage and on, either alone or combined with a trumpet or military colors. Shakespeare follows this custom by requiring drums in his histories and tragedies, but it is in a late comedy that he uses a drum to unconventional, not to say virtuosic effect. In so doing he brings the laborious, dimensional, and synaesthetic qualities of leather to performance.

The word *drum* may denote an instrument or a player or both, and *All's Well That Ends Well* demonstrates that properties and persons share the identity of sounding skins. The character in the play who is associated with drumming is Paroles: in the Italian wars he manages to lose his French regiment's precious drum and then boastfully vows to recover it. But the association of this character and this object extends beyond the plot to encompass a pattern of verbal and visual allusion. Bertram chides Paroles that "This drum sticks sorely in your disposition" (3.6.42–3) and Paroles indeed resembles a drum in many ways. Time and again he is described as a vacuous and reverberant interior over which fabric has been closely stretched: Helena finds him an overdressed fool on whom "fix'd evils sit so fit" (1.1.104), while Lafew teases that "the scarfs and bannerets about thee did manifoldly dissuade me from believing thee a vessel of too great a burthen" (2.3.202–4) and later discerns "no kernel in this light nut; the soul of this man is his clothes" (2.5.42–4). Empty vessels make the most noise, and in *All's Well* there is none emptier or noisier than Paroles. It is from this paradox that the soldiers fashion his humiliation in the form of "John Drum's entertainment" (3.6.36–7).

Appropriately, the remarkable scene in which Paroles is ambushed, hoodwinked, and tormented by his own companions is on multiple levels a performance of drumming. It opens as the braggart gives up on his drum and resolves to steal one of the enemy's, when a sudden alarum warns that what he was seeking seems instead to have found him:

First lord:	*Throca movousos, cargo, cargo, cargo.*
All:	*Cargo, cargo, cargo, villianda par corbo, cargo.*
	[They seize and blindfold Paroles.]
Paroles:	O, ransom, ransom! Do not hide mine eyes.
First sold.:	*Boskos thromuldo boskos.*
Paroles:	I know you are the Muskos' regiment,
	And I shall lose my life for want of language. (4.1.66–71)

What has happened here? In a great rush the alarum – drums struck offstage to startle and confuse – has turned into a scene of beating. The instrumental cacophony blends into the percussive rhythms of an improvised babble; the soldiers stretch a blindfold taut over their fellow's eyes like a second skin; the baffled man yields to the sounds and blows, the jabs and the jabbering. The scene simultaneously transforms Paroles into the proverbial John Drum and gives that metaphor the material form of an actor onstage. In the theater this is often the moment in *All's Well* when an audience's easy derision shifts into cautious empathy, when Paroles the caricature starts to look and sound like one of us – just a bewildered body in a bag. Only a dramatist who was also an actor would risk such discomfort, and perhaps only one who had grown up around the work of skins. In giving him a tiger's heart wrapped in a player's hide, Robert Greene insulted Shakespeare less than he acknowledged him a master leatherman, crafting emotion into action with a turn of his dyer's hand.

Notes

1. These were the views of Aubrey (*c*.1680) and Rowe (1709) respectively.
2. Edmond Malone, *The Plays and Poems of William Shakspeare* (London, F. C. and J. Rivington, 1821), 78.
3. Malone, *Shakspeare*, 82.

4. S. Schoenbaum calls Malone "the greatest of Elizabethan biographers" who "found out more about Shakespeare and his theatrical milieu than any-one before or since," and declares his *Life* "a quantum leap forward in Shakespeare studies" (*Shakespeare's Lives* [Oxford: Clarendon Press, 1970], 178).
5. Malone, *Shakspeare*, 82–3.
6. E. K. Chambers, *William Shakespeare: A Study of Facts and Problems* (Oxford: Clarendon Press, 1930), 1:12.
7. Chambers, *William Shakespeare*, 12.
8. Edgar I. Fripp, *Shakespeare: Man and Artist* (Oxford and London: Oxford University Press and Humphrey Milford, 1938), 79–80.
9. Michael Wood, *In Search of Shakespeare* (London: BBC, 2003) 24; Stanley Wells, *Shakespeare: For All Time* (Oxford: Oxford University Press, 2002), 5.
10. Wells, *Shakespeare: For All Time*, 5; Peter Ackroyd, *Shakespeare: The Biography* (New York: Nan A. Talese, 2005), 22; Wood, *In Search of Shakespeare*, 24, 38.
11. Stephen Greenblatt, *Will in the World: How Shakespeare became Shakespeare* (New York: W. W. Norton, 2004), 14.
12. Ibid., 55.
13. Ibid., 56.
14. For a subtler and more speculative approach to the problem see Katherine Duncan-Jones, "Did the Boy Shakespeare Kill Calves?", *Review of English Studies* 55 (2004): 185–93. Duncan-Jones explores the Shakespeares' ties with leather-dressers and butchers, asking if young William knew of or acted in calf-killing entertainments, and how these experiences registered in his mature writings. See also her *Ungentle Shakespeare: Scenes from his Life* (London: Arden Shakespeare, 2001), 14–16.
15. Such a genealogy is offered, in simplified form, by John W. Waterer in his *Leather in Life, Art, and Industry* (London: Faber and Faber, 1946), after 118; but his preceding chapter on "The Leather Crafts" (66–117) represents the full complexity of the shifting gild affiliations.
16. For a full account see Ralph W. Wiggett, *A History of the Worshipful Company of Glovers of London* (Chichester: Phillimore & Co., 2000).
17. Cited in Waterer, *Leather in Life, Art, and Industry*, 99.
18. This taxonomy is elaborated in Peter C. Meade, *John Waterer's Guide to Leather Conservation and Restoration* (Northampton: Museum of Leathercraft, 1986), 8–10.
19. L. A. Clarkson, "The Organization of the English Leather Industry in the late Sixteenth and Seventeenth Centuries," *Economic History Review* 13:2 (1960), 245.
20. W. G. Hoskins, "English Provincial Towns in the Early Sixteenth Century," *Transactions of the Royal Historical Society*, 5th series, volume 6 (1956), 13–14.
21. *Leather: A Discourse, Tendered to the High Court of Parliament* (London: T.C. for Michael Sparke, 1629), 10. To this survey the author adds two "upstart Trades: Coach makers, And Harnesse makers for Coach Horses."
22. *Leather: A Discourse*, 13.
23. The inventories appear most recently as Appendix 2 to *Henslowe's Diary*, ed. R. A. Foakes (Cambridge: Cambridge University Press, 2002), 316–25.
24. Foakes (ed.), *Henslowe's Diary*, 273.

25. The standard description of "prompt books" is W. W. Greg, *Dramatic Documents from the Elizabethan Playhouses* (Oxford: Clarendon Press, 1931), 189–221. Greg's use of the term "prompt book" over "playbook" has been criticized, notably by William B. Long; see his "*John a Kent and John a Cumber*: An Elizabethan Playbook and Its Implications," in *Shakespeare and Dramatic Tradition*, ed. W. R. Elton and William B. Long (Newark: University of Delaware Press, 1989), 125–43.

26. I assume that companies owned printed texts as well as manuscript copies. Certainly the term "playbook" has unstable reference in the age, as anti-theatrical texts show by confusing "playbooks" with "playhouse books"; see Heidi Brayman Hackel, "'Rowme' of Its Own: Printed Drama in Early Libraries," in *A New History of Early English Drama*, ed. John D. Cox and David Scott Kaplan (New York: Columbia University Press, 1997), 117–18.

27. On printers' purchase of pelts, leather used to tie the matrix to the mould, and the construction of leathern ink balls, see Joseph Moxon, *Mechanick Exercises on the Whole Art of Printing*, ed. Herbert Davis and Harry Carter (London: Oxford University Press, 1958), 81, 169, and 282–7.

28. Geneva Bible (Madison: University of Wisconsin Press, 1969).

29. Vulgate (Stuttgart: Deutsche Bibelgesellschaft, 1983).

30. On the partial commentary Erasmus wrote on the Psalter, see Michael J. Heath, "Erasmus and the Psalms," in *The Bible in the Renaissance*, ed. Richard Griffiths (Burlington: Ashgate, 2001), 28–44.

31. Thomas Chaloner, *The Praise of Folie*, ed. Clarence H. Miller (London: Oxford University Press, 1965), 111. Further references to this text will be parenthetical.

32. Erasmus, *Moriae Encomium*, ed. Clarence H. Miller, in *Opera Omnia Desiderii Erasmi Roterodami* 4:3 (Amsterdam: North-Holland Publishing Company, 1979), 183. My reading is indebted to the brilliant discussion of this passage by M. A. Screech in his *Ecstasy and the Praise of Folly* (London: Duckworth, 1980), 244–6.

33. Scholars are divided on whether the chief material for biblical scrolls was parchment or papyrus. For a summary of the debate and a polemical position, see Menahem Haran, "Book-scrolls in Israel in Pre-Exilic Times," *Journal of Jewish Studies* 33:1–2 (1982), 161–73. How early modern humanists viewed the matter is a subject for another investigation.

34. Desiderius Erasmus, *Adages*, trans. Margaret Mann Phillips and R. A. B. Mynors, in *Collected Works of Erasmus*, vols. 31–4 (Toronto: University of Toronto Press, 1982–1992), 31: 4. Cited hereafter as *CWE*.

35. *CWE*, 31: 3–4.

36. *CWE*, 32: 60.

37. *CWE*, 31: 24.

38. Richard Curteys, *Two sermons preached by the reuerend father in God the Bishop of Chichester* (London: J. Allde, 1576), 117–18.

39. For paleontology, see R. S. Thomson, "Tanning: Man's First Manufacturing Process," *Transactions of the Newcomen Society* 53 (1981–82), 139–40. On animal skins in the Fall, see Ann Rosalind Jones and Peter Stallybrass, *Renaissance Clothing and the Materials of Memory* (Cambridge: Cambridge University Press, 2000), 269–71.

40. Genesis 3:7 and 3:22. The Geneva Bible does not establish for certain whether leather in Eden was a divine or human product: the main text reads "Unto Adam also and to his wife did the Lord God make coates of skinnes, and clothed them," but a marginal note cautions "Or gave them the knowledge to make themselves coates." Either way, it was God's idea.

41. Phillip Stubbes, *The Anatomie of Abuses* (London, 1583), I: C3v–C4r. Further citations will be parenthetical.

42. Phillip Stubbes, *The Second Part of the Anatomie of Abuses, Conteining the Display of Corruptions* (London, [1583]), F2v–F4r. Further citations will be parenthetical.

43. Michael Bath, "Weeping Stags and Melancholy Lovers: The Iconography of *As You Like It*, II, i," *Emblematica* 1 (1986) 14; Martha Ronk, "Locating the Visual in *As You Like It*," *Shakespeare Quarterly* 52:2 (2001), 270.

44. Robert Burton, *The Anatomy of Melancholy* (London: Dent, 1972), 383–4.

45. George Puttenham, *The Arte of English Poesie* (Kent, Ohio: Kent State University Press, 1970), 202.

46. *Iliad* 17: 335–49. Cf. the English translation in *Chapman's Homer: The Iliad*, ed. Allardyce Nicoll (Princeton: Princeton University Press, 1998), 358.

47. I refer to Frances Teague, *Shakespeare's Speaking Properties* (Lewisburg: Bucknell University Press, 1991). Despite its title, Teague's study excludes "instruments used to produce sound effects" (35) and in fact explores the *visual* language of Shakespeare's props.

11
Digging the Dust: Renaissance Archivology

William H. Sherman

> There is a Supreme God in the ethnological section;
> A hollow toad shape, faced with a blank shield
> ... Let us offer our pinch of dust all to this God,
> And grant his reign over the entire building.
> — William Empson, "Homage to the British Museum"[1]

My essay takes the form of a general meditation on what is at stake in the work in and on "the archives" that has reshaped and revitalized the interdisciplinary study of texts and cultures over the last few decades. This is neither the time nor the place to attempt an overview of, or even an introduction to, the Renaissance period's own archives: much more work – by a *team* of scholars – would be needed to survey the political, architectural, and intellectual developments that led to the creation of new documentary collections in Renaissance homes, cities, and states, along with an increasingly sophisticated sense of the disciplines that we now call library science and information management (and I would put this high on my list of the great collaborative projects that remain to be done for the Renaissance period). Rather, I will look at some of the materials and metaphors that frame our work in archives and, in particular, urge us to think more deeply about the peculiar place of dust. As we shall see, this small but significant substance brings into focus a number of questions about our relationship to the past – questions that have become more pressing and more interesting with the advent of digital technology.

1. Archive fever: a Shakespearean impression

There is no better place to start than with a virtual visit to the National Archives (UK), which launched the "Documents Online" website a few

246

years ago as a repository for downloadable images of the records preserved in what used to be known as the Public Record Office (or PRO).[2]
The site allows users from anywhere in the world to explore the British
state archive in the comfort of their homes, offices, or local libraries –
provided they have access to a networked computer and can afford the
fee of £3.50 per document. At the heart of this enterprise is the class of
records most crucial to people reconstructing past lives, whether they
are professional historians or amateur genealogists: the complete run of
wills from the Prerogative Court of Canterbury between 1384 and
1858. In the 1960s, 28 of the more than 1 million wills in this collection – including those of King Henry VIII, Sir Francis Drake, Lord
Nelson, and Jane Austen – were singled out "because of the celebrity of
the testator" and put in a record group of their own (PROB 1); and in
1972 a further sixty-four wills were added to what is now known as the
"famous wills" category. Not surprisingly, these were the first documents to be digitized for the Documents Online website. But the only
item to be offered *free of charge* was the will of William Shakespeare.

If we download the pdf file, we find ourselves looking at several
time-worn pages of densely written text, in an obsolete script, filled
with odd spellings, tangled syntax, and arcane legal formulae. This
online document offers instant access to the final desires of our greatest writer (including the much-debated bequest of his "second best
bed" to his wife), and to no less than three of his six surviving sig-
natures; but it is safe to say that the text will be almost completely
illegible to most members of the general public, most students of
Shakespeare, and most professional Shakespeareans, very few of whom
are now trained as a matter of course in Elizabethan handwriting or the
legal conventions needed to make sense of a document like this one.
Given that the facsimile is not accompanied by a transcription, a paraphrase, or even a general description, what exactly are we being given
access to and what exactly are we supposed to do with it?[3] Is it meant
to serve as our own small piece of the cultural patrimony, to be cher-
ished like an old coin or venerated like an icon? Or is it a clever
reminder, on the part of the national archivists, that old documents
are very hard to decipher without the services of professionals, and
that the archives rarely give up their secrets easily?

There may be no better introduction to our current relationship to
the archives than this document – which everyone can access (and
even, in a sense, *own*) but almost no one can read – and it offers a preliminary object lesson in the Shakespearean strains of what we might
describe (following Jacques Derrida) as "archive fever." The archives

have always been associated with the work of historians but they have also served, for some time now, as one of the key sites of interdisciplinary theory and practice across the arts and humanities – at least since Michel Foucault put them at the heart of his "archaeology of knowledge" in the 1960s and 70s.[4] The History of Material Texts, New Historicism, Gender Studies and Performance Studies have all continued to prompt new questions about old archives, helping us to see them as "statements," "events," and "repertories" as well as official houses for facts, and alerting us in particular to the principles of selection and exclusion and the systems of organization that determine our very access to the past.[5] But we have still just begun to explore the ways in which archives might matter not only to social, economic, and political historians but also to students of literature, art, and music – and how, indeed, they might provide some common ground on which they can meet and consider the role played by archives (however they are defined and wherever they are found) in preserving, ordering, and authorizing the past.[6]

Discussions of the politics and poetics of the archive now tend to take as their point of departure not Foucault's 1969 book but Jacques Derrida's more recent text of 1996, *Archive Fever: A Freudian Impression*, in which he invited us to "imagine ... a project of general archiviology [or *archivology*], a word ... that could designate a general and interdisciplinary science of the archive."[7] As he so often did, Derrida deployed another general and interdisciplinary science – etymology – to lay the foundations: he began by tracing the origins of the word "archive" in the Greek root *arkhê-*. The *OED* neatly charts the word's long and circuitous journey into the English language: it derives from the French *archif*, which in turn derives from the late Latin *archivum*, which in turn derives from *arkhêion*, Greek for "magisterial residence" or "public office", which in one last turn derives from the general term for government, *arkhê*. In Derrida's account, the OED's dominant sense of "archive" as *a place in which public records or other important historic documents are kept* "comes to it from the Greek *arkheion*: initially a house, a domicile, an address, the residence of the superior magistrates, the *archons*, those who [governed] ... On account of their publicly recognized authority, it is at their home ... that official documents are filed" (2). But Derrida also reminds us that *arkhê* has another meaning that the OED leaves out, defined by the standard Greek dictionary as "a beginning, origin, [or] first cause." So just as "archaeology" is the study of *ancient* objects and "archbishop" is the *prime* ecclesiastical authority, the archive (in Derrida's terms) "refers ... to the originary, the first, the principal, the primitive, in short to the commencement" (2).

Derrida's meditation on archives was first delivered as a lecture at Freud's house (now the Freud Museum) in London; and he devotes most of his time *not* to outlining a "general project of archiviology" but rather to discussing the role of memory and mythology in psychoanalysis and to diagnosing what might be described as a psychopathology of archival life. Even after an "Exergue," a "Preamble," and a "Foreword" (which together occupy well over half of the book), we are no closer to understanding what an archivology might be or do. And that is intentional: for Derrida, the archive hides as much as it reveals. The English title *Archive Fever* perfectly captures the double-edged condition identified by the French phrase *"mal d'archive."* We are *"en mal d'archive*, [or] in need of archives" – that is, we both desire them and lack them. We are therefore possessed by a *mal d'archive*, an archival passion or malady: "It is never to rest, interminably, from searching for the archive right where it slips away."[8]

If we are looking for something like a foundational moment in the Shakespearean impression of this archive fever, we need to move forward some seven years from his last will and testament to the first collected edition of his plays, the so-called First Folio of 1623, *Mr. William Shakespeares Comedies, Histories, & Tragedies. Published according to the True Originall Copies.*[9] While scholars have tended to be skeptical about the title-page's claim for a return to authentic origins, they credit this volume with a primary role in archiving – that is, both *collecting* and *shaping* – the Shakespeare that has come down to us: as Peter Blayney has reminded us, of the 36 plays in the collection, exactly half have survived only because the First Folio was published, and of the remaining 18 all but 2 were printed there in new (and often very different) versions.[10] The volume's compilers were also responsible for ordering the plays into the three generic categories featured in its title and table of contents – an order that may or may not have mattered to Shakespeare, as an overarching design or classifying system, but that continues to determine the shape of publishing ventures, university courses, theater seasons, and so on. And, finally, they came extremely close to establishing a canon of genuine Shakespearean texts (one that privileges the playwright over the poet): many titles have been added and subtracted through the years, but the table of contents of any major one-volume edition of Shakespeare's plays will still look surprisingly similar to this one.

In their prefatory epistles, Shakespeare's former associates John Heminge and Henry Condell describe Shakespeare's legacy in terms that Derrida would have had a field day with (had he offered a

Shakespearean rather than a Freudian impression). To "the Great Variety of Readers" they wrote,

> It had bene a thing, we confesse, worthie to haue bene wished, that the Author himselfe had liu'd to haue set forth, and ouerseen his owne writings; But ... it hath bin ordain'd otherwise, and he by death departed from that right, we ... haue collected & publish'd them ... (A3r)

And to their patrons, the Earls of Pembroke and Montgomery, they continued:

> We haue but collected them, and done an office to the dead, to procure his Orphanes, guardians; vvithout ambition either of self-profit, or fame: onely to keep the memory of so worthy a Friend, & Fellow aliue, as was our SHAKESPEARE ... In that name therefore, we most humbly consecrate to your H[onours] these remaines of your seruant *Shakespeare* ... (A2v)

As Ben Jonson memorably put it in the poetic tribute that follows these letters, the First Folio provides Shakespeare with a monument that keeps him alive by making archons of each of us: "Thou art a Moniment, without a tombe, | And art aliue still, while thy Booke doth liue, | And we haue wits to read, and praise to giue" (A4r).

And do we ever. Peter Ackroyd's *Shakespeare* recently joined Stephen Greenblatt's *Will in the World: How Shakespeare Became Shakespeare* and James Shapiro's *1599: A Year in the Life of Shakespeare* as the third blockbuster biography in less than a year – and there are more in the pipeline. If the unprecedented investment of their publishers turns out to be justified (and in Shapiro's case, at least, it seems to be), there is now a greater appetite not so much for Shakespeare's plays but for Shakespeare himself than ever before. Whatever is driving this biographical feeding frenzy, it is not new archival discoveries: the basic documentary record testifying to Shakespeare's birth, life, and death has been established for decades, and it remains disappointingly (even notoriously) slim – both in quantity and quality.[11] It may come as some surprise, then, that the longest of the 50,000 entries in the new *Oxford Dictionary of National Biography* is Peter Holland's life of Shakespeare: at just over 37,000 words, it is some 2,000 words longer than the runner-up, Patrick Collinson's entry on Queen Elizabeth I.

The challenge of writing about such a famous but poorly documented life has forced biographers to focus on Shakespeare's *after*life (as Holland does), to flesh out Shakespeare's milieu with the people, places, and things we *do* know about (as Shapiro and Ackroyd do), or to read into or out of Shakespeare's *works* the experiences he *might* have had (as Greenblatt does). And the patchiness of the record has also created room for conjecture of a more fundamental sort – that a person with such an unimpressive archival presence could not possibly be the author of such an impressive corpus of texts.

Given Shakespeare's status as the *arch-author*, there has always been a lot at stake in his identity. The first serious challenger in this remarkably durable controversy was Francis Bacon, and his case was first put forward in earnest during the 1850s by an American writer named Delia Bacon. After a period of dementedly close reading, she published her magnum opus, *The Philosophy of Shakspere's Plays Unfolded*, in which she found Bacon's name and philosophy carefully concealed in the letters of Shakespeare's works. She set off for England, where her patrons Emerson and Hawthorne arranged for her to stay with Thomas Carlyle. Despite her personal letter of introduction to Anthony Panizzi, Chief Librarian of the British Museum, she preferred to work (as Carlyle wryly observed) "from the depths of her own mind, disdainful apparently ... of all *evidence* from Museums or Archives."[12] It was her desire for such evidence, however, that inspired her to move to Stratford-upon-Avon, where she convinced herself that Bacon's will and other relics – constituting what she called "the archives of this secret philosophical society" – would be found under Shakespeare's gravestone in Holy Trinity Church; and she went so far as to attempt a late-night assault on the tomb (with lantern and shovel in hand) in a futile attempt to unearth them.[13]

This was what the people who named the SARS epidemic a few years ago would call SAAF (Severe Acute Archive Fever). But it is too easy to dismiss the anti-Stratfordians as simply "mad" – in his exhaustive account of Shakespeare's afterlives, Samuel Schoenbaum groups Bacon and other non-believers under the general heading "Deviations" – and in doing so (I think) we miss an opportunity to learn about the intellectual and emotional energies invested in the sixteenth and seventeenth centuries by the nineteenth and twentieth. After all, when the New York Public Library opened its doors in 1911, the very first book requested was Delia Bacon's 1857 treatise, *The Philosophy of the Plays of Shakspere Unfolded*. And Freud himself was fascinated by the Baconian theory throughout his life and ultimately died a convert to the

Oxfordian cause, adding a little known footnote to his discussion of Hamlet in the final revision of his *Outline of Psychoanalysis*, suggesting that "The name 'William Shakespeare' is very probably a pseudonym behind which a great unknown lies concealed."[14]

2.   Can this dust live?

If we are looking for a material and metaphorical foundation for a "Renaissance Archivology," we need to turn to the dusty books and papers we spend our lives exploring and pay some attention to the dustiness itself. In doing so, we can follow the lead of contemporary artists, who have recently become obsessed with dust as material and metaphor. In 2004, the British Library gave its resident artist Rachel Lichtenstein free run of the manuscript reading room. The result was her exhibition and book, *Add[itional MS] 17469: A Little Dust Whispered*, in which she displayed images of manuscripts and users' responses to them. The items she selected were chosen primarily for the power of their physical details rather than their intellectual or artistic content – the scars and stains that remind us of the now absent people who made and used these texts.[15] The same year David Musgrave curated an exhibition at the Norwich City Gallery called *Living Dust*, in which he called our attention to the "dust of drawing" and explored the various ways in which this inanimate matter might be said to come to life.[16] In 2003 the Swiss Institute in New York mounted an exhibition called *Dust Memories*, in which a group of artists worked from Jean Dubuffet's provocative confession that "The voices of dust, the soul of dust, these interest me a lot more than flowers, trees or horses ..."[17] This show was a reprise of a 1998 exhibition in Bourgogne called *Poussière;*[18] and one of the artists from that show, Ignasi Aballí, was the subject of a major exhibition in 2005 at the Museum of Contemporary Art in Barcelona. Commissioned as part of the Year of Books and Reading, Aballí's show offered an artistic archivology: one of his pieces involved lists of people and figures of deaths or injuries cut out of newspapers and set side-by-side with inventories of languages, religions, currencies, subway systems, or breeds of dog. But much of his work explored the physical traces of the passage of time – sagging bookshelves warped by the weight of now absent books, or an empty room with white walls which became scuffed and soiled by the passage of visitors through it, or the dust that settled on his studio windows. Finally, last winter the contemporary art magazine *Cabinet* published an interview with a man named Peter Brimblecombe, professor of atmospheric chemistry at the

University of East Anglia and author of several studies on dust accumulation in the libraries of historic homes belonging to the National Trust.[19]

If this all sounds too far removed from scholarly work in libraries and record offices, it is worth considering that, in her recent book *Dust: The Archive and Cultural History*, Carolyn Steedman identifies dust as both the defining condition and the central trope of archival work. In calling for what she half-jokingly calls "Dust Studies," she cites a key passage from Jules Michelet, who gave this remarkable account of his work on "the nameless dead" in the National Archives in Paris: "as I breathed their dust, I saw them rise up. They rose from the sepulcher ... as in the Last Judgement of Michelangelo or in the Dance of Death" (a vision Steedman suggests was quite possibly inspired by an *actual* fever contracted from work with dusty documents in closed spaces). She also offers her own vivid account of the fever that sets in at night, in a cheap hotel after a day of archival research, where she is kept awake worrying about the dust of those who have slept there before her and the dust of the "infinite heaps" of "notes and traces" left behind by the people she is trying to recover in the archives.[20] And I could add my own account of a summer spent surveying more than 8,000 books at the Huntington Library in Los Angeles, collecting fragments of traces left behind by Renaissance readers: I still remember emerging each day from the cold stacks into the warm California sun, with fingers stained by the kind of dust that only old bindings give off – feeling good about getting my hands dirty but worrying about what exactly I was literally and figuratively taking away.

As that which we are all reduced to *and* that which remains after we are gone, dust is the very trace of time; and like the cemeteries and other burial grounds described by Robert Pogue Harrison in his beautiful book, *The Dominion of the Dead*, dusty books in libraries and archives testify "to an allegiance between the dead and the unborn of which we the living are merely the ligature."[21] And I would suggest that some of the most eloquent early modern writers and readers had a profound appreciation of the charged particles that serve as the interface between the dead, the living, and the not-yet-born. In this context, for instance, Hamlet's predicament comes to look more and more like an acute and ultimately fatal case of archive fever. His actions, inactions, and (above all) words suggest that he suffers not so much from a Death Drive as from a *Dust* Drive, one diagnosed at the very beginning of the play by his mother: "Do not for ever with thy vailed lids," she warns, "Seek for thy noble father in the dust."[22] In the course of the play, dust is precisely what Hamlet proceeds to dig in, stir up, and return to himself. His archive fever reveals itself to be at once a documentary impulse ("meet it is I set it down"), an obsession with setting the record straight for posterity ("Horatio, I am dead. I Thou livest; report me and my cause aright"), an unhealthy interest in decayed bodies ("Alas, poor Yorick!"), an extreme sensitivity to the hauntings of ghosts ("Remember thee? I Ay … while memory holds a seat I In this distracted globe"), and an acknowledgment that we are ultimately nothing more, and nothing less, than a "quintessence of dust."

But it was John Donne whose imagination was most occupied with visions of bodies turning (or re-turning) to ashes and dust before being resurrected, and whose sermons offered a sustained exegesis of the Christian approach to dust. In a particularly powerful passage in his final sermon, *Deaths Duell* (preached not long before his own death in 1631), Donne rehearses Hamlet's meditation on the fact that all bodies – those of paupers and princes, of mothers and sons – will mingle in the ground after death:

> Even those bodies that were *the temples of the holy Ghost*, come to this *dilapidation*, to ruine, to rubbidge, to dust … I must dye againe in an *Incineration* of this *flesh*, and in a dispersion of that dust: That a *Monarch*, who spred over many nations alive, must in this dust lye in a corner of that *sheete of lead*, and there, but so long as that lead will laste, and that privat and *retir'd man*, that thought himselfe his owne for ever, and never came forth, must in his dust of the grave bee published …[23]

For Donne, as for many later preachers and writers, the most resonant scene is that where God places the prophet Ezekiel in the valley of dry bones, where he asks:

> *Sonne of man can these bones live?* as though it had bene impossible, and yet they did; the *Lord* layed *Sinewes upon them, and flesh,* and breathed into them, and *they did live*: But in that case there were *bones* to bee *seene*, something visible, of which it might be sayd, can this thing live? But in this death of *incineration*, and dispersion of dust, wee see *nothing* that wee can call *that mans*; If we say, can this dust live? perchance it *cannot* … This death of *incineration* and dispersion, is, to naturall *reason*, the most *irrecoverable death* of all, and yet *Domini Domini sunt exitus mortis*, unto

> *God the Lord belong the issues of death,* and by *recompacting* this
> *dust* into the *same body,* and *reanimating* the *same body* with the *same*
> *soule,* hee shall in a blessed and glorious *ressurection* give mee such
> an *issue from* this *death,* as shal never passe into any other death,
> but establish me into a life that shall last as long as the *Lord of life*
> himselfe. (D4r–v)

This process of death, decay, and reanimation is a matter for Donne
not just of mystical resurrection but of "sheets," of "publishing,"
of "issues" – the very stuff of *textual* afterlives, and the means (according to one of the most common tropes of Renaissance poets) of
preserving an author's corpus long after the demise of his physical
body.[24]

Not surprisingly, those responsible for first re(-)membering Donne –
for paying tribute to him, on the one hand, and for editing and
publishing his works, on the other – picked up on precisely this
idea, and continued his play on dust. When *Deaths Duell* was
given its first, posthumous publication, the text was followed
by an anonymous "Elegie on Doctor Donne," the final lines of which
read:

> Commit we then thee to thy selfe, nor blame
> Our drooping loves, which thus to thy owne fame
> Leave thee Executor: since but thy owne
> No Pen could doe thee Iustice, nor Bayes crowne
> Thy vast desert, save that we nothing can
> Depute to bee thy ashes Guardian.
> So Iewellers no Art nor mettall trust,
> To forme the Diamond, but the Diamonds dust.[25]

So, as with Shakespeare, Donne had to be his own executor and the
author of his own enduring monument – which could only be created
from his own artistic dust. And when Donne's collected sermons were
first published in 1640 they were famously prefaced by a short biography written by Izaak Walton. Walton saw Donne's own words as his
defiant answer to the question posed to Ezekiel, "shall these bones
live?" He preached his own funeral sermon, in effect, giving himself an
issue from death.[26] Walton's closing paragraph echoed Donne's own
wording and promised a textual resurrection: "that body, which once
was a temple of the Holy Ghost … is now become a small quantity of
Christian dust: But I shall see it reanimated."[27]

3.   Dust in the age of digital reproduction

The question of reanimating the dust of Renaissance books (and the other artifacts that come down to us from the past) has become more complicated with the advent of digital technology. Computers are making our access to the archives easier than ever before, and also giving our archive fever a whole new dimension.[28] Digital resources such as ProQuest's Early English Books Online (EEBO) have made it possible to access images of virtually all of the books printed in Shakespeare's day, and to allow students with no access to rare book rooms to examine the original appearance of the texts they are reading in modern editions as well as to discover texts that have never been printed in modern editions. The impact of this development on early modern teaching and research has been nothing short of revolution- ary; and (as I discovered listening to a student presentation at a recent conference devoted to EEBO) the effect it can have on students is nothing short of thrilling. An undergraduate from Bath Spa's History Department – who had never been anywhere near a rare book library – explained how he was so electrified by his work with original materials on EEBO that he is now pursuing a PhD on Hobbes. I was genuinely moved by his epiphany, but also a bit worried by his concluding state- ment that "The best thing is you can do it all from the comfort of your front room. You don't have to go into the dusty, dirty archive."

There are certain things, as he will no doubt discover, that can *only* be found in the archive. This is not (or not just) a matter of valorizing archival labour for its own sake, the historians' equivalent of the "In my day we had to walk to school" stories with which the older have always chastised the younger. EEBO claims to reproduce "the total surviving record of the English-speaking world for 227 years" – so how might it matter that EEBO does not contain any of the period's handwritten texts (administrative records like Shakespeare's will, countless drafts of published works and copies of unpublished works, devotional compilations, and personal documents like the page from Richard Stonley's diary, accounting for one day's expenses on "Vittell," "Apparrell," and "Bookes" – including the first recorded purchase of Shakespeare's first book, *Venus and Adonis*)?[29] How might it matter that EEBO takes readers straight to the title-page and does not reproduce any bindings (which play an integral role in the production and circu- lation of books, whether functional, decorative, or both)? How might it matter that all of EEBO's images are in black and white when the Early English book, like its medieval forebear, often used colour for decoration, emphasis, and guides to navigation?[30] And how, finally, might it matter that EEBO does not contain any *dust*?

The best way of answering that question is to share one final story from the archives, by the historian and information theorist Paul Duguid:

> I was working in an archive of a 250-year-old business ... Incoming letters were stored in wooden boxes ... each containing a fair portion of dust as old as the letters. As opening a letter triggered a brief asthmatic attack, I wore a scarf tied over my nose and mouth. ... I longed for a digital system that would hold the information from the letters and leave paper and dust behind.
>
> One afternoon, another historian came to work on a similar box. He read barely a word. Instead, he picked out bundles of letters and, in a move that sent my sinuses into shock, ran each letter beneath his nose and took a deep breath, at times almost inhaling the letter itself but always getting a good dose of dust.
>
> ... Choking behind my mask, I asked him what he was doing. He was, he told me, a medical historian ... documenting outbreaks of cholera. When that disease occurred in a town in the eighteenth century, all letters from that town were disinfected with vinegar to prevent the disease from spreading. By sniffing for the faint traces of vinegar that survived 250 years and noting the date and source of the letters, he was able to chart the progress of cholera outbreaks.[31]

We have been inspired to return to the archives by a renewed emphasis on the materiality of texts; but we have done so in the context of an explosion of digital resources that (in some important ways) *de*-materializes the text. What I am suggesting is that there is a tension here that we have only begun to acknowledge; and a challenge that creators and users of the new digital archives have only begun to address.

I began with an epigraph and I will end with an epitaph. Dust made one final appearance in Shakespeare's life and writings – and this time it is his own dust that he was imagining. It is found in the inscription he allegedly composed for his gravestone (the very one that Delia Bacon almost took a shovel to):

GOOD FREND FOR IESVS SAKE FORBEARE,
TO DIGG THE DVST ENCLOASED HEARE:

BLEST BE Y^E MAN Y^T SPARES THES STONES,
AND CVRST BE HE Y^T MOVES MY BONES.

I have only begun to scratch the surface, as it were, and there is still much more to be said about Renaissance archives, archivology and dust. I haven't even gestured toward the dust that formed the ground of Renaissance archaeology, and the process of *Unearthing the Past* that Leonard Barkan (in his book of that name) finds at the heart of Renaissance art and culture.[32] But I hope I have shown that whether we are after an archaeology of knowledge, trying to bring the dead back to life, or simply hoping to scratch an archival itch – in order, as Heminge and Condell put it, to do an office to the dead, for the living – digging the dust is precisely what we have to do.

Notes

This essay began its life as the introduction to a session on "Shakespeare in the Archives" at the 2004 meeting of the Shakespeare Association of America. It draws on material presented in my inaugural lecture at the University of York (10 October 2005) and an address to the Society for Renaissance Studies (National Library of Scotland, Edinburgh, 8 July 2006). I am grateful to the audiences at each of these occasions for ideas and encouragement.

1. William Empson, *Collected Poems* (London: Chatto and Windus, 1955), 35.
2. Http://www.nationalarchives.gov.uk/documentsonline/.
3. Among the most welcome of the recent additions to the website is a page of guidance for working with old wills, with links to online tutorials for paleography and Latin.
4. See, for a start, the two special issues of *History of the Human Sciences* on "The Archive," 11:4 (1998) and 12:2 (1999); and Alexandra Gillespie, "Books," in *Twenty-First Century Approaches to Literature: Volume I, Middle English Literature*, ed. Paul Strohm (Oxford: Oxford University Press, 2007).
5. See Michel Foucault, *The Archaeology of Knowledge*, trans. A. M. Sheridan Smith (New York: Pantheon Books, 1972), esp. Part III ("The Statement and the Archive"); David Greetham, "'Who's In, Who's Out': The Cultural Poetics of Archival Exclusion," *Studies in the Literary Imagination* 32:1 (Spring, 1999), 1–28; and Diana Taylor, *The Archive and the Repertoire: Performing Cultural Memory in the Americas* (Durham, NC: Duke University Press, 2003).
6. Paul J. Voss and Marta L. Werner, eds. *The Poetics of the Archive*, a special issue of *Studies in the Literary Imagination*, 32:1 (Spring, 1999); Rebecca Comay (ed.), *Lost in the Archives*, Alphabet City No. 8 (Toronto, 2002).
7. Jacques Derrida, *Archive Fever: A Freudian Impression*, trans. Eric Prenowitz (Chicago: University of Chicago Press, 1996), 34. The book was first published as *Mal d'Archive: une impression freudienne* by Éditions Galilée in 1995.

8. Derrida, *Archive Fever*, 90–1.

9. William Shakespeare, *Comedies, Histories, & Tragedies* (London: Isaac Jaggard and Edward Blount, 1623).

10. Peter W. M. Blayney, *The First Folio of Shakespeare* (Washington DC: The Folger Shakespeare Library, 1991), 1. Cf. Anthony James West's *The Shakespeare First Folio: The History of the Book*, Volume 1 (Oxford: Oxford University Press, 2001) – the final volume of this projected four-volume study will consider the cultural history of the book.

11. It is laid out most neatly by Samuel Schoenbaum in the second edition of his *Shakespeare's Lives* (Oxford: Clarendon Press, 1991), 3–37.

12. Quoted in Schoenbaum, *Shakespeare's Lives*, 387–8.

13. Ibid., 391–2.

14. Ibid., 443.

15. Rachel Lichtenstein, *Add. 17469: A Little Dust Whispered* (London: The British Library, 2004).

16. *Living Dust*, curated by David Musgrave (Norwich: Norwich Gallery, 2004). Musgrave's essay suggests that "The mute, material aspect of [drawing] is harder to approach. It doesn't seem enough to list a range of textures, or to describe shifting densities of tone; nor is it enough to write it off as the dead carrier of living meaning. If the dust of drawing is alive, it is both because of its entanglement with language ... and its ability to elicit something less easy to articulate in words, something that happens in the blind spots of representation" (14). I am grateful to Elinor Jansz for bringing this catalogue to my attention.

17. Http://www.swissinstitute.net/Exhibitions/2003_Dust/Dust_Memories.htm.

18. François Dagognet, Cyril Harpet, and Emmanuel Latreille, eds., *Poussière (Dust Memories)* (1998).

19. Brian Dillon and Sina Najafi, "Elementary Particles: An Interview with Peter Brimblecombe," *Cabinet* 20 (Winter 2005/6): 68–70.

20. Carolyn Steedman, *Dust: The Archive and Cultural History* (Manchester: Manchester University Press, 2001), 17, 27.

21. Robert Pogue Harrison, *The Dominion of the Dead* (Chicago: University of Chicago Press, 2003), ix. For a useful survey of dust from a scientific perspective, see Joseph A. Amato, *Dust: A History of the Small and the Invisible* (Berkeley: University of California Press, 2000) – though, as the title suggests, he is interested in minuteness rather than mortality.

22. William Shakespeare, *Hamlet*, ed. Harold Jenkins, The Arden Shakespeare (London: Methuen, 1982), I.ii.70–1. All subsequent quotations cite this edition.

23. John Donne, *Deaths Duell, or, A Consolation to the Soule, against the dying Life, and liuing Death of the Body. Deliuered in a Sermon at White Hall, before the KINGS's MAIESTY, in the beginning of Lent, 1630* (London: Thomas Harper, 1632), D3r–v.

24. Jennifer Brady, "'No Fault But Life': Jonson's Folio as Monument and Barrier," in Jennifer Brady and W. H. Herendeen (eds.), *Ben Jonson's 1616 Folio* (Newark: University of Delaware Press, 1991), 192–216.

25. Donne, *Deaths Duell*, G3v–G4r.

26. Indeed, the title page to the 1632 publication of *Deaths Duell* advertised it as "THE DOCTORS OWNE FUNERALL SERMON."

27. See the discussion of this passage in Jessica Martin, *Walton's Lives: Conformist Commemorations and the Rise of Biography* (Oxford: Oxford University Press, 2001), 176–83.
28. In 1994, when Derrida wrote the lecture that became *Archive Fever*, he could already claim that "electronic mail today ... is on the way to transforming the entire public and private space of humanity" (17).
29. Reproduced in Samuel Schoenbaum, *Shakespeare: The Globe and the World* (New York: Oxford University Press for the Folger Shakespeare Library, 1979), 83.
30. On the use of red ink in early printed books see Sabrina Alcorn Baron, "Red Ink and Black Letter: Reading Early Modern Authority," in Sabrina Alcorn Baron (ed.), *The Reader Revealed* (Washington DC: The Folger Shakespeare Library, 2001), 19–30; Bianca F. C. Calabresi, "'Red Incke': Reading the Bleeding on the Early Modern Page," in Douglas A. Brooks, ed., *Printing and Parenting in Early Modern England* (Aldershot: Ashgate, 2005), 237–64; and Margaret Smith, *The Book Becomes Monochrome* (in progress).
31. Paul Duguid, "Trip Report from Portugal," in John Seely Brown and Paul Duguid, *The Social Life of Information* (Boston: Harvard Business School Press, 2000), 173–4.
32. Leonard Barkan, *Unearthing the Past: Archaeology and Aesthetics in the Making of a Renaissance Culture* (New Haven: Yale University Press, 1999).

12

Of Busks and Bodies

Ann Rosalind Jones and Peter Stallybrass

Charles:	The trouble is I need you several times a week.
Camilla:	Mmmm, so do I. I need you all the week. All the time.
Charles:	Oh, God. I'll just live inside your trousers, or something. It would be much easier!
Camilla:	(laughing) What are you going to turn into, a pair of knickers? (Both laugh)
Camilla:	Oh, You're going to come back as a pair of knickers!
Charles:	Or, God forbid, a Tampax! Just my luck! (Laughs)
Camilla:	You are a complete idiot! (Laughs) Oh, what a wonderful idea!
Charles:	My luck to be chucked down the lavatory and go on and on, forever swirling round on the top, never going down.
Camilla:	(Laughing) Oh, Darling!
Charles:	Until the next one comes through.
Camilla:	Oh, perhaps you could come back as a box.
Charles:	What sort of box?
Camilla:	A box of Tampax, so you could just keep going.
Charles:	That's true.
Camilla:	Repeating yourself … (Laughing). Oh, darling, I just want you now.[1]

Despite the chorus of scorn that followed "Camillagate," Charles and Camilla's notorious 1989 telephone conversation was one of their finest moments, in which they revealed themselves as the unabashed imitators and creative perverters of themes in Catullus and Donne. Camilla imagines Charles as the knickers that she can perpetually wear. Charles imagines himself as the man forever inside the woman, endlessly erect. But no, in this wonderful perversion of a perennial heterosexual fantasy,

261

he is soft and, alas, disposable after all. Camilla rescues the fantasy ("what a wonderful idea!") only to be met by Charles's self-mocking "my luck to be chucked down the lavatory and go on and on, forever swirling round on the top, never going down." An eternity of activity, but never even going down (the lavatory) – let alone into Camilla. But again, Camilla rescues the fantasy, picking up on Charles's ambiguous "until the next one comes through." The next tampon? And through what? The lavatory? Camilla? Camilla turns it into the latter. Charles may not be endlessly in her, but, like a box of tampons, he can multiply himself so as to be in her again and again and again: "you could just keep going," "repeating yourself." Like the best of fetishes, this is repetition without a difference: more of the same, a same that is wanted obsessively, repetitively, but now. "Oh, darling I just want you now." An impossible now for two people separated by the distance of a telephone call or a letter or a poem. Or rather a now that can only be achieved prosthetically. Othello away, Desdemona still kisses him in the form of the handkerchief that was his first gift to her. Catullus imagines himself as his beloved Lesbia's pet sparrow.

In "On his Mistress Going to Bed," Donne is luckier: he's with his mistress, so he needs no substitute. Yet the poem lingers lovingly over all the substitutes he doesn't need: her girdle, "like heaven's Zone glistering"; her "spangled breast-plate"; her "wiery Corronet."[2] All these must be undone, unlaced, unpinned, and cast aside. But even at this moment when her disposable coverings are discarded in favor of his mistress's naked body, Donne has time to cast an envious eye on one of them:

> Off with that happy busk, which I envie,
> That still can be, and still can stand so nie.

Only one of his mistress's supplements does Donne envy: her busk, which "still" (that is, "always") can, like him, be beside her but, unlike him, can "stand" long after the flagging erection of the sated lover. The busk is "happy" in a way that Donne can only dream of, even as he hastens past it to get to the "real thing." Not only is the busk always close to his mistress's body, but also it is a prosthesis larger and harder than his own penis.

In 1688, Randle Holme gave a succinct definition of a busk:

> A *Busk,* it is a strong peece of Wood, or Whale-bone thrust down the
> middle of the Stomacher, to keep it streight and in compass, that

the Breast nor Belly shall not swell too much out. These Buskes are usually made in length according to the necessity of the fullness of the Breasts, then it extends to the Navel: if to keep the Belly down, then it reacheth to the Honor.[3]

What Holme describes is something like a stiff ruler that was inserted into a thin stitched channel in the front of a woman's bodice so as to keep the body erect. This was worn in addition to any other stiffeners, such as thinner whalebone stays that could be permanently stitched into a bodice – what we would now call a corset. Busks of this kind are listed as a purchase in a sixteenth-century account book: "twelve payer busks of whales bone."[4] But the single sternum-to navel busk had the most obvious effect on the body, straightening and stiffening it vertically. This busked silhouette can be seen in the second of two prints from Cesare Vecellio's 1590 costume book: his full-bellied, empire-waisted Venetian noblewoman of 1490 contrasts strongly to the upright, busked English noblewoman of the late sixteenth century (Figures 12.1(a). 12.1(b)).[5]

The busk was fashionable in France, too. Peter Erondelle, in *The first dialogue of The French Garden for English Ladyes and Gentlewomen to walke in ... Being an instruction for the attayning unto the knowledge of the French tongue* (1605), offers the following speech from a "Lady" dressing with the help of her "wayting-woman Jolye":

> Goe fetch my cloathes: bring my petty-coate bodyes: I mean my damaske quilt bodyes with Whale-bones, what lace doe you give me heere? This lace is too shorte, the tagges are broken, I cannot lace myselfe with it ... Shall I have no vardingdale? ... doe you not see that I want my buske? What is become of the buske-poynte?[6]

The busk was a detachable accessory, with holes at the bottom through which a "point," that is, a lace, was inserted; the point, inserted into these holes through reinforced eyelets in the bodice, tied the busk in place.[7]

But literary accounts of busks are rarely simply descriptive. Even Randle Holme, as he defines the busk, simultaneously mythologizes it as "strong," "thrust down" the front of the woman's bodice. Surviving busks undo any simple opposition between material substance and mythological fantasy because they materialize those fantasies in their visual emblems and written inscriptions. A French metal busk owned by Anne-Marie-Louise d'Orléans, Duchesse de Montpensier, is inscribed:

Figure 12.1a   Cesare Vecellio [An unbusked Italian noblewoman] in *Degli Habiti antichi et moderni di diverse parti del Mondo* (1590)
Photo credit: private collection.

DONNA NOBILE INGLESE.

Figure 12.1b Cesare Vecellio [A busked English noblewoman] in *Degli Habiti antichi et moderni di diverse parti del Mondo* (1590)
Photo credit: private collection.

"How I envy you the happiness that is yours, resting softly on her ivory white breast. Let us divide between us, if you please, this glory. You will be there during the day and I shall be there at night."[8] The inscription speaks for the lover against his envied rival, the busk. He will have to make do, getting close to the Duchess by night while the busk holds her by day. More commonly, it is the busks themselves that "speak." A seventeenth-century French metal busk is inscribed: "I have from the Lady this favor: to rest long on her bosom. Whence I hear a lover sigh who covets my place."[9]

But the busk can also bear contradictory inscriptions, speaking indeterminately both for itself and for the lover. A seventeenth-century French ivory busk depicts a house with two hearts above and the inscription: "L'AMOUR LES IOINT." As the house conjoins the hearts of lover and beloved, so does the busk itself. But another inscription on the same busk reads "IVSQUES AU REVOIR," with a weeping eye. The separated lover will weep for his absent beloved, even as his substitute, the busk, will remain to enjoy her.[10] Another ivory busk has the same "L'AMOUR LES IOINT" inscription over two flaming hearts, pierced by a single arrow, and the additional inscription: "ELLE NOUS VNIT." The "elle" here must be love, often feminine in early modern French, rather than the masculine *busc*.[11] Here, too, an additional phrase, set above a flower turning to the sun, points to the alternation between union and separation of which the busk is both reminder and imagined cure: "VOIR OV MOVRIR." The lover gives the woman this busk as a material pledge that he will suffer mortally until he sees her – and it – again.

These French busks were professionally decorated and inscribed. But in William Habington's *The Queene of Arragon* (1640), Cleantha ironically praises "Lords whose heads and legges move more | Than doe their tongues" and who "on my buske, even with a pin can write | The Anagrame of my Name."[12] And in Thomas Shadwell's *A True Widow* (1679), Selfish ("A Coxcomb conceited of his Beauty, Wit and Breeding, thinking all Women in Love with him, always admiring and talking of himself") boasts to Mrs Gartrude: "my fancy always pleases the Ladies. Pretty Miss, let me see that delicate Busk, I will write a Distick upon it, and present it to you." The "very foolish and whorish" Gartrude accepts the offer, whereupon Selfish kisses "that happy Busk, that goes so near your lovely body."[13] Like a ring, a busk can be inscribed with a posy, a lover's words that, whether comically or not, corporeally touch the beloved to whom they are written.

The busk was indeed often the medium of a conventionally gendered exchange: the man acquires it (from an ebenist, jeweler or peddler) and gives it, the woman accepts it and wears it to mark, if only privately, the bond between them. But the busk could also disturb such patterns, reversing gender roles and even throwing sexual identities into complete confusion. For one thing, its properties were antithetical to the clichés of the potent, then flagging penis: ideally, the busk keeps the female body "in compass, " stabilizes it, and acts to prevent the swelling of breasts and/or belly. But phantasmatically it can have the opposite effect, turning women into men and men into women and even dissolving sexual norms entirely.

In *Christs Teares over Jerusalem* (1613), Thomas Nashe takes the busk as visual proof of women's vanity and of their disorderly lust:

> Now come I to the Daughters of Pride, whereof Disdaine is the eldest. ... [The] Daughters of Pride, delight to go gorgeously ... Their breasts they embuske vp on hie, and their round Roseate buds immodestly lay forth, to shew at their hands there is fruite to be hoped. ... They shew the swellings of their mind, in the swellings and plumpings out of their apparrayle.[14]

Nashe is imagining a busk that, pressing in the belly, pushes up and exposes the breasts. But the breasts of Pride's daughters, if they suggest sexual availability, are also depicted as threatening self-assertion. Far from reducing women to mere body, the busk materializes "the swellings of their mind."

Such "swellings" of women's minds can, in turn, be inscribed in the busk as a corporeal threat to generation and lineage. In "A Glasse, to viewe the pride of vaineglorious Women" (1595), Stephen Gosson denounces the busk as an abortifacient, leading to a sterile and venal seductiveness:

> The baudie Buske, that keepes downe flat
> the bed wherein the babe should breed:
> What doth it els but point at that,
> which faine would haue somewhat to feede.[15]

Gosson imagines a significantly different function of the busk from the one that Nashe depicts. In Nashe's denunciation, the busk forces the breasts upwards, exposing "their round Roseate buds." But in Gosson's account, the emphasis is upon the way the busk flattens the belly, "the bed wherein the babe should breed."

Busks could, in fact, be used to disguise pregnancy, as is revealed in a 1754 trial, in which Sarah Jenkins was tried but found not guilty of infanticide. Thomas Warner, a journeyman brushmaker, had "bought [Sarah] of her husband for a gallon of beer" but left her after she became pregnant. In the course of the trial, Sarah Opwood testified that she had had the following conversation with Sarah Jenkins:

> I said, I don't believe you are with child; she said, I am sure I am, but nobody can tell by my busk. I said again, I cannot believe it; then she pulled her busk out of her stays, and said, will you believe it now; then I said, I believe you are. She said, I have not above a month to go, and pulled out her left breast and milked some milk into her left-hand. She left her busk at my house two or three days, and said it hurted her.

The busk must have been made of wood, judging by the testimony of Thomas Wilks, another brush-maker:

> T. Wilks: ... [Sarah Jenkins] said she had got a busk, that keeps down her belly so flat that no body can tell that she was with child, till she comes to the last month: she lost the busk at my house, and I burnt it before she was taken up: she at that time mended her stays.
> Q: Why did you burn it?
> T. Wilks: Because I wanted something to light my fire.[16]

Unlike Sarah Jenkins, a fictional maid in Richard Head's *The English Rogue* (1668) is unable to conceal her fictional state by "[l]acing her self very streight, and keeping down her belly with three Busks." The "English Rogue" himself, Meriton Latroon, who seduced and then deserted the maid, later resorts to wearing a busk himself when he disguises himself in women's clothes. A "Bravo" who lusts after him, so disguised, comes near to castrating him when he grabs her/him by what he takes to be a "busk, which some Ladies wear very long to hide their rising bellies."[17] This substitutability of vulnerable penis and inanimate busk is the point of a joke that Edward Philips tells:

> A Lady was commanded to put her busk in a Gentlemans codpiss. Another Lady was commanded to pull it out, which occasioned some sport, for she laying hold upon somthing else, after two or

three pulls gave over, excusing her disobedience, by pretending that the busk was tackt to the Gentlemans belly.[18]

If women were suspected of using busks to hide pregnancy, Gosson equally suspects that busks turn women into men. In refusing their roles as wives and mothers, busk-wearing women refashion them-selves through the armored bodices that transform them into "*Amazones*":

> These priuie coates, by arte made strong,
>   with bones, with paste, and such like ware:
> Whereby the backe and sides grow long,
>   and now they harnest, gallants are.
> Were they for vse against the foe,
> Our Dames for *Amazones* might goe.

Busks thus simultaneously attract and repel. But as the armor that repels, they shape the body in a way that destroys lineage:

> But seeing they doe only stay
>   the course that nature doth intend:
> And mothers often by them slay
>   their daughters yoong, and worke their end.
> What are they els but armours stout:
> Wherein like Gyants, *Ioue* they flout.[19]

We are here at the opposite extreme from Donne's fantasy, in which the busk is an imagined rival of and substitute for the male lover. Gosson's busk is a means of constructing the "armours stout" that transform women first into "*Amazones*" and then into "Gyants" who "flout" Jove, not only the highest of the gods but also the one most notorious for his subjugation of women by rape.

The busk and the bodice it stiffened were seen as composing a female body that oscillated dangerously between the natural and the unnatural. Indeed, the word "bodies," far from signifying a unified corporeal presence, referred both to bodies of flesh, bone, muscle and to the two-part bodice (written as either "bodies" or "a pair of bodies" as Erondelle's gentlewoman says) that constructed a body, as if the fabricated "pair of bodies" preceded any physical body and gave shape to it. Barnabe Rich claimed that tailors had become "*Body-makers ... swarm*[ing] through all the parts of London," "more sought vnto then he that is the *Soule-maker.*"[20] If these artificial bodies constituted by bodices and busks disrupted the virginal/maternal body, they also, according to Thomas Lodge's hyperbolic claim, upset the whole balance of nature, stripping the seas of whales from which the busks were made: "since busks came into request, horne is growne to such scarcity that Leuiathan hath cast his owne beakes of late to serue the market."[21]

If the busk is repeatedly attacked by Renaissance moralists and satirists, it remains radically unclear whether it is because it threatens masculinity or femininity. In John Taylor's "A Whore" (1630), the woman's "Buske and Busk-point too" are added to the "Reliques" to which "mad men must homage dooe."[22] In doing such homage, the gallant becomes simultaneously idolatrous and effeminate. But a rhetorical distinction is usually made between busks and busk-points. If the busks threaten the corporeal order, busk-points, the laces that tie the busk in place in the bodice, are depicted as an absurd inverter of economic value. Mere trinkets and hence valueless in themselves, they become for the enslaved lover the most treasured of commodities. And as worthless busk-points are transformed into the most desirable of relics, women become gods and rulers while men become fawning idolaters. Thus, in Samuel Rowlands' "A Courtezans Humour" (1609), the courtesan boasts:

> I haue my Champions that will fight,
> My Louers that do fawne: ...
> Then comes an Asse, and he forsooth
> Is in such longing heate,
> My Busk-poynt euen on his knees,
> With teares he doth intreat:
> I graunt it, to reioyce the man,
> And then request a thing;
> Which is both Gold and precious stone,
> The Wood-cocks Diamond Ring.[23]

The ridiculous lover's worship of busk-points became a staple of Renaissance satirist and moralists. In *Lingua* (1607), the following exchange takes place between Heuresis and Phantastes:

Heu.: But what say you to the gentleman that was with you yesterday?
Ph.:   O I thinke thou meanest him that made 19. sonnets of his mistris Busk-point.

Heu.: The same, the same, Sir. You promis'd to helpe him out with
th' twentieth.[24]

And in Robert Burton's *The Anatomy of Melancholy*, included among the
"Symptomes of Loue melancholy" (1621), busk-points are among the
"remnants" of his beloved that the inamorato ridiculously flaunts to
the world:

> If he get any remnant of hers, a buske-point, a feather of her
> fanne, a shoo-tie, a lace, he weares it for a fauour in his hat,
> or next his heart. Her picture he adores twice a day, & for two
> howres together will not looke off it; a garter or a bracelet of
> hers is more precious then any Saints relique; and he layes
> it vp in his casket, O blessed relique, and euery day will kisse
> it.[25]

While Burton's lover wears his lover's busk-points as a favor in his hat,
Henry Fitzgeffey's gallant "clog[s]" his wrists "[w]ith Busk-points,
Ribbons, or Rebato-Twists."[26]

In John Marston's *The Scourge of Villanie* (1598), the pointless
"points" of a busk turn Publius into an abject idolater, despite the
fact that he hates "idolatries" and "laughs that Papists honor
Images":

> I saw him court his Mistres looking-glasse,
> Worship a busk-poynt, (which in secrecie
> I feare was conscious of strange villanie.)[27]

Marston leaves it unclear what "strange villanie" the busk-points
have witnessed. But the "secrecie" perhaps implies that the "Mistres"
has been masturbating with her busk. In the anonymous *The Maydes
Metamorphosis* (1600), Ioculo says that Mopso has "a wit, as nimble
as a Sempsters needle, or a girles finger at her Buske poynt." Mopso
responds, "Your iest goes too low sir," and Frisco adds, "O but
tis a tickling iest." The conjuncture of busks and "girles finger[s]"
suggests a world in which the inamorato is not merely absurdly
enslaved but also unnecessary. A woman can "tickle" herself – and, to
recall Donne, with a prosthesis that "still can be, and still can stand
so nie."[28]

In Thomas Heywood's *How a man may chuse a good wife from a
bad* (1602), the mirror of "Reason" is the necessary cure for the

looking-glass that holds alike the image of the busked woman and of her effeminated lover:

> ... I was once like thee,
> A sigher, melancholy, humorist,
> Crosser of armes, a goer without garters,
> A hatband-hater, and a busk-point wearer,
> One that did vse much bracelets made of haire ...
> But when I lookt into the glasse of Reason, strait I began
> To loath that femall brauery, and henceforth
> Studie to cry peccaui to the world.[29]

For satirists like Joseph Hall, though, the "glasse of Reason" has been displaced by the mirror of vanity, in which men are transformed into their opposite. In Hall's account, men now not only wear cosmetics and stiffen their torsos as women do but also assume women's roles:

> I wote not how the world's degenerate,
> That men or know, or like not their estate: ...
> When comely striplings wish it weare their chance,
> For Caenis distaffe to exchange their Lance;
> And weare curl'd Periwigs, and chalke their face,
> And still are poring on their pocket-glasse.
> Tyr'd with pin'd Ruffes, and Fans, and partlet-strips
> And Buskes, and Verdingales about their hips.[30]

These "comely striplings" invert the story of "Fond Caenis," who wished "to be a man." Caenis, a young woman, was, according to Greek mythology, raped by Poseidon. But Poseidon then offered to grant her any wish. She chose to be transformed into a male warrior, in which form she avenged herself on men by killing them in battle.[31] If women now transform themselves into Caenis, the young gallant has been effeminated, as Hercules was by Omphale. Like Omphale, the "mannish Hus-wiues" make "a drudge of their vxorious mate,"

> Who like a Cot-queene freezeth at the rocke,
> Whiles his breech't dame doth man the forrein stock.

Or, in John Caryl's take on Ovid, the gallant is a modern version of Achilles, as Briseis imagines him, melting his hours away "[i]n Loves soft joyes,"

> And so transform'd from what he was before,
> That he will fight for *Greece* or Me no more.
> ... that mighty Man
> Now weilds a Busk, and brandisheth a Fan.[32]

Busk and fan are, in fact, repeatedly conjoined as the "weapons" of the effeminate gallant or the emblems of the hen-pecked husband. In Sir George Etherege's *She Wou'd if She Cou'd* (1668), Sir Oliver Cockwood claims: "I am in my Nature as valiant | As any man." But Sir Joslyn Jolley mocks him because he is not brave enough to break his engagement for supper with his wife:

> Fy, fy, a man, and kept so much under
> Correction by a Busk and a Fan![33]

Marston's amorous fool, on the other hand, is not corrected by a woman's busk; he wants to *be* it:

> *Saturio* wish'd him selfe his Mistres buske,
> That he might sweetly lie, and softly luske
> Betweene her pappes, then must he haue an eye
> At eyther end, that freely might discry
> Both hills and dales.

The fantasy that Marston mocks, though, could become the subject of celebration. In "Writ on Clarastella's Busk," Robert Heath imagines himself transformed into the busk that Donne "envies":

> Might I o'nights in thy room lie
> 'Twixt *Stella*'s warmer mounts of snow,
> So neer her heart dissolving, I
> No higher *Paradise* would know.[34]

If, according to critics, men now "mould their [own] bodies to euery deformed shape,"[35] the molding of male desire through the prosthesis of a busk provided a vision of a "higher *Paradise*," in which a lover could for ever "discry" his beloved's "hills and dales." The busk, indeed, embodied the ambivalence of the Renaissance fetish: mocked, trivialized, feared, desired.

Notes

1. "The Camillagate Transcript," http://www.ohnonews.com/pccpbtr.html, posted 12/18/1989, accessed 11/22/2006.
2. John Donne, "To his Mistress going to bed," *Poems, &c ... To which is added Divers Copies under his own hand Never before Printed* (London: Henry Herringman, 1669), 97. This was the first printing of this poem in a collection of Donne's poems. The poem was first printed as "An Elegie made by J. D." in R. C., *The Harmony of the Muses, or, The gentlemans and ladies choisest recreation full of various, pure and transcendent wit: containing severall excellent poems, some fancies of love, some of disdain, and all the subjects incident to the passionate affections either of men or women / heretofore written by those unimitable masters of learning and invention, Dr. Joh. Donn* [et al.] (London: Printed by T. W. for William Gilbertson, 1654), 1–2. For a richly informative discussion of the busk in Donne's poem and in early modern culture more generally, see Sandy Feinstein's excellent article, "Donne's 'Elegy 19,' The Busk between a Pair of Bodies," *Studies in English Literature, 1500–1900*, 34: 1 (Winter 1994): 61–77. We are indebted to her analysis throughout.
3. Randle Holme, *The Academy of Armory, or, A storehouse of armory and blazon containing the several variety of created beings, and how born in coats of arms, both foreign and domestick* (Chester: Printed for the author, 1688), 94.
4. Egerton Ms. 2806.
5. These woodcuts are reproduced from Cesare Vecellio's *Degli Habiti antichi et moderni di diverse parti del Mondo* (Venice: Damiano Zen, 1590), sig. 92v and 369v.
6. Peter Erondelle, Dialogue 1, *The French Garden: for English Ladyes and Gentlewomen to walke in ... Being an Instruction for the attayning unto the knowledge of the French Tongue* (London: Printed by Edward Allde for John Grismond, 1621), sig. E2v, E5v.
7. For a photo of a four-holed busk, see Sandy Feinstein, "Donne's 'Elegy 19,'" p. 70.
8. French metal busk, 17th century, made for Anne-Marie-Louise d'Orléans (1627–93), Duchesse de Montpensier, Costume Institute, Metropolitan Museum of Art, New York, accession number 30. 135/32.
9. Costume Institute, Metropolitan Museum of Art, New York, 30. 135/34.
10. Costume Institute, Metropolitan Museum of Art, New York, 30. 135/20.
11. Costume Institute, Metropolitan Museum of Art, New York, 30. 135/21. For a discussion of the two genders the noun *l'amour* could have in the Renaissance, see François Rigolot, "Gender vs. Sex Difference in Louise Labé's Grammar of Love," in *Rewriting the Renaissance: The Discourses of Gender in Early Modern Europe*, ed. Margaret Ferguson, Maureen Quilligan, and Nancy Vickers (Chicago University Press, 1986), 289–92. The "elle" in this inscription probably does not refer to "la coche," a fifteenth-century term for a stiffener different from the later *busc*, a masculine noun. See Feinstein, quoting Patricia Crawford, in "Donne's 'Elegy 19,'" 64.
12. William Habington, *The Queene of Arragon* (London: Printed by Thomas Cotes for William Cooke, 1640), sig. B2v.
13. Thomas Shadwell, *A True Widow* (London: Printed for Benjamin Tooke, 1679), 36–7.

14. Thomas Nashe, *Christs Teares over Jerusalem* (London: Printed [by George Eld] for Thomas Thorp, 1613), 145.
15. Stephen Gosson, "A Glasse, to viewe the pride of vaineglorious Women," in *Pleasant Quippes for Vpstart Newfangled Gentle-women* (London: By Richard Jhones, 1595), sig. B1r.
16. Trial of Sarah Jenkins for infanticide, *The Proceedings of the Old Bailey*, 4 December 1754, reference number t17541204-33. If busks could be used to disguise pregnancy, a woman who stopped wearing a busk could be suspected of being pregnant. In John Dryden's *The Wild Gallant* ([London] in the Savoy: Printed by Thomas Newcomb for Henry Herringman, 1669), 58, Isabelle deceives Nonsuch into believing that Constance is pregnant by telling him: "she has not worn her Busk this fortnight. I think she's grown fat o' th' sudden ... She has qualmes too every morning: ravins mightily for greenfruit; and swoones at the sight of hot meat." Nonsuch responds "She's with Child: I am undone! I am undone!"
17. Richard Head, *The English Rogue Described,* in *The Life of Meriton Latroon* (London: Francis Kirkman, 1668), 84–5 and 131–2.
18. Edward Philips, *The Mysteries of Love & Eloquence* (London: Printed by James Rawlins for Obadiah Blagrave, 1685), 14–15.
19. Gosson, "A Glasse," sig. B1r–v.
20. Barnabe Rich, *The Honestie of this Age* (London: Printed by Thomas Dawson for James Adams, 1614), 20.
21. Thomas Lodge, *Wits Miserie, and the worlds madnesse discouering the deuils incarnat of this age* (London: Printed by Adam Islip for Cutbert Burby, 1596), 14–15.
22. John Taylor, "A Whore," *All the Workes of Iohn Taylor the Water-Poet* (London: Printed by J[ohn] B[eale], Elizabeth Allde, Bernard Alsop, and Thomas Fawcet] for James Boler, 1630), 111.
23. Samuel Rowlands, "A Courtezans Humour," *Doctor Merrie-man* (London: John Deane, 1609), sig. C2v.
24. Thomas Tomkis, *Lingua: or The combat of the tongue, and the fiue senses for superiority. A pleasant comoedie* (London 1607, Printed by G. Eld, for Simon Waterson), 4.6.22, sig. S2v.
25. Robert Burton, "Symptomes of Loue-melancholy," *The Anatomy of Melancholy* (Oxford: Printed by John Lichfield and James Short for Henry Cripps, 1621), 613–14.
26. Henry Fitzgeffrey, "Satyra Secunda. A Morall Satyre," *Certain Elegies, Done by Sundrie Excellent Wits with Satyres and Epigrames* (London: Printed by B. A[lsop] for Miles Partrich, 1618), sig. B5v–B6.
27. John Marston, "Satyre VII. A Cynicke Satyre," *The Scourge of Villanie* (London: Printed by J[ames] R[oberts] for John Busby, 1598), sig. F6r–v.
28. Anon, *The Maydes Metamorphosis* (London: Printed by Thomas Creede for Richard Olive, 1600).
29. Thomas Heywood, *A Pleasant Conceited Comedie, Wherein is Shewed, How a Man may Chuse a Good Wife from a Bad* (London: Printed [by T. Creede] for Mathew Lawe, 1602), sig. B3v.
30. Joseph Hall, "Satyre 6," *Virgidemiarum* (London: Richard Bradocke for Robert Dexter, 1598), 44–5.
31. *Encyclopedie van de Mythologie,* A. van Reeth (Tirion, Baarn: 1994).

32. John Caryl (trans.), "Briseis to Achilles," in Ovid, *Ovid's epistles translated by several hands* (London: Jacob Tonson, 1680), 246–8.
33. Sir George Etherege, *She Wou'd if She Cou'd* (London: Printed for H. Herringman, 1668), 40.
34. Robert Heath, "Writ on Clarastella's Busk," in *Clarastella* (London: Printed for Humphrey Moseley, 1650), 56.
35. *"Hic Mulier:* or, The Man-Woman" (1620) in *Three Pamphlets on the Jacobean Antifeminist Controversy*, ed. Barbara Baines (Delmar, New York: Scholars' Facsimiles, 1978), sig. B1r–v.

Index

225 - born into leather — Gloves
226 - Glover + butcher etc ~ list of Shenk + leather
228 - leather as metaphor (Greenblatt)
229 - range of animals used (inc. dog) + use of droppings
230 - range of trades using leather; leather links gloves,
                 theatre + printing.

231 : use of leather in book production; leather items (inc
     books) in theatre; leather pervasive in Shak's life
232 : Erasmus: leather = figure of figmation
233 : flaying of St Bartholomew
234 : Marsyas — skin = figure of natural limits
     supple hero (of leather) = insult
235-6 : Stubbes / change in his perception of leather
236 :   leather = figure of nature / culture
237 :   from pelt to parchment — central to Shak.